The History of Ancient Israel

The History of Ancient Israel

MICHAEL GRANT

CHARLES SCRIBNER'S SONS • NEW YORK

Copyright © 1984 Michael Grant Publications Limited

Library of Congress Cataloging in Publication Data

Grant, Michael, 1914-
   The history of ancient Israel.

   Bibliography: p.
   Includes index.
   1. Jews—History—To 70 A.D.   2. Bible.
O.T.—History of Biblical events.   3. Palestine—
History—To 70 A.D.   I. Title.
DS117.G894   1984   933   84-1384
ISBN 0-684-18081-2
ISBN 0-684-18084-7 (pbk.)

CONTENTS

MAPS

INTRODUCTION

This is an account of ancient Israel, extending from its beginnings to the destruction of Jerusalem and the Temple in AD 70.

Part of the tale is told by excavations, which reveal many aspects of the material culture and everyday life of those times, but by far the most significant evidence is provided by the Hebrew Bible, the Old Testament of the Christians. This unparalleled compilation, which has inspired the literature and art and ethics of half the world, includes a great deal of historical writing, almost the first that the world had ever seen.

But the purpose of the men who composed the Bible was not just to write a history. Their aim was to depict the glory of Yahweh, and to display his unceasing intervention in human affairs. This aim is of primary historical as well as religious importance because it guided the course which history took. That is to say, the ancient Israelites or Hebrews or Jews accepted the validity of this divine assessment of their destiny, and were conscious of it whatever actions they performed, so that their whole story adopted a shape it would not otherwise have possessed. However, the biblical writers, while rarely ceasing to emphasize this divine guidance, also allowed an enormous amount of 'straight' history to slip through – political and social as well as spiritual and intellectual – since all these various fields were seen as forming a single, indistinguishable unity. Thus the Bible is an overwhelmingly important source of information. Indeed, for the greater part of the period it is virtually the only source of information we possess, other than the discoveries of archaeologists.

The Bible, of course, is an enormously voluminous, massively varied compendium of anonymous books, which constitutes an entire literature in itself. And it presents the historian with a formidable and perplexing problem, because of the composite, multiple authorship, editorship and conflation that almost every one of these writings, upon investigation, is found to reflect. The number of people in the world today who are intimately familiar with all this material is smaller than it was. I make no apology therefore (except to the cognizant minority) for including summaries of certain of the biblical narratives in the chapters which follow. I do, however, have another and more serious apology to offer. Any claim, on my part, to be capable of deploying all, or most, of the modern methods of textual, literary and historical criticism that are needed for this undertaking would be rash and unwarrantable. All that I can offer, with diffidence, is one man's view of the historical situations which the Hebrew Bible, the Old Testament, illuminates.

I have tried to describe these situations as objectively as possible. This, of course, is an aim which cannot be fully attained, since every writer, however much he hopes to take a balanced view, inevitably employs procedures of selection, arrangement and interpretation which are conditioned, often unconsciously, by his or her environment and background and epoch. Nevertheless, I have endeavoured, as well as I can, to apply the techniques of a historian to the story of the ancient Israelites. Whether the supernatural interventions, in which they believed, actually took place, is not, in my opinion, for the student of history to say: an attempt to recreate the course of events and development of thought is most likely to succeed if its author, for the time being, endeavours to forget whether he himself is a Jew, Christian, Moslem, Buddhist, Hindu, agnostic or atheist – if, that is to say, he avoids presuppositions or conclusions based upon his own beliefs or disbeliefs.

Since this book is intended to present a general picture, it will not concentrate on any single theme to the exclusion of others. Yet one persistent theme does seem to emerge. This is the perpetual coexistence and confrontation, among the people of the Bible, of two diverse and apparently opposed points of view concerning foreigners. That is to say, Israel unceasingly harboured the simultaneous convictions, first, that it was an entirely unique and separate community, and, secondly, that it was a nation necessarily linked with other peoples as well, both outside its borders and within them. Israel had to be apart from the world and yet remain inside it, at one and the same time. Modern historians, noting this polarization, have either seen it as a hopeless dilemma between two contradictory opposites, or, instead, as the coexistence of two complementary, indissociable viewpoints which Judaism successfully harmonized and united. Let the argument continue. In any case, these two recurring approaches, whether compatible or contradictory, were both alike essential features of this nation's peculiar character and greatness.

And both features are still very prominent in Israel today. I did not write this book with any intention of 'updating' its contents to provide analogies with modern times, but the analogies are there, all the same. Modern Israel is only comprehensible in the light of how its inhabitants acted, and what happened to them, throughout all the centuries of the past, and particularly throughout the ancient world. Those dramatically veering fortunes and vicissitudes – including repeated, almost incredible survivals in the face of crushing obstacles – will form the subject of the chapters that follow.

This book would scarcely have been possible without Mayor Teddy Kollek's generous invitation to Jerusalem, for which I am extremely grateful. I hope he and others will be indulgent to many failings. I also owe particular appreciation to Miss Linden Lawson of Messrs Weidenfeld and Nicolson for her careful editing of the text – a task which, since new materials and interpretations continually came to light, required exemplary patience. I want to thank Father Gregory Bainbridge for offering many perceptive comments, and Mr Patrick Leeson for making the maps. For my wife's advice and help any acknowledgement is entirely inadequate.

Translations: I have for the most part employed translations, for which I am grateful, from the *New English Bible* (© 1970 by permission of Oxford and Cambridge University Presses), and the *Bible in Today's English Version* (*Good News Bible*, O.T. and 4th ed. of N.T., 1976, © American Bible Society; British edition published by the Bible Societies/Collins). At times, however, it has seemed preferable to retain the cadences of the *Authorized* or *King James Version* (1611; a somewhat modernized version has now appeared). The Jewish Publication Society of America has completed its revised translation (1962–82).

Gattaiola, 1983   *Michael Grant*

Dates in this book, until Chapter 20, are BC (BCE) *unless otherwise stated.*

Part One

THE LAND OF CANAAN

CHAPTER 1

FORERUNNERS AND ORIGINS

i. The Land and its Beginnings

A traveller moving in from the stiff, stormy line of the Mediterranean coast found the land stretching ahead of him in four successive strips. First came the coastal plains of Philistia and Sharon (less fertile then than they have been made now), terminated at the north by the promontory of Mount Carmel. Further inland, beyond the lowland moors of the She-phelah, rose the central rugged plateau (about the size of Kent or Long Island), dotted with unwelcoming thorns and scrub, seamed and broken by steep and narrow gorges, and occupied in historical times, from south to north, by the tribes of Judah, Ephraim and Manasseh (these last two forming the core of Samaria): northwards again was the land's most important inland plain Jezreel (Esdraelon), flanked by Mounts Carmel and Gilboa and merging, on its northern side, into the slopes of Galilee. To the east, the country fell sharply into the Jordan Valley, which widened, at two points, into the Dead (or Salt) Sea and the Sea of Galilee (Lake of Chinnereth, Gennesaret). And finally, to the east, came the hilly or mountainous fringe tracts, not regarded, for millennia, as genuinely Israelite: Edom beyond Judah's Negeb wilderness, and Moab and Ammon across the Jordan.

The whole complex of small but varying and often mutually hostile territories extended for about a hundred and fifty miles from north to south, and less than seventy-five across. It was a land, whether we call it Canaan or Israel or Palestine (Appendix 11), doomed by this lack of natural, geographical unity to be the land-bridge and meeting-place and battlefield of great empires – Egypt, Assyria, Babylonia, the Hellenistic kingdoms, and Rome. Their peoples and armies moved up and down the Way of the Sea which spanned the country from north to south, traversing the coastal plains and the plain of Jezreel, the site of many armed clashes. It was only, therefore, for brief periods, and in precarious fashion, that Israel became its own master, enjoying political independence and power.

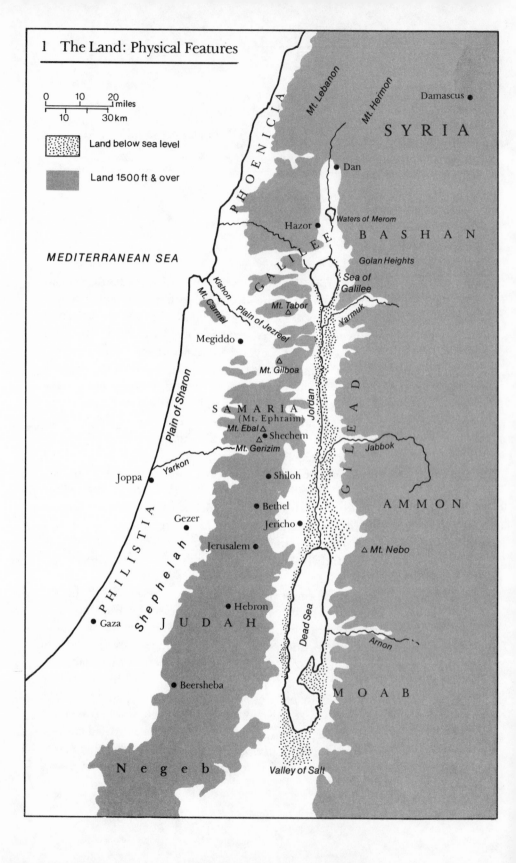

1 The Land: Physical Features

0   10   20 miles
10   30 km

Land below sea level

Land 1500 ft & over

MEDITERRANEAN SEA

PHOENICIA

Mt. Lebanon

Mt. Hermon

Damascus ●

S Y R I A

● Dan

Hazor ●   Waters of Merom

B A S H A N

GALILEE

Golan Heights

Sea of Galilee

Kishon

Mt. Carmel

Plain of Jezreel

Mt. Tabor △

Yarmuk

Megiddo ●

Mt. Gilboa △

Jordan

G I L E A D

Plain of Sharon

S A M A R I A
(Mt. Ephraim)

Mt. Ebal △
△ ● Shechem

Mt. Gerizim

Jabbok

Joppa ●   Yarkon

Shiloh ●

A M M O N

Bethel ●

Jericho ●

PHILISTIA

Gezer ●

△ Mt. Nebo

Shephelah

Jerusalem ●

Hebron ●

Dead Sea

● Gaza

J U D A H

Arnon

Beersheba ●

M O A B

N e g e b

Valley of Salt

Nor was it a very fertile land, or very rich in natural resources. True, it contained sufficient plantable areas to make two-thirds of its surface fit for human habitation, and the westerly winds of winter-time, coming in from the Mediterranean, brought rain which was caught up by the mountains and slopes, so that its crops did not need the artificial irrigation which was so indispensable in Egypt and Mesopotamia (Iraq). Yet, in comparison with other Mediterranean regions, the rain was unpredictable and could not be relied upon. It was withheld by Yahweh, concludes the Bible, when he felt displeased. To make this a land 'flowing with milk and honey', as he was said to have described it to Moses, was a challenge and a labour, like every other situation that confronted its people.

Twelve miles north of the headwaters of the Dead Sea, and four and a half miles west of the River Jordan, the extremely ancient city of Jericho emerged from the plain, one mile from the modern town that bears the name. The lush, semi-tropical oasis surrounding the place provided the most abundant water-supply in the area. And Jericho controlled not only the north–south route along the Jordan but also the gorge which penetrated the hills from east to west and provided a major trade route linking the territories across the river to the Mediterranean coast.

In what is described as the country's Neolithic epoch (c. 8300–4000), Jericho already moved decisively to the fore. By 7000, or earlier, its economy had advanced to a transitional stage between the gathering and producing of food. Pottery began to be made in about 4500. The dwellings of the inhabitants were surrounded by fairly massive walls, and enclosed a population of perhaps two thousand. Even at this early date their racial composition is likely to have been thoroughly mixed.

During the second half of the fourth millennium the first wave of Semitic-speaking peoples seems to have made its appearance. Coming from the extremities of the Arabian desert, they spread into Mesopotamia and Egypt, and then joined or displaced the Neolithic peoples of Jericho and other parts of Palestine as well. Because of the violence and destruction that these movements involved, the region suffered a material decline until about 3500 or a little later. But then many new villages came into existence, making use of copper, and displaying technical and artistic advances. An almost inaccessible cave at Nahal Mishmar, near the west bank of the Dead Sea (beside the later Masada), has yielded the finest hoard of copper objects ever found in the Near East. These objects were imported from Mesopotamia or Iran, and had perhaps, in the first instance, been brought to Engedi (not far from the cave), where a substantial stone-built shrine dates from c. 3300–3200. Meanwhile, a well-planned and strongly fortified little town had also been established at

Jawa across the Jordan, upon a basalt outcrop in the middle of the desert. This settlement housed between five and six thousand persons, who had access to a seasonal watercourse.

What is described as the Early Canaanite (or Early Bronze) Age in Syria and Palestine can be dated between *c.* 3150 and *c.* 2200. Its four successive phases formed an epoch of active trading, culture, religion and art. Population considerably increased; and city-states began to take shape, independent urban centres in control of surrounding strips of land. At Jericho, solid and substantial houses were built, including a sanctuary (others were at Megiddo and Ai). And other towns sprang up as well, constructed on defensible rock-spurs, and never far from a reliable water supply. By this time the people of the country, it would appear, predominantly spoke a Semitic tongue, one of the ancestors of the northwestern branches of this group of languages (Eblaic, Canaanite, Phoenician, Moabite, Hebrew, Aramaic).

Meanwhile in Mesopotamia the city-states of the Sumerians, a non-Semitic people, had achieved a standard of civilization unequalled in all the world except Egypt and China. The city of Kish, which has provided what may be the world's oldest inscribed tablet (*c.* 3500) displaying pictorial symbols or pictographs, yielded the supremacy to Ur in *c.* 2600. Ur's Great Palace, datable to the twenty-fourth century, is the earliest known residence set apart for the use of a king. But then in *c.* 2370 Mesopotamia was invaded by the Akkadians, speakers of a Semitic tongue (the only representative of its north-eastern group, later divided into Assyrian and Babylonian). These Akkadians overwhelmed the Sumerian communities, and under Sargon (Sharrum-kin) of Agade, an unidentified city somewhere near Babylon, welded the surrounding region into an empire, possibly the first in human history. Sargon even claimed to have conquered 'the territory of the sunset and the cedar forest and the silver mountains', meaning Syria and Palestine. And then another invader of those vulnerable lands came from the opposite direction; that is to say, from the ancient, elaborately civilized kingdom of Egypt, whose VIth Dynasty pharaoh Pepi I (*c.* 2325–2275) conducted campaigns against the 'sand-dwellers' beyond his Sinai borders.

Our knowledge of northern Syria during this epoch has been revolutionized by recent discoveries at Ebla (Tell-Mardikh), south-west of Aleppo. This locality, rising above the surrounding plateau and covering an area of 140 acres, was easily accessible to the fertile Idlib region which provided it with natural produce. At first under Mesopotamian influence, the place was already prospering in the earliest years of the third millennium, and then during its heyday (*c.* 2300) became a handsome town of towered, three-storeyed buildings. Trading extensively in timber and copper and precious stones, Ebla attained the status of a political super-power, controlling substantial tracts of Syria and Palestine and even reducing large regions of Mesopotamia to vassalage.

Excavations at this site throw back our knowledge of Semitic origins and of Palestinian civilization by a thousand years. In particular the fifteen hundred tablets that have so far come to light, inscribed with cuneiform (wedge-shaped) pictographs or pictorial symbols, provide an exceptionally rich store of information. The language they employ, pro-visionally described as Early (or Palaeo- or Proto-) Canaanite, must be added to the north-western Semitic tongues of which we have hitherto known. It may even be the ancestor of Hebrew (with Canaanite as inter-mediary, Ch.1,ii). This remains uncertain: but it does seem that the third and greatest of Ebla's kings was called Ebrum or Ebrium, akin to Eber who was reputed to have been one of Abraham's ancestors. And the Ebla tablets include specific references to place-names including Sinai, Jerusalem, Hazor, Lachish, Megiddo and Acco, and personal names including Esau, Ishmael, David, Saul and Israel (though none of these are identifiable with the later biblical personages). The unidentified place-name Yahweh has also been detected in these documents, but that is unconfirmed. In any case, it is evident that these Hebrew traditions go back a great deal farther than had hitherto been supposed.

ii. The Amorites and Egypt

During the last centuries of the third millennium the end of the Early Canaanite (Early Bronze) Age came upon the Syrian and Palestinian sites with devastating completeness. During the fourth and last phase of that Age (c. 2400–2000) almost every site in Palestine was either completely abandoned or settled on a greatly reduced scale. For, in the first place, a marked climatic change had produced far drier conditions, resulting in a large-scale supersession of productive agriculture and commercial activities by dry-farming and herding at bare subsistence level. And then, in c. 2200–2000, there arrived waves of invaders, pas-toral semi-nomads who, while destroying such settled, urban ways of life as still survived at that time, employed shaft graves and tumulus burials in a manner reminiscent of the Kurgan (tumulus or barrow) culture on the south Russian steppes.

What followed was the age of the Amorites, the Amurru or 'Wester-ners' as the Akkadians of Mesopotamia called them (the Sumerians had known them as Martu). 'Amorite' bears a variety of different and loose and blurred meanings, particularly in the Bible, but the term may be applied particularly to the Semitic-speaking groups of invaders and immigrants who began to break in from the semi-arid Arabian fringes of

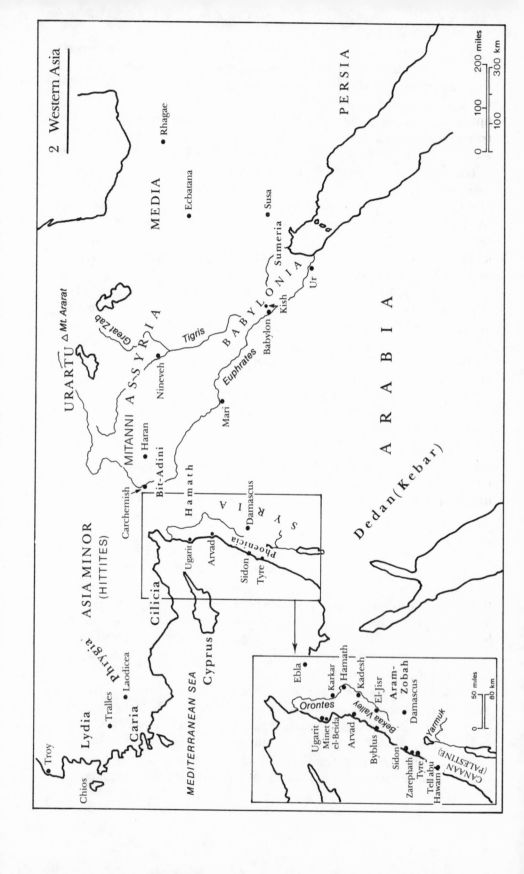

2 Western Asia

the Fertile Crescent shortly before the end of the second millennium. By the nineteenth or eighteenth century they had subjugated the whole of upper Mesopotamia, founding Babylon as the capital of a new and powerful dynasty, of which the most famous and dynamic monarch was the lawgiver Hammurabi (1728–1687).

The Amorites had made their appearance in Syria and Palestine as well during the first two centuries of the second millennium. This period of their settlement is described by archaeologists as Middle Canaanite (Middle Bronze) Age IIA; and in the epoch that followed (IIB, c. 1800–1550), when climatic conditions had greatly improved, they launched major economic and cultural advances. Indeed, this was an unprecedentedly flourishing period in the history of the two countries. It was also the first for which written documents exist; they were written in Canaanite, a north-western Semitic tongue related to, and perhaps originating from, the language already found at Ebla (and developing subsequently into Phoenician, Hebrew and Moabite). During this period Canaan, as a recognizable entity, can be said to have come truly into existence.

Particularly notable, early in this period, was the Mediterranean port of Byblus (Jebeil), on the strip of the Syrian coast later known as Phoenicia. This was already an ancient foundation, but had fallen into decline. At the beginning of the second millennium, however, the place began to recover, becoming a centre for the manufacture of quite elegant pottery, evidently made on the wheel. Ebla, too, which had been destroyed by fire in c. 2250, was reborn as an impressive city containing a substantial royal palace (c. 1900), strong fortifications, and a large tripartite temple. Once again Syria had become an important centre of material, spiritual and cultural developments.

Far inland in the same country lay the equally powerful city-state of Mari (Tell el-Harari), situated on the middle Euphrates at the intersection of major caravan routes from all points of the compass. Mari had already flourished in the third millennium, but after a period of eclipse began to rise again, like Ebla, attaining a new Golden Age in the eighteenth century under the last of its three known kings, Zimri-Lim. In his very large palace, more than 25,000 cuneiform tablets have been found. They are written in Akkadian, the Semitic language which now provided the medium of international diplomacy for many of the nearer regions of Asia, but the kings of Mari possessed a north-western Semitic (Amorite) nomenclature, and the bulk of the population, too, evidently spoke the same language. Like those found earlier at Ebla, its names display a close relation to the speech of the Israelites' ancestors: thus Mari texts speak of Abram-ram, Jacob-el, Levi and Israel, and refer to an Amorite tribe of Bene-iamina (although, as at Ebla, without any apparent connexion with the biblical stories). The same texts provide our first precise evidence for the dual society of the time, in which pastoral nomads or semi-nomads existed alongside a sedentary population, in conflict or uneasy peace. Indeed, some groups of the people living at Mari belonged to an intermediate category known as 'integrated tribes', of which one branch remained static all the year round while the other moved into the steppes or hills according to the seasons.

In Palestine, too, development became apparent as the second millennium proceeded on its way, though progress was slower and on a smaller scale. The local situation was recorded by Sinuhe, a refugee from Egypt who visited the country during the reign of the XIIth Dynasty pharaoh Senusret (Sesostris) II (c. 1897–1878). This phase is illustrated by two sets of Execration Texts (1925–1875, and second half of nineteenth century) inscribed in hieratic (stylized hieroglyphic) pictorial symbols or pictographs on broken pottery bowls, as part of a ritual designed to curse Egypt's enemies. For at this time most of Palestine's local Canaanite rulers were dependants, sometimes rebellious, of the rich and powerful Egyptian pharaohs of the Middle Kingdom (XIth and XIIth Dynasties, c. 2080–1640). This Palestinian dependence upon Egypt was not, it appears, an altogether new phenomenon, but now the Egyptians felt more than ever conscious that domination over Palestine was not only convenient for access to the timber of Phoenicia (Lebanon), but also, as Napoleon pointed out, indispensable for the safe protection of the valley of the Nile itself. Thus the coastal highway which linked the two countries, the Way of the Sea – known to the Egyptians as the Ways of Horus – was protected by their fortresses, for example at Sharuhen (probably to be identified with Tell el-Farah) and El-Arish.

The earlier group of Execration Texts shows that, during this phase, there were several chiefs or elders in each Palestinian community, at a time when the new, semi-nomadic tribal immigrants were first beginning to make contact with the settled life of their areas. The later series of texts, on the other hand, reflects a period in which each locality had come to have a single chief, indicating a fuller assimilation to sedentary life and centralized urban rule. By 1800 these Canaanite leaders were fortifying their small capitals, recreating the city-states of the previous millennium, and beginning to enlarge their dominions into minor kingdoms, increasingly capable of looking after themselves.

In the later eighteenth century, a considerable number of immigrants, traders and infiltrators moved through Canaan and gradually gained control of Lower Egypt, establishing a fortress capital at Avaris (Tell el-Debaa) in the eastern portion of the Nile delta. These new rulers of the two countries were a warrior aristocracy known as the Hyksos (*hyk khwsht*, 'rulers of the desert uplands' or 'of foreign lands'). They and their followers were of mixed stock but preponderantly used a north-western Semitic tongue, resembling the Canaanite speech.

The Hyksos (XVth–XVIIth Dynasties), from the time of their arrival in Canaan (c. 1720), controlled its city-states pretty tightly. They did not, it is true, effectively dominate the whole land, but their fortresses at Tell el-Ajjul (Beth-eglaim, the predecessor of Gaza) and Joppa (Jaffa) enabled them to control the coastline – which provided their major route to the north – and kept intruders out of the plains of Sharon and Jezreel; while Lachish (Tell ed-Duweir) in the interior also received impressive fortifications. In general, recent excavations at Palestinian sites of this period suggest that the Hyksos rule conferred greater and more widespread prosperity than later Egyptian tradition wished to suggest.

The Hyksos remained in power from c. 1720 until c. 1580 (or c. 1567), when they were driven out of Egypt by Ahmose, founder of the XVIIIth Dynasty and brilliant New Kingdom. On expulsion from the country, the Hyksos managed to retain their stronghold at Sharuhen, but were driven out of it after about three years. It has been conjectured that the destruction of many important Palestinian cities dates from this troubled time. However, within a century or two (in the Late Canaanite period, c. 1550–1200), most of these places had recovered. Their recovery was, once again, the work of the Egyptians, whose XVIIIth Dynasty pharaoh Thothmes (Tuthmosis) III (1504–1450), the most imposing ruler they ever possessed, asserted full control of Palestine and Syria in the course of no less than seventeen campaigns, starting with the battle of Kadesh on the River Orontes against 330 Canaanite chiefs (c. 1479) and continuing for over thirty years. Amenhotep II (1450–1424) sent punitive forces not only to north Syria but also to Palestine, with the Jezreel plain as one of his principal objectives.

Light is thrown on subsequent developments by a series of more than three hundred and fifty cuneiform tablets from Tell el-Amarna in Upper Egypt, written in a Semitic jargon of a scholastic or diplomatic nature – bad Akkadian with a strong Canaanite admixture. These tablets, archives from the Foreign Office of the pharaohs, date from the reigns of Amenhotep (Amenophis) III (c. 1417–1379) and his son Amenhotep IV (c. 1379–1362), the religious revolutionary who renamed himself Akhenaten, after the sun-god Aten. The Amarna letters include numerous reports from local rulers in Canaan. They reveal a marked weakening of Egyptian control, manifested in local revolts and intrigues, incursions of nomads and semi-nomads from the fringes, and pressures and subversive actions from other imperial powers. Amid widespread recrimination, corruption and rapacity, complaints and appeals to Egypt went unanswered.

CHAPTER 2

THE CANAANITES

i. Canaanite Civilization

Canaan was indeed in a ferment, but by this time its city-states had built up a strong enough civilization to survive the successive storms. As we have seen, the middle years of the millennium, before the troubles recorded in the Amarna letters, had witnessed a gradual revival of town life at many sites. Admittedly, the population was mostly concentrated on the plains and in the valleys: the hill-country on either side of the Jordan was still very sparsely settled. Nevertheless, a way of life had now developed which, although the country was still a poor relation of Egypt, was distinctively Canaanite and indigenous, reflected in a language which formed one of the main north-west Semitic tongues.

The cities of Canaan, each ruled by a king, were fortified by a new kind of massive rampart, surmounting a bank of earth (glacis) and adjoining an exterior ditch or fosse. This technique, designed to resist attacks by battering-rams and horse-drawn chariots, was probably brought to Palestine in Hyksos times (late eighteenth century) from north Syria, where Ebla and Carchemish provided conspicuous examples of similar defences. They had learnt about fortifications of this kind, and about the chariots that necessitated their construction, from the kingdom of Mitanni, north of Assyria, upon what are now the frontiers of Turkey and Syria. This powerful imperial state was ruled, between the eighteenth and sixteenth centuries, by an invading caste known as the Hurrians, who were migrants of Indo-European speech from the highlands of Armenia; one of their cities is now being excavated, at Kahat (Tell Barri). Their development of the chariot created a feudal society consisting of a hereditary nobility and military élite (the *maryannu*), and a half-free, Semitic-speaking class of dependants (*khupshu*) – excavations suggest that there was no middle class in between.

Mitanni, at its height, extended downwards at least as far as the fringes of the city-states of Canaanite Palestine, and influenced their social structure and legal institutions (as well as those of the Hyksos in Egypt). For, in this period, Canaan, as the Amarna letters make clear, likewise possessed a class of graded feudal barons, probably for the most part of non-Semitic stock, ruling over a much larger population of oppressed Semitic speakers, often employed in the forced labour (*corvée*) which David and Solomon subsequently imitated. Documents indicate that the local kings settled privileges and fiefs on this warrior aristocracy.

It appears from our sources, and excavations confirm, that the most powerful city-states of the epoch included (from north to south) Hazor, Megiddo, Beth-shan, Shechem, Gezer and Jerusalem.

Hazor (Tell el-Kedah), in Upper Galilee, stood on a small hill rising above the river route between the Sea of Galilee and the Waters of Merom (Lake Huleh), at a point where trade routes from many points come together so that the town spanned and controlled the highways from Damascus to the Syrian ports, whose culture and religion it shared. Mentioned in Mari texts of the eighteenth and seventeenth centuries as an important commercial centre (the recipient, it is recorded, of three successive consignments of tin), Hazor became the largest city in the whole country, with a uniquely extensive urban area capable of housing 30,000 or 40,000 inhabitants. Its monarchs were the overlords of a substantial part of northern Canaan, and are rightly described in the Bible as heads of a number of kingdoms.[1] Their power was evidently on a par with that of important contemporary rulers at places such as Ebla and Carchemish in northern Syria. Although they were granted a title of exceptional esteem in Egyptian sources, the Amarna letters portray them emancipating themselves from Egyptian suzerainty.

Megiddo (Tell el-Mutesellim), south-west of Hazor and not far from the modern Haifa, rose upon a spur of the ridge of Mount Carmel. Commanding a view of almost the whole Jezreel valley, the place presided over the vital north-south Megiddo Pass, where the Way of the Sea, the coastal route from the Sharon plain, penetrated the neck of the Carmel range. This strategic location meant that Megiddo was fated to witness frequent clashes of armies (under the name of 'Armageddon' it was thought of as the scene of the final great conflict on the Day of Judgement). The town was surrounded by a massive wall, originally thirteen feet thick and later strengthened to twice that width; so that the XVIIIth Dynasty pharaoh Thothmes III, despite his victory over the Canaanite coalition at Kadesh (*c.* 1479, Ch.1,ii), was unable to capture the fortress.

Megiddo possessed an efficient water supply which testified to its rulers' authority, persistence and skill. They were also able to profit from the trade and culture of the maritime colony of Tell Abu Hawam, a settlement of the proto-Greek Mycenaeans, whose imposing civilization dominated the Greek mainland. Megiddo was only ten miles away from this port, and the rectangular, Egyptian appearance of some of its houses reflects international contacts. The fifteenth-century palace presiding over the city, constructed round several courtyards, was found to contain a rich hoard of gold, lapis lazuli, and over two hundred carved and incised ivory objects. On one of these ivory reliefs, dating from the close of the Late Canaanite epoch (c. 1200), a king is shown sitting on a richly sculptured throne, reviewing prisoners of war to the accompaniment of music and dancing.

East of Megiddo, at the far end of the Jezreel plain, rose the stark, steep, imposing eminence of Beth-shan or Beth-shean (Tell el-Husn), visible for many miles around. The place was located in a well-watered, fertile area with good rainfall, near a perennial tributary of the Jordan – which could easily be crossed at a point not far away. The conspicuous natural advantages of this site had been exploited for centuries: its great mound of rubble was found to contain no less than eighteen levels of successive habitation, going back to the fourth millennium. The Canaanite city which constituted several of these levels was fortified with an inner and an outer wall, linked with cross-walls forming small rooms. The position of Beth-shan earned it the role of the Egyptians' principal base in the interior of the country, probably from the time of Thothmes III onwards.

To the south-west of Beth-shan stood Shechem (Nablus), below Mount Gerizim. Not far off, between Gerizim and Ebal, was the pass through which ran the longitudinal thoroughfare along the central highlands of Samaria: an east–west route is also readily accessible. This crossroads location, with its international potentialities, explains why cylinder seals with Mesopotamian (Akkadian) motifs and inscriptions have been found at the place. Shechem became a city soon after 2000, and acquired formidable walls. It was destroyed (by unknown attackers) in the mid-sixteenth century, but soon rose to importance again. We learn from the Amarna letters[2] (Ch. 1,ii) that in the fourteenth century a chieftain named Labaya or Labayu, the 'Lion Man', gained control over Shechem, and built up a kingdom extending as far as the Mediterranean coast. Labaya, who, although his name was Hurrian, fostered a network of Canaanite allies and clients, refrained from grovelling to the Egyptians like many other local chiefs, but did not, on the other hand, openly secede from them like his fellow monarch at Hazor. That is to say, he alternated between conciliation and truculence, encouraging nomad raiders to encroach on Egyptian possessions when he felt so inclined. He died a violent death; but thereafter his sons played an equally active part.

Gezer was further south, upon one of the few bastions the hill country of Ephraim throws out towards the west. Although not standing very high, it enjoys an unimpeded view in all directions, and presides over the junction of two ancient trade routes, the coastal highway and the road leading inland from the sea up to Jerusalem. The place, which enjoyed fertile, well-watered surroundings, had been occupied since before 3000. In Canaanite times its twenty-seven-acre site was enclosed by a wall thirteen feet broad, followed after destruction by another of even larger dimensions.

Up the pass eastwards from Gezer lies Jerusalem, which like Shechem was not only situated on the central ridge and the north–south route, but also formed a staging point on the road running eastwards from the Mediterranean towards the Jordan. The town, inhabited in the later second millennium by Jebusites (a people of uncertain origin), stood on the rocky plateau of Ophel, protected by deep valleys, with access to the adjacent Gihon spring. 'Salem' (meaning 'peace' – or the name of a Canaanite deity) was the city of Melchizedek ('monarch of right-eousness') in the early second millennium, later honoured as the ideal priest-king. Jerusalem is also mentioned in the Execration Texts; and the Amarna letters show Abdi-Hiba, the governor of 'Urusalim', writing repeatedly to the pharaoh Akhenaten asking for Egyptian troops.

The road eastwards from the city towards the Jordan led to Jericho, which gained a fresh and novel lease of life during this period. In the south (Judah), the only important town to survive the disturbances accompanying the expulsion of the Hyksos was Beth-eglaim (Tell el-Ajjul, near Gaza), which became a rich and important place, and was selected, in the time of Thothmes III, to become the capital of the entire Egyptian province. The slightly later Amarna letters also mention Gath, Ashkelon and Lachish in this region, cities subsequently occupied by the Philistines (Ch.6,i).

Basing their military power on the employment of chariots, the Canaanite rulers relied increasingly on bronze tools and weapons. Much of their copper came, by courtesy of the Egyptians, from an exceptionally large mining complex in the Timna valley, eighteen miles north of the Gulf of Elath (Eilat) or Akaba. There the pharaohs employed not only casual Negeb labour but also skilled metallurgists (itinerant Kenites, related to the Midianites) to obtain the copper that was to be found in abundance. Because of these mines, the inscriptions of Rameses III show a new interest in the adjoining regions of Edom and Moab. Additional copper came to Canaan from the island of Cyprus, which was only sixty miles from the Syrian coast. And it is possible that they obtained further supplies of the metal, together with the tin with which it was alloyed, from Khurasan in Iran. In return they were able to offer purple dye (murex), oil and wine, ivory, and woods for construction and ornament. They also made use of a new range of pots, well turned on a flat wheel;

sixteenth-century examples, suggestive of Greek wares, were inspired by Mycenaean settlements at Syrian ports such as Tell Abu Hawam. As their geographical situation suggested, the Canaanites played an important part as commercial, diplomatic and cultural middlemen between Mesopotamia and Egypt.

It was in aid of this function that they devised the alphabet. Already by c. 1800 (?) a simpler script than the old Egyptian hieroglyphic (pictorial) had appeared at Byblus in Phoenicia. This script consisted of eighty signs, each probably representing a syllable, and it interlarded characters derived from the hieroglyphic symbols with others of a linear, geometric appearance which still seem to be depicting natural objects, but in an increasingly stylized fashion. A more completely abstract linear script of about the same date, once again likely to be syllabic, has been found on a piece of pottery at El-Jisr in the Bekaa valley of Lebanon. Then at Serabit el-Khadem, in the western part of the Sinai peninsula, Semitic-speaking (Canaanite) labourers working in turquoise mines under Egyptian control made use of what has been called a 'Proto-Sinaitic' script, at some date between 1600 and 1450. Here only thirty signs, or fewer, are to be seen. Once again Egyptian pictographs are combined with conventional linear symbols. The latter (including most of the characters subsequently found in Hebrew writings) may still represent a syllabary, in reduced and streamlined form, but they have, alternatively, been interpreted as 'acrophonic', i.e. representing the initial sound of a syllable or word, and if that is correct, this script has achieved the status of a purely alphabetic medium.

More definite evidence of the same phenomenon soon becomes apparent at Ugarit (Ras Shamra) on the north Syrian coast. Equipped with a harbour (Minet el-Beida) which, like Tell Abu Hawam, possessed a Mycenaean quarter – it was the main port of entry for copper ore from Cyprus – Ugarit stood at the crossroads of many trading routes and was courted by great powers to north and south, whom its rulers played off against one another with skill. Forty seasons of excavations have yielded our most revealing glimpse of Canaanite culture and prosperity at its height. A royal palace of over sixty rooms, disposed around five courtyards, includes four separate quarters reserved for business and governmental archives. The inscribed tablets that have emerged from this site mainly belong to the fourteenth and thirteenth centuries. Their signs are wedge-shaped (cuneiform), as in ancient Mesopotamia. Yet here, whether by descent from the 'Proto-Sinaitic' script or through another channel, we seem to have arrived at a fully developed alphabet, like that of the later Hebrew language (Ch.8,ii). Displaying two versions, one a contraction of the other, twenty-seven of the thirty Canaanite characters represented consonants (the Semitic vocabulary is built up of regular sets of consonants, very often three in a word; its three primary vowel-sounds were not thought to need inclusion). The remaining three Canaanite letters stood for glottal stops (the sounds produced by the closure of the glottis, the opening between the vocal chords).

This extraordinary feat of dissecting the sounds of human speech into so few and convenient elementary constituents was the crowning contribution of the Canaanites to the world's culture. Writing, now infinitely more accessible, enabled Ugarit not only to amass archives but also to create an entire literature. This was composed partly in a Hurrian dialect and partly in Ugaritic, a north-western Semitic tongue related to (or possibly a dialect of) Canaanite. It was a language which lent itself to a splendid poetic style, foreshadowing early Hebrew verse, and was readily set to music, which apparently became the other major Canaanite art – though we cannot judge its quality, since it is all lost.

ii. Canaanite Religion

What has survived of the literature of the Canaanites is rich in myth, epic, saga and ritual, and provides an arresting picture of their religion, which so enormously influenced the faith of the Hebrews, both by direct derivation and by hostile reaction.[3]

These Canaanite documents make it clear that their authors were religious people who believed in the existence of deity, a belief concerned, in origin, with coercing and enlisting divine favour, to get it on one's own side. Most other ancient peoples, too, believed, like the Canaanites, that a supernatural power or powers, which could somehow be approached, presided over the world. 'Fools say to themselves, "There is no God",' declares a Psalmist.[4] But this scepticism was evidently rare: beliefs in the existence of a divinity guided the history of the ancient Canaanites, and then of the Israelites too, with overwhelming force.

The Canaanite version of this conviction, emanating from Mesopotamia, was polytheistic, in contrast to the strict monotheism of later Israelite theologians. The monotheist finds that the universe is inexplicable (and its guarantee of our own security imperfect) unless regarded as the product of a single, all-creating, all-controlling deity. The polytheist notes the diversity of phenomena, and frequently the conflict, between them (including, as sophistication grew, the conflict between good and evil) and is unable to conceive that such diversity could have been created, or could be controlled, by any one single power.

In polytheistic Canaan, as in many other countries, each locality and settlement and craft and aspect of life had its own deities. They included minor gods, to whom ordinary men and women liked to attach themselves, as protectors of their interests. But there were also high gods, with universal aspects, although their omnipotence and domination over humankind seemed diminished by the rival existence of their fellow divinities. This was a doctrine which mirrored the inter-state and inter-city wars people saw raging around them. It scarcely made for psychological security. Yet it did satisfactorily account for the diversity of phenomena. Moreover, the essentially agricultural basis of Canaanite life, as of the life of Mesopotamia and Egypt, involved a close view of nature's manifold, varied expressions, which prompted the assumption of a divine division of labour.

A comprehensive account of religion in the cities of the Canaanite-Phoenician coast, attributed to a certain Sanchuniathon who supposedly lived in the eleventh century, has only survived in some fragments of a work by Philo of Byblus (1st century AD);[5] but what he reports is now regarded as fairly reliable. Canaanite religious practices also receive abundant mention in the Bible, though these are often fragmentary, hostile and biased, but the voluminous second millennium archives of Ugarit and elsewhere enable the balance to be redressed.

The beliefs of Ugarit envisaged a pantheon of more than thirty gods and goddesses, anthropomorphically conceived and endowed with human passions and weaknesses. Assessments of their personalities, relationships and functions seem to have been curiously fluctuating and fluid. The leading deities, however, are of great relevance to this study, since their influence subsequently appears in Israel again and again. This applied particularly to El, the Mighty One, the head of the Canaanite pantheon, the final authority in all human and divine affairs. He is the 'Creator of Created Things' (*bny bnwt*), the majestic Father and King of Gods and of Men. 'El' meant 'god' in almost every Semitic tongue, and in Canaan, as elsewhere, became the generic term for a super-god, for the Canaanites had borrowed from earlier civilizations, and considerably sharpened, the concept of a supreme, living God who had made the world, and embodies the ultimate explanation of the universe beyond human life.

In the Ugaritic epics, El sat in royal state amid a cosmic paradise, 'at the confluence of the two streams' (where the upper and lower waters meet and mingle), beyond the menace of any evil power. He is the Bull, because of his mighty strength. But he is also, like Yahweh after him, all-powerful – and wise, beneficent, kindly and merciful. He is the supreme judge, and stresses justice, charity, hospitality and decency as qualities human beings must endeavour to possess, so that the Canaanite kings, presiding over the rituals of their city-states, were in duty bound, as representatives of the divine will on earth, to show fairness and charity to the underprivileged and defenceless. Moreover, the monarchs performed rites with the specific aim of securing forgiveness for their sins and offences. These religious and moral concepts of kingship were destined to provide Israel with one of its most substantial Canaanite heritages.

Such insistence upon moral rectitude among men and women came about *as a result* of the attribution of the same qualities to El himself. Thus, the Canaanites belonged to that section of humanity which considers morality to be directly derived from religion, and only able to exist at all because of religious sanctions. Despite opposition, this remained the general inheritance of the Jews and Christians, and the whole non-pagan and post-pagan west.

Among the Canaanites, however, this potentially monotheistic aspect of El was blurred and clouded by the localizations of his cult. As the Bible, much later, had still not forgotten, he was worshipped in or near Hebron (at Mamre?) as El Shaddai ('of the plains, fields, steppe'; mainly poetical, perhaps of Akkadian origin); and he was venerated, also, at Bethel ('House of God') as El Bethel (likewise perhaps Akkadian), at Beersheba as El Olam (the Eternal One), at Kadesh-barnea as El Roi ('El sees me'), and at Jerusalem as El Elyon (the Most High). It is true that El Elyon could be described, in universal terms, as 'creator [*or* owner] of heaven and earth',[6] but it was only to be expected that popular, polytheistic belief should, by way of contrast, tend to regard these regional cults as representing local deities (which, indeed, they had once perhaps been) rather than as manifestations of a single all-powerful god.

Besides, El's omnipotence was further qualified by the Canaanites' acceptance of other powerful gods within their pantheon. His son Baal is the deity of whom, eventually, we hear most. He is youthful and vigorous, the Mighty, Mightiest Hero, Prince, Lord of Heaven. His name Hadad – to whom Hazor's most important temple was dedicated – expresses the clash of thunder that accompanies the winter rain. Assuming El's role, he is god of the mountains where the storms build up; he is the terrible, raging Rider of the Clouds. These flashing tempests echoed the wilderness round about; but Baal's worship also became adjusted and assimilated to the sedentary agricultural life adopted by the Canaanites, so that he next became the god of the vegetation promoted by the tempests over which he presided.

Taking his name from a common noun meaning owner, master, or husband, Baal was originally, it appears, associated with specific places and sanctuaries; in an Ugarit temple he is linked or equated with Dagon, who had been the high god of Ebla. But his cult became widespread throughout Canaan, where one could talk of a Baal in every field or ford or spring. That was befitting to the Lord of the Land's fertility cult, the master and dispenser of the land's earth and water.

This role explained the mighty battles he was believed to be incessantly fighting, incessantly engaged in conflict with the forces of disorder and chaos against whom he emerges triumphant – monsters like the Leviathan and Behemoth of later biblical literature. But his principal enemy is Mot or Death, the god of the dried-up summer soil. In this annual struggle Baal, like so many of his counterparts in other near eastern regions, met his death when the vegetation perished every year, descended into the underworld, and rose to life again when the winter was over. This constant struggle between life and death was a dramatic myth by which the emotions of the people were profoundly excited and purged. Baal's enemies had done their worse – and their power was exhausted.

Thus the religion of Canaan was anchored in the annual, cyclical, movements of nature, overridingly preoccupied with the productiveness of flock and field, upon which the lives of the people depended. This productiveness could be secured and maintained by sympathetic, imitative magic, designed to attract the goodwill of Baal and his fellow deities, seen as unpredictable outsiders who needed to be appeased, rather than as the protective power by whom the Israelites later believed they had been specially chosen and singled out. Moreover, the Israelite prophets savagely attacked the cyclical nature cults of Canaan, since their own Yahwist religion was not so much rooted in nature as in the alleged events of their national history, directed towards a determined end (Ch.4,ii; 5,ii). Yet the faith of the Canaanites lived on and on – as long as the prophets themselves – because it was so securely anchored to their own daily existence, binding gods, human beings and nature in a stable order of security, procreation and unity in this life upon earth (like the Hebrews, they saw the afterlife as wholly insubstantial). It was to maintain this indispensable unity – to control the natural forces that shape people's lives – that the colourful, dramatic myths and rituals and festivals of Canaan were evolved, passionately plunging its whole people into these annual, life-giving, elaborately orchestrated dramas.

We have news of such Canaanite forms of worship as late as in the sixth century; and it happens to come from a group of women.[7] Fertility rites were obviously of special importance to their sex, and there were deeply revered female divinities. These sixth-century women had been worshippers of the 'Queen of Heaven', Ashtoreth or Anath or a blend of the two. Ashtoreth, Asherah and Anath – not always distinguishable one from the other – were all mother figures, goddesses of sexual intercourse. But at the same time, they were also bloodthirsty patrons of the wars that were needed to preserve all this fertility for the faithful. Asherah was known to the Bible as Baal's consort, though at Ugarit she had been El's, the mother of seventy sons. Her name means 'upright', for she was a tree goddess, represented either by a tree or by a sacred wooden pole or pillar, that was called *asherah* after her (mistranslated 'grove' in the Authorized Version of the Bible). But Asherah was duplicated (and eclipsed) at

Ugarit, in her capacity as Baal's lover and sister, by the young, beautiful, desirable, life-giving Anath, upholder of justice and law, who annually rescued Baal from his enemy Mot, and was therefore especially revered at the annual fertility rites. And the Canaanites' worship of the just and kindly sun-god Shemesh and the moon-god Yerah was once again founded on a total preoccupation with the powers that give fruitfulness to earth, trees, and flocks.

Tablets found at Taanach, near Megiddo, read 'if the finger of Ashirat points',[8] suggesting that she was believed to give forth oracles; and the other divinities, too, were oracular. There were prophets at Ugarit, as there had been at Mari, for the Canaanites, like the Israelites after them, sought to learn the will of their deities through the voice of prophets or seers citing inspired, ecstatic visions and voices, in contrast to the 'technical' methods of diviners gazing at entrails, flights and stars. And another means of seeking unification with the supernatural powers, much favoured by Canaanite religious authorities and devotees, was the ritual performance of the sexual act. Guilds of consecrated female and male prostitutes (*Qedeshoth* and *Qedeshim*) were appointed to the holy places, in order to carry out this intercourse with worshippers as a form of sympathetic magic, to imitate and stimulate the processes of natural fertility. These practices, which persisted for as long as the cults themselves lasted, were seized upon by biblical writers as an exceptionally scandalous proof of the essential, disgusting error of the entire Canaanite religious system, and a striking demonstration that its claims to moral standards were false.

When the monarchs of the Canaanites sought to get in touch with their deities, they did so, like the Israelites of later days, not only by the methods that have just been described but by offering sacrifices, often accompanied by ritual ablutions. The gods lived off the smell of the offerings, and these also helped to unify the people who performed the sacrificial acts, since by partaking together of one and the same animal the community was reintegrated, one member with another. In grave corporate emergencies, or to accompany the foundation of important temples or cities, the surest way of all to appease the divine power was to sacrifice a human being, especially a son or a daughter – and best of all a first-born. Babies' skeletons found at Tirzah and Shechem, and infants buried in jars in the subsoil of Gezer, evidently testify to this custom. A ninth-century king of Moab, Mesha, was still offering sacrifices of a similar kind. And the ostensibly Yahwist kings of Judah, two hundred years later, were accused of doing the same.

Such were the rites performed at Canaanite temples of the second millennium. Places where the remains of such shrines have been found include Hazor (no less than six!), Beth-shan (two?), Shechem, and the southern fortress of Lachish, at which the discovery of many precious objects testifies to a variety of cult practices. But the characteristic Canaanite places of worship were what the Bible, speaking of them with horror, has accustomed us to describe as 'high places' (*bamoth*), not necessarily on hill-tops – they could even be in a valley – but artificial or natural mounds or knolls or raised platforms standing above the levels of their surroundings. One great stone mound was at Megiddo (*c.* 1900); on another high platform at Gezer stood nearly a dozen monoliths (*masseboth*), the standing stones or 'sacred pillars' denounced by Israelite prophets, symbols of the male deity as the pillars of Asherah stood for his female counterpart.

Part Two

FROM ABRAHAM TO THE JUDGES

CHAPTER 3

THE PATRIARCHS

i. Abraham, Isaac, Jacob

Throughout the greater part of the second millennium, many nomadic or semi-nomadic bands of refugees, brigands and rebels were continually drifting out of the eastern steppes into the hilly fringes of the settled Canaanite states and neighbouring kingdoms. Some of the immigrants served these established communities as mercenaries, others were forced into slavery, others again remained free, raiding and destroying wherever they could. Such landless, stateless individuals or groups, who stood outside the recognized social system for one reason or another, were known to the local officials and populations as *apiru, hapiru, habiru*; the term appears in Egyptian, Canaanite, and other texts. Sometimes, evidently, this shifting population became important enough to fulfil a political role. For example, Labaya, 'the Lion Man' who seized Shechem (Ch.2,i), is reported to have handed the place over to the *habiru*; and he may even have been one of their number himself.

They were probably not a homogeneous group, but of extremely mixed race. Their name has been identified, with some probability, as Hurrian (Ch.2,i), but many of them must have spoken Semitic languages and dialects, and etymological and historical links between *habiru* and 'Hebrew' have been claimed. Indeed it may well be that the Israelites, who made their first appearance in Palestine during this period – the people represented in the biblical story by the patriarchs Abraham, Isaac and Jacob – were *habiru*, not by any means the whole of the *habiru*, however, but part of a much wider socio-economic class of 'sojourners' bearing that name. It was perhaps because they belonged to this class that all the references to 'Hebrews' in the Jewish Bible (except one) allude to events before 1000. Abraham himself is singled out as 'the Hebrew',[1] while the name of one of his supposed ancestors, Eber, seems to be linked philologically with the same root (*ibri*) (cf. Appendix 11).

When these Israelites of the patriarchal age first made their appearance in the country is disputed. Abraham, Isaac and Jacob are ancient names, transmitted by an early tradition; and some believe they were immigrants who arrived before the third millennium was over. But their coming is more generally ascribed to some date, still uncertain, between the nineteenth and sixteenth centuries. In this case they are to be seen as a second or later wave of north-western-Semitic-speaking peoples, invaders or infiltrators, following after the Amorites (Ch.1,ii), or even forming part of the same movement; Jacob, and perhaps Abraham and Isaac too, were Amorite as well as Israelite names. Moreover, later biblical compilers were well aware that their patriarchs had been *gerim* (aliens) in Canaan. They and their dependants can be thought of as semi-nomadic groups with small herds of sheep and goats coming in from the desert in search of summer pasture, penetrating farther and farther through the peripheral zones year by year, and finally, despite the opposition which strangers would inevitably encounter, settling down into groups based on the *beth-ab*, the father's house – in which the head of the extended family had undivided authority – and partially fusing with the local population and its language.

So anachronistic and inconsistent and aetiological (seeking to explain names or phenomena) are the profuse legends that have gathered round the figures of the patriarchs that it cannot even be stated for certain that they ever existed at all – just as Agamemnon and Menelaus, of Greek mythology, may never have existed. Perhaps their names are those of families or clans or tribes, or of groups or sections of tribes, or even of Canaanite gods, rather than of individual persons. Nevertheless, the unanimous weight of tradition still makes it more reasonable to suppose that Abraham, Isaac and Jacob were real individuals – the chiefs or ancestors or founders of tribal units of some sort – and that these men, with their followers, dwelt in Canaan for a longer or shorter time before the final Israelite settlement of the country.

At some early stage, the names of each of them have been associated with a specific sanctuary of pre-Israelite origin: Abraham with Mamre (beside Hebron, in Judah, the southern region of the country), Isaac with Beersheba (farther still towards the south), and Jacob originally with Shechem (in the central highlands). In any case, the existences and traditions of these patriarchs and their adherents seem to have been originally quite separate from one another and unrelated. It was only much later that the compilers of the Bible wove their stories and genealogies together into a single theological construction, the 'patriarchal period', which was usually understood as including Jacob's sons as well, and was hailed as marking the true beginnings of Israel's salvation history.

By the time it reached the Bible (Ch.9,i; 11,iii, 14,iii), the tale of Abraham went as follows. Originally known as Abram, he was said to have come originally from 'Ur of the Chaldaeans', a Sumerian city of Mesopotamia near the head of the Persian Gulf. With his father Terah, his wife Sarai and his nephew Lot, he moved up the Euphrates valley until they came to Haran, a trading centre in northern Aram (Syria). Terah died there, and God, it was said, appeared to Abram and called upon him to move to Canaan, where he would found a great nation, and so, with Sarai and Lot, he journeyed to Canaan, and built altars at Shechem and Bethel. But then famine drove him onwards to Egypt. There, according to the story, the pharaoh of the time admired Sarai and brought her to his court, but later, afflicted by God with plagues, requested the party to leave the country. Returning from Egypt to Canaan, Abram and Lot agreed to part because the grazing was insufficient. Abram settled in the plain beside Hebron, and Lot moved away to Sodom near the southern extremity of the Dead Sea, where his uncle rescued him from marauding local chieftains or kings.

As Sarai had given him no children, Abram took her servant-girl Hagar to his bed, and she bore him a son, Ishmael. But when Abram was ninety-nine and Sarai ninety, God granted them a son, Isaac. It was now that Abraham was given his new name Abraham, meaning – as 'Abram' had, in fact, already meant – 'the father [the deity] is exalted'; but according to popular etymology 'father of a multitude' – 'for I make you the father of a multitude of nations'.[2] And Sarai was renamed Sarah (princess). When the child was born, at Sarah's insistence Abraham sent Hagar and Ishmael away (they are revered as the ancestors of the Arab race). God made a covenant with Abraham and (according to a story to which we shall come later, Ch. 11,iii) tested his obedience by ordering him to sacrifice Isaac, only bidding him to desist when the knife was ready to strike. After Sarah's death at Hebron, Abraham bought the cave of Machpelah as a burial place and interred her there; and he himself was later buried beside her, when he died at the age of a hundred and seventy-five.

Abraham came to be regarded as a figure of overwhelming religious significance, the recipient of God's call, who responded to it with total submission, and received the divine promise of Israel's future destiny. It was claimed, therefore, that his life was a supreme embodiment of the principles by which God's people should live – faith and obedience. This enormous significance encrusted his career with countless folklore motifs and legendary, miraculous stories, and Jews in their daily prayers still refer to him as 'Father', the first man to renounce idolatry and recognize one God, just as to Islam he is the most revered biblical personage, God's friend, *El Khalil*.

But saga, like history, often starts off with an event, and the historian has to give due weight to the tradition that Abraham – viewed as leader of a party of Semitic-speaking men and women who subsequently became known as the Israelites – came originally from Mesopotamia. His reported places of origin are two, 'Ur of the Chaldaeans' in the extreme south of the country and Haran in the extreme north, Lower and Upper Mesopotamia respectively. The introduction of the Chaldaeans or Chaldees was a later anachronism, since Ur was Sumerian and had no connexion with the people known as the Chaldaeans until a thousand years after any possible date to which Abraham can be attributed. Yet Ur itself deserves more careful consideration, for it had been reduced to insignificance long before the Bible was written; and if it had nothing to do with the original events, it is difficult to see why such an unexpected place-name should have been introduced into the story. Besides, certain names in the tale can be paralleled at a suitably early date in Lower Mesopotamia – notably names from the moon cult (Terah = Yerah, the moon), which was Ur's principal worship (and it was by night and moonlight that Abraham must have travelled with his flocks). As for Haran, the place does not seem to have become an important caravan centre until towards the end of the second millennium, long after the presumed date of Abraham. Yet the nomenclature ascribed to Abraham's ancestors significantly corresponds with the names of towns in its neighbourhood. Indeed, it is not impossible that the entire patriarchal tradition originated there. Others would prefer to believe that it took shape on the semi-desert fringes of north Syria or Transjordan, which are known to have been frequented by quasi-nomad groups resembling Abraham's supposed following.

Hebron, the Palestinian sanctuary-town with which his sagas had the closest associations, stood upon the major route commanding the approaches from the Dead Sea and Jordan valley into the central hills. The valleys around are fertile and fruitful, and Hebron's market was within hail of the desert and its trade. After arriving in this southern area, a group such as Abraham's would be very likely to have made forays into Egypt in search of better grazing grounds, and it was probable enough that some of his followers would have remained in that country once they had reached it.

The biblical account of Abraham's son Isaac proceeds as follows. Abraham sent a servant to his kinsmen in Haran to find a wife for Isaac, and the messenger returned with Rebecca. After many years God answered Isaac's prayer for a son, and she gave birth to twins, Esau and Jacob. God bestowed upon Isaac the same blessing that he had given to his father Abraham, but when Isaac, living in the region of Beersheba, had become old and nearly blind, he was tricked into passing the blessing on to Jacob instead of to Esau, his elder brother. Esau settled in the land known as Seir or Mount Seir and founded the nation of Edom, while Jacob, in order to escape his vengeance, moved on towards the north.

The story of Isaac's deception by Jacob is a relatively late part of the narrative. In general, the traditions concerning this second patriarch do not leave the impression of a personage to whom very deep or widespread reverence was accorded. Such traditions, however, as existed were attached, as we saw, to a sanctuary at Beersheba, the capital of a highly strategic southern border area of Canaan. Its massive, sandy-coloured mound rose above a fertile oasis, famous for its wells, including especially the Well of the Oath or Seven (from which the place was said to have taken its name), adjoining a major Canaanite shrine.

The Bible goes on to tell the story of Isaac's son Jacob. On his way northwards to Haran to escape the anger of his brother Esau, Jacob dreamt he saw a ladder rising to heaven (Jacob's ladder), and heard God speak to him and promise he would bring him back to Canaan. First, however, he worked for twenty years as shepherd for his uncle Laban (meaning 'white' = moon) at Haran. There he married Laban's two daughters, Rachel and Leah, and they and their maids Bilhah and Zilpah (both of mixed race) gave him twelve sons (described in a poem, the Blessing of Jacob[3]) and a daughter Dinah. While finally returning home, Jacob wrestled with a mysterious stranger in the deep gorge of the Jabbok River, a tributary of the Jordan, and God bestowed upon him the new name of Israel. He was welcomed by Esau in Edom with unexpected warmth, but then the brothers parted company, and Jacob lived in Canaan until Joseph, one of his two sons by Rachel, invited him and his family to settle in Egypt, to which he moved, dying at the age of a hundred and forty-seven.

The Jacob traditions that originated at the sanctuary of Shechem were augmented both in the Transjordanian lands and at the shrine of Bethel, where he was said to have built an altar and offered sacrifice (as he had also done previously at Shechem). Bethel, ten miles north of Jerusalem, stands 2,900 feet above sea-level on the watershed of the hill country, with many springs round about. As its name ('House of God') suggests, it was already – like Shechem – a Canaanite sanctuary. Jacob's actions seem to reflect traditions relating to the earliest Israelite settlement of the central massif.

His struggle with a stranger beside the River Jabbok may be connected with legends of river gods who accost strangers but must vanish by dawn. But somehow the struggle came to be linked with the name 'Israel' (Appendix 11) which Jacob was said to have been given by God, as symbol of a new covenant between him and his people. 'Israel' was interpreted as meaning 'the man who prevails with God [and men],[4] but its original significance is lost. It was probably a local name indigenous to the north-central hill country of Canaan and especially related to the inhabitants of the Shechem area, but soon it became regarded as the alternative name of Jacob, from whom all the tribes were supposed to have been descended, the 'children of Israel' (*Bene Yisrail*).

The religion brought into Canaan by the group represented by the patriarchs was based on the 'God of the Fathers' – 'my', 'your', 'his' etc. father – originally the deity of one's immediate father and then extended to more remote forebears. This was a different sort of faith from the religion of nature which these people found among the Canaanites with whom they settled (Ch.2,ii) because it was tied to people rather than places, being based on the divinity's protective relationship with persons, the clan-father and other members of the tribes, rather than with the soil or any fixed point within its borders. Each Israelite clan, it would appear, originally had its own family divinity: the God of Abraham, the 'Fear' or 'Kinsman' of Isaac, the 'Mighty One' or 'Bull' of Jacob, the 'Shepherd' of Israel: all these deities later merged, more or less, with one another.[5]

The introduction of a religion of this kind was appropriate to the mobile patriarchal groups, in contrast to the settled character of the Canaanite population which they joined. Or, perhaps one should say, the patriarchal immigrants *re*introduced this kind of faith. For it is likely enough that earlier waves of Semitic speakers from the fringes, such as the Amorites, had cherished similar beliefs, but that these had become absorbed within the Canaanite nature worship, and had vanished or become dimmed. Indeed this is what nearly happened to the religion of the patriarchs as well, for the continuing recollection, in much later biblical times, of the Canaanite supreme god El, and his local manifestations El Shaddai, El Bethel, El Olam, El Roi and El Elyon (ch.2,ii), shows that the patriarchal worship became substantially assimilated to the cults and local sanctuaries of Canaan. It is symbolic of this situation that King Melchizedek of Jerusalem, we are told, called down the blessing of El Elyon upon Abraham. Yet the basic concept of the patriarchal God of the Fathers, linked to people rather than places – and unconnected with any polytheistic pantheon – did not die, and was destined to bear mighty fruit in the religion later developed by the Israelite people.

ii. Joseph

The Bible next turns to the story of Joseph, the first son of Jacob and Rachel after many years of waiting. According to one of the numerous legends associated with his name, he was presented with a special coat of many colours, or a long-sleeved robe, as a sign that he was his father's favourite. Sent from Hebron to Shechem to help his brothers and half-brothers mind the family flocks, he made them jealous, especially by telling them his dreams, in which they had bowed down before him; and they planned to put him to death. But one of their number, Reuben, persuaded them to wait, and Judah suggested that instead of killing him they should sell him as a slave. So Joseph was enslaved and taken to Egypt, and his brothers dipped his coat in the blood of a kid and showed it to their father, declaring that he had been torn to pieces by a wild animal. In Egypt Joseph was bought by Potiphar, the captain of the pharaoh's guard, and placed in charge of his household. But Potiphar's wife claimed he had tried to rape her, and he was cast into prison. Two years later, however, he was released and sent for by the pharaoh to interpret his dreams – and became the chief minister of the land. After a famine, he made the country rich. Meanwhile, however, the land of Canaan, too, had been struck by a famine, and Jacob sent his other sons to Egypt to buy grain. After testing them, Joseph told them who he was, and invited them to bring their families and their father to Egypt, where they took up residence, and their descendants continued to live.

Joseph died, at the age of a hundred and ten. But then, after the accession of a new pharaoh, 'who knew nothing of Joseph',[6] the fortunes of these Israelites in Egypt underwent a change. They were oppressed and persecuted, and set to work as slaves on the construction of two royal cities, Pithom and Raamses. Finally, the monarch decreed that all their male offspring should be killed at birth, and thrown into the Nile.

This is evidently, for the most part, a fictitious story, or rather, a collection of such stories that were originally separate one from another, but were woven together into their final, complex, elaborately finished form at a much later date (Ch.9,i). It was, however, a historical fact that Semitic-speaking groups (notably the party travelling with Abraham) had already been moving into Egypt – and either staying there or moving out again later – for many centuries past. They had been prompted by the vicissitudes of seasonal pasturage and the need to find food, supplemented at times by an interest in trading, and by the desire to escape from disturbed conditions further north; while a number of pharaohs had added to their number by forcibly removing local Palestinian notables to Egypt.

Tomb-paintings of c. 1900–1890 at Beni-Hasan, two hundred and fifty miles up the Nile, portray a group of thirty-seven of such aliens, led by a certain Ibsha or Abishar (a Semitic name) and accompanied by donkeys bringing lead sulphide (*galena*) from the Red Sea.[7] From the time of the Hyksos onwards (themselves intruders from outside, Ch.1,ii), movements of this kind evidently increased in importance, since Canaanite influence on Egyptian ritual and cult became more and more apparent.

Such are the traditions that lie behind the saga of Joseph. The migrants associated with his name, and those who took the names of his father and brothers, were probably, in fact, quite distinct, unconnected groups. But Joseph's historical existence, and appointment to some sort of high Egyptian office, need not be doubted. According to the Psalms, he and his people lived 'in the land of Zoan',[8] that is to say close to the important city of Tanis (San el-Hagar) in the eastern delta. When they arrived there, we cannot tell. Perhaps this happened during the reign of the pharaoh Seti I (c. 1304–1290), son of Rameses I who was founder of the XIXth Dynasty. Seti I re-established Egyptian suzerainty over Canaan, regaining control of the coastal road, the Way of the Sea or 'Ways of Horus'. It was also he who moved his capital to Tanis, near which Joseph and his followers resided.

Joseph was said to have married an Egyptian woman Asenath (a classic mixed marriage, to be discussed by those who later considered the pros and cons of such unions), and it was claimants of descent from this match who preserved the Joseph tradition, that is to say, the descendants of their sons Ephraim and Manasseh, who gave their names to the central hill country of Samaria. This was the land of Shechem, where Joseph's story began, and where, according to one account, he was buried (a rival claim was put forward by Hebron, where other patriarchs were supposedly interred). The tradition, on the other hand, of the descent to Egypt of those who became known as his father and brothers seems to have originated from separate sources connected with Beersheba, Jacob's point of departure.

The Bible declares that the House of Joseph in Egypt, although consisting of only seventy persons at first, became very numerous and powerful. No doubt they grew considerably in number, but only a very few of them, or none at all, are likely to have become as important as Joseph. They dwelt in Egypt, it was asserted, for four hundred years, though so long a duration is improbable. At any rate, their stay concluded in a crisis which nearly caused disaster. The pharaoh who 'did not know Joseph' and began to oppress the Israelites – recruiting them, that is to say, to carry out his grandiose building projects – may have been (despite arguments to the contrary) Rameses II (c. 1290–1224) of the XIXth Dynasty, who spent much of his long reign contending against a series of revolts in the cities of Palestine. He also fought against the dominant state in Asia Minor, the kingdom of the Hittites whose allies in central Syria, at their instigation, invaded Transjordan. Rameses II moved northwards and confronted the Hittites at Kadesh on the Orontes (c. 1287/6), the site of another encounter two centuries earlier (Ch.1,ii). The famous battle which ensued, despite loud claims of Egyptian victory, appears to have been indecisive, but it resulted in a non-aggression treaty which remained effective for three quarters of a century

It was also Rameses II (or conceivably one of his predecessors) who built Pithom and Raamses, the two places where the Israelites were set to work as slaves. Pithom-Teku (Tell er-Rataba) was at the mouth of the Wadi Tumilat, near the Salt (Bitter) Lakes; the town contained granaries, and it was no doubt on their construction that the Israelites were employed. The location of Raamses (Pi-Ramesse) – one of a number of places known by that name – is uncertain; but it was perhaps the new designation of the city of Avaris, reconstructed as part of a great urban and palace and storage complex centring upon Khatana (Qantir), fifteen miles south of Tanis. The indication that forced labour was imposed on the Semitic-speaking immigrants into Egypt is plausible enough, since many other sectors of the population had to endure similar compulsion. Besides, the later Hebrew writers who reported this Egyptian bondage are unlikely to have made it all up. People do not invent stories of their ancestors' shameful and dishonourable foreign servitude out of nothing at all.

The pharaoh who had begun the oppression of the Israelites died, and another took his place, the monarch whose reign witnessed the Exodus, the escape from the country of this particular group of Israelites belonging to the House of Joseph. If the first oppressor had been Rameses II, the pharaoh of the Exodus was his successor Merneptah (c. 1224–1211).* It so happens that a large black granite stele of Merneptah, inscribed with an account of an alleged military victory, has something to say about Israel. 'Israel is laid waste,' the stele announces; 'its [grain] seed is not.'[9] The word 'Israel' is written with an inflexion indicative of 'people', not of 'country' like other names mentioned in the same inscription, so that the term may, perhaps, not be describing a community already settled in Israel, but a party of wanderers in that country, without a permanent home. Whether the name alludes, however, to the House of Joseph (after its members had undertaken the Exodus), or to some other group of Israelites who arrived in Canaan separately, we cannot tell.

---

* Some place these pharaohs about eleven years earlier or later.

CHAPTER 4

MOSES

i. The Exodus

The Bible's narrative of the Exodus describes how the oppression of the Israelites conducted by the new pharaoh of Egypt, perhaps identifiable with Merneptah (c. 1224–1211), came to an end owing to God's intervention. In the previous Egyptian reign, the story recounts, a son had been born to Amram, of the House of Levi, and his wife Jochebed. When he was three months old, in order to avoid his inclusion in the massacre of Israelite infants, his parents concealed him among the reeds beside the bank of the Nile. However, the pharaoh's daughter found him and later adopted him as her son, naming him Moses. When he grew up, in the new reign, he attacked and killed an Egyptian overseer who was beating an Israelite, and had to flee into the desert. There he dwelt with Jethro, a priest of Midian (east of the Gulf of Elath (Eilat) or Akaba at the northern end of the Red Sea), whose daughter Zipporah became his wife.

After Moses had moved on, the Bible continues, God's voice came to him out of a burning bush and told him that he had been chosen to return to Egypt and lead his compatriots out of their oppression. God gave him magic signs to convince his fellow Israelites and the pharaoh, and he and his brother Aaron returned to Egypt and were received by the monarch, who, however, was not willing to let them go. In consequence God inflicted a series of ten plagues on the country. The last was the most crushing of all: the slaying of every Egyptian first-born son. This made the ruler change his mind: on the night when the slaughter had taken place he sent for Moses and Aaron, and demanded that they should take their people away from the country at once.

So they all set out together, with their dependants and flocks and herds. The party came to an expanse of water, later described (in the Greek Bible) as the Red Sea; but what the original writers had in mind was the north end of the Gulf of Suez, or one of the Salt (Bitter) Lakes, or possibly the Gulf of Elath. At all events, a strong wind had temporarily converted the water into dry land, so that they were able to get across. The

38

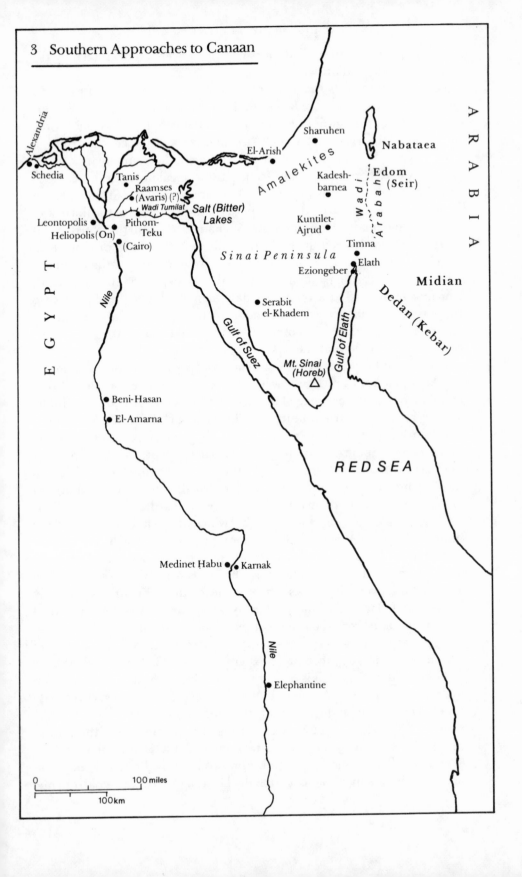

3 Southern Approaches to Canaan

Egyptians, on the other hand, pursuing them, were all overtaken by the returning flood, and drowned.

For ever afterwards this triumphant deliverance was hailed as God's supreme, miraculous act of favour to the people of Israel, and the Exodus from Egypt of this group of Semitic-speaking people, consisting of the members of the House of Joseph (the ancestors of the central tribes of Ephraim and Manasseh), is likely to be an event that actually took place. On many occasions, as we have seen, Semitic-speaking migrants came to Egypt, and subsequently departed. There are Egyptian traditions of such Exoduses. One is described on a papyrus of the last years of the thirteenth century,[1] and a later Egyptian historian named as Manetho noted an expulsion of Jews. Indeed the biblical narrative itself, in the form in which it has come down to us, seems to combine two originally distinct presentations, one concerning a flight and the other an expulsion (Ch.9,i; 11,iii), which were merged at a very early date: namely, the flight of Moses (to the Egyptians, an annoying defection of useful forced labour), and a separate deportation of another Semitic-speaking group, presumably regarded as trouble-makers.

It is not to be supposed that all such escapes or ejections of Semitic-speaking peoples from Egypt were by the same, single route of Moses' flight, involving the crossing of the stretch of water described in the Bible. Thus certain of the tribal units or collections of clans which found their way from Egypt to Canaan do not seem to have taken part in the Mosaic Exodus at all. Some of them may well have left Egypt, by flight or expulsion, before Moses did. A number of these groups probably travelled up the Mediterranean coast by the land-road; the recent failure of archaeologists to find any relevant traces is hardly surprising. This might, for example, be the route by which the whole or part of the southernmost tribe (or confederation) of Judah (which always felt distinct from the the rest of the Israelite population) reached its ultimate destination. And there could easily have been a third exodus, and a fourth. Moreover, the ancestors of some of the other tribes (notably Reuben and Gad across the Jordan) probably arrived in their historical settlement areas from the fringes of the desert, without ever having been in Egypt at all. In addition, some people descended from the groups of Abraham, Isaac and Jacob had no doubt remained in Canaan all along.

As for Moses himself, it is harder to conclude that he never existed than to decide that he did. We do not know, however, what he was originally called. The Bible indicates that the pharaoh's daughter, when she adopted him, named him Moses, 'because I drew him out of the water'[2] (from the Hebrew *mashah*, to draw out). That is an unacceptable etymology. The name is, instead, almost certainly Egyptian, not connected with the sun, as has occasionally been suggested, but a patronymic meaning 'son of' or 'is born'. This was a component of names such as Ahmose and Thutmose (Thutmosis, Thothmes): probably Moses' name likewise had an original preceding syllable indicating the god of whom he was declared to be the son, but this was later dropped when he moved out of Egypt.

The group led out of that country by Moses, according to the Bible, entered the wilderness of Sinai, where he performed miracles to provide them with food and water. After travelling for nearly three months, and repelling marauders, they camped before Mount Sinai (or Horeb), to which Moses had gone before the Exodus. This time, God called him up the mountain-top and ordered him to tell the Israelites that if they would listen to him and keep his covenant, they should become his special posssession, his kingdom of priests, his holy nation. They were ordered to wash and purify themselves for two days. On the third day, amid thunder and lightning and the loud blasts of a trumpet, they came and stood at the foot of the mountain, which was covered in a dense cloud; and then the voice of God himself was heard. Leaving Aaron and Hur (reputed by Jewish tradition to be the husband of his sister Miriam) in charge of the camp, Moses climbed up to the top of the mountain again, disappearing into the cloud that still covered its peak. There he remained for forty days and forty nights, communing with God, who pronounced the Ten Commandments. At the end of this time God gave him two tablets of stone, on which were inscribed 'the law and the commandment [presumably meaning the Ten Commandments] ... written with the finger of God'.[3] When Moses came down from the heights, he found revolt and relapse among his people, and smashed the two tablets in disgust. But after he had passed another forty days on the mountain-top, God inscribed and entrusted him with new ones.

After the Israelites had spent nearly a year beneath Mount Sinai, they moved onwards, and after further vicissitudes came to Kadesh-barnea, near the border of the promised land of Canaan. The question whether they should go further aroused violent disputes. But God, it was said, became so displeased with their lack of obedience that nearly four decades went by before they were able to move on. The Bible records Moses' capture of Heshbon, headquarters of an Amorite King Sihon across the Jordan. Balaam, a prophet in Moabite employment, was also said to have been encountered. Finally, Moses was given a distant view of Canaan, the Promised Land; and then he died.

Whatever miraculous accretions were subsequently added, the tradition that this group of Israelites, the House of Joseph, passed by Sinai or Horeb is probably based on a historical fact, since no external parallel to the unique events associated with their presence there can be quoted. Some have sought to locate the mountain in Jethro's Midianite country, east of the Sinai peninsula, but the ancient tradition relating the story to one of the formidable peaks in the gravelly, dusty southern portion of the peninsula itself may be accepted.

Kadesh-barnea, where Moses and his people next made their appearance, was located at the north-eastern extremity of the Sinai peninsula, fifty miles south-west of Beersheba. Ain Kadeis, which bears its name today, is just an obscure waterhole, but Ain el-Kudeirat, only five miles away, provides the amplest water-supply in the entire area, and the name of Kadesh-barnea was probably extended to the whole relatively large oasis which spread round about, a piece of land which was more fertile then than now and produced good yields of wheat and barley. The place was also an important crossroads, from which routes run in every direction. The emigrants' sojourn in Kadesh-barnea may have enabled them to become fused into a more or less united group. An alleged subsequent detour, to avoid the powerful 'cities' of the Edomites and Moabites, has been doubted on the grounds that no traces of any urban life of the appropriate period have come to light in those countries. Yet even if, as thus seems likely, the peoples in question were still nomads at the time the Israelites might still have wished to avoid them.

Perhaps Kadesh-barnea was regarded as a potential base for an Israelite attempt to invade Canaan. At all events, the Bible declares that before Moses died Yahweh permitted him to see that promised land. This was after he had gone up 'from the lowlands of Moab to Mount Nebo, to the top of Pisgah, eastwards from Jericho', near a site where he had once camped long before. His body was buried in a valley in the land of Moab, opposite Beth-peor, 'but no man knows the place of his burial to this day'. And there was a later tradition that he ascended to heaven.

The Bible records that the Israelites wept and mourned for Moses for forty days: and 'there has never yet risen to Israel a prophet like Moses, whom the Lord knew face to face: remember all the signs and portents which the Lord sent him to show in Egypt to pharaoh and all his servants and the whole land: remember the strong hand of Moses and the terrible deeds which he did in the sight of all Israel.'[4]

Every year, to this day, the Jews commemorate the Exodus in the seven-day spring festival of the Passover (Ch.5,ii), as enjoined by the Bible. For to them, as to all their forerunners from a very early date, this event is the central moment in all history. It was the happening by which they had become a nation, the nation God had set aside as his own, and indeed it is through the Exodus, the writers of the Bible insisted, that the whole of world history is to be interpreted and given its meaning. So those who claim descent from Moses and his followers regard him as the greatest leader the human race has ever known.

ii. The Religion of Moses

Although it was the members of the House of Joseph whom Moses was believed to have led out of Egypt, Moses himself, according to tradition, belonged to another group, descended from Levi, Joseph's half-brother. It has been suggested that the House of Levi had settled near Kadesh-barnea and was among the tribes which had never gone to Egypt at all, but that one of its tribesmen, Moses, was later represented as having done so in order that the credit for the Exodus could go to the Levites. But on the whole it seems easier to suppose that certain of Levi's descendants, including Moses, had been in Egypt along with the descendants of Joseph. Later, the tribe of Levi became a wholly distinct unit, allotted no specific territory but devoted to the priesthood. Moses' brother Aaron, described by the priestly writer (Ch.14,iii), somewhat anachronistically, as the first 'high' priest, and known as the father of priests, personified piety and the spirit of peace in later legends. But Moses, too, came to be regarded as primarily a priest, the true founder of the Yahwist faith.

Indeed, it was largely upon this religious achievement that his renown among his own people rested. And just as it seems more plausible to suppose that Moses existed than to believe that he did not, so, too, it is hard to believe that *all* the mass of religious institutions ascribed to Moses was really the work of other men, the anonymous product, that is to say, of natural, gradual growth over a period of centuries. After all, Zoroaster, Gautama Buddha and Jesus were historical figures, despite the legends attached to their names. And the Mosaic religion contained astonishing novelties which look as though they reflect the thought of one single, decisive individual.

The God to whom Moses devoted himself can be defined as a blend between the 'God of the Fathers' worshipped by his patriarchal forebears and El who had long been the supreme deity of the Canaanites. The subsequent compilers of the Bible were extremely well aware of this dual heritage. For, on the one hand, God was said to have explicitly declared to Moses, 'I am the God (Yahweh) of your forefathers, the God of Abraham, the God of Isaac, the God of Jacob.'[5] Yet, on the other hand, the Bible still abounds in references to El, whose cosmic, royal character was inherited by the God of Israel; and there were still Israelite memories of El's local manifestations such as Shaddai, Bethel, Elyon, El Roi, connected with revered sanctuaries. The local cults, it was seen (Ch.2,ii), tended to make people think not only of a single El but in polytheistic terms as well. And indeed, centuries later, one of the major Hebrew historians (the 'Elohist' or northern historian, Ch.11,iii), though he identifies El with Yahweh, still employs the plural form *Elohim*, while nevertheless ungrammatically treating the word as a singular noun: an anomaly which vividly reflects the transition from a belief in many gods to a belief in one who embraces

43

them all (like equally transitional references to 'the sons of God' sharing out the nations[6]). This was only one of many ways in which the Israelites continued to use Canaanite imagery to convey the might and majesty of their God. For example, they still saw him as a divinity of the storm (Hadad): and, more particularly, they took over the idea that he was the universal Father and Creator.

Moses, it would appear, understood that this blend of the patriarchal and Canaanite ways of regarding deity required a new definition, foreshadowing according to the Bible (or perhaps rather following) what seemed to him and his people the unique, supernatural experience of salvation which had been vouchsafed to them in the Exodus, an experience which had widened and deepened and transformed their knowledge of his character and power. According, therefore, to the Elohist and another biblical writer, the priestly historian (Ch.14,iii), this God now became known under a different name.[7]

His designation, in the vowelless Hebrew language, was YHWH (sometimes shortened to YHW, YHH, YW). How the word was pronounced is not quite certain, because an aversion to uttering it subsequently developed, partly because, as we saw, the comprehensive-sounding Elohim seemed better suited to express universal sovereignty, and partly also because of a feeling that YHWH was too sacred to utter. Later Jews therefore tended to replace it by Adonai (Lord), though this is misleading, because the substitution does not bring out the fact that YHWH is a specific name. Probably it is best transcribed as 'Yahweh'. (The erroneous version 'Jehovah' arose when medieval Christians inserted the vowels from 'Adonai' between the consonants YHWH – the 'e' in Jehovah being the indeterminate Hebrew vowel which appears as initial 'a' in Adonai.)

God himself, it was declared, had revealed his new name of Yahweh to Moses. This supposed revelation was the equivalent to the disclosure of his real nature, since a name was regarded as an effective expression of the character of the being it described. Words were power, conveying a sense of forces and energies: knowing the name of a god or spirit might give the knower some control over his or its activity, so that knowledge of the name of Yahweh meant that Moses and his people were initiated into a secret which conferred on them special and potent insight into his purpose. A new name must have seemed a new god, a god at least equal to the chief gods of the defeated Egyptians.

If not entirely new, 'Yahweh' was at least – contrary to the 'Yahwist' or southern historian (Ch.9,i) – a relatively unfamiliar designation, since a survey of recorded personal names (which often incorporate part of the name of a deity) shows that its distinctive element scarcely makes its appearance in pre-Mosaic times. A possible exception is the name of

Moses' own mother, Jochebed: but it is not certain that this incorporates 'Yahweh', and even if it does, she, like Moses himself, may have abandoned her old name (unknown) in favour of a new one. And this change of name, if it occurred, may have happened at Sinai, for it was probably during their sojourn beside the mountain that the Israelites renamed their God and called him Yahweh. That may well be why he is described as the One of Sinai (*zeh Sinai*), the God of Sinai, the God who came from Sinai, in certain passages of the Bible, including the Song of Deborah which is one of the very earliest Hebrew poems (Ch.5,i).[8] A god of mountains, he dwelt above all on Mount Sinai or Horeb, the place, men said, where Moses was granted the divine revelation. Moses had been there before, and on that occasion he may already have formed a connexion with the Yahweh cult, existing, at the time, as a purely local institution. This could have been why he returned to the mountain, straight from the miraculous escape of the Exodus: because he believed that it was Yahweh, god of those heights, who had saved him and his people.

It has been suggested that the word YHWH may come from the same root as *ehyeh*, the verb 'to be' in north-west Semitic speech. In any case, according to the northern, Elohist historian – though the tradition may well go back to Moses himself, or at least to a time very close to him – Yahweh defined himself in terms of this verb. For it is declared that he told the Israelites *ehyeh asher ehyeh*, 'I am who I am', 'I am; that is who I am', or 'I am the one who is'.[9] His essentially unchangeable continuity of existence, that is to say, can be seen at all times, including the present, here and now: there is no need for a divine mythological history like those attached to the gods in whom other peoples believe, because his character is revealed in his actions. However, a rival, alternative translation is also possible. This is because the two (perfective and imperfective) aspects of the Hebrew language – which lacks the tenses of Indo-European tongues – do not discriminate between past, present and future, leaving the context to determine the time relation. That is to say, *ehyeh asher ehyeh* may be intended to possess not so much an exclusively present as a future significance, bearing the meaning: 'I shall be what I shall be'. God, in other words, will be revealed by his future presence: just as he has granted salvation to the Israelites in the past, so he promises them salvation in the days to come; the Israelite people, as it goes forward into the future, will be accompanied by his protection and will gain ever deeper knowledge of his purpose. But the mystery, inherent in this formulation of an ineffable, metaphysical concept, cannot be said to have been dispelled.

The mystery was also deliberately increased by a specific, striking and permanent innovation. Yahweh must be imageless: this simplest form of the second Commandment (see below) forbidding images of the deity is very likely to go back to Moses himself. This, as far as we know, is something unprecedented. The veto on images of other kinds as well[10] – notably, artistic representations of human beings and animals – was a later and secondary (and not invariable) development, but images of Yahweh were taboo from a very ancient date, because they tended to *localize* his divinity. People accustomed to the Canaanite attachment to places – and to the statues and statuettes of gods and goddesses – must have found this hard to accept or understand. But the point was that nothing in all nature can be compared to Yahweh, or can represent him. Nor was he himself visible. 'My face you cannot see, for no mortal man can see me and live'[11] (and the biblical editors were later inclined to expurgate or trim suggestions that, on any occasion, God *had* been seen).

Contrary to views that have sometimes been expressed, the Israelites did not yet clearly think of Yahweh as relating himself to the whole world – even if, on occasion, he could be described as its creator and master, like the Canaanite El before him. For the people of Israel concentrated exclusively upon his role as protector of themselves, though this might well involve him in dealing with other nations. And dealing with other nations meant suppressing them, for Yahweh, throughout history, continued to be regarded (like his Canaanite forerunners) as a warlike god, presiding over a warlike people. And 'Yahweh's wars', sacred conflicts followed by the sacrifice of all prisoners and loot to himself, became a prominent idea in the era of fighting that lay not far ahead.

It is true that Egypt out of which the Israelite group led by Moses made its way had not long previously been the temporary scene of a sort of theoretical solar monotheism, among the priests of the XVIIIth Dynasty pharaoh Amenhotep IV or Akhenaten (*c.* 1379–1362), but that movement had arisen among a people far more advanced than the early Israelites, and the hypothesis that such ideas influenced Moses, even indirectly, remains dubious. For he does not seem to have been a monotheist, but a believer that Yahweh was the God of his own people: to call him an incipient, implicit, relative, seminal or practical monotheist does not produce enlightenment.

But was he perhaps, if not a monotheist, at least a henotheist (believer in one God, without actually asserting that he is the only God), and a practiser of monolatry (the worship of only one God)? The intensity of his religious experience may well have made him move a long way in that direction – the first Commandment 'thou shalt have no other god [or gods] to set against me' is ancient. Nevertheless, the Bible's continuing tendency to speak of God by the local names of El (representing, almost, local deities as well as local manifestations of the supreme deity) shows that this henotheism was for a long time modified and qualified by surviving polytheistic elements. The biblical writers, for centuries, did not suggest that other divinities had no existence at all.

All the same, whatever others might believe, Moses was convinced that the people of Israel must concentrate totally on the worship of Yahweh. That is the meaning of the six Hebrew words known as the Shema, and translated 'Hear, O Israel, the Lord is our God, one Lord' (or 'The Lord, and the Lord alone, is our God', or 'The Lord our God, the Lord is One'). And this is added: 'You must love the Lord your God with all your heart and soul and strength.'[12] That was the ringing manifesto of a religion worshipping a God who is described as uncompromisingly, forcefully, passionately jealous and exclusive, *el ganna*, the one who tolerates no rival.

Employing Moses as his intermediary on Mount Sinai, Yahweh was believed to have sealed his exclusive link with the people of Israel by pronouncing a formal, solemn pledge or oath or obligation (*berith*), a term usually translated, not altogether satisfactorily, as 'covenant', binding them to himself with the promise: 'I will adopt you as my people, and I will become your God.'[13] And this assurance, the tradition asserted, was repeated over and over again from one generation to another, in many variant forms. The formulations are sometimes much later, as their treaty-type shape and style show (Ch.14,ii), but it is generally agreed that the core of the tradition goes back to the very earliest sources: perhaps it goes back to Moses himself. The Sinai covenant has a twofold meaning: it is a pledge undertaken, as an act of grace, by Yahweh himself following up his salvation act of the Exodus. And at the same time it is an obligation imposed on the people to whom the pledge is addressed. What precedents there were for such a conception remains unknown, since covenants said to have been entered upon with figures of the past – Noah and the patriarchs – were only legendary, and in any case were only believed to have been contracts made by Yahweh with a single, chosen person, but the covenant of Sinai was not only individual but collective, involving *all* members of the community; it was a proclamation that effectively elevated worship from mere appeasement of haphazard forces to a close, dynamic mutual arrangement and nexus between the deity and his entire people.

Loyalty (*hesed*) to the covenant, a difficult and exacting path to follow, is presented as the first and most necessary of human virtues: 'I will honour those who honour me.'[14] And this loyalty was held to require obedience to a stringent system of ethical requirements. The Canaanite religion, from which the Israelites inherited so much, had already possessed ethical features, declaring that God the Father was virtuous, compassionate and merciful, and that people on earth were in duty bound to follow his ways (Ch.2,ii). The Israelite religious leaders, too, pursued both these insistences – upon the morality of God, and upon the morality of his people. And they probably went further than Canaanite codes in their emphasis not only upon piety but upon moral and humane conduct as well, regardless of social rank and status.

The most fundamental of these Israelite requirements is to be found in the Ten Words or Ten Commandments (Decalogue), believed to have been inscribed on the tablets Moses received from Yahweh. The Commandments are recorded in the Bible in two somewhat different formulations, an 'ethical' and a 'ritual' form. The 'ritual' form is more suitably framed for a settled agricultural community, so that it seems the later of the two. The earlier, 'ethical' Commandments begin with precepts of a non-ethical type relating to the exclusive acceptance of the Israelites' One God, who had brought them out of Egypt, and must not be represented by images, and is jealous. But then follow six moral injunctions:

> Honour your father and mother.
> You shall not commit murder.
> You shall not commit adultery.
> You shall not steal.
> You shall not give false witness against your neighbour.
> You shall not covet your neighbour's property [which is specified in detail].

These commandments and prohibitions are in the form known as 'apodeictic', that is to say they are absolute and categorical and unconditional, without any of the provisos concerning mitigations or special situations ('when a man does so and so') characteristic of the alternative, 'casuistic' type of regulation. Casuistic laws were familiar enough to the Canaanites, but the Ten 'apodeictic' Commandments seem to be distinct from the Canaanite tradition. They may therefore be identified as original Israelite contributions – datable, with reasonable probability, to the period before the Israelites entered Canaan, that is to say (even though our evidence for Hebrew writing only begins at a later date, Ch.8,ii), perhaps to the time of Moses himself: who may have enunciated them as principles when he was settling disputes between tribes, clans and families at the 'justice spring', *en mishpat*, at Kadesh-barnea.

CHAPTER 5

CONQUEST AND SETTLEMENT

i. Joshua and the Judges

After the death of Moses, according to the Bible, Joshua the son of Nun, to whom he had entrusted his mission, was commanded by Yahweh to lead the people into the Promised Land of Canaan. After crossing the Jordan, Joshua set up an altar of twelve stones (taken from the river) at Gilgal, and captured the city of Jericho, of which the walls fell miraculously at the sound of his trumpets. Then he went on to take Ai, not far from Bethel, by a trick, and built an altar on Mount Ebal near Shechem. Subsequently he defeated an alliance of southern monarchs, led by Adonizedek, the king of Jerusalem, and defeated a coalition of northern kings as well. The second part of the *Book of Joshua* begins with a list of the districts not yet conquered – comprising the plain and valley regions and the coast – and the areas allocated to the Israelite tribes, on either side of the Jordan, are also enumerated. Joshua is said to have delivered great harangues: a speech on Mount Ebal warning his followers against falling away from the faith, and an address to a national assembly at Shechem recalling Yahweh's past mercies and ordering the people to pledge allegiance and obedience to a new covenant. Although the book named after him contains important and ancient material, Joshua's reported achievements include substantial exaggerations and inventions: what had been, in fact, a much more complex series of events is telescoped (amid serious contradictions) into the story of his own single, heroic figure (Ch.9,i).

The House of Joseph was becoming divided into two groups named after his sons, Ephraim and Manasseh. Joshua, who had succeeded Moses as leader of all these immigrants, was evidently an Ephraimite: the place where he was buried in the Ephraim hills, when he died at the alleged age of a hundred and ten, was 'within the border of his patrimony'[1] – in the richest and most advanced region of the country. And it is likewise evident that his historical activities were mainly concerned with the settlement of these two sets of people. It took place in the hilly but not unfertile or unprosperous core of Canaan, from which the

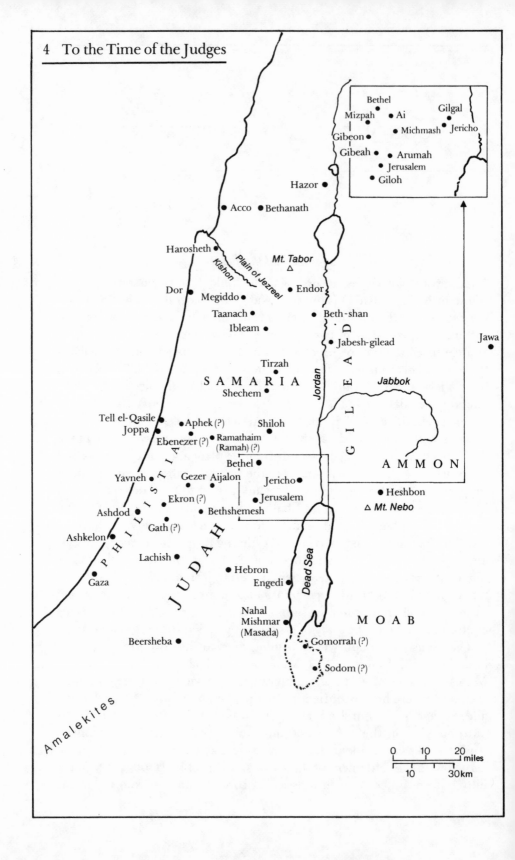

4 To the Time of the Judges

Bethel
Mizpah ● Ai   Gilgal
Gibeon   ● Michmash Jericho
Gibeah
● Arumah
● Jerusalem
● Giloh

Hazor ●

Acco ● ● Bethanath

Harosheth ●

Kishon
Plain of Jezreel
Mt. Tabor △

Dor ●   ● Endor

Megiddo ●

Taanach ●   ● Beth-shan

Ibleam ●

● Jabesh-gilead

G I L E A D

Tirzah ●
S A M A R I A   *Jabbok*
Shechem ●

Jordan

Tell el-Qasile ● ● Aphek (?)   Shiloh ●
Joppa ●
Ebenezer (?) ● Ramathaim   A M M O N
(Ramah) (?)

Bethel ●
Yavneh ● Gezer Aijalon   Jericho ●
● Ekron (?)   ● Jerusalem   ● Heshbon
Ashdod ●   ● Bethshemesh   △ *Mt. Nebo*

Gath (?) ●

P H I L I S T I A
Ashkelon ●

Lachish ●   ● Hebron

J U D A H   Engedi ●

Gaza ●

Dead Sea

Nahal
Mishmar ●   M O A B
(Masada)

Beersheba ●   Gomorrah (?) ●

Sodom (?) ●

Jawa ●

A m a l e k i t e s

0   10   20 miles
10   30 km

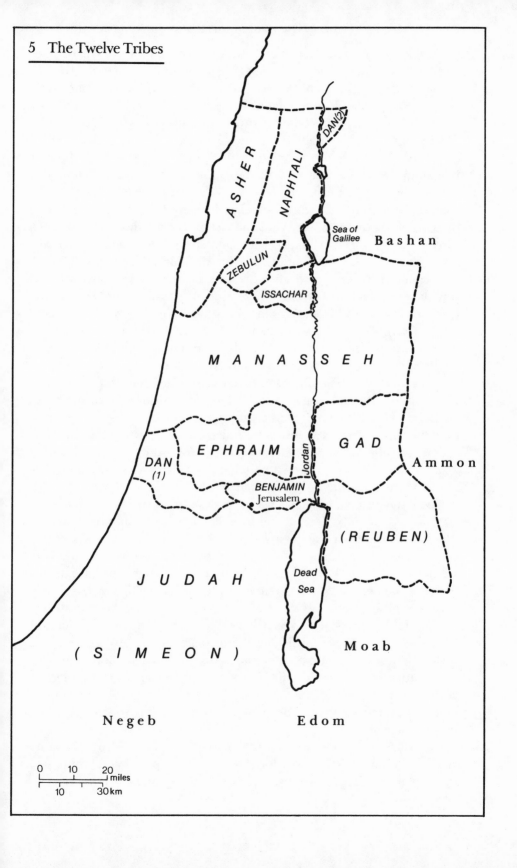

ASHER

NAPHTALI

DAN (2)

Sea of
Galilee

Bashan

ZEBULUN

ISSACHAR

MANASSEH

EPHRAIM

GAD

DAN
(1)

Jordan

Ammon

BENJAMIN
Jerusalem

(REUBEN)

JUDAH

Dead
Sea

(SIMEON)

Moab

Negeb

Edom

0   10   20 miles
   10   30 km

new settlers expanded later to the lowlands and peripheries, where other Israelites, too, had made or were making their appearance (Ch.4,i).

Their clans (*alafim*) were already, no doubt, grouped together into more or less distinguishable autonomous tribes, whose members believed they were descended from a common ancestry. And now, as the final settlement progressed, gradually it became possible to count twelve of these tribes. At first there were eleven, named after Joseph, his full brother Benjamin (their mother was Rachel), and nine of his half-brothers: namely the sons of Leah, who were Levi, Simeon, Reuben, Judah, Issachar and Zebulun; the sons of Bilhah, who were Dan and Naphtali; and the sons of Zilpah, who were Gad and Asher. It was when Levi, to which Moses had belonged (Ch.4,ii), became a special priestly unit excluded from the territorial distribution that the division of the tribe of Joseph into separate tribes named after his sons Ephraim and Manasseh was completed, since this conveniently retained the sacred number of twelve (the term 'Mount Ephraim' is sometimes loosely employed to cover both those areas). A very early document, the Song of Deborah (see below), only mentions ten of these tribes, and (amid fluctuations of identity and territory) the final configuration, familiar from modern maps, may not have been established until some centuries after the time of Joshua. Meanwhile, although some of the tribes, as the same poem indicates, could be induced to join together in temporary coalitions, for the most part they long remained mutually independent. Despite biblical indications to the contrary – the suggestion, for example, that Joshua's assembly at Shechem was on a national scale – there was still no single, united Israelite nation for a long time to come.

No archaeological trace has yet been found of the initial, partial penetration of Canaan by Joshua and his following. The tradition, however, that they forced their way westwards across the Jordan, somewhere near Gilgal, may well be correct; the place soon became an important shrine. Joshua's capture of Jericho, encrusted with a mass of heroic legends, has been doubted on the grounds that excavations have failed to disclose the existence of any such city at the time (the last having been destroyed before 1300). Others, however, believe that a small settlement or fort still existed, and the place, furnishing the strategic key to further conquests west of the Jordan, would have provided Joshua with a natural target. But his capture of Ai (Aiath, Aija, Ha'ai) – where the pass from Jericho emerges on to the plateau north of Jerusalem – seems to be a biblical invention, intended to provide an explanation of the place-name – which means 'heap of ruins'.

The story also offers an account of Gibeon (Tell el-Jib), a trading centre – perhaps fortified not long previously – upon an outcropping of the hills five miles from Jerusalem, beside the strategic west–east route from Jericho to the coast. It was a treaty the Israelites made with its ruler, we are told, which provoked the king of Jerusalem, Adonizedek, against them; and there seems no good reason to doubt this tradition.

At Hazor, in the extreme north, the Bible reports two successful Israelite engagements at different times, the first fought by Joshua and the second after his death. It looks as if the earlier of these battles was invented for the specific purpose of glorifying Joshua, who in historical fact did not penetrate so far. Certainly, excavations suggest that Hazor was destroyed before 1200; and they also reveal the destruction of many other cities of Canaan as well, in the thirteenth or early twelfth centuries to which Joshua and his settlement may be attributed. But whether, in those troubled times, the destroyers were Israelites or others, we cannot tell.

The *Book of Joshua*, despite extolling that hero's successes, nevertheless permits Yahweh to comment, when he was already old, that 'much of the country remains to be occupied.'[2] It is later explained that Yahweh *had* kept his promise to give Joshua and his people all the Promised Land, but that nevertheless certain peoples had been left unconquered in order to 'test' those Israelites who had not taken part in the operations. That comment was made in the *Book of Judges* by the southern historian (Ch.9,ii), dealing with the period immediately following Joshua's death. *Judges*, for all its evident desire to present a fully national picture, on the whole offers a more realistically fragmented (and older) version of events, according to which individual tribes or smaller groups had been and still were moving separately into particular areas on their own initiative, with varying success. In the words of a psalmist, 'the people were few in the land, strangers in the land of Canaan they wandered.'[3] They were held up and kept apart by lines of important cities that still stayed under Canaanite or other alien control. They included Jerusalem, Aijalon (near Gibeon) and Gezer – a wedge cutting the country almost in half. And then, further north, there were other alien strongholds, such as Dor, Megiddo, Taanach, Ibleam and Beth-shan, dominating the plain of Jezreel to which the Israelites still did not enjoy access, as well as Hazor beyond.

What Joshua himself seems to have achieved, amidst all these foreign cities, was to establish himself at Shechem as successor to the kingdom which Labaya and his sons had created and kept outside Egyptian control (Ch.2,i). Shechem was still a very important sanctuary. However, like the shrines at Gilgal and Bethel, it was subsequently outranked by Shiloh (Khirbet Seilun) a little to the south. Centrally situated in the territory of Ephraim, Shiloh staged an annual harvest festival (the Feast of Tents or Books or Tabernacles, Ch.8,i), much frequented by pilgrims; and its priests traced their ancestry back to Moses' brother Aaron. The Israelite tribesmen resorted to the keepers of such shrines to settle their disputes, so that these holy places gradually brought the still disunited tribes into a closer association.

It remains to be decided whether the early settlements were mainly conducted by victorious military force, or arranged by peaceful means. The Bible, for reasons of national pride, usually tends to take the former view. Thus even the *Book of Judges*, despite its more realistic recognition of the gradual nature of the process, provides a striking recital of relentless warfare between the Israelites and the hostile Canaanites whose lands they were trying to take over. It is true that the Israelite tribesmen must often have been severely at odds with the dwellers in Canaanite cities. But much of the emphasis on triumphant fighting by a series of biblical historians was due to animosity towards the religion of Canaan.

In contrast to this militaristic interpretation, most students are now disposed to agree that, although striking victories were won, authentic examples of such operations are rare–the capture of Jericho may have been one of them – and most of the military successes, and sharp hostile relations that prompted them, should be attributed to a subsequent stage. In other words, the initial settlement was largely peaceful, conflict being the exception rather than the rule. In parts of the central zone the immigrants were moving into largely uninhabited or sparsely populated country, and elsewhere they must very often have gradually reached some accommodation with the Canaanite townsmen and villagers, to whose settled way of life they soon began to approximate. The Bible itself, in a number of passages, reveals that such immigrants were actually welcomed by local leaders (presumably as potential subjects), provided that they had substantial herds to contribute, and were prepared to open up uncultivated territory.

After all, Canaanites and Israelites spoke related tongues; and Shechem, for example, was inhabited by both groups, and possessed a thoroughly mixed religion (Ch.5,ii). And an Israelite personage from Manasseh, of whom we shall shortly hear more, possessed both a Yahwist and a Canaanite name, Gideon and Jerubbaal (though the Bible chooses to give the latter an anti-Canaanite significance).[4] He took a Canaanite woman from Shechem as his concubine, and their son Abimelech was willing and able to exploit the connexion. The two peoples were threatened by common external enemies, and there was obviously a great deal of ethnic intermixture. This was a matter on which the Bible, owing to the hostilities that gained force later, was unlikely to dwell, but many centuries later the prophet Ezekiel still saw fit to puncture Jerusalem's exclusiveness with the sharp words: 'Canaan is the land of your ancestry and there you were born; an Amorite was your father and a Hittite your mother.'[5]

The *Book of Judges* recounts the sagas of twelve national heroes after Joshua's death, who were *shophets*, 'judges' of Israel. Six of them, the 'major' judges, Othniel, Ehud, Deborah, Gideon, Jephthah and Samson, were ascribed exploits which earned descriptions of considerable length. To judge, in this context, means to govern, though judging, too, was part of these chieftains' job, since wise arbitrators, such as Deborah, gained renown for their wisdom and impartiality. These judges, then, were local, tribal, small-scale rulers, belonging to various regions, whom the Bible later endowed with an artificial framework, sequence and chronology, and regarded as the originators of the 'First Commonwealth' of the Israelite people.

This fragmented tribal rule continued for more than a hundred and fifty years, during the twelfth and eleventh centuries BC. In relatively quiet times, the tribes were administered by councils of elders, but judges were temporarily appointed when menacing external attackers – Canaanites and others – demanded such an emergency measure. Although the judges varied in origin and office and character, they shared a common reputation as demonstrable, or potential, deliverers and saviours. They were held to have been marked out for their calling by the special intervention of Yahweh – his spirit 'came upon' Othniel, and 'suddenly seized' Samson (Ch.6,i): a violent seizure conferring super-human strength.

One judge, Gideon-Jerubbaal of Manasseh, had to deal with a danger-ous, indeed nearly fatal, threat that had arisen from a nomad people described as Midianites (the northern branch of that tribal group, far from their Sinaitic kinsmen). For seven years past, we are told, these oppressors had asserted total dominance over all, or nearly all, the areas settled by Israelite tribes. Gideon engaged the forces of Midian on Mount Tabor, a perilously exposed region for such an enterprise since it was close to the plain of Jezreel, still under Canaanite occupation; and, besides, the enemy had introduced a new and formidable element of mobility into the warfare of the region by their employment of camels. So when Gideon, exploiting surprise guerrilla tactics and making skilful use of terrain, put them to rout, this was a major landmark in the history of the Israelites, who were now in a much better position to deal with the Canaanite cities of the neighbourhood. As a result of Gideon's success, the tribes of Asher and Zebulun offered him some sort of monarchical rule, including the assurance that, although not yet described as 'king', he might be permitted to found a dynasty of his own. It was said that he declined the offer and retired into private life, though this cannot be regarded as certain. In any case, after his death, his son Abimelech established autocratic rule, launching a murderous *coup d'état* at Shechem and ruling for three years at the adjacent hill fortress of Arumah before suffering a fatal injury during the course of a siege.

The mother of Abimelech was a Canaanite, and a more respected figure, too, the judge Jephthah, was likewise born to a non-Israelite woman, the wife of his father Gilead (after whom an area east of the Jordan was named). These are classic cases of the external dilemma encountered by the Israelites, hinging on the extent to which they should remain apart from all other peoples, or associate (in these instances intermarry) with foreigners (Appendix 4). The name of Jephthah also came to be associated with a story involving the sacrifice of his daughter, a mythical incident from which a four-day annual festival for unmarried girls – mourning her death as Syrians mourned for the death of Adonis – was believed to have originated; it took place at Ramath-Mizpah, which has not been identified with certainty. Despite such legends, however, Jephthah is likely to have been a historical figure, a bandit and cunning bargainer who repelled not only the non-Israelite Ammonites on his own far side of the river, but also his own hostile (Ephraimite) compatriots on the nearer bank. Here was a situation in which the peoples of Israel, so far from being united, were even, on occasion, fighting one against the other. Thus the tribe of Benjamin too – occupying a diminutive territory sandwiched between Ephraim and Judah – was savaged by a temporary grouping of certain other tribes, ostensibly because of its own brutal behaviour, but also because its smallness made it a tempting and vulnerable target to its stronger fellow Israelites on either flank.

The story of Deborah, the only woman judge, and the first of many women who receive conspicuous honour in the Bible, is told twice over, in a poem and a somewhat divergent prose version derived from these verses.

Towards the north of the country, once again in the tense region round the plain of Jezreel, Deborah had became a local leader, and called upon a military man, Barak, to confront a hostile foreign coalition. This enemy force was led by Jabin, king of Hazor (not crushed by Joshua, as the Bible reported) and by his general Sisera – a non-Semitic name – from Harosheth 'of the Gentiles' (in the poem Jabin does not appear, and Sisera is the king).

At Deborah's prompting, Barak raised what must have been an unusual, and indeed probably unprecedented, alliance of no less than six of the Israelite tribes: four others of the twelve held aloof, and two are not mentioned. Then at Taanach, on the southern fringes of the Jezreel plain, the Israelite army fell on their foes, at a time when they were terrified by a fierce thunderstorm. The enemy's chariots proved useless on the sodden ground, and the swollen River Kishon swept their fugitives away. Sisera took refuge in the tent of a certain Heber (a Kenite, migrant from the northern fringes of Arabia), whose wife Jael, with a tent-peg, broke Sisera's head open as he lay asleep.

Deborah and Barak did not succeed in finally dislodging the

Canaanites from the Jezreel plain. Nevertheless, their military success was a remarkable one, perhaps the first the Israelites had ever gained over Canaanite forces in a pitched battle. The occasion was also of exceptional significance because the Song of Deborah, commemorating the engagement, has survived.

> Down marched the column and its chieftains,
> The people of the Lord marched down like warriors....
> Kings came, they fought:
> They fought the kings of Canaan
> At Taanach by the waters of Megiddo....
> The stars fought from heaven,
> The stars in their courses fought against Sisera.
> The torrent of Kishon swept him away,
> The torrent barred his flight, the torrent of Kishon:
>   March on in might, my soul!
> Then hammered the hooves of his horses,
> His chargers galloped, galloped away.[6]

Allowing for a certain amount of later elaboration, the basic structure and content of this poem are agreed by scholars to be contemporary with the victory it celebrates: it may even have been sung at the camp feast immediately after the battle, to the accompaniment of music and choral dancing. The Song, notable for its dramatic vitality and rapid, impressionistic contrasts, purports to be Deborah's own composition, although the allusions to her authorship which occur in its text may have been subsequently interpolated. That the Hebrews employed writing as early as the time of Deborah is not susceptible of demonstration (Ch.8,ii). But in any case there is good reason to regard her Song, not only as an invaluable testimony to the epoch of the judges, but as the earliest example of Hebrew verse and literature that has come down to us. It includes terms and metaphors and other stylistic elements strongly reminiscent of Ugaritic verse (Ch.2,i), and it is to these rich influences and models that we must ascribe the beginnings of Hebrew poetry.

There are other biblical poems, too, with equally strong Canaanite characteristics, which may likewise go back to the time of the judges, notably certain Psalms (in whole or part), the oracles of the prophet Balaam, the Songs of the Red Sea attributed to Moses and Miriam, and, less probably, the Song and Blessing ascribed to Moses shortly before his death.

The Israelites of the House of Joseph, when they came out of Egypt, had already no doubt spoken some Semitic tongue – we do not know its detailed characteristics – dating back to the patriarchal period, with subsequent accretions added. But after arrival in Canaan, while still retaining elements of this earlier speech, they gradually developed biblical Hebrew, out of a dialect of the north-western Semitic language spoken by the Canaanites, which their own speech continued to resemble closely in syntax, style and metre.

It became a medium which particularly lent itself to poetry, taking the form of a kind of heightened prose; and the poetry of the Israelites and their descendants, which forms a large part of the Bible, and often precedes its prose sections in date, is one of the supreme products of that people's genius. This can even be seen from translations, if they are good enough. True, the success of the Authorized Version of 1611 in reproducing the dignified sonority of the Bible has rarely, if ever, been repeated, though more accurate versions have been subsequently produced. Complete accuracy, however, still remains hard to attain, and the meaning of many passages is still disputable. The distinctive feature of the language is its flexible structure, based on sense: form becomes determined by content. For example the typical parallelisms of Hebrew poetry – echoing, balancing, synonymous, repetitive or antithetic units of two short, paratactic sentences, such as had also been characteristics of Canaanite verse – depend essentially on a pattern of *thoughts* which are expressed in strong, clear, concrete images, drawn systematically from the facts of agricultural and, later, urban life.

Excavations have now revealed ample evidence of widespread new Israelite settlements of the time of the judges (among the latest to be discovered is Giloh, just south-west of Jerusalem). It has become clear from these finds that the settlers, or their descendants, were by this time adopting the fully sedentary way of life they had learnt from the Canaanites, congregating in villages and towns. Plaster-lined, non-porous, watertight cisterns were now to be seen, so that people could live in areas where a permanent water-supply had hitherto been lacking.

Moreover, the Iron Age in Palestine may be said to have started in *c.* 1200, as knowledge of the metal filtered through from the Hittites in Asia Minor. Iron plough tips – replacing tips of holm-oak and copper – made it less laborious to clear the forests, and facilitated the production of crops. But iron only came into use gradually and partially; at the end of the second millennium it was still something of a rarity. Archaeologists detect signs of a recovery in trade, but it was evidently produced by the Canaanites rather than by the tribes of Israel, which still remained far behind them in material civilization.

ii. The Cults of the Settlers

In religious and legal and social developments, the time of the judges is now seen to have been highly significant. The covenant between God and the Israelites, entered into by Moses, was now, after partial occupation of the Promised Land, proclaimed afresh, supposedly by Joshua himself; and thereafter it was often proclaimed over again, probably at annual meetings attended by representatives of some of the still politically disunited tribes. A particularly favoured location for these assemblies was Shechem, with which the memory of Joshua was so closely associated: indeed, that may be why the shrine for which the place was famous actually bore the name of the covenant (El-Berith or Baal-Berith).[7]

These renewals of the covenant, at a revered sanctuary within the Promised Land itself, intensified the Israelites' belief, already stimulated by the Exodus, that they were recipients of Yahweh's special care and committed love, *hesed* – and recipients of his wrath, too, whenever they deserved its infliction. That is to say, they were his Chosen People, his *holy* people, holy to God (*kadosh*), dedicated to him and separate, a people 'dwelling alone, high above all the nations',[8] set apart with a peculiar vocation and a hard, inescapable responsibility.

It was to mark this special, apart character, sealed by the covenant, that the Israelites adopted their characteristic rite of male circumcision, the removal of the foreskin. This practice had been known in the east since at least the third millennium, and the Bible (referring to the employment of Stone Age flint knives for the operation) recognizes its existence among foreign peoples, notably those of the desert and its fringes. The biblical tradition also maintains that the Israelites had practised circumcision ever since the time of Abraham. This is doubtful, but in any case the custom was introduced, or reintroduced, after the move from Egypt into Canaan. In its earliest beginnings it had been an initiation rite at puberty and before marriage, presenting a grown man to the obligations of the clan's adult communal life by the transference of his rude unconsecrated sexual potency to the god of the entire group. But the Israelites moved circumcision forward to earliest infancy. Henceforward, that is to say, every male would be made over to Yahweh, from his very earliest days.

Another institution which they likewise saw in terms of their exceptional status was the Sabbath. This, once again, came into its own during the settlement of Canaan. Yet the Sabbath may have originated at least as early as the time of Moses, seeing that it is mentioned in the ethical Ten Commandments (Ch.4,ii). Or, indeed, Sabbath observance may even be a good deal earlier still, going back to patriarchal times. The custom seems to derive from a day set apart by the Babylonians and Canaanites, in connexion with their cult of the moon. The Babylonians had seen the Sabbath as a day of danger, and the Israelites pursued this idea by relating it to their own perils at the Exodus, relating its meaning 'cease' to their deliverance into a 'place of rest'. Thus it became an integral part of the covenant, but was enlarged in meaning to become a joyful day 'blessed and declared holy' by Yahweh,[9] to whom it belonged: a tithe on time, as later theologians saw it, proclaiming his lordship over the whole of history, reminding the Jews of their unique separateness, and only to be flouted on pain of death.

The simple laws which had accompanied the covenant of Moses were greatly amplified and extended in the time of the judges. Our knowledge of these precepts mainly comes from literature of a much later date (Ch.14,iii), but they themselves were early and fundamental, and formed the nucleus and basis of the Torah, the first five books of the Bible, that gradually developed around them. Law was indissolubly connected with religion, and that in turn was welded together with ethics in the sense of practical behaviour. For faith (*emunah*) is not merely a creed or belief; the Israelites were people who *saw* and *felt*, rather than embraced doctrines, so that faith automatically implied a firm, zealous adherence to a revealed course of action and a specified code. 'O how I love thy law!' declares a later psalmist. 'It is my study all day long. Thy commandments are mine for ever, through them I am wiser than my enemies.'[10]

In Mosaic times the covenant had already been accompanied by 'apodeictic' laws, direct, unconditional, unapplied statements of principle that seem to go back to the earliest dates that we can trace (Ch.4,ii), but bracketed with them, before long, were far more numerous and detailed 'casuistic' laws, provisions for every kind of situation which could arise as a result of an action or an omission. Many of these 'casuistic' laws seem to have been laid down in the time of the judges, being evidently applicable to a people that was no longer semi-nomadic, but had begun to consist of agriculturalists, living in settled communities.

The contents of such regulations, and the precise and compact style in which they are framed, bear a close relation to the legal systems of earlier near-eastern civilizations, from the Sumerians onwards – notably the famous code of the Babylonian monarch Hammurabi (*c.*1728–1683). However, Hammurabi's prescriptions had insisted on the paramountcy of property rights, protected by severe sanctions, whereas the Israelites showed a greater tendency to emphasize the essential rights and obligations of the individual. Besides, whatever debts to Babylonian legislation can be traced in their contents, the casuistic laws of Israel were, naturally enough, much more often and more directly derived, and indeed on occasion borrowed wholesale, from the Canaanites whose neighbours they now were, and whose sedentary way of life they were adopting.

Indeed, a number of Israelite centres continued to retain the designations of the shrines of the Canaanites, in which the word 'house' (Beth, in modern Hebrew Bet, in Arabic Beit) is followed by the name of a Canaanite deity: Bethel, Bethshemesh, Bethanath; not to speak of the inextricable blend of the two cultures at the sanctuary of Shechem, which, combined in its name, as we have seen, allusions to the Canaanite gods (El, Baal) and the Yahwist covenant (*berith*). Indeed, the name 'Jobaal', at the same city, actually means 'Yahweh is Baal'; and Gideon, who also possessed a Canaanite name (Jerubbaal, Ch.5,i), would not have found this strange. Although the Bible declares it to have been a stark choice between Yahwist monotheism and Canaanite polytheism, the situation was in reality much more blurred. Many people, while accepting Yahweh's pre-eminence, continued to worship the deities of Canaan, on whose side wealth and science and culture stood; while others worshipped Yahweh himself as though he was a Canaanite deity.

And yet, in sharp contrast, the Israelites (or some of them) also manifested, at this same time and for evermore, the fiercest reactions against tendencies towards any such blends. Thus Yahweh was not only equated with El and Baal, but was frequently differentiated from them as well, with the utmost vigour and violence, for, after all, there was a fundamental distinction. The Canaanite gods belonged to places and to the soil and to natural, cyclically recurrent phenomena, whereas Yahweh, on the other hand, was a god of people and of the linear, progressive movement of history, which unfolded his purpose – an interpretation that had been so sensationally displayed by the stress laid upon the significance of the Exodus by Moses and those who came after him.

Gradually the tendency to differentiate between the two religions, instead of identifying them, began to prevail among the people of Israel. The tendency to see Yahweh as the God who manifested himself in their own past, present and future national history – and who alone gave that history its meaning – intensified. It seemed clearer and clearer that the Exodus and subsequent entry into the Promised Land were indeed the unmistakable unfoldings of the divine plan, a plan that would vanquish nature, whose slaves the Israelites would never consent to be; they would go on the way mapped out for them by Yahweh despite whatever nature seemed to ordain in contradiction.

So although they inherited or took over fixed Canaanite sanctuaries, the people of Yahweh at the same time deliberately stressed their detachment from such geographical place-related ties by revering a mobile shrine which some of them carried with them, or lodged at successive places (Shiloh, in the last years of the judges). It was a tent (tabernacle), like those used for similar purposes by other ancient peoples (Semites and Egyptians alike): a holy place, and protective sacred standard of war. The surviving descriptions of the Israelite Tent are much later, and include anachronistic elaborations; but they go back to very ancient times. It was the repository of another traditional object, the sacred Ark or Chest. Contradictory ideas were at work here. It was possible to suppose that, just as Egyptian gods were believed to dwell in the portable shrines of their country, so too the Ark was, or contained, a kind of throne which was actually the dwelling of Yahweh. It could therefore be asserted by one school of thought (the priestly historian, Ch.14,iii) that Yahweh might reveal himself and 'meet the Israelites' in the Tent, which was consequently known as *Ohel Moed*, the Tent of the Presence or Meeting.[11] But that very different and increasingly strong trend of opinion which disliked the idea of Yahweh's appearing in visible form (Ch.4,ii) preferred to speak of 'the Ark of the Covenant of Yahweh',[12] containing, not the person of Yahweh himself, but the tablets of stone, setting down the covenant that he had bestowed upon Moses (to whose time both the Ark and the Tent were traditionally attributed).

This increasing religious divergence between the Israelites and Canaanites was, of course, exacerbated by growing political and military tensions. The narrators of the strife between Cain and Abel, Esau and Jacob – nomad and farmer – are at pains to make the point. Such writers were well aware that the Israelites were becoming assimilated to their enemies' agricultural life. Indeed, the assimilation made matters worse, since competition for the land increased jealousy and conflict, or produced them when they had not existed before. No wonder, then, that the Bible seized, with furious disapproval, upon such aspects of Canaanite religious practice as were most manifestly vulnerable (Ch.2,ii). Magic fertility rituals, for example – such as boiling a kid in its mother's milk – are specifically forbidden. Moreover, it was the figurines of Ashtoreth that prompted the Israelite veto on images (Ch.4,ii), or at any rate greatly encouraged it, and temple prostitution is rejected with horror (directed with special severity towards its male version, since homosexuality meets with total condemnation). The strict and meticulous sexual regulations of the Bible represent a deliberate recoil from the ways the Canaanites had followed.

Their human sacrifices of children, too, are condemned as abominable. As for sacrifice in general, a practice going back in many countries to the remotest antiquity, the detailed biblical regulations do not reject the primitive doctrine that costly service to Yahweh will win a reward, or the conception that the very sacrificial act constitutes an atonement in itself. Nevertheless, by way of reaction against Canaanite ideas, progress was early made towards the association of sacrifice with more spiritual ideas of reverence, communion, gratitude and submission.

The Israelites took over, after their fashion, the three great annual, seasonal festivals of the Canaanites: Unleavened (unfermented) Bread (Massoth), when springtime brought the winter rains to an end, 'and the sickle was first put to the standing corn'; Weeks or Pentecost (Sharuoth) in the early summer ('with the first fruits of your sowing'); and Ingathering in the autumn ('when you bring in the fruits of your work on the land'). These ceremonies were seen as admission into the presence of Yahweh, and every adult male had to attend them, while many pilgrims flocked in to the sacred places for the same purpose.

The festivals were enlivened by the impressive and varied music that was a Canaanite heritage, and indeed it was the Canaanites who had taught the Israelite tribesmen how to perform the agricultural tasks that the festivals celebrated. Yet the people of Israel, or more particularly at first the House of Joseph, also introduced characteristic innovations of their own, by explicitly relating each of these cyclical occasions to the linear *historical* events through which Yahweh had brought them salvation. Thus the Feast of the Ingathering, especially associated with Shiloh, was renamed the Feast of Tents or Booths or Tabernacles (Succoth), and transformed into a joyful reminder of their dwelling in huts during their march with Moses through the desert. The Weeks or Pentecost festival was ingeniously subjected to a similar reinterpretation, in order to bear witness to the covenant, believed to have been granted at the same time of year.

The festival of Unleavened Bread, too, came to be joined and united with another occasion for celebration, the Passover (Pesah), which immediately preceded it in the calendar. Alone, perhaps, among the major festivals of the Israelite religious year, the Passover goes back to pre-Canaanite times. It was originally a pastoral rite – the nomads' spring sacrifice of a young animal to bring fecundity to the flock. However, literary Hebrew sources once again related the festival to an occasion of salvation instead – the most momentous of such occasions, the Exodus: on the grounds of Yahweh's fierce assertion that 'on that night I shall *pass through* the land of Egypt, and kill every first-born of man and beast', or alternatively, because he 'passed over' (left untouched) the houses of Israelites in Egypt when he slew the Egyptian children and animals as a punishment for the pharaoh's recalcitrance.[13] However, the true etymology of the word 'Passover' is no longer detectable.

Originally it had not been an occasion for pilgrimage, though it later became one. It was celebrated in the home, and both there and at public services a series of psalms, known as the Hallel, were sung. A remarkable combination of a national and family festival, the Passover, like the three festivals taken over from the Canaanites, invited and invites each successive generation to think back on its people's slavery and liberation and divine selection.

Part Three

THE UNITED KINGDOM

CHAPTER 6

THE PHILISTINES,
SAMUEL AND SAUL

i. The Philistines

The settlement of Canaan by the Israelites does not seem to have been greatly impeded or affected by the Egyptians, whose control over the country had become little more than nominal. In the same year as the XIXth Dynasty pharaoh Merneptah (c. 1224–1211) claimed 'victories' in Canaan (Ch.3,ii), he also had to confront a violent combined incursion of Libyans and 'Peoples of the Sea'. Then Rameses III of the XXth Dynasty (c. 1185–1152) recorded a vast poetic tale of his achievements at Medinet Habu, in which he declared, with the aid of illustrative reliefs, that in his fifth year he had won a Libyan war, and then, three years later, had repelled 'the Great Land and Sea Raids'.[1] These seem to have consisted of a combined attack by a variety of marauding foreigners during a period when the eastern Mediterranean region was convulsed by such violent movements (of which the Homeric account of the Trojan War preserves an echo). Rameses III succeeded in re-establishing Egyptian suzerainty as far north as the plain of Jezreel, but his success was only temporary. The romanticized but basically historical travelogue of Wen-Amun, a Karnak official sent north on a mission by Rameses XI (c. 1100–1085), shows that effective Egyptian domination was by that time virtually at an end.[2]

For one thing, certain of the 'Sea Peoples' had come to stay. Among them were the Philistines (Peleset). Depicted on the monumental frieze of Rameses III as tall, slim warriors wearing tasselled kilts and distinctive ribbed caps or helmets, they had originated from Cyprus or Crete, or for the most part, it seems, from south-west Asia Minor (Caria), where their non-Semitic language appears to have originated. It was written in a syllabic script like the Carian speech, and like the language of Cyprus, but the characters of this script also echo the writings of Mycenaean Greece: for the Philistines possessed strong cultural affinities with the Mycenaeans (speaking proto-Greek) whose powerful city-states in Greece were suffering destruction at about this time. Sea Peoples, including apparently the Philistines, had already been settling in Canaan before the time of Rameses III, at the expense of the Canaanites. And then he himself was evidently forced to allow them to settle in the country in more substantial numbers, hoping that they would serve as his vassals and mercenaries, but they soon threw off Egyptian allegiance.

The principal area in which they established themselves was the southern part of the Canaanite coastal plain, a fertile strip forty miles long and fifteen or twenty miles deep. There, in the course of time, they founded five strong city-states – perhaps encouraged by their former masters the Egyptians, in order to check Canaanite and Israelite aspirations. Three of these states, Ashkelon, Ashdod and Gaza, were beside the coastal road. Ashkelon (Ascalon), rich in wells though it lacked any spring, had long possessed a harbour – though harbours at this time were somewhat rudimentary – and enjoyed a prosperous trade. The same was true of Gaza (the successor of Beth-eglaim) which disposed of useful military resources. So did the fortress and commercial centre of Ashdod (Tell Mor, Minet el-Kalah), three miles from the coast, which the Philistines had destroyed, but subsequently rebuilt. Another of their fortresses, Gath – a generic name meaning 'wine-press' – lay a little further inland (at Tell Gat or Tell es-Safi [Zafit]); and so did Ekron (probably Akir). Moreover, in addition to the five recorded city-states, there were other Philistine settlements as well. Conspicuous among them was the fertile, populous town of Yavneh (Jamnia), which in ancient times included a kind of port, and another harbour town at Tell el-Qasile – its ancient name is unknown – near the northern extremity of Philistine occupation, on the bank of the River Yarmuk. Excavations, and the report of the Egyptian envoy Wen-Amun, show that the Philistines founded the place, and used it for profitable maritime commercial relations with Phoenicia up the coast – and for active competition with the Phoenicians for control of the lucrative sea-trade. Moreover, this Philistine trading was conducted not only by sea but by caravans moving into the desert interior. Such commercial activities were encouraged by the introduction of a new and distinctive form of pottery, which at first echoed the styles of Mycenaean Greek lands, and especially of Cyprus, though subsequently a closer approximation to Canaanite and Israelite products appears.

Perhaps the foundation and maintenance of Yavneh and Tell el-Qasile were combined efforts by the feudal princes of the various Philistine city-states. The same applied to their annual council and unified military command, presiding over a well-armed and trained professional, feudal military class dominating the local Canaanite populations. The army depended upon a monopoly of the iron which had been recently reaching the country (Ch.5,i). This monopoly, we are told, meant that they denied blacksmiths and iron weapons and tools to their Israelite neighbours,[3] and, no doubt, as far as they could, to the Canaanite city-states as well.

Nevertheless, over the years in which they were settling down in their new homes, the Philistines gradually became assimilated to the civilization of the Canaanites, and presumably intermarried with them as well; even their language was eventually replaced by a local Canaanite dialect. Excavations at Ashdod have shown how many Canaanite elements became blended with their originally non-Semitic way of life. Thus the gods of Aegean origin whom they had brought to the country were given the names of Canaanite deities. These included Dagon – formerly Mesopotamian – who became their chief god, with Ashdod as his main centre; Baal, worshipped at Ekron as Baalzebul, the prince (mockingly transformed by the Israelites into Baalzebub, Lord of the Flies); and the goddess Ashtoreth.

Nevertheless, the city-states of the Philistines, operating more or less in unison, became increasingly important independent military powers. As time went on, their attempts to expand into the hill country inevitably involved them in open conflict with the Israelite tribes.

These hostilities are mirrored in the story of Samson, coming from the tribe of Dan (which was forced by the Philistines to leave the foothills and migrate to its eventual home much further north). Samson was said to have killed a thousand Philistines with the jawbone of an ass (an attempted explanation for the name Ramathlehi, 'the hill of the jawbone'). But the sagas relating to his exploits also declared that he had a weakness for Philistine women: every one of them proved treacherous – here was a familiar moral concerning the danger of foreign females – and finally he found himself trapped by the temptress Delilah, who cut off his hair, the source of his strength, while he slept: but later, when he grew it again, he pulled down the whole temple of Dagon at Gaza, killing its occupants and himself. His long hair (like the sun's rays?) has caused some scholars to regard him as a mythical figure etymologically related to the Canaanite sun-god Shemesh, whose shrine Bethshemesh or Irshemesh was in the centre of Dan's original territory.

At all events, Samson became known as a boisterous, Herculean, folk-hero of fabulous strength and bawdy pranks. But he was probably a historical individual, all the same: not perhaps, one of the judges, as the Bible regards him, but a tough resistance leader who made a name for himself. He also earned admiration because he was one of the Nazirites (whose hair must not be cut). These were holy men set aside by their possession of 'the spirit of Yahweh', displayed by ecstatic frenzy and ascetic abstinence. Originating from Canaanite fertility worships (Ch.2,ii), the Nazirite movement was converted by the Israelites into an instrument designed to destroy those very cults, and the cults of other foreigners such as the Philistines. For the Nazirites were deeply involved in the fervent fury of those conducting Yahweh's Holy Wars. And it was resistance warriors like Samson who took the lead in whipping up the Israelites' hatred against the Philistines, whose uncircumcised state seemed detestable. Israelite patrols imperilled Philistine caravans coming in from the desert, and threatened to make descents into the plain; while the Philistines, for their part, established inland frontier posts, which seemed to the Israelite tribes to presage invasions of the hill country that was the nucleus of their settlement.

One of these frontier stations was the ancient walled city of Aphek, where the foothills meet the plain. That was where the Philistines mustered an army in c. 1050, confronted at Ebenezer, not far off, by most of the Israelite tribes – or even, perhaps, by all twelve of them, combining against this common enemy for the first time. In the engagement that followed, the Israelites were rash enough to put their trust in a regular pitched battle, and suffered total defeat. After the disaster, records the Bible, the Israelite elders sent for the Ark of Yahweh (Ch.5,ii) from Shiloh (which had fallen to the enemy), in order to raise the spirits of their shattered troops. If so, the measure proved ineffective, because a second crushing setback rapidly followed. The Ark itself was captured by the enemy and taken to Ashdod; and a solid, symmetrical Philistine fortress was constructed at Gibeah (Tell el-Ful), a key point of the tribal land of Benjamin.

Thus the conquering Philistines had established themselves in the very heart of Israelite territory. It was not the first time that the tribes of Israel had suffered a grave military reverse; at an earlier date, many or most of them had succumbed to Syrian (Aramaean) invaders for a period of years, but on that occasion they had recovered. Now, however, there seemed little hope that they could ever do so again. It almost looked as if they had come to the end of their brief independent existences.

ii. Samuel

Yet it turned out that, after all, the Israelites were just strong enough to survive, guided by new leaders of remarkable calibre.

The first of these men was Samuel, son of Elkanah in the Ephraim hills. The *First Book of Samuel*, which describes his career, is thickly encrusted with miraculous legends emerging from a series of different cycles and scattered, contradictory traditions, but certain facts seem to emerge. In the first place, he was a Nazirite, like Samson before him (Ch.6,i). He had spent his youth as a priest, at the sanctuary of Shiloh, assisting the local priest Eli, who was descended from Aaron. When Shiloh fell to the Philistines after the battle of Aphek, Samuel became the leader of a group of tribal units which still managed precariously to remain outside the sphere of enemy control – a judge, that is to say, of the type of Gideon and Jephthah and the rest: though eventually he attracted a larger body of followers than they had ever possessed. His headquarters were initially at Mizpah (Tell en-Nasbeh) on the borders of Benjamin (eight miles north of Jerusalem), and then at his own birthplace Ramathaim or Ramah (Beit Rima?) on Mount Ephraim, while his sons acted as his deputies at the southern centre of Beersheba, safely distant from the Philistine city-states.

But that was by no means the sum total of Samuel's position. For he was an 'emergency man' of a very peculiar kind. In his own country, and at Shechem, he enjoyed fame as a holy man and a giver of oracles, a soothsayer and a prophet.

Prophets, supposedly conveying the will of the god or gods through the medium of oracles, had long been known elsewhere in the near east. Already before 2000 Ipu-Wer, a priest-prophet of Egypt, was denouncing evil in places high and low, and in the eighteenth century his compatriot Nefer-Rohu foretold punishment and restoration: the pharaoh is seen taking down his message on papyrus, though Nefer-Rohu prudently lies prostrate before him. There had been Canaanite seers, too (Ch.2,ii), and a Phoenician prophet was encountered by the Egyptian envoy Wen-Amun at Byblus. Prophecy is also mentioned on the inscription of a Syrian monarch, and the Bible gives an account of a Mesopotamian (?) prophet named Balaam, said to have been hired by King Balak of Moab.[4] He was attributed to the time of Moses: and Moses too was likewise declared to have been a prophet, as was Abraham before him. These descriptions are probably anachronistic. But the woman judge Deborah enjoyed a prophetic reputation and employed it to turn the power of Yahweh against her foes.

To the accompaniment, often, of suitable music, prophets of both sexes screamed out their visionary, loosely versified, traditionally phrased oracles, falling, or seeming to fall, into a frenzied, trance-like condition in which they seemed no longer to be themselves. People might think that these weird and alarming men were drunk (sometimes a correct conclusion, according to Isaiah), or that they were traitors, madmen, or fools, for such people were hard for polite society to absorb. Yet they gained extremely widespread respect and fear because of the exciting manner of their speech and behaviour, which seemed to prove that they were the genuine mouthpieces of Yahweh, 'standing in his Council',[5] extensions of his personality, through whose voices he himself seemed to give utterance: *nabi* (prophet) signifies 'a person who speaks for [God]', and an earlier term, *roeh*, may well mean the same. As God's spokesmen, the prophets could intercede with him on behalf of their people. In later days the prophets of Israel became, above all else, foretellers of the future, and in early times, too, they had no doubt fulfilled such a role on appropriate occasions – though they also sometimes interpreted the past, when this was necessary in order to illustrate Yahweh's purpose.

This being their awesome role, if their assertions became critical of national or tribal leaders, it would be hard (and unpopular) to keep them quiet. But in the more ancient periods this was not very likely to happen, for early prophets (such as Nefer-Rohu in Egypt), although their messages sometimes contained disturbing elements, were closely associated with existing political institutions – and with religious institutions, too, since many of them, like Samuel, may well have been priests as well as prophets. In their prophetic capacity, such Israelite personages often belonged to groups or guilds, each presided over by a Father – institutions already in existence, according to the Bible, as early as Samuel's time. They were not so much schools, at first, as wandering bands, with no territorial ties, who kept alive the primitive conscience of the Children of Israel, 'coming down from the hill-shrine, led by lute, harp, fife and drum, and filled with prophetic rapture'.[6]

Samuel's role as a prophet earned him reverence first from the people of some town (probably Ramathaim) where he accepted money for his services, and then far and wide. What gained him this repute was not only his purposeful oracular gift, but his dedication, like that of Samson in slightly earlier times (Ch.6,i), as a Nazirite. It was a Nazirite's fanatical fury which caused Samuel to declare that a hostile semi-nomadic people, the Amalekites (related to the people of Edom), should be annihilated by Yahweh's will.[7]

The Nazirites' claim to be the spokesmen for Yahweh brought them close to the prophets, as the Bible noted; and Samuel was evidently able to fulfil both roles at the same time. A priest in his early days, it looks as though he gradually distanced himself from the priestly hierarchy, replacing it, as a major public force, by a group of prophets. It was they, more than the priests, who were to become the recognized successors to the judges as messengers of Yahweh, and forerunners of the social and political prophet reformers of the future.

Samuel's other significant initiative was of a political nature: his successful plan to make Saul king – because a unified military command was needed in order to drive the Philistines out of Israel's hills. This initiative receives curiously puzzling treatment in the *First Book of Samuel* because that work incorporated, and imperfectly conflates, two parallel and irreconcilable sources (Ch.9,i). The first and earlier source, more or less favourable to the monarchy, tells how Samuel, by the promptings of Yahweh, brought Saul before the people as King of Israel at Mizpah, in Benjamin. According to the second source, however, the demand for a king had come from the people itself (that is to say, presumably, from the tribal elders), whereas Samuel at first resisted the suggestion on the grounds that the only monarch the Israelites could ever possess was Yahweh; only with the utmost reluctance, according to this account, did he finally give way and arrange Saul's elevation to the throne, which he subsequently regretted. This second source dates from a later time when the kingship had fallen into disrepute, so that the reluctance it attributes to Samuel is of doubtful authenticity; though its further assertion that he and Saul differed sharply – because Saul thought it stupid that the punishment inflicted on the Amalekites should include the slaughter of their cattle – does not sound incredible. In the face of these conflicting traditions, all that can be safely said is that Samuel created the monarchy, presenting Saul to the population as its first national monarch.

Thus Samuel succeeded in combining political and religious leadership as none of his compatriots in Israel ever had before. And so he became honoured, when all the strands of the story came together, as a uniquely versatile, multiple figure whom Yahweh had singled out; judge, military chief, Nazirite, priest and prophet. And despite modern attempts to cut him down to size, that seems to have been what he was.

iii. Saul

Saul, the son of Kish, a Benjaminite, came to the newly created throne late in the eleventh century. His first important military victory was against the semi-nomad Ammonites across the Jordan, who had threatened to wipe out Jabesh-gilead, centre of the Transjordanian section of the tribe of Manasseh. Then followed a ceremony of royal acclamation at the ancient shrine of Gilgal, designed to stress continuity with the sacred Israelite past. It was thereafter that he proceeded to 'cut the Amalekites to pieces', treating them, however, with less ruthlessness than Samuel had wished. But Saul's real challenge came from the Philistines, whose efficient, united forces still held down the greater part of the country. However, in this apparently desperate situation, he engaged and defeated them in at least three major battles, including an important encounter at Michmash, south of Bethel. These decisive successes apparently compelled them to withdraw their garrisons, for the time being, from the inland regions they had occupied; so that their monopoly of iron, which had deprived the Israelites of that vital metal, could no longer be enforced.

But now the clouds began to gather, and Saul's internal political strength went into decline. Out of the complicated, contradictory biblical story, two main reasons for this deterioration emerge. The first was his quarrel with Samuel, although after Samuel's death (the account continues, with a blend of piety and pagan superstition) Saul regretted the loss

73

of the holy man, and induced the witch of Endor to conjure up his ghost. But the Bible also gives a second reason for Saul's loss of influence, namely, his jealousy of his own youthful protégé David, who eventually became a dangerous rival and open rebel. These strains, it appears, caused Saul to suffer some kind of psychological collapse, but he lived on to fight another pitched battle against the Philistines, beside Mount Gilboa overlooking the plain of Jezreel. It proved a total catastrophe. In the rout three of Saul's sons were slain – including Jonathan his heir – and Saul himself, wounded in the stomach, committed suicide by falling on his sword. The Philistines set up his severed head in the temple of Dagon, nailed his body on to the city wall of Beth-shan and displayed his armour in the shrine of Ashtoreth. And they reoccupied the greater part of the country. Saul's attempt to dislodge them had ended in abysmal failure. His reign was said to have lasted for two years; though its real duration may have been a good deal longer.

Despite this lamentable end, he remained a figure of major importance, because he had been the first king of Israel. Legend depicted him as the man who had set out to consult Samuel about some lost donkeys, and had found a kingdom instead – which then continued to exist for four centuries. It was convenient that Saul came from Benjamin, which was too insignificant to provoke jealousies among the other tribes, and it was in Benjamin too, at Mizpah and Gilgal, that his national kingship was inaugurated. He built himself a residence in the same territory, at Gibeah; it has been discovered by excavators, a small rectangular citadel of rough stone blocks, the reconstruction of a Philistine building. Benjamin and neighbouring Ephraim had suffered worst from the Philistines, and it was they that formed the power base upon which Saul depended, together with the Israelite settlements across the Jordan, to which his relief of Jabesh-gilead had endeared him. He also possessed a valuable link with the people of Judah to the south. Although their relations with the northern tribes were never close or friendly, they admired the way in which, until the final disaster, he had repelled their hostile Philistine neighbours.

Under Saul's monarchical rule, the Twelve Tribes had been able to assume their final shape as a single political unit, comprising all Israel. Despite surviving inter-tribal enmities, national unity of a kind was at last in existence. In order to achieve it, each of the tribes had been forced not only to forgo its own local, centrifugal ideals of independence, but also to accept instead the foreign institution of national monarchy – 'like other peoples'[8] and more particularly like the Canaanites, from whom this was one of Israel's most substantial heritages. Moreover, even if lip-service was paid to the 'popular', conditional character of Saul's régime, he surely intended, riding on the crest of his military successes, to establish a dynasty, under his son Jonathan, had he not fallen at Mount Gilboa together with his father.

Owing to the conflicting emotions Saul's monarchy aroused in later biblical writers, the part played by the already powerful prophetic groupings in his kingship is hard to disentangle. The equivocal role of Samuel has already been mentioned, but in addition, we are told, either before or after his accession, the king encountered a group of prophets and fell into an ecstatic trance, dancing and shouting like them, and, in one version, tearing off his clothes. This caused onlookers to utter the cry that became proverbial, 'What can have happened to the son of Kish? Is Saul also among the prophets?'[9] The story suggests that Saul found it diplomatically advisable to identify himself with the prophetic movement, to which he had not belonged before.

Clearly, he had to take other measures as well, in order to maintain his rudimentary military kingdom. For one thing, he amply rewarded those who were loyal to him, thus creating a new class tied to the court rather than to any specific tribe. Samuel allegedly forecast that Saul would behave oppressively, interfering in the private lives of his subjects. How far that is what actually happened we cannot tell. We are informed, however, that he recruited professional soldiers (David was one of them) and enlisted mercenaries to supplement the national levy of his own Israelite population. The judges and their contemporaries, such as Jephthah and Abimelech, had to some extent done the same, but Saul, employing his cousin Abner as general, became the true founder of Israel's professional and mercenary army. Against the Philistines (although they adopted similar methods) his military successes were spectacular, but then the pattern was entirely reversed by their decisive victory at Mount Gilboa. They had moved north to the attack because David's defection had depleted the Israelite army. At the end of the battle, their chariots and horsemen were seen closing in on the wounded Saul. This means that he must have allowed them to lure him down from his own hill country into the plains, where they could be reinforced by Saul's Canaanite and other enemies – and his own personal heroism could do nothing to help him.

The Bible pours a good deal of cold water upon his entire career and rule. Anti-monarchical influences were at work upon this version (Ch.14,ii). And, besides, he had to be belittled as a prelude and contrast to the glory of David – who had to be displayed as the archetypal hero. Moreover, the picture was blackened further by pious Yahwists, since Saul's relations with religious leaders had been far from satisfactory. His efforts to secure the support of the prophets had evidently met with questionable success, and the priests, sons of Samuel's patron Eli, had incurred his disfavour. Indeed, when people at the priestly shrine of Nob, near the capital, were suspected of having supported David's rebellion, he commissioned a professional assassin, Doeg the Edomite, to massacre the inhabitants. In the slaughter, no less than eighty-five of the priests of Yahweh lost their lives.

Saul, that is to say, was by no means a whole-hearted Yahwist. He stood very close to primitive, popular beliefs of another nature altogether. It is true that he ordered necromancers to be banished – no doubt he regarded them as subversive – but this, we are told, did not prevent him from personally consulting the witch of Endor. Furthermore, he was deeply influenced by Canaanite religion. One of his Benjaminite clansmen was called Bealiah ('Yahweh is Baal'); and two of his own sons likewise incorporated the name of Baal in their names: Eshbaal ('Baal exists') and Meribbaal ('Baal rewards'). It seems that Saul worshipped Yahweh and the Canaanite gods at one and the same time, and treated them as indistinguishable parts of one and the same religion. So did many other kings of Israel and Judah in the centuries to come. They earned the sternest possible rebukes from chroniclers and prophets, but it is evident that they saw no other way to make a political success of governing their ethnically mixed country; and that must have been Saul's attitude too.

In the Bible as we have it, these hostile assessments of Saul appear side by side with the relics of lost earlier accounts, including the Book of Jashar[10] (the Upright? or the Book of Heroes?), which pay, or imply, tributes to his personal bravery and magnetic leadership. This juxtaposition of contradictory versions, in the hands of the biblical historians, presents an arresting picture, not too far, perhaps, from the complexity of the historical truth – and not too far from Greek tragedy either: Saul becomes the greater-than-ordinary tragic hero, who is splendid and able and powerful and tries to be fair, but becomes a prisoner of his own evil spirit and can do nothing right, and therefore paid for his mistakes, since 'pride goeth before a fall'.[11] Despite his brutality and eventual downfall, he had justified the experiment of the united kingship.

CHAPTER 7

DAVID

i. The Empire of David

David was the youngest of the eight sons of Jesse of Bethlehem. This was a small town near the northern borders of the territory of Judah, spread over a hill top looking down into fertile, well-watered glens, and commanding a major route which linked the Jordan valley with the central part of the country.

He began his career as a handsome, bright-eyed, ruddy-cheeked boy, when he was invited to join Saul's entourage. Soon afterwards he began to gain a considerable military reputation, reflected in the picturesque and variously told saga of his successful duel in the valley of Elah with the giant Philistine warrior Goliath of Gath. David was given Saul's daughter Michal in marriage – buying her hand for the foreskins of a hundred slaughtered Philistines. He was also appointed commander of the royal guard. The women sang a song telling how 'Saul made havoc among thousands, but David among tens of thousands'. This popular renown, however, earned him the jealous anger of his master, and, forewarned by the crown prince Jonathan – with whom he had formed an intimate friendship – he concluded that it was prudent to move away from the court. In the company of the priest Abiathar, a refugee from Saul's massacre at Nob, David fled to the cave of Adullam in the southern wilderness, where he collected together a band of disaffected adventurers and debtors; and his marriage to Abigail, a wealthy herdsman's daughter, won him supporters in Judah. Then he enrolled himself under the Philistine Achish, king of Gath, who granted him the town of Ziklag as his personal property; and in this mercenary capacity he enhanced his renown as a soldier and diplomat.

When Saul was defeated and killed at Mount Gilboa, and his heir Jonathan lost his life in the same battle, Saul's fourth son Eshbaal survived to inherit the kingdom. But it was greatly diminished in size, since the Philistines were in occupation of most of the land, including Galilee and Transjordan, while David, as their vassal, moved to Hebron and ruled over Judah. Then, after seven years – perhaps still with Philistine support – he succeeded in supplanting Eshbaal, whose chief supporter Abner, the former military commander of Saul, was assassinated by David's general Joab. Denying complicity in the murder, David was anointed king over the whole country (c. 1000).

He immediately took steps to convert this claim into reality. Moving from Hebron, he captured Jerusalem, overcoming the Jebusites (Ch.2,i). Next, in successive stages, he evidently conquered the various Canaanite city-states around the country. He won decisive battles against the Philistines, and fought unprecedented wars of conquest against semi-nomadic Edom (where there were mines of copper and iron) and Moab (rich in cattle) and Ammon (land of a roving and predatory people), and against the Ammonites' ally Aram-Zobah (in Syria). These territories were incorporated, in the vastly enlarged Israelite dominion, as subjects or dependent clients.

To link together all these various elements, David enlisted numerous wives – in addition to Michal and Abigail – from various Israelite and foreign territories alike. In consequence, family and political dissension abounded, including dangerous revolts by the king's own sons Amnon and Absalom (put to death by Joab, to David's sorrow), and Adonijah (whom Joab supported). David then proceeded to crown another of his sons, Solomon – offspring of his Jebusite wife Bathsheba – as his eventual successor. Then he died, having ruled over the country for about thirty-five years.

The decisive moment of David's reign had been the capture of Jerusalem. Taking over the Jebusites' massively terraced town on the rocky plateau of Ophel, he enlarged it to a considerable extent by the construction of a new royal city that extended over eleven or twelve acres across the ridge of the hill; masonry that has now been discovered, including the remains of solid walls braced across by transverse structures, may bear witness to his work.

Jerusalem was David's by conquest, so that he could truly make it his own: a thousand paeans in the Bible honour its holiness. The selection of the place as his capital was a masterstroke, because it stood right outside Israelite tribal zones and rivalries. And it was conveniently located in between the northern tribes and Judah, whose mutual animosity was only precariously deferred by the king's personal ties with north and south alike.

His conclusive victories over the Philistines likewise represented the beginning of a new era. They had been provoked by his capture of Jerusalem, which brought his amicable relations with their leaders to an end. 'As soon as you hear a rustling sound in the treetops', declared Yahweh to David, 'you shall give battle, for God will have gone out before you to

Plan of Jerusalem

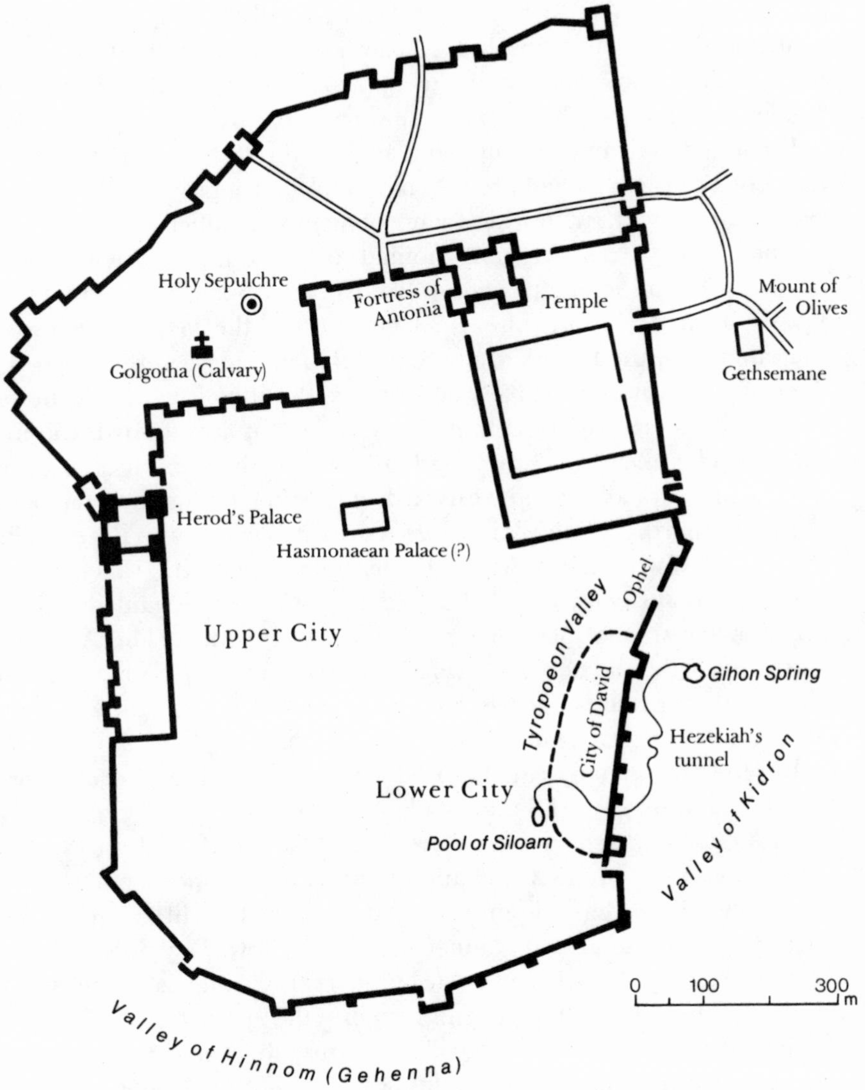

Holy Sepulchre ⊙

Golgotha (Calvary) ✝

Fortress of Antonia

Temple

Mount of Olives

Gethsemane

Herod's Palace

Hasmonaean Palace (?)

Upper City

Tyropoeon Valley

City of David

Ophel

Gihon Spring

Hezekiah's tunnel

Valley of Kidron

Lower City

Pool of Siloam

0   100   300 m

Valley of Hinnom (Gehenna)

defeat the army of the Philistines'.[1] So David, we are told, drove their soldiers in flight from Gibeah (or Gibeon?) to Gezer. He also captured their city of Gath, whose king had formerly befriended him. But it is not certain that he annexed the town (for another Gath, in Judah, see Ch.12,i), and the remaining Philistine city-states, too, escaped formal annexation, probably because Egypt would have resented any such step. However, they had been completely deprived of their power: pinned into a narrow strip of territory, they lost both their maritime and land traffic to David, and their trading town of Tell el-Qasile became a commercial centre of the Israelites instead. A new sort of Israelite pottery, derived from Philistine models, began to appear, with a hand-burnished slip coloured dark-red with haematite (natural ferric oxide).

David's bloodthirsty campaigns against the three main semi-nomad tribes of Transjordan had brought him into confrontation with the Syrian state Aram-Zobah, with which some of them were allied.

These Aramaeans, originally nomads of mixed ethnic origins, spoke a north-west Semitic tongue (not unlike Hebrew), for which a great future lay in store (Ch.16,i). They had constituted the last major wave of migrants from the fringes of the Syro-Arabian desert, in the wake of the Amorites, Canaanites and so many others. Profiting from the decline and collapse of the Hittite, Egyptian and Assyrian empires towards the end of the second millennium, they had pressed northwards into the Meso-potamian river valleys and westwards into Syria, taking their name from the fertile north Syrian plain *Aram Naharain*, Field of the Rivers. There they gradually settled down and intermarried, herding sheep but also engaging in agriculture and the caravan trade, which gained in impor-tance owing to the increased employment of camels. The Aramaeans worshipped Babylonian and Assyrian gods, and then Canaanite deities as well; their principal goddess was a fusion of the Canaanite Ashtoreth and Anath. In due course, too, they absorbed the Canaanite material culture of the Syrian regions in which they settled, and established a number of quite powerful independent kingdoms.

Aram-Zobah, rich in copper, was one of them. Based on the Bekaa valley between Mounts Lebanon and Anti-Lebanon, north-west of Damascus, it bordered upon the northernmost Israelite tribes and had already come into armed conflict with Saul. Now, David decisively de-feated its monarch Ben-Hadad I (Hadadezer), seizing his copper supplies and other lucrative plunder, and bringing the entire territory under his own control. He also reduced to client status (short of actual annexation) a second Aramaean kingdom, Hamath, beside the Orontes, which had access to Syrian elephants and conducted a profitable ivory trade. David's domination of these Aramaean monarchies – facilitated by the temporary power vacuum among the great surrounding empires – had enabled Israel, unprecedentedly and uniquely, to assert its control over the greater part of Syria.

Almost the whole of the first two decades of David's reign had been spent in aggressive wars. Assisted by Joab, who was ruthless and jealous but a highly competent general, he had begun to conscript the Israelite population. But he also inherited from Saul a professional and, in particular, a mercenary force, which he greatly enlarged, by recruitment from Philistines and others. These were the men he employed for his bodyguard, keeping them under his own close personal supervision.

The only important part of Syria or Palestine which had not come under David's control was Phoenicia, the coastal area of the modern Lebanon, for he dealt with that region in a different way. Its people were Canaanites by origin, and spoke a north-west Semitic language which (like Hebrew) had developed from the Canaanite tongue. The encroachments, immigrations, settlements and aggressions of Sea Peoples (Philistines and others), Israelites and Aramaeans had deprived the Canaanites, taken as a whole, of three-quarters of their territory and nine-tenths of their grain-land. Virtually all that remained to them was the central, Phoenician coastal strip, together with its immediate hinterland, a region full of mountain forests, which could be settled and exploited for timber.

On this shore stood the well-protected, immensely active maritime cities of Byblus, Sidon, Tyre and Arvad (Aradus). Their governments and business men exploited the general chaos pervading the near-eastern world before and after the turn of the millennium, and converted it to their own advantage. Constructing impressive merchant fleets, they built up a sea trade, which the alarming raids of the Sea Peoples only temporarily damaged. Egypt, although much weakened, could still intervene to a certain extent. Thus the ancient port of Byblus, which quickly re-emerged as a lumber port, may have accepted nominal Egyptian sovereignty in order to escape encroachment by Sidon. Tyre, a little to the south, had been founded by Sidon as a colony, but in due course surpassed its mother city. Originally a fishing port, it was hailed by the Bible as a place of merchant princes. Its ruler Hiram I the Great (c. 970–936) – conqueror, builder and suppressor of rebellions – was delighted by David's subjugation of the Philistines, which had helped his maritime commerce, by enabling him to utilize the port of Joppa (Jaffa) for the disembarcation of the wood he exported; and he also wanted access to the inland trade routes which were now under David's control. So the two monarchs made a treaty together – and we are told that they became close personal friends. Thus the process of civilizing Israel's material life developed under strong Phoenician influence. By forming this judicious diplomatic alliance to supplement his conquests, David's

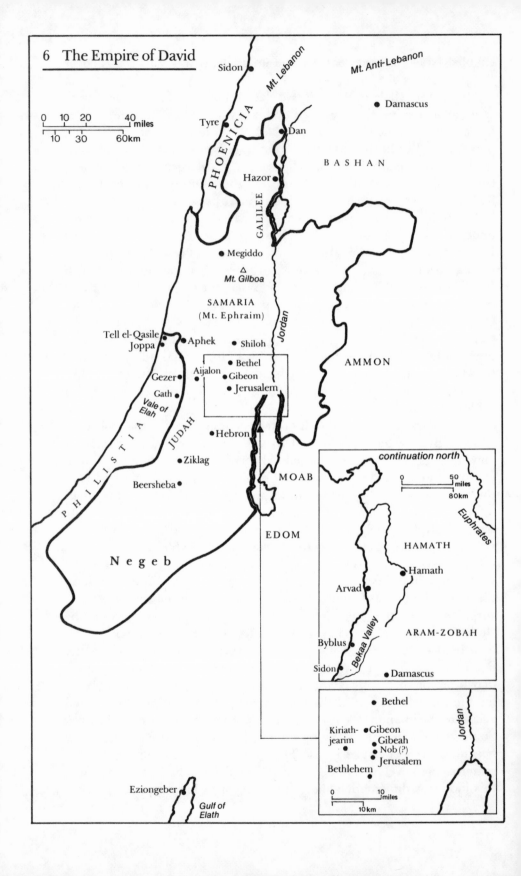

6 The Empire of David

0 10 20 40 miles
10 30 60km

Sidon
Mt. Lebanon
Mt. Anti-Lebanon
Damascus
PHOENICIA
Tyre
Dan
BASHAN
Hazor
GALILEE
Megiddo
△ Mt. Gilboa
SAMARIA
(Mt. Ephraim)
Jordan
Tell el-Qasile
Joppa
Aphek
Shiloh
Bethel
Aijalon
Gibeon
AMMON
Gezer
Jerusalem
Gath
Vale of Elah
JUDAH
Hebron
Ziklag
MOAB
Beersheba
PHILISTIA
EDOM
Negeb

continuation north
0 50 miles
80km
Euphrates
HAMATH
Hamath
Arvad
Byblus
Bekaa Valley
ARAM-ZOBAH
Sidon
Damascus

Bethel
Kiriath-jearim
Gibeon
Gibeah
Nob (?)
Jerusalem
Bethlehem
Jordan
0 10 miles
10km

Eziongeber
Gulf of Elath

imposing dominance now extended, without a break, from the Gulf of Elath right up to the upper Euphrates. For the first and only time in history, Israel had become a major political power, a complex near-eastern empire.

But this novel and sensational development created many problems within the Israelite homeland itself. Saul had already taken what steps he could to integrate the old tribal ideals with the new concept of monarchical centralization. Now came the even more serious question of reconciling those same antique ideals with the requirements of the new empire. In order to tackle this problem, and govern and tax his territories on viable modern lines, David was obliged to create a considerable bureaucracy. This institution of 'servants of the king' was based on sophisticated Phoenician models and drew also on the larger experience of Egypt, from which officials were imported to act as advisers. They and their Israelite colleagues, appointed to fulfil these varied duties, soon came to comprise a small but powerful and wealthy urban ruling class. Ordinary people, on the other hand, saw few of the benefits of the new imperial order. What they had to do was to pay up – and provide forced labour as well, an ancient institution borrowed from Canaanite models.

Nor did the ordinary Israelite benefit greatly from David's substantial building programme, of which traces have been detected by archaeologists. The various envoys whom Hiram I of Tyre dispatched to give him help included carpenters and masons to build a new royal residence at Jerusalem. In Megiddo, too, a couple of palaces, and a storage building, and a fine small gate may belong to a reconstruction of the city undertaken during David's reign. Certain of these structures were partly composed of stones cut into accurate rectangles fitted together with precision. The technique was evidently of Phoenician origin, but our earliest instances of its employment happen to come from sites in Israel. The same may be said of the stone column-capitals ornamented with volutes or 'palms' (misleadingly described by classical students as 'Proto-Aeolic' or 'Proto-Ionian') of which early examples appear at Megiddo, at Hazor and elsewhere. More than thirty of these capitals have been found in the country, dating from the period of David and his successors. Their ultimate models may have been wooden capitals in north Syria, though the Phoenicians probably served as intermediaries. Large gates at Dan (Tell el-Kadi) and Beersheba, at the northern and southern extremities of the Israelite homeland, are also attributed to David, though this is not quite certain.

ii. The Religion of David

David's immense success seemed to indicate that he was the special recipient of Yahweh's favour, a situation of which he took ample advantage, interpreting the kingship in religious terms, and claiming that it enjoyed the authority of divine grace. Furthermore, he skilfully revived and renewed the Mosaic covenant in order to depict his own special relationship with Yahweh, whose partner in the agreement was no longer the people of Israel, but David himself. 'I have made a covenant with him I have chosen,' psalmists make Yahweh declare; 'I will name him my first-born, highest among the kings of the earth. ... Your royal sceptre is a sceptre of righteousness.'[2]

To set the seal on this novel situation David brought the Ark of the Lord to Jerusalem. Captured by the Philistines at Aphek and then released, it had been transferred by the Israelites to Kiriath-jearim or Baalah-judah near Gibeon (? Kuryet Enab or Khurbet Erma), and from there David had the sacred object brought in pomp to Jerusalem. It was all the easier to exalt the place as a holy city – described by the prophets as 'Zion' when they wished to stress its spiritual significance – because its ancient monarch Melchizedek had achieved legendary fame as a priest and a king, in the service of El Elyon (Ch.2,ii). So David, his position sanctified by Yahweh's renewed covenant, could be presented as a priest-king of the same kind: 'You are a priest for ever, in the succession of Melchizedek.'[3]

Yet here the psalmist was indulging in a poetic exaggeration, since a difference remained: for David, although a sacred person performing religious functions, never, in fact, became a priest-king, or high-priest (the term only originated much later), or any sort of priest at all. The distinction between spiritual and temporal leadership may have become somewhat blurred, but it did not vanish. That is to say, David, being king, left the principal priesthood to others, Zadok and Abiathar jointly, both claiming descent from Moses' brother Aaron. Abiathar, however, became involved in the abortive revolt of Adonijah, which brought his career to an end. And it may have been in David's reign, too, that the power of the priestly Levites was weakened, by distributing them throughout the country (Ch.4,ii).

David relied on the invaluable services of the prophet Nathan. Saul had already tried to form links with the prophetic movement, but David went further. Following the tradition of older civilizations, he successfully attached prophets, including Nathan, to his court; this was perhaps one of the principal keys to his successful conduct of affairs. Biblical writers, conscious of the later role of prophets as the critics of kings (Ch.11,i), liked to imagine Nathan speaking out against David – for instance, when the king had Uriah the Hittite killed, in order to transfer his wife Bathsheba to his own harem. The Bible also declared that after David had bought the threshing-floor of Araunah at Jerusalem and built an altar there, in time of plague, Nathan had cautioned him not to construct a temple as well, which (it was asserted) he had planned to do. This could be true, not so much for the reasons stated, which are contradictory – because Yahweh needed no localized shrine, or because David had fought and shed blood – but because a temple with a fixed location looked too reminiscent of Canaanite religious influences and intrusions.

For David, like Saul before him, was demonstrably prone to such influences. Indeed, he himself may originally have borne a Canaanite name, (El-Hanan 'grace of El');[4] so did one of his sons, (Beeliada, Eliada). His 'leaping and capering before the lord', to musical accompaniment – which his wife Michal (embittered because of the eclipse of her House of Saul) rebuked as ludicrously undignified – was a ritual that went straight back to Canaanite practices. And the state religion over which he presided was not purely Yahwistic at all, but a mixture of Yahwism and Canaanite cult.

These were considerations which made later biblical writers eager to see Nathan, retrospectively, as a stern moral critic of the king. In fact, however, he seems rather to have been a court prophet in the old, loyal style. For he solemnly pronounced that Yahweh's covenant was pledged not only to David himself but to his house for all time to come: 'Your throne shall be established for ever'[6] – with immeasurable repercussions upon future Jewish and Christian history. For like Saul, but even more insistently, David intended to establish a dynasty invested with divine sanctions. However, as in other near-eastern hereditary monarchies, no clear rule of primogeniture was introduced, and the ageing David would not or could not name an unchallenged heir. As a result, his last years were a grim tale of hesitations, savage intrigues and bloodthirsty rebellions, until in the end, with the support of Nathan, Zadok, and his own wife Bathsheba, he designated her son Solomon as his successor: his favourite among his sons, though not the eldest.

David's daemonic energy and versatile genius had bestowed upon Israel an unparalleled epoch of prolonged peace and prosperity; so that his reign, for all its bloody acts which the court historian (Ch.9,ii) admitted, was looked back upon as the type and harbinger of Yahweh's future Golden Age.

One of his many outstanding qualities, and one of his greatest contributions to his country, was a passion for music, inherited from a long Canaanite and Israelite tradition. He was a skilful harpist, and that was how as a youth, according to the story, he had first attracted the attention of Saul, but above all David was renowned as a poet and singer. A song reputed to be his work commemorated his delivery from his enemies, including Saul, after their friendship had broken up: 'The Lord is my fortress, my rock and my deliverer.'[7] And we have the dirge that he composed, probably for antiphonal singing, to lament the death of Saul, and particularly of Saul's son Jonathan:

> Thy love for me was wonderful,
>   Passing the love of women.
> How are the mighty fallen,
>   And the weapons of war perished![8]

This lamentation recalls the Mesopotamian Epic of Gilgamesh, grieving for his friend Enkidu.[9] But it has a poignant authenticity all its own, which gained it inclusion in the Bible, despite its unabashedly secular tone.

However, it was as a singer and poet of religious themes that David gained particular fame among posterity: 'With his whole heart he sang hymns of praise, to show his love for his Maker.'[10] And in particular, he came to be honoured, by Jews and Christians alike, as the composer of the entire contents of the Psalter, the Book of Psalms gathered together in the Bible. In fact, nearly all the psalms are demonstrably later (Ch.13,iv). However, there are passages in a few of them that may well go back to David himself;[11] and others were attributed to his contemporary Asaph the Levite. Asaph was his musical director, and the leader of a choir and orchestra, five thousand strong, according to tradition. The figure must be exaggerated. Yet David evidently assigned an enormous importance to music, as part of the rites of his religion. When the Ark was brought to Jerusalem, he 'and all Israel' danced before it to the accompaniment of harps and lutes, tambourines, castanets and cymbals[12] – the sort of display his wife Michal deplored.

CHAPTER 8

SOLOMON

i. The Policies of Solomon

The Deuteronomic Historian (Ch.14,ii), as he shaped the *First Book of Kings*, put together a neatly, too neatly, balanced picture of the reign of Solomon (*c.* 965–927). The initial ten chapters are designed to indicate that his reign had been peaceful and prosperous. We are told, moreover, that he himself was not only exceptionally wise but also exceptionally rich. He formed an alliance with the Egyptians, and sealed it by marrying the daughter of the reigning pharaoh and receiving from him, as a dowry, the Canaanite city of Gezer, which had evidently remained an enclave under Egyptian control up to that time. Solomon also preserved and developed David's friendship with King Hiram I the Great of Tyre, with whom he maintained close commercial collaboration. Helped by Hiram, Solomon became an outstanding builder and rebuilder of cities. At Jerusalem itself, he spent thirteen years constructing a palace complex, including the Temple (the 'First Temple'), which took seven and a half years to build.

It was mainly because of this achievement that one of the traditions preserved in *Kings* is so favourable to Solomon. Another contributor, however, dwells on a blacker side of the picture, though an editor of his narrative has, unhistorically, concentrated these unsatisfactory events into his last declining years. We are told that Solomon's political position suffered a setback when Edom seceded, becoming independent under its chieftain Hadad. In Syria, too, the Aramaean kingdoms are stated to have regained control over their own affairs, the lead being taken no longer by Aram-Zobah but by an even more powerful state with its capital at Damascus. And, in addition to losing all this territory, the king had to offer twenty towns in Galilee to Hiram of Tyre, in order to settle his debts. Moreover, his succession had been a tricky affair – and troubles continued. His older half-brother Adonijah, who had revolted against David, soon had to be got rid of. And his own claim to the throne was by no means strong – especially as his mother Bathsheba was a Jebusite and a foreigner.

Nevertheless, these difficulties did not prevent him from developing a very vigorous commercial policy. With assistance from Hiram, he built a fleet of trading vessels at Eziongeber near the head of the Gulf of Elath. This port was probably on the island of Jezirat Fara'un, on which the remains of strong fortifications are visible, though they cannot be dated with certainty. Tell el-Kheleifah, on the adjacent mainland – hitherto a bone of contention with Edom – was not a copper refinery of Solomon's as has been sometimes supposed, but a fortress and storehouse and granary. It stood beside a major land route into the heart of the country, by way of the Negeb.

Back to Eziongeber from Ophir (perhaps Suppara near Bombay) came cargoes of gold and silver, precious stones and ivory, valuable woods and peacocks and apes. His chariots Solomon bought from Egypt, and his horses from Egypt and Coa (Kue, Cilicia in south-eastern Asia Minor). For the first time Israel had been brought fully into the mainstream of near-eastern big business and diplomacy, as the accounts (even if exaggerated) of his 700 wives and 300 concubines, many of them foreign, effectively confirm.

The saga of the visit of the Queen of Sheba (Saba, in the Yemen), famed for her beauty in Arabic literature, is intended to make the same point. This visit, allowing the biblical writers to enlarge upon her admiration of Solomon's wisdom and wealth, contains fictitious elements, but the tales reflect a commercial relationship between Solomon and south-western Arabia that is likely to be authentic. The Sabaean Arabs, speaking a south-east Semitic tongue, had established a strongly expanding kingdom astride the spice and incense routes leading to Palestine and Mesopotamia. Solomon controlled significant portions of these routes, and it was sensible for the two countries to come to an agreement. An early south Arabian clay stamp of not very much later date – belonging, in fact, to the following century – seems to have been found (and not just 'planted', as some thought) at Bethel.[1] The millennial relationship between the Hebrews and the Arabs had begun.

In order to keep all this external activity going, Solomon was obliged to maintain a powerful army. David had largely relied on mercenary infantry, but under Solomon, this was overshadowed by a formidably enlarged force of chariots. It was stationed in the much strengthened fortress of Gezer (Solomon's gift from the Egyptians), in Hazor, and in Megiddo. At Megiddo he seems to have built a new town, partially replacing the constructions of David. It contained impressive palaces of Syrian type, and was protected by a solid wall possessing a triple gate flanked by square towers.

By these and other ambitious enterprises, the face of Israel was transformed. At Jerusalem, the foundations of Solomon's citadel have now been discovered. But his greatest hopes were set upon the new Temple on Mount Moriah, of which the massive platform (the Haram al-Sharif) still survives. Whether David had wanted to initiate the project or not (Ch.7,ii), the monarch who carried it out was Solomon, whom it made famous for ever. The Temple, which formed part of an elaborate palace complex, was described by later biblical writers in great detail, and with substantial exaggeration. However, it must have been an impressive building. Its threefold partition can be partially paralleled elsewhere in Palestine and Syria. In general, the plan seems to have been modelled on the sanctuary at Shiloh (for another shrine at Arad, see Appendix 6). Shiloh had been designed on Canaanite lines; and the construction of the Temple, too, was entirely Canaanite, that is to say Phoenician. For Hiram I of Tyre, who had helped build David's palace, likewise sent cedar and fir-wood, as well as labour teams, for the construction and adornment of Solomon's Temple, in exchange for wheat and olive oil.

In the absence of a native Israelite visual art – either because the second Commandment was interpreted as vetoing all images, or because of a lack of talent, or both – the entire scheme of decoration, too, was Phoenician in character. Hiram dispatched bronze and gold for the purpose; and the two giant cherubim of gold-plated olive-wood, whose wings roofed the Ark in the Holy of Holies, resembled the fantastic composite figures found at Byblus and Megiddo, which displayed a human head and a lion's body and the wings of a bird, and were sacred to Ashtoreth. The Temple also no doubt contained specimens of the low reliefs which were a speciality of the Phoenicians, developed from the furniture-making at which the availability of high-class Lebanese woods enabled them to excel. They were a people who, as visual artists, lacked originality, but proved skilful, tasteful assimilators and adapters and blenders of Mesopotamian, Hittite, Mycenaean and Egyptian motifs.

This same Phoenician element was also abundantly present in the worship practised in the Jerusalem shrine. Its bronze pillars were like the standing stones (*masseboth*) which the Phoenicians had inherited from the Canaanites (Ch.2,ii). Moreover, the temples of those peoples had been built as residences for their deities, and at Solomon's Temple, too, many people still found it easier to believe that Yahweh was actually there, in the Holy of Holies, than to consider him incorporeal and transcendent (Ch.5,ii). The same sort of fusion of Yahwist and Canaanite ideas was abundant in spectacular ritual, directed by Solomon's appointee to the priesthood, Azariah the son of Zadok, in whose line the office was long to remain. The old festivals, adapted from Canaanite origins, were transformed into a series of magnificent national occasions, designed to attract popular devotion to the crown, and Solomon's feast, when the Temple was dedicated, seemed just like the feasts which celebrated the completion of sanctuaries of Baal.

For despite pious, manful attempts, on the part of later writers, to praise the founder of the Temple, Solomon (only half Israelite himself) was even less of a thoroughgoing Yahwist than Saul or David had been. Certainly, he worshipped Yahweh – and even, at times, superseded his priest, as his predecessors had never ventured to do – but he also worshipped quite other, foreign deities as well, on a very large scale indeed. The Deuteronomic historian is quite clear about this, and names them with appropriate horror; Ashtoreth the immoral goddess of Sidon, Chemosh the loathsome Moabite deity, Moloch the cruel god of the Ammonite people.[2] Indeed, Solomon even erected new shrines for these divinities – at Gezer for example, excavations suggest; and the Bible declares that he built others for Chemosh and Moloch at Jerusalem itself, on the Mount of Olives just opposite the Temple hill. The Bible appeals to the principle of *cherchez la femme*, blaming his numerous, exotic wives and concubines for this outrageous behaviour. It would be truer to say that both phenomena alike, cosmopolitan harem and religious eclecticism, formed interlocking parts of the same policy, directed at bringing his Israelite and Canaanite and other subjects and foreign allies together in a single national and religious entity. This was anathema to strict Yahwist theologians of all times and epochs, but it was the pragmatic formula chosen by Solomon, even more emphatically than by his predecessors, to control a large imperial state of mixed race and religion.

The population of this empire was rapidly rising. In Israel alone there may have been as many as 800,000 inhabitants, twice the number of the period just before the monarchy began. The cities, too, were now much larger, attracting many people from the countryside. Novel and improved methods of governing this far more elaborate state had to be found. True, to ensure as much continuity as possible, Solomon was careful to employ men who had served David, or to appoint their sons in their place, and he left municipal government in the hands of local officials. At the higher levels, however, he vastly and expensively enlarged David's bureaucracy, making even more substantial use of foreign organizational models, and foreign functionaries to ensure that they were followed. These powerful bureaucrats, chosen without regard to birth or race or wealth, had to pilot decisive changes in administrative structures and methods. In particular, the country was divided into twelve new administrative prefectures, only six of which were named after the old Israelite tribes, so that Solomon evidently took a decisive step towards weakening or dissolving the tribal parochialisms of the past.

The duties of the prefectures included the collection of taxes, which had to be increased to pay for the new chariot army; and funds were also needed to compensate for the loss of Edom, Aram and part of Galilee (lost because Solomon found such difficulty in repaying his debts to Tyre). Royal trading monopolies came into being, and customs and excise duties were considerably augmented. And so, above all, was forced labour. David had borrowed this institution from the Canaanites, and Solomon made much greater use of such practices – interpreting them as an extension of the military levy. The labourers were set to work on the construction of public works and defences. Canaanites and other non-Israelites were enrolled for these purposes, being virtually reduced to state slavery – a practice which was still maintained in later centuries, according to the *First Book of Kings*. But the further assertion, in the same passage, that Israelites, under Solomon, were not compelled to suffer the same experience is evidently an inaccurate attempt to whitewash the king, for it is contradicted by another passage in the same work: 'King Solomon raised a forced levy from the whole of Israel amounting to thirty thousand men.'[3] They were employed for the construction of the Temple, after a period of training and quarrying in Phoenicia, where they were sent in relays of ten thousand at a time.

This forced labour took many workers away from the land, impairing agricultural efficiency. It was also highly unpopular among the liberty-loving Israelite tribesmen, and liable to increase the ever deepening gulf between the new, rich, governing class and the rest of the people. An attempt at geographical discrimination also had explosive results, for the list of Solomon's twelve prefectures does not include Judah, which appears, that is to say, to have been exempted from his various exactions. For the capital, Jerusalem, looked towards Judah, whose men predominated in the higher levels of the government. Among the excluded northerners – never favourably inclined to Judah – it was in Ephraim, the core of the Mosaic settlement, that the grievance and unrest were strongest. Finally one of its people, Jeroboam, commander of the local labour force, began to launch a plot against the king. He was forced to flee to Egypt; but not before Ahijah, a priest in the sanctuary of Shiloh, had promised him the support of the northern population.

Indeed, they were already disquieted for another reason as well: for Solomon's loss of control over Aramaean Damascus had confronted them with a menacing neighbour. Damascus lies on the edge of the eastern desert beside two rivers and at the meeting point of roads running west, south and east, the only city in Syria that has always been important. Succeeding to Aram-Zobah's wealth of copper, it developed a chariot force capable of taking on Solomon's; and its rulers controlled the fertile wheat-crops of Bashan, running down to the eastern shores of the Sea of Galilee. From now onwards, Damascus became a major, hostile, perilous factor in all Israel's calculations and vicissitudes. Whether, in Solomon's time, the state became formally independent or merely autonomous, he had lost it, as he had lost Edom. So the writer of *I Kings*, when he claimed that Israel still ruled over the whole of the Levant, was exaggerating. The account of Solomon's wealth also seems to be overstated. It is true that his successful trading placed him among the wealthier monarchs of the day, but his riches were not extravagant or fabulous, nor, by the same token, was the prevailing peace so universal, continuous and gloriously idyllic as those who eulogized him chose to assure us.

David's reign and his form the two halves of that brief period in history, spanning three or four generations, when Israel was a united state and an imperial power, under worldly kings: David's regime had witnessed the rise of that power, and Solomon presided over its mature continuance, though not without signs of stagnation and incipient decline. About his personal character the strong legendary element in our Hebrew tradition (unchecked by any foreign sources whatever) makes it hard to speak with any assurance. One modern writer likes to see him not as a hawk or dove but as an octopus. It seems possible, perhaps, to detect in his behaviour a peculiar blend of sybaritic regal excess and cool, calculating astuteness.

ii. Solomon's Wisdom: Proverbs

But posterity, and probably his contemporaries as well, saw much more than astuteness in Solomon. For they found him a paragon of wisdom, as the stories of the Queen of Sheba and the judgement of Solomon show. The latter tale describes how cleverly he decided between the demands of two women who claimed the same child. It is framed in proverbial, legendary terms, but the persistent tradition that he possessed unusual gifts presumably had some historical basis.

The time was precisely ripe for ambitious intellectual development among the Semitic-speaking peoples. This was because of the Canaanites' epoch-making introduction of an authentic alphabet, consisting of twenty-seven letters and three glottal stops (Ch.2,ii). But it had still consisted of the relatively inconvenient cuneiform characters, suitable only for incision in clay; and now the Phoenicians, improving upon tentative innovations that had appeared elsewhere in their neighbourhood, devised a more streamlined script of only twenty-two characters, which could easily be inscribed on papyrus, leather and wood. This new alphabet, suitably modified, came to be employed to write down other Semitic languages; and then, by way of the Greeks who added vowels, it was adapted to transcribe Indo-European tongues as well.

Among the Semitic languages using a version of the script was Hebrew, at the time when the Israel of David and Solomon was coming under pervasive Phoenician (and Aramaean) influence. This convenient Early Hebrew alphabet, consisting of letters that were wider and shorter and more squat than those of the Phoenicians, spread quite rapidly and greatly stimulated the culture of the Israelites, whose cultural originality – like that of their Canaanite forerunners – was so pre-eminently literary rather than artistic. A few of them may already have used writing towards the end of the epoch of the judges, when the Song of Deborah was preserved; and historical prose works, such as the Book of Jashar, were possibly initiated at about the same time. But we only have positive evidence for written Hebrew in the years following 1000. It is provided by the 'Gezer calendar'.[5] This consists of a small flat piece of soft, chalky limestone, incised with a concordance table harmonizing the twelve lunations (times from one new moon to the next) with the periods of the agricultural year. The language can already be described as a form of Hebrew; most of the letters are still nearly identical with those of earlier Semitic inscriptions, though some signs have already taken on the distinctive shapes of the early Hebrew alphabet. The 'calendar' may be a school exercise, to be learnt by heart, but if literacy already existed at this unpretentious level, it must also have been present, as the Bible suggests, in the more highly educated circles connected with the court.

Solomon's famous wisdom was celebrated by the ascription to his brain and voice not only of 1,005 songs (making him the true son of his highly musical father) but of 3,000 proverbs as well.[6] And indeed the *Book of Proverbs* in the Bible was known as 'The Proverbs of Solomon' (*Mishle Shelomoh*). In fact, a great proportion of its contents has to be assigned to a much later date; but not all.

This kind of instructional wisdom literature was a very ancient phenomenon in the near east, where sages had been accustomed to offer their views not only about technical matters (medicine, biology, zoology), but also about the general standards according to which life should be lived. The biblical writers were well aware of this tradition among foreigners – to whom, indeed, they often explicitly ascribed the sources of their own writings of this kind – so that Solomon's exceptional wisdom, 'as wide as the sand on the sea-shore', was specifically compared (to his advantage) with 'that of all the men of the east and of all Egypt'.[7]

Among the Egyptians, especially, a rich tradition of wisdom literature had existed for a very long time. In *c.* 2400 Ptahhotep, a Vth Dynasty vizier, drew up an ethical treatise in the form of a collection of proverbial sayings (founded, no doubt, on centuries of oral transmission) counselling how to attain the good life. Then in *c.* 1250 appeared the *Instruction of Amenemopet* of Thebes (?), preserved in a document dating from about the turn of the millennium.[8] Drawing upon Ptahhotep, and following a common Egyptian formula of father offering counsel to son, Amenemopet provides advice about integrity, honesty, kindliness and self-control. His 610 pieces of wisdom are closely followed in the biblical *Book of Proverbs*, where a collection of 'thirty sayings' deliberately echoes the 'thirty chapters' of Amenemopet.[9]

In Mesopotamia, too, there had been wisdom literature right back as far as Sumerian times. Subsequently, the Semitic-speaking Babylonians produced the Poem of the Righteous Sufferer, dating back to an original of the fifteenth century. This composition, beginning with the words, 'I will praise the Lord of Wisdom', bears considerable resemblances to one of the most important Hebrew wisdom works, the *Book of Job* (Ch.15,i). And *Job* also echoes the Babylonian Theodicy, or Dialogue about Human Misery (*c.* 1000).[10] A similar tradition had also been strong among the Canaanites of Ugarit and elsewhere, whose imagery constantly reappears in the wisdom books of the Bible; while many of its other books too, even when they cannot be classified specifically as wisdom literature, are nevertheless pervaded by the same kind of theme.

The wisdom books themselves, led by *Proverbs*, are based on the traditional *mashal*, an aphorism or riddle or allegory. These proverbial statements are set out in a series of short, sharp phrases, sometimes taking the form of question and answer, which present dramatic, keenly observed, often unforgettable miniature scenes related to the actions of daily life. This language of Hebrew humanism is a much more pragmatic affair than the abstractions of Greek philosophers, whose influences only appear at the very end of the story.

Certainly, the *Book of Proverbs* stresses the moral excellence of such virtues as humanity, patience, respect for the poor, and loyalty to friends – and even decency to enemies. But it does so in strictly concrete terms: 'If your enemy is hungry, give him bread to eat; if he is thirsty, give him water to drink'.[11] That injunction (directly foreshadowing the Christians' 'turn the other cheek') seemed sensible, because unchecked brutality in war, advocated by fanatics, was counter-productive, inviting reprisals. The wise man and woman in *Proverbs* are generally those who show empirical, realistic, intelligent common sense. Fools, we are told, can never catch up. Do not drink too much, or next morning you will feel you have been bitten by a poisonous snake. You can get a prostitute for the cost of a loaf, but not a married woman – for the book contains a great deal of talk about women, and their power for good and ill, and how they should behave and how to treat them. Adultery is described as a mistake, owing to the remarkable inconvenience it causes.[12] And, besides, such anti-social actions should be avoided because they rock the boat. For *Proverbs* is the most prudently conservative book in the whole of the Bible. New ideas are dismissed as antique, resurrected fallacies. Much better to aim at preserving stability. 'I hate subversive talk.'[13]

This is a group ethic or class ethic, the gradually amassed product of successive, authoritative, senior élites, who felt themselves to be endowed with the responsibility of an inherited tradition and training, needed to keep their people on the right lines. The guides in this directive activity were known as *hakamim*, sages. For in Israel, as in Edom, there appeared a special class of these sage counsellors, who may be regarded as forerunners of the later scribes (Ch.16,i; 18,ii) and evidently exerted a widespread influence in the community. The prophets, when they came to write their oracles down, made very extensive use of this wisdom approach. Yet they also, quite frequently, reprimanded the sages as well. For a prophet found their attitude altogether too hard-boiled and realistic; and besides, they seemed to pay too little attention to Yahweh and his purpose. Certainly, by the time of the final compilation of *Proverbs*, he had become recognized as the source of all wisdom. But the earliest passages of the book, like Egyptian and Canaanite writings of the same kind, are much more secular and man-centred. What is done, these wise men tell us, leads to natural, practical results, rather than to divine rewards and retributions. The basic wisdom writings stand outside salvation history, representing an alternative way of life and thought and speech.

The *Second Book of Samuel* contains curious passages describing professional sages (of the female sex) in two towns of Israel as early as the reign of David.[14] At any rate such wise men and women can surely be attributed to the court of Solomon, where they formed part of the new cosmopolitan, intellectual class employing the new script that was now readily accessible. Their grouping in schools – academies for the education of state functionaries – is only attested at a later date, but once again these academies may well have gone back to Solomon, whose new system demanded a multiplication of educated officials.

Furthermore, that would fit in very well with his reputation for great wisdom – and his reputed utterance of numerous proverbs, and authorship of *The Book of Proverbs* itself. The use of the title the 'Proverbs of Solomon' to head the whole book was the work of a later editor, but at some earlier stages two substantial sections of its contents had already been ascribed to his authorship, one directly and the other through the intermediary of copyists employed by Hezekiah (king of Judah in the eighth century). It is the first of these sections that comprises the thirty 'sayings', in the form of parallel couplets, which echo the thirty 'chapters' of the *Instruction of Amenemopet*. And the second section, including four-line stanzas in addition to couplets, resembles the first in spirit and form.[15] Both show sound practical psychology and observation, conveyed in forceful antitheses, and may well be surviving examples of the Solomonian Enlightenment.

CHAPTER 9

THE INVENTION OF HISTORY

i. The Southern History ('J')

The reign of Solomon may also have been the time when not only the earliest Israelite proverbs, but also the earliest Israelite history, came to be written down.

The first five books of the Bible, the 'Books of Moses' or the Torah or Pentateuch, provide immensely rich historical material, but each is a mass of legendary and mythical as well as historical material, brought together and imperfectly blended, edited, interpreted, expanded and contracted by a succession of unidentified historians and editors.

They relied, to some extent, on orally transmitted material from earlier times, surviving, for example, in liturgies. But written history, too, was not unfamiliar in the near east. True, it had not greatly interested the Egyptians, whose world view was largely static, but in Mesopotamia a historical prologue usually stood at the beginning of collections of royal laws. However, it was the Hittites of Asia Minor whose monarchs – Mursilis II (1339–1306), Hattusilis III (1275–1250) and Telepinus (c. 1100) – showed the first real awareness of writing down history, and doctoring it to suit their own point of view. The early Israelites, too, themselves had their own early official histories, now lost, but occasionally cited by the biblical writers: the Book of Jashar, the Book of the Wars of Yahweh, the Book of the Acts of Solomon, the Chronicles of the Kings of Israel and Judah.

In the century before our own, critical experts decided that the early books of the Bible consisted, for the most part, of material coming from three documentary sources, which they called J (Yahwist), E (Elohist, Ch.11,iii), and P (Priestly Writer, Ch.14,iii), supplemented by D (the Deuteronomist, Ch.13,i) for the epoch of Moses. After endless subsequent discussion, it is still not agreed that any one of these symbols exactly corresponds to, or defines, a separate and distinguishable documentary source. Nevertheless, the general conclusion that these four main authorities, or something like them, once existed and form the basis of the biblical books has on the whole stood the test of time. The 'Books of Moses', that is to say, were not written by Moses, but as a workable hypothesis we can suppose that they consist of material derived from J, E, P and D.

J looks as if he was a single writer (though some say two), using both oral and written traditions. He seems to have started his narrative in the most antique times, and carried it forward through the Exodus down to the founding of the monarchy. Lists of probable, though sometimes arguable, J material have been drawn up.[1] He shows a keen interest in the southern region of the country, namely Judah; he seems only to have known the north from the outside. Although much of his material is of earlier origin, he himself belongs to the period of the early monarchy, and probably lived during the tenth century. Attribution to the reign of Solomon, when literary life seems to have been well under way (Ch.8,ii), appears a likely conclusion. We can see him, very tentatively, as a man of Judah at Solomon's court, inspired by his pride in royal and united Israel to compile this national, epic history proclaiming the glories of his country's past – half a millennium before Herodotus and Thucydides wrote their histories of the Greeks.

J provides a fascinating, transitional blend between folklore materials and the advanced literary histories of the future, but, above all else, he writes a religious kind of history. Its character is suggested by his belief, almost certainly erroneous, that God's divine name Yahweh had been known from the earliest primeval times (Ch.4,ii) – that is why we know him as J (Yahwist). In accordance with this emphasis on the deity, his record of events is by no means secular in purpose. Its aim, instead, like the aim of most Israelite history, is to show Yahweh's unceasing protective intervention in all the past, present and future affairs of his chosen, covenanted, unique people Israel – his tremendous promises and their tremendous fulfilment, requiring a total obligation and obedience in return.

Nevertheless, one can often discern, through the chinks in the edifying framework, the course of secular events as well. This is a collection of momentous, thematically interconnected short stories telling of human beings, some legendary but some also historical, loving and hating and fighting and rejoicing and suffering. J writes with picturesque artistry and confident exuberance, not unmixed with a tinge of pragmatic, detached irony. His fast-moving, economic directness takes us unswervingly right to the heart of a scene: and very often it is a scene of stern pathos, or heart-rending intimacy. The simple, candid manner in which J recounts and transforms the sagas he has gathered from his various sources is not the simplicity of naïveté, but his chosen vehicle for profound and mature reflections. He is not only almost the earliest but also one of the very greatest of the writers who gave the ancient Hebrews their superlative literature.

In order to set the history of Israel in its widest context, J begins his tale at the beginning of the human race, with the myth of Adam and Eve. He tells how Yahweh created the first man, Adam, out of dust from the ground, forming him in his own image, and breathing the breath of life into his nostrils. Yahweh set Adam in the Garden of Eden, and formed Eve out of one of Adam's ribs to be his companion. He also brought all the animals and birds, which he had likewise created, to Adam, who gave them their names. Adam had been warned not to eat the fruit of the tree of the knowledge of good and evil, but the serpent tempted Eve to eat the fruit, and she gave some to Adam. Because of this disobedience, they became ashamed of their nakedness and covered their private parts with fig-leaves, and hid from Yahweh's sight. Whereupon Yahweh cursed the serpent, and pronounced to Eve that she would bring forth children in sorrow and that her husband would be her ruler. And to Adam he declared: 'By the sweat of your brow you shall gain your bread till you return to the ground ... You are dust, and to dust you shall return.'[2]

Adam in Hebrew was originally just 'the man', humankind in general terms. For the God who made him was seen to have made the whole world, so that Israel was not his only concern – an attitude familiar to the Canaanites too, though they had accompanied and overlaid this universalism by polytheistic ideas (Ch.2,ii). Adam emerges from the dust of the ground, the *adamah* or mother earth. He is made in God's image, which perhaps originally meant 'physically like him', but was probably intended to imply, in addition, that he was capable of conducting a dialogue with Yahweh, and able to participate, however inadequately, in his purpose. When the animals are brought to him so that he can name them, the influence of the wisdom tradition (Ch.8,ii) is apparent: *Proverbs*, too, was very interested in pictures of man dominating the created order. The name of Eve (*Hawwah*) was supposedly derived from *hay*, life, since she was 'the mother of all who live'. She is of one flesh with man, which suggests equality, but she is of one flesh because she has been taken from *his* flesh, a secondary creation, thus reflecting (like the maleness of God himself) the inequality between the sexes that prevailed in ancient society. In the end, she is condemned to accept man as her master.

The Garden of Eden, like rustic bowers painted on the walls of Canaanite Mari, is an idyllic oasis, such as might have been glimpsed by early immigrants from the desert. It is also the paradise that might have been, if human history had not decided to reject it. The tree of knowledge is the world tree, or tree of life, the 'great cedar tree' of the Epic of Gilgamesh, like 'a tree of great height at the centre of the earth' in the *Book of Daniel*.[3] But J calls it the tree of knowledge of 'good and evil', for man is tempted to grasp arrogantly at total knowledge, which only God can possess.

As for the serpent, the Bible sometimes employs it to symbolize healing and genuine wisdom, but its subtlety is usually sinister. For it came straight from the abhorred fertility cults of the Canaanites and Aramaeans. ('Eve', originally, may not have been derived from *hay*, life, after all, but from *hiwya*, the Aramaic for snake.) Israel itself, in early days, had borrowed the worship of a magical, curative bronze serpent from the Canaanites; no wonder one of its pious later kings, Hezekiah, broke the object to pieces. But J improves on all these traditions by using the serpent to stand for the duality of good and evil, which was familiar to the Persians, and later firmly found a way into the Hebrew religion (Ch.18,ii).

There were many near-eastern folk-tales telling how men and women had once almost had immortality, or divine prerogatives, within their grasp, but were tricked out of the gift by frightened or malicious spirits that tempted them to fatal arrogance. J shows that they are not entitled to any such prize: they are creatures, not creators. But by dabbling in superstitious Canaanite cults, represented by the serpent, they have revolted against this subordinate status, and thus against Yahweh himself, whose purpose alone gives history its meaning. So they find themselves naked and expelled from Eden, and all the sorrows of life and death lie in store for them, all the intractable problems and distresses that fell upon Israel, who were Yahweh's chosen people, but have only rewarded him with rebellion.

The belief in an initial rebellion, that of Adam, seemed a philosphical and theological necessity, in order to answer the appallingly difficult question (with which Jeremiah and Job were to wrestle so forcefully) of how a good and omnipotent God can allow evil in the world: this was not – J tells us – because of his inability to master it, but was due to Adam's disobedience. For this disastrous lapse was followed, in later generations, by others, and then by others again, crisis upon crisis; and the whole of future history is a series of laborious, painful attempts – with the aid of Yahweh's encouragements and rebukes – to get back to paradise lost.

St Paul, in agreement with some but not all Jewish writers of his own far later time (*II Esdras* against *II Baruch*), transformed this conception into a doctrine of original sin, according to which Adam's offence had plunged the whole world into a state of perpetual imperfection and guilt; from which it could only be redeemed by the atoning death of Jesus (Appendix 9). The writers of the Hebrew Bible, on the other hand, while they admitted that human beings need Yahweh's assistance to overcome evil, had believed that such assistance was automatically furnished once a man strives to do good; and they increasingly denied (from *Deuteronomy* onwards) the ancient popular belief that one might have to pay for the sins of one's fathers, insisting instead that every individual was personally responsible for his own sins, despite the effects of Adam's fall.

The first disaster, which that fall had foreshadowed, came very soon indeed. J goes on to tell how Eve bore two sons to Adam, first Cain and then Abel. Cain became a tiller of the soil and Abel a shepherd. When they went to sacrifice to Yahweh, Abel brought young lambs, while Cain offered the first products of the field. Yahweh accepted Abel's gift but rejected Cain's. Thereupon Cain persuaded his brother to come into the fields – where he put him to death. Yahweh cursed Cain and declared that his land would no longer bear fruit, and that he himself must henceforth be a wanderer over the face of the earth, but when Cain protested that anyone whom he encountered would kill him, Yahweh set a protective mark upon him so that this would not happen.

The story symbolizes a clash between the two ways of life in the country, the settled (Canaanite) agricultural population and seminomad (Israelite) herdsmen, represented by Cain and Abel respectively. The result is curiously equivocal. On the one hand, Cain's brutality prevails, consummated in the murder of his brother – which is rooted in primitive Canaanite human sacrifices, to ensure the fertility of the soil. This dreadful deed was the first inexorable sequel of their parents' primal disobedience. It would seem, from its outcome, that the farmer had vanquished the shepherd: and that was true to the extent that in settled Israel outright nomadism could no longer hope to prevail. And yet, all the same, our sympathy is with Abel. Not only was he the victim, but Yahweh accepted his animal sacrifice, whereas Cain's agricultural offering was refused. J is nostalgically idealizing the pastoral ways which produced Yahwism, at the expense of the Canaanite contamination that he saw all around him, especially in the highest circles of the land.

But the tale also deplores the guilt of shedding innocent blood. Because of this, Cain is doomed to loneliness, the greatest misfortune that man can suffer. It is he, the settled farmer, who becomes the wanderer that his brother had been. His ejection goes back to the very ancient Canaanite belief that the eldest son could become a scapegoat, a 'first fruit' that had to be given back to God.[5]

J then tells how the disobedience of the human race continued on its corrupting way. As punishment for such evil deeds, Yahweh decided to destroy all life on earth by means of a flood. But Noah, of the tenth generation after Adam – grandson of the 969-year-old Methuselah – had led a blameless life, and was therefore saved from the flood by being allowed to set out upon its waters in the ship, or ark, he had constructed. His wife and three sons (Shem, Ham and Japheth) and their wives accompanied him, and so did a pair of every sort of living creature. After the ark had come to rest on Mount Ararat (the ancient Urartu, now on the Turco-Soviet border), they all re-emerged on dry land.

Stories of great floods had long been familiar, particularly in Mesopotamia where they were a matter of life and death. An independent poem, later incorporated in the Epic of Gilgamesh, narrated the saga of a flood, from which Ziusudra, after building a huge boat, emerged alive. A Babylonian myth of the seventeenth century gave the survivor's name as Atrahasis, 'the exceedingly wise' (in a later Assyrian version he is Utnapishtim, the 'faraway'). Though floods on a Mesopotamian scale were not to be expected in Canaan, these antique narratives duly found their way into its traditions. Yet they had all been filled with the whims and squabbles of the gods, whereas the Bible, when it took such sagas over and adapted them, injected a moral and theological purpose of an unfamiliar kind. In this process J, although his work has to be disentangled from the contributions of subsequent narrators and editors, appears to have taken a leading hand.

Yahweh was pleased by Noah's sacrifice, 'when he smelt the soothing smell'.[6] So he set in action the whole process of nature once again – harnessing the Canaanite cycle to his own historical purposes. But the new era did not begin well. For Noah planted a vineyard, and drank too much of its wine; the old lure of the Canaanite agricultural life had proved to have deplorable effects. His son Ham saw him lying naked in his tent in a drunken stupor, and Noah cursed Ham and Ham's son Canaan, declaring that their descendants would be slaves to the descendants of his brothers.[7] So the Canaanites were doomed to eternal subordination, especially to the house of Shem, the ancestor of all the Semitic-speaking peoples – including Eber to whom the Hebrews traced back their name.[8]

After the Flood – J went on to recount – when people still spoke a single language, they planned to build a city on the plain of Shinar (Sumer) in Mesopotamia, and to make a tower, the Tower of Babel (Babylon), that would reach upwards to heaven. Yahweh censured these pretensions and brought the work to a standstill by confusing their speech, so that people henceforward spoke different, mutually incomprehensible tongues and were 'scattered all over the face of the earth'.[9]

The Tower of Babel was inspired by the enormous platform shrines (ziggurats) of Mesopotamian cities, including Ur, where a structure of this kind had been erected at about the end of the third millennium BC The account given here is conflated from two distinct tales. One set out to explain how these ziggurats originated. The other sought to describe why the human race possessed such a large number of languages. This multiplicity was interpreted as a decline into religious corruption: a single speech, explained the prophets, had meant 'pure lips' and a unanimous, harmonious, worship of God. Babel, Babylon, means 'the gate of God', but was associated by the Hebrews with a word of their own signifying confusion. The ziggurats were held to be links between heaven and earth, but Babel was godless.

It is J, too, who sets down the main features of Abraham's travels and conquests (described in an Old Akkadian literary form, the *Naru* or glorification of monarchs). He focuses with overwhelming emphasis on the promise and blessing accorded him by God: 'I will make you into a great nation ... I give this land to your descendants.'[10] The covenant of Moses, renewed and adapted by David, is retrospectively, mythically, thrown back as far as Abraham. He ceases venerating other gods in order to become a worshipper of Yahweh instead – thus beginning to lead humankind back to the obedience from which Adam had deviated. Abraham is the exemplar of a man who ventures out into a new life, not knowing where he would settle, but placing absolute faith in the divine call he has received, a call which is presented as a free and unsolicited gift, unexplained and mysterious, for he had not done anything to deserve it. But it symbolized the whole meaning of the nation's future history.

J also tells, at length, the curious, moralistic, story of Lot. Abraham and his nephew Lot had migrated together to Canaan, but there was not enough grazing for both of them, and friction broke out among their herdsmen. So they parted, and Lot headed eastwards to Sodom and Gomorrah, which, although not identifiable with certainty, lay among 'the cities of the plain' beside the southern end of the Dead Sea. Later, two visiting strangers disclosed to Abraham that they were angels sent by Yahweh to destroy these two cities because of their wickedness, notably the homosexual practices with which Sodom became synonymous. Abraham interceded for the sinners, but in vain. Lot himself, however, and his wife and their two unmarried daughters were permitted to escape – provided that they did not look back. So they set out for the neighbouring town of Zoar. Then Yahweh annihilated Sodom and Gomorrah with fire and brimstone. But as Lot and his family were fleeing, his wife flouted the divine order and looked behind her, and she was turned into a pillar of salt; 'remember Lot's wife'.[11]

The rest of the party moved onwards to the mountains. There Lot's daughters, believing that no one else was left alive in the world, made their father drunk and seduced him, subsequently giving birth to sons, Moab and Ben-ammi, from whom the Moabites and Ammonites respectively were descended.

The story of the destruction of Sodom and Gomorrah is, as so often, aetiological, providing the answers to questions about 'causes' – in this case, perhaps, a geological subsidence or an earthquake, that had once occurred at the southern end of the Dead Sea (or Salt Sea or Sea of Arabah, known to the Arabs as the Sea of Lot). But the tale of Lot is also resonant with moralistic themes. One was divine wrath and punishment for disobedience. Another was condemnation of Sodom and Gomorrah as representatives of Canaanite religion. The shrines of Canaan harboured male prostitutes (Ch.2,ii), the cities of the plain became emblems of the homosexuality that Yahweh so strongly condemned. And at the same time the author, who is especially interested in the south, manages to explain why the Transjordanian Moabites and Ammonites, though evidently related to the people of Israel, were at least half-foreigners, manifestly of second-class status. For they were declared to be the products of an incestuous relationship.

The narrator goes on to recount that God sent three angels to Abraham, in order to declare to him that his wife Sarah would bear a son, despite their great age. This son was named Isaac, and became revered as the second of the patriarchs. The legends surrounding Isaac, centred upon Beersheba, seem originally to have been separate from those attached to Abraham (Ch.3,i). They describe how Isaac's wife Rebecca bore him twins, and how the younger of them, Jacob, tricked his elder brother Esau, a red-haired hunter, into handing over his birthright – in exchange for some lentil soup. And then Jacob performed a second piece of deception: dressing in Esau's clothes, and covering his hands and neck with the fleece of a kid, he induced his blind old father to give him, the younger son, the paternal blessing, which should have gone to Esau. So Esau became destined to live far away and depend on the sword, and serve his brother; and his descendants were the half-alien, inferior Edomites of the desert – inferior like the Moabites and Ammonites.

The story of the lentil soup seems to come from an early tradition which J borrowed and incorporated into his own narrative, whereas the account of the deception of Isaac represents a blend of J with a later source. Here we have the theme of Cain and Abel again, the primitive rejection of the first-born son, made scapegoat and victim. And here is repeated, once more, the duality of Cain and Abel, farmer and nomad shepherd – though this time more or less in reverse, since the simple nomad hunter Esau (meaning 'hairy, shaggy') is defeated by his twin, the sedentary farmer Jacob ('supplanter'). J and those who came before and after him made an extraordinary character drama out of these tales. They seem to have felt a measure of admiration for the cunning Jacob, rather as Greeks admired the wiles of Odysseus.

Yahweh, we are told, gave Jacob the new name of Israel, though the traditions regarding the two names may originally have been separate, applying to a pair of different, legendary or half-legendary personages. Israel, as a geographical designation, may originally have been applied, not to the whole of the country, but to the hilly tribal districts of Ephraim and Manasseh, which formed the nucleus of the settlement by the House of Joseph (Appendix 11). Here, then, is a central Palestinian tradition which J blended with his other and more southern material, probably in order to legitimize the united monarchy, which included Judah along with all the other tribes.

J's account next reached a period which can, to a limited extent, be regarded as historical. Abraham, Isaac and Jacob, as figures in human history, had been pretty dim, dubious and symbolic. But Joseph and those who came after him form slightly more substantial bridges between legend and fact (Chs.3–4). That does not, however, really mean that their stories are any less thickly encrusted with antique folklore motifs. Joseph's career illustrates the well-worn fable of the 'Success of the Unpromising'. It also directly echoes many fairy-tales taken from Egypt and other lands of the near east.

The basic features of our Joseph tradition seem to go back to the time of David or Solomon. Much of it is likely to have been compiled by J, with supplements by the later northern historian E (Ch.11,iii). They relied on different forms of a single oral tradition; as before, one strand relates to the south, and the other to the central region of the country: particularly the area round Shechem, where the story begins and Joseph was buried.

Out of this varied, fragmented, rambling material someone – apparently J in the first place – has constructed a carefully unified, taut, well-polished, sophisticated romance, one of the most artistically composed narratives in the whole of the Bible. The plot, subtle and complex and yet admirably clear, is spiced with dramatic suspense and exotic local colour: a true precursor of the novel (Appendix 4). The generous Joseph is presented with psychological sympathy. Yet, behind all the picturesque details, there is a strong, if unobtrusive, religious purpose, for the tale provides an outstanding example of the way Yahweh can turn evil into good.

The story of Moses was first distinct from those of the earlier patriarchs, as the division between *Genesis* and *Exodus* still recalls. Once again the mass of legends with which we are provided seems to contain a factual core, centred upon a faintly seen but apparently authentic, personage (Ch.4,i,ii), and once again the J and E threads are hard to tell apart. But it seems to have been J who, employing earlier written sources, now lost, or drawing upon fragmentary oral traditions, triumphantly confirmed Moses' role as the central, towering, dominant figure of the entire Hebrew past. As a matter of historical fact, the group who escaped from Egypt with Moses was only one of several major components of the later Israelite people; it was probably J who did more than anyone else to ensure that they became known as the *only* significant component. This meant that the Israelite nation, because of this unique happening, were able to see themselves as the specific, special people on whose behalf God had intervened in human history with stupendous force, at this crucial point to which all creation had been leading, and from which the whole of subsequent history progressively developed. This concept that Israel was Yahweh's chosen people may very well go back (though not all agree) as early as the tenth century, and can thus be attributable to J.

Yahweh had now displayed his power. Yet it cannot be said for certain that J was a thoroughgoing universalist or monotheist. True, he described his God as the 'judge of all the earth',[12] and recognized him as its creator, but so had the Canaanites, who at other times were thoroughly polytheistic. And Yahweh had also been seen to intervene in non-Israelite communities, Sodom and Gomorrah – though only to fight against them and destroy them. Other peoples, J no doubt believed, had their own gods as well, but Israel would ensure, with Yahweh's continued help, that such deities remained in their inferior place – a fitting deduction from the Solomonic imperial universalism of J's own day, though Solomon himself, for political reasons, was more permissive.

The Exodus, interpreted by J as a flight and not an expulsion (as in E), and linked with the Passover, was logically followed by Moses' encounter with Yahweh on Mount Sinai. Some have believed that the two traditions were separate, the product of different Israelite groups, until J brought them together. One early description of the Mosaic covenant seems to go back to him, though he does not mention it in so many words; and so may the 'ritual' version of the Ten Commandments[13] (though the 'ethical' version may be earlier still, Ch.4,ii).

Traces of J, as of other historians, can be extensively detected in the *Book of Joshua* also. And the mainly rational, historically realistic summary of the conquest in the first chapter of *Judges* (Ch.5,i) – later overlaid by the neater, 'unitary' view of a once-and-for-all annexation by Joshua – seems to be derived from the same source. However, it may also have been J who, more misleadingly, knitted together the separate tales of the judges into a single, edifying succession of national deliverers, foreshadowing and legitimizing the united monarchy. And in the dramatically balanced or even self-contradictory presentation of Saul that we find in the *First Book of Samuel* (Ch.6,iii), the source favourable to the monarchy may have been J once again.

ii: *The Court History*

Another admirable piece of biblical historiography (*2 Samuel*, 9–20, *1 Kings*, 1–2) is the account of David's career, known as the Court History or Succession Narrative. This must have been a single composition, since the various incidents are dovetailed together to form an integral whole. While basically a story about David as king, its climax is the elevation of Solomon to the throne, preceded by the elimination of his half-brothers (Ch.7,i).

Although later editors have left their mark, the writer's evident first-hand knowledge shows him to have been contemporary with the events he is recording. On the basis of two passages which seem to contain personal reminiscences, it has been suggested that he may have been Ahimaaz, son of the Temple priest Zadok,[14] setting himself to this task in order to explain how it came to be Solomon who was privileged to build the shrine. Be this as it may, the court history can be ascribed to the reign of Solomon, or, possibly, to the decades immediately following his death. The author seems to be familiar with the international, and now Hebrew, wisdom tradition which is displayed, for example, in a parable about a rich man's unscrupulousness attributed to the prophet Nathan (allegedly remonstrating with David for his seizure of Bathsheba from her husband Uriah, though the story is improbable, Ch.7,ii).[15]

The court historian's prose is simple and superb, his style dazzlingly concise. He is a master of sustained dramatic flow, of piquantly contrasting perspectives, of vividly illustrative detail. He handles innumerable, richly varied sub-plots, involving a shattering succession of rape, incest, murder and savage intrigue, without ever losing sight of his principal themes. Nobody understands better than he does the subtle intricacy and ambivalence of situations. He brings forward a huge cast of unmistakably differentiated personages, and relates them sharply to the rapid course of events. And with magisterial skill, typical of Hebrew narrative at its best, he makes all these people speak for themselves. Some would prefer to label his work biography rather than history. And indeed his assessment of David is uncannily perceptive. The narrator not only makes his greatness and nobility evident, but reveals with equal force the major flaws in his character, displayed in a series of absorbing dramas: so that he becomes the most fully and vividly presented human being in the whole of the Bible.

Yet to describe J's masterpiece as a model of objective factual reporting would be going too far. For one thing, the motifs and methods of the old *raconteurs* are still to be seen. And the tale of David's seduction of Bathsheba, for example, cannot be based on observed fact, since some of its incidents took place in circumstances that must have been private. Certainly, from a political viewpoint, the work is a great deal more balanced and objective than the crude court flattery of earlier Egyptian compositions devoted to royal men and women, but that is because the court historian is not very interested in politics. He wants to demonstrate, it is true, that Solomon is the legitimate successor to David – yet that is not for political but for religious reasons, because Solomon's succession was what Yahweh had willed. Even David himself is shown, *with the aid of Yahweh*, to be capable of rising above his many faults. For the story, like other Hebrew stories, is dominated by the concepts of divine government and recompense: it insists that in the long run no one can escape the ordinances of Yahweh. And the principal characters of this tale, although so plausibly portrayed, are in fact made use of, with tactful persistence, to exemplify moral, religious precepts and viewpoints. Nevertheless, secular events often burst through – as they had burst through in the work of J as well – and once again this is historiography of the very highest order.

Part Four

THE DIVIDED KINGDOMS

CHAPTER 10

THE NORTHERN MONARCHY: ISRAEL

i. The First Northern Kings

The death of Solomon in c. 927 was followed by the Disruption – the division of the land into two kingdoms: Israel comprising the territories of the ten northernmost tribes, and Judah in the south consisting of the tribal area of that name and the small land of Benjamin.

The Disruption meant not only the abandonment of all imperial pretensions, but also the end of any real freedom of action for the two small states that had now come into being (the larger of them, Israel, only measured some sixty miles by forty). Although they managed to drag out their existence for some centuries, it was only for brief periods that they ceased to be at the mercy of more powerful neighbours. We learn something of their histories from the Deuteronomic historian and the Chronicler (the two *Books of Kings* and two *Books of Chronicles*), but in specialized form, because these writers, like others before and after them, had a strong religious viewpoint to express (Ch.14,ii;16,i).

When Solomon died he was succeeded by his son Rehoboam. But at a meeting at Shechem the northern tribes – whose tendencies to separatism his father and grandfather had warded off by patient diplomacy – produced a list of demands for relief from discriminatory forced labour and tax burdens. These requests goaded the young monarch to a futile attempt to browbeat them into obedience. Thereupon they vociferously rejected the rule of the House of David altogether, and instead chose Jeroboam I, the son of Nebat, as their king[1] (c. 927–907: for the dating see Appendix 1 and its note 1). Appointed by Solomon to direct the labour force in his native Ephraim, Jeroboam had engaged in a plot, and found himself compelled to take refuge with the XXIInd Dynasty pharaoh of Egypt, Sheshonk (Shishak) I (c. 945–924). Now Jeroboam had returned to his country, and was elected the first ruler of a separate, northern kingdom of Israel. His own tribal area of Ephraim, which had been somewhat eclipsed by Judah in the time of the united monarchy, became the nucleus of the new state.

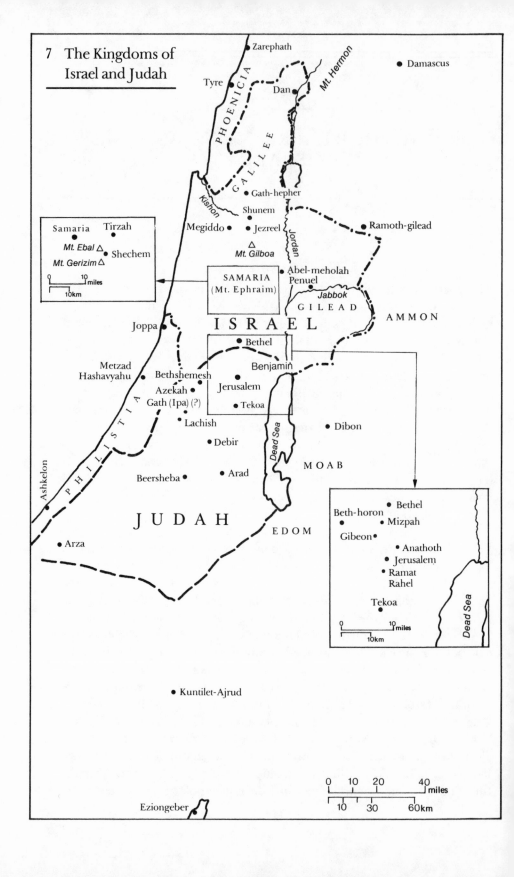

7 The Kingdoms of
Israel and Judah

Zarephath

Damascus

Tyre

PHOENICIA

Dan

Mt. Hermon

GALILEE

Kishon

Gath-hepher

Shunem

Samaria   Tirzah

Mt. Ebal △

Mt. Gerizim △ Shechem

0   10 miles
10km

Megiddo   Jezreel

Mt. Gilboa △

Jordan

Ramoth-gilead

Abel-meholah

Penuel

SAMARIA
(Mt. Ephraim)

Jabbok

GILEAD

AMMON

Joppa

I S R A E L

Bethel

Benjamin

Metzad
Hashavyahu

Bethshemesh

Azekah

Gath (Ipa) (?)

Lachish

Jerusalem

Tekoa

Dead Sea

Dibon

M O A B

Debir

Ashkelon

PHILISTIA

Beersheba

Arad

J U D A H

EDOM

Arza

Beth-horon

Bethel

Gibeon

Mizpah

Anathoth

Jerusalem

Ramat
Rahel

Tekoa

0   10 miles
10km

Dead Sea

Kuntilet-Ajrud

0   10   20   40 miles

10   30   60 km

Eziongeber

His election was a conscious attempt to get away from the hereditary principle, in order to return to the old idea of kingship founded on personal merit and conferred by Yahweh on the basis of a decision by the whole community, or at least by its elders. The continuing persistence of this idea meant that Israel would tend towards more autocratic regimes than Judah. It was also the 'older sister' – and stood a better chance of success. Its population was four times larger, and its territory, round the central heights of Ephraim (together with Gerizim and Ebal), yielded more abundant crops. Moreover, while Judah was encircled by unfriendly states, Israel was more accessible to the outside world, and could trade more freely by land and sea with western Asia.

Jeroboam I, however, did not possess Jerusalem. Instead, he moved from one less distinguished capital on to another. First he chose Shechem, where his new kingdom had originated. The Bible states that he rebuilt the town, and remains of a large government warehouse and wall with a casemate (vaulted chamber) seem to testify to his work. Then he moved seven miles north-east, to reside for at least part of each year at Tirzah (Tell el-Farah). A former Canaanite centre, which may never have been fully incorporated into the tribal system of Israel, the place stood on a plateau, jutting out like a peninsula and commanding both the north–south highway through the hills and a pass leading down to a crossing of the Jordan. On the other side of the river, too, he built a town at Penuel (Tulul edh-Dhahab esh-Sharkiya) on the River Jabbok. It was intended as a second capital – safely remote from Egypt, and well placed to control his Transjordanian territories.

It was important for Jeroboam I to wean his subjects away from the glamour of Solomon's Jerusalem Temple. This he attempted to do by reviving the historic sanctuaries at Bethel and Dan, at the southern and northern extremities of his kingdom. He expelled the priestly Levites, who were too loyal to the dynasty of David, and in their place recruited priests of local origin. They came from all classes of the people; but those at Bethel claimed descent from Moses' brother Aaron, and their colleagues at Dan asserted that their ancestor was Moses himself. However, the priests at Jerusalem, and their supporters, rejected these pedigrees. For they were entirely unwilling to recognize any shrines at all except their own – and besides, Bethel drew off the lucrative pilgrim trade.

The complaints of the Jerusalem hierarchy directed against the northern shrines found their way into the Bible. It tells us a lot about these deplorable 'high places', on hilltops or mounds. At Dan the remains of one such sanctuary have been discovered. Situated near the foot of Mount Hermon, close to one of the sacred sources of the Jordan, it was designed to serve the religious needs of the most northerly tribes, which had always tended to maintain a certain detachment from Ephraim. Excavations have revealed a massive twin-towered gate over a processional route winding up a fifty-acre mound to a wide, flat platform, the central feature of a stone-paved open-air sanctuary. No doubt Jeroboam duly dedicated it to Yahweh, but the author of *1 Kings* (deeply prejudiced against his entire régime) saw such high places as Canaanite and sinful. Sinful too were the 'golden calves' (gilded statues of bulls) which the king set up both at Bethel and Dan. Like the adornments of the Ark in Solomon's Jerusalem Temple, these images honoured the presence of Yahweh, symbolic and invisible, or (to the less philosophically minded) actual and present. A long passage was later inserted in *Exodus* to condemn such objects as idolatrous Canaanite infringements of the second Commandment.[2] And indeed, Jeroboam's high places, with their equivocal implications, did smooth the way for a resurgence of Canaanite religion. Like the kings of the united monarchy before him, he felt that a certain blend of Yahwist and Canaanite religious institutions was desirable, in order to endear his régime to people of both faiths.

Such unity was particularly important, since his reign witnessed a sharp revival of the Egyptian threat to the country, after hundreds of years of quiescence. The invader was Sheshonk or Shishak I (*c.* 945–924). As a refugee, Jeroboam had received asylum from Sheshonk, but now he came under attack from the same quarter. The biblical account only mentions the pharaoh's assault upon Judah, but his own version, preserved on the Temple of Amon at Karnak, displays 156 captives, each representing a Palestinian town – and the list makes it clear that Israel, as well as Judah, suffered serious devastation.[3] Jeroboam may well have encouraged Sheshonk to invade Judah, but the Egyptian, presiding over a new and a much more dynamic and aggressive régime, had evidently been tempted by the weakness of divided Palestine to bring down destruction upon Israel as well. Fortunately, however, a crisis in his homeland meant that he had to retreat.

Equally ominous, for the future of Israel and Judah alike, was their own shortsighted hostility towards each other. Throughout the entire first half-century following the Disruption, border warfare between the two states was almost continuous. These conflicts, together with the general dislocation caused by the invasions of Sheshonk, perilously encouraged encroachment by the Aramaean state of Damascus. This, after disengagement from Solomon's control, had become a power very much to be reckoned with (Ch.8,i). And when Baasha of the tribe of Issachar (906–883), superseding the Ephraimite house of Jeroboam I on Israel's throne, established a fortified post at Ramathaim (Ramah) on the frontier of Judah, the king of that country, Asa, bribed Ben Hadad I of Damascus (*c.* 885–870) to invade Israel from the north, so that Baasha found himself obliged to retire. He lost parts of northern Galilee to Damascus, and also had to evacuate Moab and other Transjordanian territories.

ii. The House of Omri

This threatened disintegration of the kingdom of Israel was halted by Omri (c. 882–871), an able military commander who proved more than a match for a rival claimant, Tibni. A remarkable thirty-four-line inscription of King Mesha of Moab, found at the Moabite capital Dibon (Dhiban), shows that Omri had been able to recover that country.[4] Wisely, too, he concluded peace with Judah. And, in addition, he effectively contained the menace of Damascus, first by winning a series of military victories, and then by permitting the businessmen of the defeated state to establish a trading quarter in Jerusalem. He also gained an important ally, and secured access to the sea, by renewing David's and Solomon's friendship with Tyre in Phoenicia, which was now enjoying a revival. Omri sealed the alliance by obtaining Jezebel, the daughter of its priest-king Ittobaal (Ethbaal) (c. 873–842), as the bride of Ahab, his eldest son and heir.

At first Omri continued to reside at Tirzah, where traces of a new, royal quarter, constructed on his initiative, have come to light. But the palace was abandoned before completion, because six years later he moved ten miles to the west and built an entirely new capital at Samaria (Shmer, 'Watch Tower'), on the western side of the Ephraim massif. The site, which had previously housed an unfortified village or town, was a round, prominent, isolated summit beside the main highway from north to south, in reach of a spring and enjoying a spectacular view of the coastal road, the Way of the Sea. For Omri intended to break free of the confining hills, and turn his face towards Phoenicia and the Mediterranean world. Samaria was also defensible, for the hill on which it stood, although not very high, fell steeply on three of its sides, and, now or a little later, was made virtually impregnable by the construction of a thick wall of carefully squared stone blocks.

Omri, followed by Ahab, converted the entire summit of the hill into his regal residence. Excavations have revealed the mansions of his family and courtiers, storehouses, reservoirs and granaries. This was the first and last major city the ancient people of Israel ever founded from nothing. Perhaps its lay-out echoed Solomon's Jerusalem, which Omri deliberately intended to outdo. Moreover the new Samaria also included a quarter lying further down the slopes, for the housing of its poorer population. This was protected by an outer wall of its own, though its more perishable materials have yielded few or no remains. At Tirzah, too, beside the palace, there had been a humbler city for the poor. A novel and rapidly growing class distinction was now apparent. It augured badly for the social coherence of the country.

From an ethnic point of view, on the other hand, Samaria represented an attempt to safeguard the unity of the kingdom: for it was meant to ensure that the Canaanites, as well as the Israelites, enjoyed a worthy and significant rôle in a personal union under the monarchy. Omri had purchased the site, as his private possession, from a Canaanite, by a transaction according to Canaanite law. There seems to have been, at this stage, no cult of Yahweh in this new Samaria. Yet, as we shall see shortly, there were cults of Canaanite gods – and the furniture inlays and ivories adorning the palace, following the precedents of Solomon's Jerusalem and Megiddo, were purely Canaanite in style.

However, Omri (or Ahab) also acquired yet another capital, Jezreel (Zer'in) at the foot of Mount Gilboa, which, instead, was built not on Canaanite but on Israelite property (belonging to the family of Baasha). In Jezreel, then, it would seem, the kings were to appear as the monarchs of their Israelite subjects, whereas in Samaria they were the rulers over the Canaanite population. His worship of Yahweh, that is to say, only represented about half of his political philosophy and calculation. According to *1 Kings*, therefore, 'He outdid all his predecessors in wickedness.'[5]

Omri's son Ahab (871–852) maintained and further developed his father's policies: constructive co-existence with Judah; intimate association with the Phoenicians, because of the threat from Aramaean Damascus; and skilful handling of that kingdom itself. First of all, two military victories were won against the monarch of Damascus, Ben-hadad, probably the second of that name (*c.* 870–842). But then the two rulers agreed to the establishment of an Israelite trading quarter there, to balance the Aramaeans' similar quarter in Jerusalem.

These friendly relations led to a result which we learn about from Assyrian sources. For Assyria, of which the nucleus was in the angle between the Rivers Tigris and Great Zab, had now become a great military power again – the most menacing that the near east had ever experienced. Its tough and soldierly people, speaking a north-eastern Semitic language descended from Akkadian, showed an explosive desire to expand. The first great Assyrian empires had crumbled in the twelfth and eleventh centuries, latterly under Aramaean pressure. But eventually the fortunes of the country began to rise again. Ashurnasirpal II (881–859), famous for the brutality of his military methods, struck out at the smaller kingdoms of the region, absorbing them into a ring of provinces and client states. With his eye on the timber of Phoenicia, he undertook a campaign to the Mediterranean coast, 'washing his weapons in the sea' and extracting tribute from the local Syrian rulers. Then his successor Shalmaneser (Shulmanu-Asharidu) III, as we learn from Assyrian records, pushed westwards again with even greater determination.[6] He conquered the nearest of the Aramaean kingdoms of northern Syria (Bit-adini, Beth-eden), and then moved into the centre of that country, threatening Hamath and particularly directing himself against Damascus.

In this extreme crisis, Ahab came to the aid of the Aramaeans, sending a contingent of 2,000 chariots and 10,000 infantry (unless some of them came from Judah). In 854–853, the first certain date in Hebrew history, this coalition fought a major engagement against the Assyrians at Karkar (Khirbet Qerqur) on the lower Orontes. Shalmaneser III, as was usual on such occasions, pronounced that he won. But since he did not follow the battle up, the result was probably indecisive. The opposing alliance, while it lasted, had displayed a gallant, rare and long overdue attempt at Syro-Palestinian unity. But almost immediately afterwards Israel and Judah broke with Damascus, coming to blows with its army at Ramoth-gilead across the Jordan; and Ahab lost his life. During his reign, Israel had been forcibly pitched into the larger near-eastern scene and all its perils, which from now onwards would never again be far away.

Meanwhile, Ahab's internal policy had been equally energetic. His father's building programme was vigorously pursued. A considerable and perhaps major portion of the royal acropolis at Samaria seems to date from his reign. He reconstructed and resettled Jericho. A large citadel and military stock-houses, and a superbly ingenious water-system, were created at Hazor, which was doubled in size. Another protected water-tunnel, and further storerooms, were brought into being at Megiddo, which was also equipped with massive fortifications. These measures, although they required heavy taxation, all served to strengthen the country.

But they were disastrously outweighed, in the eyes of orthodox Yahwists, by Ahab's keen adherence to his father Omri's policy of combining the Israelite and Canaanite populations in a partnership, on more or less equal terms. It seems to have been Ahab who greatly enlarged the high place at Dan, which had already generated so much misunderstanding and disapproval. What is more, he himself, in person, 'went and worshipped Baal; he prostrated himself before him and erected an altar to him in the temple of Baal which he built in Samaria',[7] the city Omri had founded as the capital for his Canaanite subjects. This Baal was probably equated with the Tyrian god Melkart, and the biblical writers were no doubt right in supposing that his Phoenician wife Jezebel played an active part in this encouragement of foreign religion; though whether (as was said) she maintained as many as 450 priests or prophets of Baal and

400 of Asherah (Ashtoreth), and whether she was allowed to massacre numerous devout adherents of Yahweh,[8] must be regarded as doubtful, for Ahab still maintained the cult of Yahweh – and gave his sons Yahwist names. Indeed, he was eager to play a prominent part in the Yahwist priestly cult; all too eager, in the eyes of the prophets, who disapproved of any suggestion of a royal priesthood among the northern kings.

However, Elijah (Ch.11,i) was right to complain that Ahab deliberately 'sat on the fence'. There are traces, in the Bible, of a rival tradition which treated him in more complimentary fashion, displaying his dealings with Ben-hadad II of Damascus, for example, in a favourable light, but the overwhelmingly predominant conclusion was that 'he committed gross abominations in going after false gods. ... He did more that was wrong in the eyes of Yahweh than all his predecessors.'[9]

iii. Revolution, Recovery and Fall

After the deaths of Ahab and his son Ahaziah (852–851), and the succession of another son Joram (851–845) (who helped Judah to invade Moab), the Yahwists took their revenge. This took the form of a coup launched by a senior officer named Jehu (845–818). Dashing fifty miles in his chariot to Jezreel, Jehu slew the fleeing Joram with an arrow. Jezebel was hurled out of a window, and Jehu drove over her body, leaving it to be torn apart by dogs. Joram's brothers were slain by the upstart's followers, and their heads stacked in two heaps at the city gate. The late monarch's close friends were likewise massacred, and so, with his entourage, was the new king of Judah, called Ahaziah like a slightly earlier ruler in Israel, to whose brother and successor he happened, fatally, to be paying a visit. The slaughter was also extended to the priests of Baal at Samaria; and the ruins of their shattered temple were converted into a latrine.

Behind this unprecedentedly ferocious revolutionary purge stood the legendary figure of the prophet Elisha and the extremist, reactionary Yahwist sect of the Rechabites, founded by Rechab whose frightening son Jonadab had now succeeded to his position. Successors of the puritan Nazirites (Ch.6,i), the leaders of the sect came out of the cattle-raising fringes of the country, professing nomadic ideals and reviling the settled residential and agricultural ways – inherited from the Canaanites – since no provision for such a life had been made in the precepts of Moses. The poor and landless, suffering from raw new class distinctions, debts, droughts and perversions of justice, found that these ideas exercised a considerable appeal.

So the Rechabites, by a special summons from Yahweh, brought Jehu to power, but his later conduct, the Bible remarks, failed to satisfy the orthodox after all (Ch.14,ii). His own motives for rebellion may have been more sophisticated, in terms of international politics, than those of his fanatical religious backers. A black obelisk from the Assyrian city of Nimrud shows a personage specifically identified as Jehu ('Ya-ú-a') lying on his stomach in front of the Assyrian monarch Shalmaneser III, while behind the recumbent figure stand servants carrying tribute (described in detail).[11] Jehu, an experienced military man, must have seen that the multiple convulsions produced by his own revolt had brought Israel to the verge of total ruin. That is to say, submission to the Assyrians – who invaded Syria in 841 and issued threats against Israel – had become imperative if the obliteration of his kingdom was to be avoided. Indeed, one of the purposes of his rising may have been to suppress the anti-Assyrian faction in his own ranks.

His recognition of the weakness of his new régime was soon to be abundantly justified, for this vulnerability induced Hazael, who had ascended the throne of Damascus, to launch a violent and overwhelming attack on Jehu's remaining Transjordanian possessions, which were almost wholly lost; Mesha of Moab, already autonomous, announced his total independence.[12] Moreover, under Jehu's son Jehoahaz '(c. 818–802), Israel virtually became the vassal of Hazael, on whose orders its armed forces were cut down to nothing; so that Jehoahaz felt obliged to abandon his father's exclusively Yahwist policies and accept Aramaean and Canaanite influences (a step which, according to the Bible, was the cause of his failures). It was therefore a stroke of luck for Israel when Damascus was crippled by an Assyrian assault in 802. This enabled Joash (802–787), the son of Jehoahaz, to win three victories against Hazael's successor Ben-hadad III, recapturing a number of towns. Joash also fought a battle against Judah at Bethshemesh, with such success that he was even able to force his way into Jerusalem itself, plundering the royal and Temple treasures.

But the most triumphant of all the northern kingdom's monarchs, in terms of territorial expansion, was Jeroboam II (c. 787–747), the son of Joash. Continuing his father's aggressive policy towards the debilitated state of Damascus, Jeroboam II reannexed extensive Syrian territories, in which the whole of the Bekaa valley may well have been included. He also reoccupied areas east of the Jordan. These conquests made him the most powerful monarch since the beginning of the Disruption, and the strongest ruler of his day in all Palestine and Syria. He also maintained excellent relations with the king of Judah, Uzziah. By such means he markedly enlarged the resources of his state, although (as the prophet Amos pointed out) the affluence was still very unevenly distributed (Ch.11,ii).

The 'Samaria ostraca' (fragments of earthenware), inscribed in ink and paint, may belong to this reign.[13] They comprise sixty-three invoices for wine and oil received at court from the managers of crown lands, probably in payment of taxes. The ostraca also suggest why Jeroboam II, in spite of all his achievements, is nevertheless ranked by the Bible among the numerous kings who did evil in Yahweh's eyes. For the word 'Baal' is still incorporated in forty per cent of the personal names of the people whom these documents mention. That is to say, Jeroboam II continued to water down or reverse Jehu's austerely Yahwist programme, in the interests of internal harmony.

After the death of Jeroboam II, marking the termination of Jehu's dynasty, a rapid succession of kings of Israel plunged its foreign affairs into unmitigated disaster. Assyria, which had seemed moribund, experienced a formidable revival under Tiglath-Pileser (Tukulti-apal-Esharra) III (745–727). His huge and strongly centralized empire, extending from the Persian Gulf to Armenia, included a corridor right through to the Mediterranean coast, from which he dominated all Syrian and Palestinian territory. King Menahem of Israel (c. 747–738) was one of his vassals, paying a tribute of one thousand talents of silver, raised by a levy from every man of property in the kingdom. Prompted by indignant nationalists, however, an army officer named Pekah (735–732) murdered Menahem's son Pekahiah and struggled to form an alliance to repel the Assyrians. Judah refused to cooperate (and was invaded by Pekah), but the coalition was joined by Damascus, Ammon, Moab, Edom and some of the old Philistine cities.

Ahab's similar coalition in the past had not fared badly. But now the enemy was altogether too strong. Tiglath-Pileser III obliterated Damascus and killed its king (c. 733), carving his state into four Assyrian provinces and deporting much of its population to Iran. Israel, likewise overrun and devastated, was reduced to a small territory not extending beyond the immediate neighbourhood of Samaria, and many of its inhabitants were exiled to Assyria. Hoshea ('salvation' in Hebrew) (731–723) murdered and took the place of Pekah, who had brought about these disasters, and reverted, at first, to the policy of submission to Assyria. After the death of Tiglath-Pileser III, however, he made a futile attempt to throw off Assyrian domination. Encouraged by Tyre, he also appealed to Egypt for help: 'Ephraim [Israel] is like a silly dove, without understanding,' declared the prophet Hosea: 'they call unto Egypt, they go to Assyria.'[14] However, the Egyptian pharaoh was too weak, or unwilling, to respond; and Shalmaneser V, on succeeding to the Assyrian throne (c. 727–722), invaded what was left of Israel, captured its king, and lay siege to Samaria.

The siege dragged on for three years, but finally in 722, either at the end of Shalmaneser's reign or soon after the subsequent usurpation of Sargon

II, resistance collapsed. The city was burnt to the ground; and the state of Israel was abolished and absorbed into the Assyrian empire. No less than 27,290 of its inhabitants – and perhaps the figure does not include women and children – were reportedly taken off to Assyria and Media.[15] There, in due course, they and earlier deportees vanished completely from view – the 'Lost Ten Tribes': probably they became assimilated with the local populations, which was all the easier, because many of them had been pro-Assyrian at home. To take their place in their former homeland, people were brought in from various regions of the Assyrian empire, including Syria, Arabia, Babylonia and Media.

CHAPTER 11

NORTHERN PROPHECY
AND HISTORY

i. Elijah and Elisha

The ninth century witnessed the rise of a new and impressive kind of prophet in the kingdom of Israel. Among the Canaanites, and under the united monarchy, the most frequent rôle of such men had been as advisers, adjuncts and on the whole supporters of the royal court. In the time of Ahab (Ch.10,ii), however, there seems to have been an abrupt change, or perhaps the result of a gradual shift became more clearly visible. For the two prophets who arose in the reigns of Ahab and his successors, Elijah and Elisha, were extremely hostile to royal policy, and showed their hostility as clearly as could be. Out-and-out Yahwists, they raised violent and unrelenting objections to the kings' policy of tolerating Canaanite religious practices alongside Yahwism.

It is difficult, however, to disentangle Elijah and Elisha from the mass of legends that immediately gathered around their uncompromising, mysterious personalities, and are incorporated in the work of the Deuteronomic historian (Ch.14,ii). Elijah appeared suddenly out of Tishbe (unidentified) in Gilead, east of the Jordan, upon the desert's edge. Because of the worship of Baal and other Canaanite gods by Ahab and his wife Jezebel, Elijah was sent by Yahweh, we are told, to inform him that there would be a terrible drought. Having conveyed this message, he avoided the king's wrath by moving across the Jordan to the brook Cherith, where ravens brought him food. Later he moved to Zarephath (Sarepta) in Phoenicia to dwell with a widow, whose food supply was miraculously renewed; and when her son died, Yahweh answered Elijah's prayer and brought him back to life.

In the third year of the drought Elijah received a divine order to go back and confront Ahab again. After an angry exchange, the monarch agreed to a trial of strength between Elijah and Jezebel's priests of Baal and Ashtoreth, estimated, as we saw elsewhere, as numbering 450 and 400 apiece. The priests leapt and ranted and raved and slashed themselves, but elicited no divine response, and Elijah had them dragged to the brook Kishon and put to death in the valley. When Jezebel threatened him with a similar fate, he once more fled for his life, taking refuge in the southern wilderness; but after a series of wondrous occurrences Yahweh spoke to him, and ordered him to go and anoint Hazael and Jehu as kings of Damascus and Israel respectively (a taste left for Elisha).

Later, when Ahab had the Jezreel landowner Naboth killed in order to seize his vineyard, Elijah warned the king that Yahweh, condemning the murder, would destroy the entire royal family – a moral story in the wisdom tradition. Then Ahab's son and successor Ahaziah, who had sent messengers to consult the alien god Baalzebul at Philistine Ekron, felt the weight of the prophet's displeasure as well. Not long afterwards, knowing his end was near, Elijah came to the banks of the river Jordan, and was taken up to heaven in a chariot of fire.

Being a product of the cattle-raising periphery of the country, Elijah blamed all contemporary evils on the Canaanite ways of agricultural and urban life. He lived the life of a Yahwist solitary, and may have been a dedicated Nazirite (Ch.6,i). Yet he spoke for many priests and prophets when he protested to Ahab, which he did with such violence that the king angrily called him a 'troubler of Israel'. (Another critical prophet, Micaiah, was struck in the face by a colleague who supported the king, and cast into prison.)[1]

These anti-monarchical views were voiced at a time when current droughts were reflecting badly on Baal, supposedly the god of fertility and storm and rain. For his challenge to the god's power Elijah chose the summit of Mount Carmel, symbol of strength, beauty and natural richness, but also the place where Baal's ritual dances were staged. There the prophet ordered the people not to submit to Ahab's collaborative, permissive ideas but to make a direct choice: 'If Yahweh is God, follow him; but if Baal, then follow him', and his followers gladly slaughtered the prophets of Baal, roaring out, 'Yahweh is God! Yahweh is God!'[2]

If there is some kernel of truth in this epic trial of strength – as seems likely – the Yahwists, under the leadership of Elijah, had for the time being won a notable victory. The event also confirmed a perceptible shift, among the population, towards monotheistic thought. It is true that the prophet's concept of Yahweh as the bloodthirsty war-god of vengeance goes back to the old ideas of tribal deities, one for each group. Nor is it probable that, in historical fact, Elijah did more than stress the *supremacy* of the God of Israel rather than emphasize his universality; 'Yahweh is God' can also mean 'Yahweh is *my* God', allowing room for other deities. Nevertheless, his insistence that Yahweh was great enough to interfere in the affairs of a foreign state such as Damascus, and his uncompromising assertion that Baal could do nothing against him, prepared the way – like the similar reflections of the southern historian (Ch.9,i) – for the more thoughtful universal monotheism that the later prophets were to provide before long.

Yahweh, we are told, spoke personally to Elijah: a very rare event in Hebrew religious history. And the divine words were not brought by wind or earthquake or fire, but in a pronouncement that can be variously translated as a 'low muttering sound', 'a still small voice', 'the soft whisper of a voice', 'a voice of gentle silence'.[3] This was an endeavour to show that he worked his will in a less noisy and primitive fashion than the old thunderous storm-god of Canaan. His, in complete contrast, was a low, quiet speech that could be heard if one devoted oneself to listening for it.

This passage, pointing towards a more spiritual and transcendent concept of Yahweh, was written after Elijah was dead, but may embody a tradition going back to his own time. The same relatively sophisticated approach is seen in reflections on the legal and moral relationship of citizen to state prompted by the prophet's career. But alongside appears primitive folklore material stressing savage bloodshed and wonder-working excitement and dervish-like oracular utterance.

The sudden arrivals of this eerie, gaunt figure from the wilds, this 'hairy man with a leather apron round his waist',[4] caught the fancy of later generations, who hailed him as an archetypal hero. His austerity epitomized other-worldly values. His miracles demonstrated that holy men could work their will on natural phenomena. Prophets saw him as the very model and image of their order. His rescue of his people from Canaanite corruption ranked him with Moses; and like Enoch, Methuselah's father, who walked with God – like Moses too, as some said – he ascended to heaven. Orthodox Judaism rejected the idea, but the story was designed to show the possibility of an after-life, and there was a persistent belief that Elijah would one day return as a great helper in the ultimate time of crisis: indeed John the Baptist and Jesus were sometimes believed to be his reincarnations.

Yahweh was said to have declared to Elijah that Elisha, the son of Shaphat, a farmer from Abel-meholah in the Jordan valley who was present at his end, would continue his mission; and so it came about.

He became the hero of two groups of stories. One consisted of tales that depict him as a political figure: saving the Israelite army from dying of thirst; helping his people against enemy invasions, notably during the siege of Samaria by King Ben-hadad II of Damascus; overthrowing Ben-hadad and Joram of Israel, and placing Hazael and Jehu on their thrones instead; telling Joash he ought to have fought Damascus harder. The second series of narratives was planned to illustrate his supernatural powers. When boys mocked him for his baldness, he cursed them in Yahweh's name, so that she-bears came out of the wood and mauled forty-two of them to death,[5] but generally he appears in a more beneficent rôle: he brings back to life the dead son of a woman from Shunem (near Afula); he miraculously multiplies food for the prophetical guilds and their adherents; he cures Naaman, Damascus' commander-in-chief, of his leprosy, by ordering him to wash seven times in the Jordan – a procedure related to the ritual ablutions (to remove spiritual impurities or annul contact with things unclean) which were a feature of the Yahwist religion.

The tales describing his political interventions appear to be more or less historical. Elijah, too, had already influenced state affairs in the most forthright fashion, when religious considerations seemed to him to require this, and Elisha carried the process much further by openly organizing Jehu's revolutionary *coup*. For it was Elisha, according to the biblical writer, who helped to bring the House of Omri down in a torrent of blood in collusion with the fanatical Rechabite sect, and then proceeded to anoint Jehu as 'king over Israel, the people of Yahweh'.[6] No longer were the prophets just the advisers of monarchs; nowadays they overthrew monarchs, and set them up. They formed a second centre of power in the land, almost equal to the kingship in strength, and superior to it in popular reverence. And Elisha was perfectly prepared to interfere equally forcefully at Damascus as well. Well might Ben Sira declare, many centuries later, 'Throughout his life no ruler made him tremble; no one could make him subservient.'[7]

The same writer went on to speak of the miracles the prophet performed – the themes of the second set of colourful stories and character sketches clustering round his personality. Sometimes these tales are duplicates of the Elijah saga, but usually they are cruder – and may sometimes be older. They are popular anecdotes, which circulated widely and perpetually. The shocking account of his alleged massacre of the mocking boys shows how completely its narrators were prepared to sacrifice every sort of consideration of humanity and ethics to Elisha's renown as a performer of miracles.

One of the stories refers to a company and community of prophets,[8] the sort of body which Elisha evidently employed as a power base. It is reasonable to suppose that this whole collection of sagas, gathered orally at first, was put together by someone attached to such a guild, though the sequence in which it has come down to us may be the result of subsequent editorial changes. The narratives relating to Elijah and Elisha became manifestos of a kind of opposition party located in rustic or semi-desert communities, combating non-Yahwist customs and rituals and resisting class oppression, in sympathy with the Rechabites' demand for a return to nomad simplicity.

ii. Amos and Hosea

In the course of the eighth century these developments led to the rise of another and different sort of prophet, of whom we know more because their views, for the first time, were set down in literary productions. In that sense, they were the first 'writing' prophets, though they did not write down their prophecies themselves. The first leaders of the movement were Amos and Hosea. Once again, they were severe critics of the kings, but now their criticism was uttered in more reasoned and intellectual terms. It was also voiced in tones of alarmingly pessimistic gloom, for they proclaimed the startling, outrageous message that Yahweh's people were gravely at fault, indeed that they were guilty of such intolerable sins that he was going to withdraw his support from the two kingdoms, and obliterate them.

The *Book of Amos* begins with a prose introduction describing the prophet's profession and background. He came from the village of Tekoa in the Judah hills, where he was a sheep farmer and dresser of sycamore figs. Then he moved into the northern kingdom of Israel, no doubt in order to get a better price for his wool; and so he appeared as a prophet at one of Israel's chief sanctuaries, Bethel.

After this preface, most of the work consists of poetry. First we have a series of prophecies directed against neighbouring nations: on account of their violations of the laws of humanity, Yahweh will destroy them, one and all. But these forecasts reach their dismaying climax in the denunciation of Yahweh's own worshippers. Other prophets had attacked them for turning away from him to worship Canaanite idols, but Amos prefers to stress the moral and social decline into which he believed that this practice had plunged them: they had become hard and callous in their dealings with the poor and oppressed; they had indulged themselves with Temple prostitutes, and they had prevented Yahweh's spokesmen from making themselves heard. In fact, they had broken the covenant he made with their ancestors, and could in no way escape the punishment he was determined to bring down upon their heads. Yahweh would shatter to pieces the debased shrine of Bethel, and scarcely a trace would survive of Samaria to bear witness to its former wealth.

For the much vaunted religion of the Israelites, the prophet went on to pronounce, was only an empty façade. By famine, drought, blight and disease, Yahweh had warned them where they were heading, but all to no avail. Yet he still appealed to them to save their lives, even at this late date, by becoming loyal to him once again; which meant, not a plethora of sacrifices at the country's corrupt sanctuaries, but a truly reformed way of living – a thoroughgoing return to Yahweh's standards of just and right behaviour in private and public life alike. Otherwise the coming Day of the Lord, on which the people of Israel, after their enemies had been crushed, expected to enter an era of blessed perfection, would prove to be the exact opposite: a time of lamentation and darkness and destruction. Prosperous, comfortable living had bred security and self-sufficient pride, which was totally unwarranted. Judgement would not be delayed for ever.

The priest Amaziah, continues the book, had ejected Amos from the royal sanctuary of Bethel, bidding him pack up and take his message back to his native Judah. But Amos, still speaking as the mouthpiece of Yahweh, declares that an invading army will rape Amaziah's wife, slaughter his children, seize his land, and dispatch him into exile to die in misery. People like to think that their wrongdoings are too small for Yahweh to notice, but he sees every one of them, without fail. And the poor, who always come off worst, remain his special care. Then comes a word of limited hope. True, for the people as a whole, punishment cannot be averted: Yahweh will deal with them as he deals with any other nation. Yet the faithful few, the Remnant, will win their blessed reward.

Amos appeared in the northern kingdom for a sensational few years towards the end of the reign of Jeroboam II (c. 787–747), a century after the encounters of Elijah and Elisha with Ahab. When Amaziah told him to stop 'drivelling on' and get out of the sanctuary of Bethel, he replied by endeavouring to explain himself: 'I am [or was] no prophet, nor a prophet's son; I am [or was] a herdsman and a dresser of sycamore figs; but Yahweh took me as I followed the flock and said to me, "Go and prophesy to my people Israel." '[9] He had not been a prophet at first, that is to say, but became one – of a kind. Amaziah remained sceptical. For how could one discover if someone was an authentic prophet, if he had not been trained in a prophetic guild?

And that raised a deeper question still. Even if a man did belong to such a guild, how on earth was it possible to tell if he was a true prophet or a false one? – of whom there were many about, insistently claiming to speak on Yahweh's behalf. As violent disputes in the time of Ahab had shown, the kings and their friends thought that the false prophets were the ones who spoke against the policies of the court. No doubt the unprivileged classes took precisely the opposite view. Isaiah suggested that false prophets drank (vomiting all over the table). Micah (Appendix 5) thought you could distinguish when they were fraudulent because they would not offer optimistic forecasts unless you gave them food. Another writer ascribed to Moses the idea that you can only tell 'true' prophecy because it comes true.[10] Yet there may be a long time-lag in which the outcome cannot be seen, and in any case actual prediction was only one of the tasks of a prophet (Ch.6,i). In the end it all hinged on belief. Amos, Hosea and the rest were only 'true' prophets because the Bible tells us so.

But in any case they were astonishing thinkers. Amos's humble origins made him somewhat averse to theoretical speculation. Yet to judge from the distinctive tone of his reported oracles (even if their balanced classical language is a later development), he was by no means an uneducated rustic. He reveals more than a touch of irony: and he echoed the wisdom tradition (Ch.8,ii). But there must have been something especially compelling about his claim to have seen visions and to have heard Yahweh's voice. He compares this direct, violent encounter, involving the submersion of his own personality, to the terror inspired by a roaring lion.[11] This was in the tradition of the earlier ecstatic prophets. Yet Amos's sense of vocation was highly distinctive and all his own.

He also advances further along the path which his predecessors – the southern historian, and Elijah – had started to follow, towards the idea that Yahweh is supreme not only over Israel, but everywhere else as well. For Amos recalls that Yahweh has helped and saved other nations too, and now, in a series of oracles of doom (a literary form that became a prophetic tradition), he ritually denounces their iniquities as rebellions *against Yahweh*. The gods whom other people worship are not worth serious discussion. And indeed, unlike Elijah and Elisha, Amos is scarcely interested in attacking these gods, for what he, much more disturbingly, wants to do is to criticize the current practice of Yahwism itself. To him, this religion was nothing better than a formal, useless sham unless it could be accompanied by an overwhelming moral and social improvement, a 'turning back' foreshadowing the demands for repentance made by Isaiah and Jeremiah (Ch.13,ii,iii). And above all, in the *nouveau riche* capital of Samaria, Amos helped to create a splendid Jewish tradition of the future by his denunciations of social inequality and oppression: 'They grind the heads of the poor into the earth.'[12] This, he believes, is an offence against Yahweh himself. But the time will come when all the luxury-loving women, who demand that their husbands should keep them well supplied with liquor, will be dragged away with hooks, like fish, and hurled through the nearest hole in the wall.

This is just one of the many forcible acts of retribution which will take place on the inevitable Day of the Lord. It had become an entrenched popular hope, by Amos's time, that Israel would eventually have the happy experience of a Last Day on which Yahweh would scatter its foes. Amos startlingly and brutally reverses such a view, for 'On that day', declares Yahweh, 'the songs in the palace will become cries of mourning. There will be dead bodies everywhere. They will be thrown out in silence.'[13]

And Amos clearly sees that Yahweh's agents in this work of destruction will be the Assyrians, although he does not actually mention them by name. His prediction was to be fulfilled when Samaria fell before thirty years had passed (Ch.10,iii). To the many who must have protested, in dismay, that such things could not happen to Yahweh's chosen people, the prophet declared that it was precisely because of Yahweh's uniquely intense concern for them that Israel was doomed to suffer penalties of peculiar severity.[14]

Nevertheless, the book ends with a final divine assurance that a Remnant would be spared from the destruction: David's fallen House will be restored and rebuilt, and the people will once more be planted on their own soil, and will never be uprooted again. This doctrine of a saved, saving Remnant became and remained very important to Israel, but it may have been a later addition inserted into the *Book of Amos* by subsequent editors, because they found the original text too disquieting. Amos had not been, by nature, a purveyor of comfort, but a prophet who provided a ferocious indictment and a devastating shock.

Even in its original form the book was not written by Amos himself. No doubt his prophecies, which it contains, had at first circulated orally, but after he had been silenced at Bethel and expelled from its shrine, his hearers and disciples – probably members of one of the prophetic guilds – evidently felt that it had become a matter of urgency to write his sayings down. And so they were collected into something like the book that has come down to us.

Very shortly afterwards came the message of another prophet, Hosea, who concentrated in more traditional fashion on launching violent attacks upon Canaanite cults, although he does so in extremely unusual and novel terms.

Hosea, of uncertain origin, began to prophesy in the northern kingdom of Israel towards the end of the reign of Jeroboam II (c. 787–747), and continued to do so for about twenty years, during the period of unstable, depressing vacillations which immediately preceded the fall of Samaria to the Assyrians. The biblical book that bears this prophet's name contains, like the *Book of Amos*, some subsequent editorial amendments. Yet it, too, may already have been brought to a state not far removed from its final form before the eighth century was over, that is to say, when authentic memories of the prophet were still alive. It resembles *Amos* in another respect also: for both books mainly consist of poetry.

We are informed that Yahweh astonishingly commands Hosea to marry and have children by Gomer, who is a whore and an adulteress. She gives birth to three children, and each is given a name which tells of the divine message to Israel. All this is a way of declaring that Yahweh vouchsafes his people a last opportunity to change their ways before judgement descends upon them: so that when the Last Day brings peace throughout the earth, Israel can become the beloved bride of Yahweh once again. Next, it is recounted that Gomer, who has seemingly become the slave of another man, is brought back and placed on a kind of probation: and in the same way the Israelites too, after living for a long time without their true Lord, 'will seek him once again, and turn to him anxiously for his bounty in days to come'. Meanwhile, the prostitution of religion, by the acceptance of repulsive Canaanite practices, has led Israel (and Judah too) into sexual degradation, symbolizing the breakdown of social order and decency of every kind.

Hosea knows he is Yahweh's watchman and will not hold his tongue: the country will become a slave to the Assyrians as it once was to Egypt, and desolation will ravage its people. Yet although they deserve no mercy, Yahweh still shrinks from their final, total annihilation. For the survivors, his punishment will not be an end but a hopeful beginning, based on an altogether new relationship with himself.

This has sometimes been called the most obscure book in the whole Hebrew Bible. Its strangest feature is Hosea's sustained imagery relating to his alleged marriage to the harlot Gomer. Her disgusting immorality is dwelt upon at length and in detail. However, this is not just a painful personal reminiscence on the part of the prophet, since Gomer stands for Israel who has forsaken her husband Yahweh for adultery with Baal and the deities who are worshipped along with him.

Of all the great prophets, Hosea is the most deeply revolted by the Canaanite religion. The people who follow it, he declares, are nothing better than idolaters, 'asking advice from a block of wood and taking their orders from a fetish'. Gomer's selling of her body is just the same as the filthy sacred prostitution in Canaanite temples (Ch.2,ii). And yet that is the religion into which the people of the northern kingdom, 'mumbling their prayers', have guiltily and deplorably fallen, abandoning the God who brought them out of Egypt. Hosea sets Yahweh and Baal in the sharpest opposition, and goes out of his way to deny the widespread feeling that produce and fertility come from Baal. That, he points out, is what Gomer so mistakenly believes, but she is wrong. It is Yahweh, not Baal, who is the giver of all the riches of nature and of the soil. *It is to me*, he declares, *that you owe your fruit.*[15]

Yet the prophet combines this far-fetched, near-eastern allegorical way of speaking with a notably direct and poignant apprehension of what Yahweh's divinity means. It means the loving, tender fatherhood that he had manifested time and time again. That is why, although the nation is so corrupt and disobedient that it has to be destroyed, he cannot, and will not, annihilate all of it for ever, for Hosea's message of hopefulness is more manifestly authentic than the similar words attributed to Amos. Indeed he declares that the men of Israel will one day become the masters of the whole earth, raised up 'on the third day',[16] an echo of the cyclical Canaanite fertility cult which was to seem to the Christians a fore-shadowing of Jesus' resurrection.

Although Hosea may himself have come from a priestly, Levitic back-ground – which provided him with a more extensive education than Amos had ever enjoyed – he declares that priests, and prophets too, will be no help at all. 'Priest? By day and night you blunder on, you and the prophet with you.... Priests are banded together to do murder.... The prophet shall be made a fool and the inspired seer a madman (*meshugga*) by your great guilt.'[17] No, the new, repentant start that is necessary must be based on something that should come, not from any priest or prophet, but from within the individual heart of each separate member of the community: namely *hesed*, warm and steadfast, unwavering love felt for Yahweh, and completely changing one's whole way of life. Once again the note of repentance, sounded by Amos and re-echoed by many later prophets, is heard with unmistakable clarity. *Hesed* is Hosea's lasting contribution to the Hebrew faith. It is what Yahweh bestows upon men and women, so that they, too, unreservedly, must lavish the same devotion upon him in return. Only thus will they regain their lost position as his chosen people. When their obedience is resumed, Yahweh 'will be as dew to Israel that he may flower like the lily.... They shall flourish like a vine and be famous as the wine of Lebanon.'[18]

In considering this happy future time, Hosea, the un-political prophet, strays for a moment, like so many others of his profession, into politics. He mocks the vacillating foreign policy of the kingdom, courting now Assyria and now Egypt. Moreover, unlike Elisha, he detests King Jehu's bloodbath, seeing violent usurpations of the throne as a sin against Yahweh and a sign of his anger. Hosea's own political panacea for the future is the reunification of Israel and Judah; their Disruption, he rightly maintained, was what had caused their hopeless weakness, but this or any other solution will only be achieved by exclusive obedience to Yahweh, or, as Hosea – in the terms of his usual insistent personal imagery – prefers to express it, Gomer 'shall call me "my husband" ... and I will wipe from her lips the very names of the Baalim'.[19]

iii. The Northern History ('E')

The great southern historian of Israel's origins is known to us as J (Yah-wist), because he believed that Yahweh had been known under that name from the very beginning, from the time of the patriarchs onwards (Ch.9,i). Now the northern kingdom, too, produced a significant historian, who goes by the designation of E, because, in contradiction of J (and more plausibly), he asserted that the name of Yahweh was only revealed to the Israelites in the time of Moses, before whose time they had described the Godhead as Elohim, the plural form of the Canaanite divine name El (Ch.2,ii). Despite a great deal of argument, this overall division between J and E remains valid. Thus it can still be conjecturally concluded that E, like J (and like the later P, the Priestly source, writing about the same periods, Ch.14,iii), may have been a single person, and a tentative identification of E (as of J) passages in the Bible can be offered.[20]

Although E, once again, draws on very early stories – by no means all of them known to J and some no doubt (like his own tales) handed down by oral transmission – it does not seem likely that any of his material relates to the most primeval mythical periods of all, purporting to describe the ancestors of the entire world; E scarcely shares J's universal dimension. Thereafter, however, he plays a considerable part in building up the sagas of the patriarchs. In these narratives, he follows tradition by invariably stressing Yahweh's special purpose which set the Israelites completely apart from other nations. And once again this purpose is displayed in the providential deliverance after their expulsion (not flight, as in J) from Egypt, as a preparation for their entry into the Promised Land: events which the disclosure of Yahweh's name to Moses significantly emphasizes. The decisive rôle of Moses as the unique, unrepeatable, mediator between man and God is heavily stressed – with an eye on times much nearer to the epoch of E himself, for, unlike J, he deplores the existence of the kingship, and wants to show that Yahweh had worked through ancient institutions of quite a different sort. To E, history was merely the setting in which Israel either showed obedience or disobedience to Yahweh's will. In this picture, the kingship was a failure. The arch-hero had been Moses, who was never a king.

And so we are shown a nostalgic picture of Mosaic Israel in which faith and the Law had been practised in all their purity. E adds much to J in his presentation of Sinai. The covenant and the 'ethical' version of the Ten Commandments mirror the conditions of a settled agricultural community, and replace merely ritual commands by mature prescriptions that strike much deeper. Moral judgements are more frequent and thoughtful, and the spicier lapses of the patriarchs' behaviour are ignored. Again, of course, there is fierce denunciation of Canaanite rituals, which had been so recently tolerated by Omri and Ahab, and even thereafter were by no means discarded. E is still heavily reliant upon miracles, but theological thought is developing. The distance between Yahweh and humankind has widened. He is farther away, in heaven, making less direct contacts with men, to whom he conveys his orders by angels or prophets or dreams. It was E who tried to explain the character of the divinity by ascribing to him the solemn, cryptic assertion 'I am what I am', which possibly went back to Moses himself, and apparently signified that Yahweh is the God who manifests himself in the course of events (Ch.4,ii).

Although the style of this northern historian is not so powerful or vivid as J's, he displays considerable psychological subtlety. He likes showing how the obedience of human beings to Yahweh is tried by grim tests. And it is perhaps in the alarming, question-provoking story of the test he imposed on Abraham that E's peculiar flavour emerges most vividly. Ordered by Yahweh to sacrifice his son on Mount Moriah at Jerusalem, Abraham built an altar, bound his son, and had the knife ready in his hand when Yahweh reprieved him by substituting a ram.[21]

E has made use of a primitive tale. Human sacrifice, undertaken to ward off the wrath of the gods, had been familiar to the Canaanites from very ancient times. And there was also an antique belief, recorded in the *Book of Exodus*, that a man's eldest son was a firstfruit or scapegoat to be given back to God or the gods – the idea is apparent in the rejections of Esau and Cain; and Jephthah the judge was said to have sacrificed his daughter. These customs, by no means altogether forgotten or obsolete, are known to E, who finds them terrible, yet retains them, duly disguised, in the form of myths. In the original version, almost certainly, the savage sacrifice had been duly carried out, but E is glad to record that, owing to the intervention of Yahweh, no such thing happened. His repudiation of the grim climax probably reflects what had actually happened in one of the great sanctuaries where human victims were at some stage replaced by animal sacrifices. E also seizes the opportunity to explain a place-name, Yahweh-jireh ('The Lord will provide').

But his major intention, in serving up this old, savage narrative, is far more serious. Abraham had received the most appalling divine order it seemed possible to conceive. Yahweh appeared to have utterly forsaken him. Yet Abraham complied, without counting the cost, and in so doing he provided his people with a supreme model of unreserved faith and obedience. That was why Yahweh, after showing Abraham mercy, then proceeded to bless all subsequent generations of his House, and promise them the cities of their enemies. The Binding of Isaac (Akedah) has played a major part in the ritual of Jewish synagogues, and Arab mosques, throughout the centuries. St Augustine explained it as a classic case of 'troubles sent to try us', but the nineteenth-century Danish philosopher Sören Kierkegaard declared that the incident revealed an unbridgeable gulf between ordinary human morality and the morality of a God who could impose a test of such a kind. In E's mind, however, quite other considerations were paramount. Yahweh was a righteous God, he knew, but his righteousness demanded, in return, the austerest possible code of submission from his chosen people.

E's attribution to the northern kingdom of Israel is based on his particular interest in the central and northern tribes, and especially in Ephraim, whose shrines at Bethel and Shechem make prominent appearances. But the state of Israel was obliterated in 722 (Ch. 10,iii), so that E was probably active before that event. Indeed, the absence of any allusion to an Assyrian threat suggests a date not later than the first years of that century. Perhaps he was working even before 800, since the perversion of the monarchy by Omri and Ahab often seems, by implication, to be in his thoughts; and his protests against pagan religions recall the Elijah sagas. In any case he was writing at a time when prophecy was much respected; and he takes care to describe both Abraham and Moses as prophets.

After the fall of Samaria, it can be supposed that refugees migrating southwards to the kingdom of Judah brought with them what E had written, or the material he had collected. There they found the J tradition already established, and in due course, perhaps quite quickly, the two versions became amalgamated – with E as the junior partner.

CHAPTER 12

THE SOUTHERN MONARCHY:
JUDAH

i. The First Southern Kings

Although the Disruption left the southern kingdom of Judah with nothing more than the tribal territories of Judah and Benjamin – and the number of its inhabitants amounted to barely a quarter of Israel's – yet there were important compensations. It proved an inestimable advantage that the royal capital of Jerusalem was retained, and the people showed a stubborn loyalty to the dynasty of David, so that, although quarrels existed within the royal house, rebellions and usurpations from outside its ranks were far fewer than those that disfigured the history of Israel. Moreover, in a modest way, town and village life flourished, because the secluded geographical situation of the kingdom made it less vulnerable to external aggression.

However, the reign of Judah's first monarch, Solomon's son Rehoboam (c. 926–910), provided a strong reminder that this lack of exposure was only relative. For the pharaoh Sheshonk (Shishak) I of Egypt, on his way to invade Israel, launched a very severe assault upon Judah as well. Many of its towns were overrun, and many of the treasures of the Temple and palace had to be handed over as a ransom. After Sheshonk's withdrawal, Rehoboam surrounded his frontiers with a string of fortresses, many of them only a few miles apart. To the south, Arad in the Negeb, inland from Beersheba, could serve not only to stop the Egyptians but to repel threatening nomad invaders from across the Jordan. To the west, defences were also needed, since after the Disruption all the Philistine cities had reasserted their independence, depriving Judah of its access to the sea. However, the list of Rehoboam's fortresses, provided by *2 Chronicles*, includes a number which were clearly intended to keep the Philistines in check. One of them is stated to have been Gath or Ipa (seemingly different from the Philistine Gath, and farther inland), and Lachish (Tell ed-Duweir): its man-made mound – a hundred and twenty feet high, the highest in Palestine – was protected by a nineteen-foot-thick wall around the summit, and a stone and brick rampart lower down on the slope. On his northern border, facing Israel, Rehoboam constructed another fortress at Azekah (Tell Zakaryah), comprising a strong inner keep fortified with eight substantial towers.

But the population of Judah, like that of Israel, was extremely mixed, and Rehoboam, in common with his fellow monarchs in the north, believed in a policy of supporting Canaanite as well as Yahwist religion. So the Deuteronomic historian (Ch.14,ii) writes with great disgust of 'hill-shrines, sacred pillars and sacred poles on every high hill and under every spreading tree', and of male prostitutes in the temples. 'The people adopted all the abominable practices of the nations whom Yahweh had dispossessed in favour of Israel.'[1]

Rehoboam's son Abijah (c. 910–908) claimed the entire territory of both kingdoms on behalf of the house of David, and was able to make a start in that direction by gaining temporary possession of Bethel, but he soon died, leaving fourteen wives, twenty-two sons and sixteen daughters.

The son who succeeded him was Asa (c. 908–868). Threatened with a counter-attack from Baasha of Israel, Asa successfully appealed to Ben-hadad I of Damascus for help. Baasha withdrew, and Asa built a strong wall around the strategically located fortress of Mizpah in Benjamin. He also reconstructed the citadel of Arad. Asa reversed the pro-Canaanite religious policies of Rehoboam, destroying idols and expelling male prostitutes from the shrines, and his grandmother, the Maacah, a title that may be of Aegean (Philistine) origin, was demoted. She lost her rank as Great Lady (gebirah) because she had honoured the cult of Ashtoreth by the erection of an obscene image, which Asa cut down and burnt. He thus became one of the very few kings to win praise for devotion from the Bible, which declared that he was pious 'like his ancestor David'.[2]

His son Jehoshaphat (c. 868–847) continued to institute pro-Yahwist reforms. Civil legislation was codified by a national judicial commission, including among its members not only the heads of families but priests and Levites as well. Nevertheless, the Deuteronomic historian was not entirely satisfied with his policies, for this monarch incurred clerical disapproval by arranging an alliance with the more powerful kingdom of Israel, by means of which Athaliah, the daughter (or sister?) of its king Ahab, became the wife of Jehoram, his own son and heir. Jehoshaphat also joined Ahab in an attempt to recover Ramoth-gilead across the Jordan from Damascus. Ahab was killed in the battle, but Jehoshaphat survived and, in association with Ahab's son Joram, embarked upon an invasion of Moab. He also attempted to revive trade by reactivating Solomon's Red Sea harbour at Eziongeber. Some of the ships he constructed or renovated were wrecked. Nevertheless, Jehoshaphat became very rich, and his reign witnessed increasing general prosperity, at least among the ruling classes.

Jehoram reigned in his place (c. 851–845), and was succeeded by his son

Ahaziah, murdered by Jehu while visiting the northern kingdom. At this point the throne of Judah was seized by Jehoram's widow Athaliah (845–840), profiting by her position as Great Lady. This was a bloodthirsty break in Judah's peaceful sequence of royal successions. It brought a woman to the throne, the first female monarch ever to rule in the country, and the last for nearly eight centuries to come. She launched a violent attack on the Yahwist religion, 'breaking into the house of God and devoting all its holy things to the service of the Baalim'.[3] Or, at least, like her kinsmen in the north, she encouraged the coexistence of Yahwism with Canaanite and Aramaean cults. Certain tombs at Silwan, opposite Jerusalem's Ophel hill, display foreign influences, and may have belonged to Athaliah's Phoenician courtiers and friends.

However, Jehoiada, the priest of the Temple, brought her down by a successful intrigue. He also caused his principal Canaanite rival, Mattan, to be put to death, and the temple of Baal was levelled to the ground. The queen herself fell to assassins at the Horse Gate of the palace, and Jehoiada, with the help of mercenaries from Crete or Caria (Asia Minor), succeeded in gaining the throne for her seven-year-old grandson Jehoash (840–801). When he grew up, he subjected the Temple's suspect finances to a tighter control, and sharply diminished the power of its priests, stoning Jehoiada's son and successor Zechariah to death because he had criticized the court's Canaanite deviations. However, an invading force under King Hazael of Damascus, on the way to attack the Philistine city of Gath, caused great carnage among the officers of Judah's army, and exacted a humiliating and crippling ransom. Jehoash, severely wounded, succumbed shortly afterwards to a plot by two palace officials, connived at by the priesthood.

His son Amaziah (c. 801–773) claimed leniency and religious correctness because he had executed his father's assassins, but not their sons as well. After carrying out a census, he crushed and massacred the people of Edom, in order to safeguard his trade routes to the south and south-east. However, he then brought back images of their gods to Jerusalem and worshipped them himself, thus earning the gravest disapproval in Yahwist circles. The action was a conciliatory gesture towards the Edomites intended to secure his rear against Joash of Israel, with whom hostilities were now beginning. In the disastrous war that followed, Jerusalem itself suffered temporary capture, and Judah was virtually reduced to a tributary state. Amaziah, captured but released, lived on for many years to come, but was finally killed at Lachish, where he had fled to escape a conspiracy. His son Uzziah (c. 787–736), by a reversal of policy, enjoyed an excellent relationship with his northern contemporary Jeroboam II, which encouraged him to return to the attack against Edom. Uzziah also expanded to the east, where he unprecedentedly reduced the Ammonites to vassalage, and advanced westwards into Philistia as well, where Gath and

Ashdod and Yavneh finally passed into Judah's possession. Jerusalem and other cities were extended and refortified, and the armed forces were reorganized and re-equipped as a fully professional body.

From a material viewpoint, too, Uzziah's reign proved impressive. The population of the kingdom considerably increased, and so did its commercial and agricultural activity. The port of Eziongeber was restored and refortified, so that the trade routes leading up to Phoenicia could be revived. At Kuntilet-Ajrud, where the road branches up towards Gaza, a number of cosmopolitan inscriptions have come to light; the place seems to have been a caravan station with important religious associations. In many such conquered or re-captured semi-arid zones farmers were settled. Gibeon made good wine for the whole of Palestine. Beth-ashbea, in the south, manufac-tured the finest kind of bleached linen. A specialized woollen textile industry was developed at Debir (Tell Beit Mirsim), a town where ex-cavations have revealed a high degree of social homogeneity in its population, although prophets denounced luxury elsewhere. However, Uzziah himself became a leper, and was obliged to remain in seclusion. The *Second Book of Chronicles* (Ch.16,i) though conceding that he had made a pious beginning, blames his illness on a presumptuous ritual action: he had sacrificed incense in the Temple, thus usurping a prerogative of the priests.

His son Jotham, who had acted as his regent and finally ascended the throne in his place (*c.* 756–741), continued his successful policies, enlarging and strengthening Jerusalem, building new fortresses elsewhere, and making a financial profit out of the subjection of the Ammonites. But under his son Ahaz (*c.* 741–725) the tide turned against Judah once again. The Philistines regained lost territory, and Edom successfully revolted, so that Eziongeber passed into alien hands. Pekah of Israel and Rezin of Damascus, angry because Ahaz would not join them against Tiglath-Pileser III of Assyria, dealt him a severe military blow. Thereupon Ahaz turned to the Assyrians for help: and Tiglath-Pileser duly smashed Damascus, crippled Israel, and having thus isolated Ahaz by his own fault, ungratefully subjected him to massive payments of tribute. The Assyrian army also, it ap-pears, occupied Philistia, where excavations have shown that Arza (Yurza), just south of Gaza, became an important Assyrian base, de-signed to threaten the frontiers of Egypt. Ahaz felt it necessary to pay a friendly visit to Assyria; and on his return, he installed in the Jeru-salem Temple an altar in the Assyrian style. Earlier, according to the Bible, he had practised Canaanite or Aramaean religious customs, including the human sacrifice of a son of his own[4] – a traditional rite in serious emergencies.

ii. Reform and Collapse

Early in the reign of his son Hezekiah (c. 725–697), the Assyrians completed the conquest of Israel, leaving Judah as the only surviving independent state in the region. Hezekiah was at first very careful not to offend them. Instead, he concentrated on strengthening his own kingdom. A tunnel (improving on an earlier version and still surviving today) was built at Jerusalem from the Spring of Gihon to the Pool of Siloam, to ensure that spring water would still be accessible in time of siege. In the southern part of the country, the frontier was pushed forward; a good deal was done to strengthen border defences. The king also preceeded to overhaul the state's entire administrative and fiscal structure, and reserves of grain, livestock, wine and oil were amassed in specially constructed storehouses.

Then, in 705, the Assyrian monarch Sargon II died, and Hezekiah, supported by nationalistic public opinion, decided it was the time to take a calculated risk, for the new ruler of Assyria, Sennacherib, found himself challenged on either side, both from Babylon and Egypt. In this encouraging situation the Philistine cities, led by Ashkelon, felt emboldened to join the Egyptians in a rebellion against him; and Hezekiah, too, was persuaded to contribute his army, largely consisting of conscripts, to the alliance. Sennacherib responded by a violent invasion in 701 (or, some say, by two successive invasions, in different years). He inflicted a crushing defeat on the coalition, and claimed on a triumphal relief, perhaps with some exaggeration, to have captured forty-six fortified towns of Judah, and to have deported 200,150 of its inhabitants.[5] The relief also shows, in detail, that the climax of the campaign was the siege and capture of Lachish. Hezekiah, taken prisoner, offered the capitulation of his forces and the payment of tribute, but Sennacherib demanded the surrender of Jerusalem as well – pointing out that none of the other peoples conquered by the Assyrians had been saved by their deities. But before the city fell, suddenly and amazingly they went back home. A miraculous plague had smitten their troops, said the Bible, and an epidemic may, indeed, have been the cause of the withdrawal.

Although Hezekiah fell a victim to ulcers, he now believed that peace and security, however precariously achieved, would last out his lifetime; and he was right. Nevertheless, Jerusalem, its population trebled by an influx of refugees, seemed all too vulnerable, and he surrounded it with a new wall twenty-five feet thick. Furthermore, the apparently miraculous deliverance from the Assyrians prompted him to embark on a new religious policy. The biblical historian dates this to his eighteenth year, prior to Sennacherib's invasion. But even if the reforms had their beginnings at that early date, they must have subsequently derived great momentum from the vast prestige gained by Hezekiah when the Assyrians abandoned their invasion.

At all events, departing sharply from his father's policies, he devoted himself entirely to the strengthening of Yahwism. Canaanite and Aramaean and other external elements were ruthlessly purged; it was these, declared his advisers, which had been the cause of the downfall of their northern neighbour Israel. Moreover, although complete centralization was evidently impossible, Hezekiah sought to revive the status of the Temple as the supreme cult centre of the nation, and even sent messages to the towns of occupied Israel inviting them to send pilgrims to the Jerusalem festivals.

But his son and successor Manasseh (c. 696–642) wholly reversed his father's religious course. Non-Yahwist cults were allowed to proliferate in an openly polytheistic atmosphere. Excavations have revealed their sanctuaries not only at Beersheba but even at Jerusalem itself, less than three hundred yards from the precinct of the Temple, and pagan altars and images, we are told, were even admitted within the shrine itself. Moreover, Manasseh was said to have offered up his own son as a human sacrifice, in the Canaanite fashion. Earlier kings, too, had allegedly done the same, but whereas they had seemed chiefly concerned to strike a diplomatic balance between Yahwism and Baalism, we have the impression that Manasseh was far more in sympathy with the latter. Or, as the biblical historian put it, 'He misled his people into wickedness far worse than that of the nations which Yahweh had exterminated in favour of the Israelites.'[6]

Assyrian cults, too, found their way into the country once again. And the king, according to an Assyrian record, appeared among dependent monarchs summoned to Nineveh.[7] For its rulers were glad to retain him as a vassal, in order to prevent any revival on the part of Egypt, which they had defeated in c. 663. By such means, even at this late and fragile stage of Judah's existence, he retained its throne for more than fifty years.

His son Amon, who succeeded him (c. 641–640), was almost immediately assassinated, no doubt by pro-Yahwist elements. But the murder evidently proved unpopular, and the dead man's eight-year-old son Josiah (c. 639–609) was elevated in his place.

However, Josiah, when he came of age, reverted dramatically to an out-and-out Yahwist policy. In the eighteenth year of his reign, the priest of the Temple Hilkiah showed Shaphan, the royal secretary or adjutant-general, a 'Book of the Law' (or 'of the covenant') which he had discovered in the building while it was being repaired on the king's orders.[8] It was probably an early text of *Deuteronomy* (Ch.13,i), perhaps composed in the dangerous times of Manasseh as a secret rallying point for the faithful Yahwist underground.

Shaphan read the holy text to Josiah, who was shocked to learn how extensively current religious practice had deviated from its precepts. The prophetess Huldah, wife of the keeper of the royal wardrobe, was consulted, and confirmed the authenticity of the work. She also foretold (it was said) that Yahweh in his anger would obliterate the kingdom of Judah, though not in the lifetime of the pious Josiah. Then, after reading out the book to a great concourse in the Temple, Josiah launched a programme of reforms like those of his great-grandfather Hezekiah, but much more far-reaching, and indeed of revolutionary scope. Every conceivable Canaanite, Aramaean and Assyrian religious practice was forcibly extirpated, and a centralization of Yahwist cult in Jerusalem, even more decisive than Hezekiah's, seems to have been put into effect. Next, the people of the entire country were summoned to the greatest Passover celebration of all time, in the reconstructed Temple. These thoroughgoing reforms represented a deal between the priests and the prophets. Such a programme had long been favoured in prophetic circles, and Hilkiah and his fellow priests were supporting it on the condition that priestly interests were safeguarded. Yahwism had been very severely eroded in recent years, and without Josiah's strong actions it might never have survived.

They earned him a tremendous reputation. And he may also have been a more democratic ruler than most. It seems to have been some sort of ground-roots movement among the pro-Yahwist section of the population that had brought him to the throne. Furthermore his public recitation of the sacred book implied deference to the principle that the people have a right to know about documents of national importance, and the prophet Jeremiah, not an easy man to please, pronounced that the king dealt justly and fairly, with due attention to the lowly and poor.[9]

His freedom of action had been increased by a current eclipse of Assyria's fortunes, for the very existence of that country was now fatally threatened by the rising power of the Babylonians, and indeed, acting together with their allies the Medes (in northern Iran), they succeeded in capturing the Assyrian capital Nineveh in 612. Josiah exploited this turn of events by extending his influence northwards into the former kingdom of Israel, as the Assyrians' grip on that area weakened. He also enlarged his territory in the Red Sea region, and expanded in Philistia as well, where discoveries of pottery at Metzad Hashavyahu near Yavneh suggest that he was assisted by Greek mercenaries. The Egyptian pharaoh Necho II, of the XXVIth Dynasty, felt deeply alarmed by what was happening in Mesopotamia, and wanted to come to the help of the Assyrians, who were still attempting to resist. Josiah was determined to prevent this, but in 609, at the pass of Megiddo, he was severely defeated by the Egyptians, and died of his wounds.

This disastrous setback, which seemed to make nonsense of the biblical idea that virtue and piety would earn their rewards, dispelled any dreams of a new Davidic empire. Indeed, it also meant that Judah could never be truly independent again. This at once became abundantly clear, for the dead man's son Jehoahaz, after reigning for only three months, was deposed by the pharaoh and deported to Egypt, together with a number of his subjects. In his place they gave the kingship to his half-brother, Jehoiakim (608–598). The new monarch, a forceful character, embarked upon an ambitious building programme. Arad, destroyed at the time of Josiah's defeat, was reconstructed. Jehoiakim also gave Jerusalem a new citadel, which has now been brought to light by excavation, and he built himself a new palace at the military strongpoint of Ramat Rahel (on the road to Bethlehem), where his steward's seal has been found.

In 605 the Egyptians, together with their Assyrian allies, were heavily defeated by the Babylonian army at Carchemish (on the northern borders of Syria). The crown prince Nebuchadrezzar (Nebuchadnezzar), who had been the author of the victory, became king shortly afterwards, and three years later Jehoiakim started a rebellion against him. The Babylonians sent their Ammonite, Moabite and Edomite vassals to wear him down; and then his son Jehoiachin, the next monarch of Judah, had to capitulate to Nebuchadrezzar himself (597). The palace and Temple at Jerusalem were plundered, and a substantial part of the population suffered deportation, including the king himself, together with his family.

The Babylonians appointed his uncle Zedekiah in his place. For nine years the new monarch remained quiescent. But then, with the encouragement of the XXVIth Dynasty Egyptian pharaoh Hophra (Apries), he ill-advisedly launched a revolt against Babylonian encroachment. However, Egypt's intervention proved ineffective, and Nebuchadrezzar descended upon Judah again. A series of eighteen inscribed pieces of earthenware (ostraca) casting light on the campaign that followed have been discovered in a guardroom on the city wall of Lachish. These documents mostly consist of reports to the military governor of the city from the commander of one of its outposts to the north.[10] The tone is deeply pessimistic, with every justification. As excavations confirm, Lachish and one city after another fell into Nebuchadrezzar's hands, including Jerusalem itself, after a two-year siege (587). By this time, the inhabitants were starving. Zedekiah got away; but the enemy caught him. First he was forced to witness the deaths of his children, and then his captors blinded him and transported him to Babylon, where he perished.

The kingdom of Judah had survived the kingdom of Israel by 135 years, but now it, too, was at an end; and so was what is called the 'First Commonwealth', the whole period of national independence that had begun half a millennium previously in the time of the judges.

CHAPTER 13

SOUTHERN LEGEND
AND PROPHECY

i. Deuteronomy

The small, harassed kingdom of Judah, like its northern neighbour Israel, derived glory not so much from its kings or politicians or generals as from its uniquely distinguished religious writers – historians and prophets and poets. They invariably represented, not the Canaanite viewpoint so often favoured by the court, but the uncompromising Yahwism which utterly opposed such tendencies.

Among them was an author who gathered together and reinterpreted the traditions about Moses. The work that emerged was the book of Debarim or Devarim ('Words'), of fundamental importance to the whole future development of the Jewish religion. Its later Greek name *Deuteronomy* ('Second Law') is derived from a mistranslation of a Hebrew term in its text.[1]

The book begins at the camp of the Israelites in Moab before their entry into Canaan. Moses delivers three great speeches or sermons, which are set down at length. The first of these addresses recalls the main events in the Israelites' journey onwards from Mount Horeb (Sinai) (Ch.4,i,11), and concludes with an exhortation to serve Yahweh and obey his Law. The second oration, which is much longer, starts by reminding his audience of the terms of the covenant, which demanded exclusive allegiance to their God. It is upon this that their future possession of the Promised Land will depend. A varied array of prescriptions then follows, intended to maintain and strengthen the covenant relationship; their neglect, it is added, would bring disaster. Moses' third address reiterates the stark choice that confronts the people of Israel. It is between obedience and disobedience. But even if they are punished for disobedience, emphasizes Moses, a repentant attitude will still restore their fortunes. A series of appendices deal with the writing down of the Law, its lodgement in the Ark, the appointment of Joshua as the next national leader, and Moses' Song and Blessing and death and burial.

Following after the historians J and E (Ch.9,i,11,iii), the author of *Deuteronomy* represents the third of the four principal strands that make up the first five books of the Bible, the Torah or Pentateuch (another, the Priestly historian, is still to follow, Ch.14,iii).

In an earlier, briefer form, this seems to have been the 'Book of the Law' brought to notice by the Temple priest Hilkiah in the eighteenth year of the reign of King Josiah of Judah (*c.* 639–609, Ch.12,ii), for the reforms which, as *2 Kings* informs us, Josiah went on to introduce correspond substantially to what is prescribed in *Deuteronomy*. Out of its thirty-four existing chapters, the scroll to which Hilkiah had drawn attention included at least sixteen and perhaps twenty-two, including the most important legal regulations.[2] These contents were not by any means entirely of recent date, for they often display a pronounced archaic flavour, and evidently go back to earlier sources transmitted, in some cases, by word of mouth. A substantial contribution, written or oral or both, was provided by refugees from the north; this often bears a relation to the work of E, the northern historian.

Perhaps the scroll that came to light in the reign of Josiah dates back, for the most part, to the time of his grandfather Manasseh (*c.* 696–642), when Yahwism had been obliged to have recourse to concealment. Whether Hilkiah literally found the scroll, or knew about its whereabouts already and 'found' it at what he judged to be an appropriate moment, cannot now be determined. Perhaps the discovery was made the occasion of a new and amended edition. In any case, other such editions followed later.

Deuteronomy represents an ambitious endeavour to systematize and unify the religious traditions of the people of Yahweh, insisting that they make their devotions to no other god but himself, and worship him with total, responsive, undivided respect and submission. The biblical doctrine that this was the only recipe for prosperity, and provided the only means of avoiding catastrophic divine retribution, reaches its formidable climax in this book. The theme of repentance, so prominent in the prophets, makes itself heard. The code is seen as the complete expression of Yahweh's will. The paradoxical election of the lowliest nation of all, the Hebrews, as his chosen people – through no merit whatsoever of their own – is given the clearest expression it had ever received.[3] Because they have been chosen, it is incumbent on them to lavish their love upon Yahweh.

His saving acts of the past are traced yet again, with a new freshness and vigour. Exodus, Sinai (with which the book begins) and conquest are all recalled with superb vividness, forming the eloquent theme of a 'Short Historical Credo', which the Deuteronomist has taken from an earlier source.

Did Yahweh not make you and establish you?
Remember the days of old,
Think of the generations long ago:
Ask your father to recount it,
And your elders to tell you the tale.[4]

If you neglect this message of destiny, his people are told, you will be showing the basest ingratitude to Yahweh, and you will invite his severe retaliation. That is what the covenant of Moses is all about. Reformulated in language, this time, not so much archaic as reminiscent of contemporary treaties between political suzerains and their dependent states, for the first time the covenant becomes a truly central concept.

Such sentiments brought the Deuteronomist very close to the prophets. In particular, the injunction to love Yahweh is reminiscent of Hosea (Ch.11,ii), and later prophets, too, would often depend on what this writer had laid down. For example, he insists (despite a contradictory gloss) that every man is responsible for his own actions (rather than the inheritor of his ancestors' guilt).[5] Jeremiah was to say just the same. Indeed, the Deuteronomist may have been a prophet himself. Or he may have been a Levite and a priest. In any case, he collaborated with prophets and priests alike – both groups that had suffered from Manasseh.

The love, he insists, which every one ought to feel for Yahweh in his heart must be expressed in a cult of unmitigated purity, strictly controlled at one single, central sanctuary, and entirely purged of Canaanite, Phoenician and Aramaean elements or rituals. For these, the writer declares, are so detested by Yahweh that the people who have fallen back to wallow in such dirt deserve nothing better than to be stoned to death.

Violent sentiments of this kind sometimes appear to involve the Deuteronomist in contradictions. One of these concerns the Canaanites, whom the people of Israel had encountered and supplanted in the Promised Land. Moses is made to forecast their extermination by divine command.[6] Yet elsewhere in the book we are told that Yahweh 'loves the alien who lives among you, giving him food and clothing. You too must love the alien for you once lived as aliens in Egypt.' Whatever the cause of this apparent inconsistency – editorial adjustment or concern for some special group of aliens that did not include the Canaanites – it sums up vividly the dilemma that beset Yahweh's people throughout their ancient history: whether to be receptive to the ways of foreigners, including those in its midst, or to reject them with total exclusiveness. Indeed, the Deuteronomist himself seems embarrassed by the dilemma, for he concludes (no doubt in line with the practice of other nations) that any welcome to aliens must be subject to very definite economic reservations, in order to ensure that their status remains inferior. 'At the end of every seventh year you shall make a remission of debts. .... You may press foreigners; but if it is a fellow-countryman, you must remit all claim to it. ... You may charge interest on a loan to a foreigner but not on a loan to a fellow-countryman.'[7]

Elsewhere, on the other hand, the Deuteronomist reverts to being liberal and compassionate. He appreciates that the suppression of local shrines will deprive provincial priests of a living, so the Temple will have to pay them their salaries. And in more general terms, too, the biblical tradition of a strong humanitarian concern for the poor and oppressed is fully maintained: Yahweh is 'no respecter of persons and not to be bribed'; he secures justice for widows and orphans. This author likes to stress the part ordinary people had played under Hezekiah, Jehoash and Josiah. Nor does he fail to see the less attractive underside of Solomon's royal glamour. He proposes laws, encouraging kings to do their duty. True, these measures often sound rather utopian, yet despite all his deliberately nostalgic touches, the writer has succeeded in replacing the old, narrow, cultic perspectives of the Law by a more socially conscious breadth of vision. Wisdom thinkers (Ch.8,ii) must have found his insistence on divine retribution somewhat naïve and credulous. Yet when he makes use of their own tradition – as he does – he seeks, when he is at his best, to rise above the humdrum special knowledge or cunning, which they had sometimes appeared to be purveying, and to advocate standards of decent behaviour and morality in much wider terms.

The Deuteronomist's uniquely blended, all-embracing care not only for ritual but for moral precept as well, for outward act and inward motive alike, gained him extraordinary authority, enhanced by an appealingly distinctive, emphatic style. Although rhetorical and didactic, his preaching flows onwards with a simple, urgent intensity, rich in drama and pathos, displaying a single-minded determination which decisively helped the Yahwists of Judah in their desperate struggle to survive, as a religious entity, the successive crises that afflicted and finally engulfed their cult and state.

Deuteronomy eventually gained inclusion in the Torah because it seemed to provide the written constitution that the Hebrew community needed; so it was placed at the end, as a recapitulation of the four previous books (with which the reader is assumed to be familiar). Previously, only a kind of fragmented Bible had existed, comprising a diffuse, separate group of writings believed to be the product of divine inspiration. It was the appearance and acceptance of *Deuteronomy* that gave shape to the Torah – to which it directly refers, as a work that must be thoroughly known[8] – as a single, complete *canonical* unit, comprising the five books that came to be attributed to the authorship of Moses himself (though *Deuteronomy* records his death).

These books form the foundation of the Jewish religion, and everything else in all other scriptural writings was held to be revealed or implied in their contents. 'Torah' is often translated as 'Law', but its meaning is much wider – since law and religion and morality were inseparable. In origin, the term probably meant 'instruction', especially in practical conduct, with particular emphasis on the rules of the cultic worship. But then the use of the word became extended to every conceivable form of teaching that emanated from Yahweh's direction, designed to train the people in holiness and conformity with the covenant. And so, eventually, it came to be understood in terms of the whole vast interlocking system of observances (oral as well as written) upon which the continuity of Judaism has depended throughout the ages. The Torah contains doctrine and creed, regulation and ritual, history and prophecy, memory and aspiration, proverbs, riddles, legends, myths, aetiologies, fables, short stories and novellas.

ii. Isaiah

The *Book of Deuteronomy* spoke for an age not only of kings but of prophets. Like the Deuteronomist, these brilliant men were totally dedicated Yahwists, fiercely hostile to Canaanite cults and rites. This brought them into inevitable conflict with the bi-partisan policies of the kings. Yet the popular reverence accorded to those two legendary figures Elijah and Elisha in the kingdom of Israel showed that the state's power to check them was limited. Their successors, prophesying in the same kingdom, were Amos and Hosea, the first 'writing' prophets in the sense that biblical books purporting to contain their oracles have come down to us (Ch.11,ii). The most important, slightly later, counterparts of these spiritual leaders in the southern kingdom of Judah were Isaiah and Jeremiah.

Our information about Isaiah is to be found in the first thirty-nine chapters of the book bearing his name, known as one of the three Major Prophetic Books (the others are named after Jeremiah and Ezekiel).

The book begins with prophecies of Yahweh's judgement, not only against other nations, but upon Judah and Jerusalem, because of their arrogance, depravity, social injustice and perverted cult. Writing under the shadow of the Assyrian menace, Isaiah sees hope ahead, forecasting that a young woman shall conceive a son named Immanuel; the child who is born shall be 'the prince of peace'; and an ideal king shall come from David's line, for a Remnant of the chosen people will be spared. Practical counsels and warnings regarding the foreign policy of Judah are added, within the general framework of Yahweh's sovereignty over historical events. A final narrative section deals especially with Isaiah's part in the crisis resulting from the invasion of Judah by the Assyrian monarch Sennacherib (701).

These chapters are highly composite, and only achieved their present form after a long period, during which prophecies attributable to Isaiah were supplemented by material compiled in later centuries. *Chs.1–12**are to a large extent, though not *in toto*, authentically Isaianic. The description of the devastation of Judah in *Ch.1* is probably to be dated after Sennacherib's invasion of 701. (But a prophecy of a religious confederation of peoples, also found in *Micah* [Appendix 3], is not necessarily attributable to Isaiah himself; nor is a eulogy of Zion's blessedness after the purifying judgement.) The story of the prophet's divine call (*Ch.6*) must originally have formed the prologue to a separate collection of oracles. *Chs.7–8*, including the promise of the blessed child Immanuel, belong to a period when Syria and Israel were unsuccessfully endeavouring to enrol King Ahaz of Judah in an alliance against Assyria (*c.* 735).

Then follows a poem, with a recurrent refrain. Its opening verses insist that Yahweh uses foreign, heathen power to chastise his own people. Nevertheless, a series of subsequent oracles foretells doom upon foreign peoples as well, when the Day of Yahweh shall come. Certain of these prophecies (directed against Assyria, Philistia, Damascus and Israel) appear to belong to the time of Isaiah, while others (against Babylonia, Moab, Edom and Arabia) are later; denunciations of Egypt could belong to either category, or both. *Chs.24–7* form a distinct section stressing catastrophic world judgement and the deliverance of the Jews; it is known as the 'Isaiah Apocalypse' but dates from long after his time. *Chs.28–33*, however, referring to foreign relations, belong to the teaching of Isaiah himself. The final narrative account (*Chs.36–9*) was taken by a later editor from a passage in *2 Kings* (unless both come from a single common source). (The authors of the sayings preserved in the remaining chapters of the *Book of Isaiah* were different and subsequent prophets, Second and Third Isaiah (Ch.15,ii, Appendix 3).

Isaiah was born in Jerusalem in about 765, and began to receive prophetic visions in about 742. He probably helped to inspire the reforms of Hezekiah (*c.* 725–697), and still remained active at the end of the century; a tradition, of uncertain reliability, records his execution by the anti-Yahwist monarch Manasseh (*c.* 696–642).

The record of his oracles includes our earliest reference to a prophet writing down part of his message[9] – unless the reference is figurative. But even if it is, his prophecies evidently appeared in written form at a fairly early stage. (The discovery of a twenty-three-foot-long leather scroll at

---

* Chapter references *in italics* refer to the book of the Bible being discussed (*Isaiah*), those in roman figures refer to chapters in the present book.

Qumran (Ch.18,ii), containing the whole of the book in fifty columns of Hebrew – the longest and best preserved manuscript of the Bible in existence – has carried our knowledge of the text back by a millennium.)

The difficulty of determining what parts of the book are attributable to Isaiah himself can be sufficiently overcome to enable a remarkable picture of the man to emerge. This picture displays a preacher of startling messages in language unsurpassed in the entire Hebrew Bible, displaying the concentrated energy of the national genius in its tersest, most vivid, and most clear-cut form. Isaiah skilfully adapts his manner to a huge range of subjects. His style is scintillating and torrential, and often rises to sublimity.

His central thought is the terrible majesty and righteousness and above all *holiness* of Yahweh, confronting and confounding and annihilating any feeble human attempts to live up to such a model. Holiness had not been much selected by earlier prophets as a quality attributable to Yahweh. But 'Holy, holy, holy', repeat the seraphim in Isaiah's oracles, 'The Lord Almighty is holy! His glory fills the world!'

And so the prophet finds himself swept up into an incomparably exalted vision of this overwhelming, luminous presence. He is one of the few who claimed, and were allowed to claim, that Yahweh had appeared before them: 'With my own eyes, I have seen the Lord Almighty – the *King*',[10] in a sense that left all living monarchs in the shade. Isaiah, above all others, is the prophet of faith and confidence in the divine purpose. He sees that Yahweh will become the redeemer (*goel*) of Israel from its iniquities, as one buys back a slave or a parcel of land: the metaphor comes from commercial law, but the idea of the *goel* is of Canaanite and even earlier origin (having often been associated with the next of kin's duty to avenge murder). Another ancient idea prominent in the thought of Isaiah, which had likewise appeared in Canaanite texts, is *forgiveness*. Thus, when confronted with Yahweh, he cries out: 'I am a man of unclean lips and I dwell among a people of unclean lips.' But a seraph touches his lips, and declares his sin has been wiped away. For 'though your sins are scarlet, they may become white as snow'. That is to say, you must cease to commit them, and repent – the turning back (*teshubah*) that Amos and Hosea and the Deuteronomist had urged, and Jeremiah was to stress with even greater emphasis.[11]

For each and every believer in Yahweh is declared to be personally, inescapably responsible for his own actions – as the Deuteronomist, too, had insisted. Employing a second, and frequently recurrent, legal metaphor, Isaiah sees the entire people summoned to account for their behaviour, as though in a court of law. For he is a moralist of the most uncompromising character, who has given sharper form and intensity to Canaanite and Mosaic ethical teaching, defining human problems firmly as conflicts between evil and good. Yahweh himself, of course, is seen as the author of this entire moral system, being himself the fountain of rectitude, and the model of fairness. So Isaiah attacks the rich (savaging fashionable ladies like others before him) and champions the poor, not, like Amos, by identifying himself with their distress, but by conveying his profound conviction that justice is the very essence of the holiness of Yahweh. 'He yearns to have pity on you: for the Lord is a God of justice.'[12]

Isaiah, attempting to convey his message to an unreceptive people, is well aware of the danger of being *rejected*.[13] Yet he knows he has been called by Yahweh to become a prophet; and he may even have been the head of a prophetic school in Judah. However, he thinks nothing of contemporary prophets, or, for that matter, of priests. 'They have drunk so much wine and liquor that they stumble in confusion. The prophets are too drunk to understand the visions that Yahweh sends, and the priests are too drunk to decide the cases that are brought to them.'[14] They also seemed far too devoted to external forms of ritual and cult.

Like other prophets, Isaiah often depended, though never uncritically, upon the forms, themes and vocabulary of the wisdom tradition that has been traced back tentatively to Solomon's entourage (Ch.8,ii), and he himself may well have been, for a time, a member of the Jerusalem court. At any rate, he was by no means unwilling to offer the kings the benefit of his views about foreign relations, however irritatingly unwelcome this counsel may have been. Thus when Ahaz (741–725), threatened by a coalition of Damascus and Israel, appealed to Assyria for help, Isaiah declared that the king had made the greatest mistake. Speaking as a theologian, he pointed out that the royal appeal to this foreign power showed a lamentable lack of faith in Yahweh. But Isaiah also believed, quite correctly, that any such attempt to enlist Assyria's uncontrollable force was found to end in disaster.

And he also went a good deal further. For after the northern kingdom had fallen to Assyria, he believed, and loudly stated, that his own rulers need not bother about futile Egyptian alliances, for the very adequate reason that Judah was in any case destined, like Israel, to be totally obliterated by Assyria. This defeatist view must have caused great shock and anger in governmental circles. And worse still, Judah's defeat – he went on to say – would be entirely its own fault because of its own moral failures, so that Yahweh, far from helping his chosen people in this desperate emergency, would actually, instead, be assisting the Assyrians to mete out amply deserved punishment.

Nevertheless, when Sennacherib surrounded Jerusalem in Hezekiah's reign (701), 2 *Kings* is careful to insist that Isaiah remembered his practical patriotic duty after all, in time to advise King Hezekiah to stand firm. And since the Assyrians surprisingly retired, this contradiction of his earlier attitude stood the prophet's political reputation in very good stead. Directed by a brain of commanding range and power, he had subjected the contemporary scene to a series of penetrating political scrutinies, which, in the extreme crisis, had proved justified by events.

Yet even at an earlier date, while damping the expectations of Ahaz, he had alleviated his gloomy predictions by offering a word of hope – though of a somewhat long-term character: 'Yahweh himself shall give you a sign: "Listen, house of David. ... A young woman (*almah*, a girl of marriageable age, single or married) is with child, and she will bear a son, and will (*or*, you will) call him Immanuel ('God is with us').'' Desolation, Isaiah added (unless this is the insertion of a later editor), would fall upon Damascus and Israel before the child had begun to grow up. Christian writers, following translators who rendered *almah* as *parthenos* (virgin), were to hail these words as a forecast of the birth of Jesus (Appendix 9). But Isaiah appears, more immediately, to have been referring to a son who would be born to King Ahaz, probably his successor Hezekiah, who is then, after his birth or accession to the throne, described by the prophet (perhaps originally in a different context) as 'a son given to us to bear the symbol of dominion on his shoulder ... Father of a wide realm (*or*, for all time), Prince of Peace'.[15]

And in due course, too, there will come a 'shoot that shall grow from the stock of Jesse (David's father)', who will possess every virtue. Here the thought is of some other, remoter successor of Hezekiah in time to come, a future member of David's House which is seen as divinely blessed, and ruling over a divinely blessed city, and due to endure for evermore, long after the strutting, insecure kings of Israel have vanished. It cannot be regarded as certain that this passage goes back to Isaiah himself, since it may instead, like that other oracle mentioned above, have been added by a later editor. But it is the prophet himself who, in terms seen by the Christians as Messianic, once again, looks forward to a return of peace and perfection, when 'the wolf shall live with the sheep, and the leopard lie down with the kid; the calf and the young lion shall grow up together'.[16]

Isaiah is looking forward far beyond the flawed and fated little nations of the present, to the time when an elect residue, that pure Remnant of Yahweh's people so dear to Hebrew thought, would survive all current disasters and win through to the new epoch of happiness. Naming his own son Shear-jashub, 'a Remnant shall return', he imagined this community narrowed down to a vital nucleus which, by turning back to Yahweh, could retain the Israelite inheritance and finally take its place in the restored Garden of Eden.

But this new paradise will be for survivors, not only from Yahweh's chosen people but from all the nations of the world: 'For the earth shall be full of the knowledge of the Lord, as the waters cover the sea.'[17] Isaiah was certain that the deity who struck and destroyed other nations was not any god of their own but Yahweh himself. And by the same token the Golden Age that lay in the future would extend to the whole world. This universalism is more explicit and distinct, it would seem, than anything that had so far been envisaged (Ch.9,i;11,i). But it can only come about when the other nations, after acting as Yahweh's tools, but nevertheless not escaping the vengeance that they merited, have in the end been converted to his faith, and earn his blessing.

iii. Jeremiah

The other outstanding prophet of the southern kingdom was Jeremiah. The book bearing his name is divided into two halves. After a preface referring to his origins from Anathoth ('the sign of Anath', now Anata) in Benjamin, not far from Jerusalem, and describing his divine call, the visions narrated in the first half of the work consist mainly of threats and warnings and laments addressed to Judah, on Yahweh's behalf, during the three final reigns of Jehoiakim, Jehoiachin and Zedekiah before the Babylonians extinguished the kingdom. Ch.2 launches a series of denunciations of Judah's sins, and Chs.4 and 6 contain prophecies of foreign invasion and its catastrophic aftermath, accompanied by indictments of the corruption of all classes at Jerusalem. Ch.7 is a prose sermon which singles out for attack those who trust falsely in the Temple and the sacrificial system. After an assault on idolatry (which may be a later interpolation), Ch.11 tells of Yahweh's call to Jeremiah to bring Judah back to the covenant, and enlarges on the evil behaviour into which the country had fallen.

Then follows the story of a plot against Jeremiah's life at his birthplace, Anathoth, raising the problem of why the wicked prosper. A description of a drought in Ch.14 introduces a series of passages known as the Confessions of Jeremiah. Ch.21 contains a forewarning of the fall of Jerusalem delivered in response to an enquiry from King Zedekiah (597–587), and further forecasts predict the coming scion of David. Other prophets are denounced. Then Jeremiah refers to those of his compatriots who accompanied King Jehoiachin (c. 598) into exile, comparing them favourably with those who stayed behind. Ch.25 contains a familiar list of the nations whom Yahweh intends to punish.

The second part of the book largely concentrates on Jeremiah's own career and vicissitudes at court, though these happenings are not told in the order in which they were supposed to have occurred. Ch.26 describes how his straight speaking in the time of Jehoiakim (c. 608–598) nearly cost him his life. But *Ch.27* passes on again to the time of Zedekiah; and we are shown Jeremiah voluntarily walking the streets with a wooden yoke round his neck, symbolizing the necessity of submission to the Babylonians. A rival prophet, Hananiah from Gideon, likewise claiming to speak for Yahweh, bitterly opposed him; but the subsequent course of events, the book points out, proved that Jeremiah was right. In *Ch.29* he advised the deportees to Babylonia, who went with Jehoiachin, to settle down in their new homes. After seventy years, however, declares a passage described as the 'Little Book of Hope', the exiles will return (*Chs.30–3*), and this remnant will need, and be vouchsafed, a new version of the covenant. *Chs.34–9* consist of a series of stories which mostly relate to the siege of Jerusalem in the time of Zedekiah, but *Ch.36* intersperses reminiscences of an earlier time when Jehoiakim destroyed Jeremiah's prophetic scrolls, and the prophet's secretary Baruch wrote them out again, with additions. But then we jump ahead, once more, to the reign of Zedekiah, when the prophet was thrown into prison as a defeatist and a traitor. Next follows a picture of the final fall of the city to the Babylonian besiegers: the victors offer Jeremiah a place at their court, but he refuses the offer, and decides to remain behind in Judah.

Chs.40–4 record the fortunes of this community that had stayed on in Judah, under Gedaliah whom the Babylonians had installed as their governor at Mizpah. But Gedaliah fell a victim to assassins; whereupon a group of men, women and children fled the country and made for Egypt, taking with them the unwilling Jeremiah. There he made his last recorded pronouncement, criticizing the Egyptians but assailing the Jews in their country as idolatrous. In *Ch.45* Yahweh promises the secretary Baruch that he will be able to survive. A second series of predictions of doom against foreign nations (*Chs.46–51*) is now inserted, and the book concludes (*Ch.52*) with another account of the fall of Jerusalem, parallel to a passage in *2 Kings* (like the epilogue to the prophecies of Isaiah, only shorter).

So the *Book of Jeremiah* is a bewildering mass of material. Brought together with a total disregard for chronological sequence, it provides a mixture of the most diverse literary forms – prose and poetry, taunt and lamentation, biography, autobiography, history and acted parable. Earlier prophets, and the wisdom tradition, and especially the Deuteronomist (Ch.13,i), have all exerted their influences. Since later generations became eager to attach Jeremiah's name to their own aspirations and hatreds, doubts have been expressed whether the evidence about his life contained in these chapters is authentic. Certainly, editors have by no means resisted the temptation to touch up this incident or that, yet it does seem as if we are being given an unequalled chance to watch, at close quarters, a prophet conducting his mission.

The book contains the Hebrew Bible's first explicit reference to the writing down of a whole collection of oracles, for Jeremiah, who although a priest had been banned from the Temple area, dictated what he had to say to his secretary Baruch. This Baruch was sent to recite the scroll to a crowd of worshippers on a fast day. Officials, after a second reading held at their own request, urged both men to go away and hide, but the document was then read out to King Jehoiakim, who, as we saw, angrily had it destroyed. He also ordered that its perpetrators should be arrested. They could not, however, be found, and Baruch rewrote the scroll in expanded and more menacing form. (A second collection, including Jeremiah's later prophecies, may have been formed towards the end of his life.)

It has been suggested that this whole theatrical story may have been invented at a later date in order to credit the preservation of the book to the scribes, preservers of the wisdom tradition, with whose order Baruch was identified. The *Book of Jeremiah* brackets wise men and scribes together, and refers to the wise, the priests and the prophets as separate, distinguishable classes. The scribes, however, are described as liars, and the wise men as witless.[8] This may be because scribal circles were rent by factions, with Baruch, as a follower of Jeremiah, belonging to one such group, and hostile critics to others.

The book starts with the assertion that 'the word of Yahweh' had come to the prophet in 627–626, during the reign of Josiah. But probably this was, instead, the date of his birth, and it may have been only under Jehoiakim (608–598) that he began to prophesy. This would explain the warning ascribed to Yahweh: 'I bring disaster out of the north, and dire destruction',[19] since the Babylonians were at hand at that later time. Such words did not endear Jeremiah to Jehoiakim; but his subsequent relations with Zedekiah were even worse. For the prophet, quite rightly, did not believe that the Egyptian pharaoh Hophra (Apries) would intervene with sufficient effectiveness to call the Babylonian army off; he saw him as 'The Noisy Braggart who missed his chance'.[20]

So Jeremiah, parading the city with a yoke about his neck, preached total obedience to Babylon until Yahweh should decree otherwise, which would not be until after the catastrophe which lay ahead. As a result of this openly defeatist attitude, an attempt to leave the city to see to some family property in his village caused him to be arrested as a deserter. He was cast into prison, and subsequently let down into a muddy pit in the guard-house courtyard. Later on, he was hauled up again, and taken to a room above ground, but remained in detention until after the city fell. He proved more fortunate than another collaborationist prophet, Uriah, who had been brought back from Egypt by Jehoiakim and put to death.

Scattered throughout a number of chapters of the *Book of Jeremiah* are the dramatic thoughts, meditations, comments and poetical prayers and lamentations to Yahweh, that bear the name of his Confessions. Their nucleus, despite suggestions to the contrary, seems to be original and authentic. These intimate outpourings – which influenced many of the Psalms – reveal a singular power of expressing emotion. They also testify to a violently distressed state of mind. His enemies seem to be everywhere: they are not only the kings and their courtiers, not only hostile wise men and scribes, but even his own fellow villagers from Anathoth, whom he believed to be whispering against him and bent on his destruction, 'on the watch for a false step' – and Jeremiah demands Yahweh's savage vengeance against them.[21]

He felt a degree of social isolation rare and terrible for a man of his people and religion. His refusal to get married did not help; for that was equally rare. But his fears were more than just baseless persecution mania, because the sort of assertions he made could not fail to arouse the bitterest hostility. Yet behind the abrasive manner was a lonely, self-doubting and sensitive person, whose up-hill, unpopular task left him desperate. 'Why is my pain unending, my wound desperate and incurable? ... A curse on the day when I was born!'[22]

This dark night of the soul was something he felt powerless to overcome. And he blamed its horrors unequivocally on Yahweh. It was through 'uttering the word of Yahweh' that all this anguish had befallen him, in such sharp contrast to the prosperity enjoyed by the wicked.[23] It was Yahweh who had led him like a sheep to the slaughter. 'You have duped me,' he declares, 'I have been your dupe. ... I will dispute with you, plead my case before you.'

Jeremiah saw his relationship with Yahweh not merely as a routine obligation but as a fierce and exacting struggle. Yet it was a struggle conducted within the framework of extraordinarily close intimacy. 'The word of Yahweh came to me', and *dabar*, word, also means 'thing' – this is a concrete experience, overwhelmingly potent. For in spite of everything, it is still 'to you that I have committed my cause'. It was because of that tormenting yet peculiarly inseparable relationship that he was racked by an obsessive agonized need to give utterance:

> Oh, the writhing of my bowels
> And the throbbing of my heart!
> I cannot keep silence.[24]

Like Isaiah, Jeremiah was a powerful preacher of divine universalism. That is to say, he saw himself as a prophet 'to the nations'. It seemed self-evident that the whole world lay under the sovereignty of a single God: who was Yahweh. As so often, therefore, the idea of Canaanite and Aramaean gods is regarded with intense disgust and hatred, and the time has now come when these deities are clearly seen, not just as 'powerless to help', but as totally non-existent and imaginary: 'hot-air' gods (*hebel*), or 'logs of wood, which can no more speak than a scarecrow in a plot of cucumbers'.[25] Yet Jeremiah also repeatedly reminds us that very many people still regarded these objects with reverence, and worshipped them[26] – for example, a crowd of female fellow-refugees in Egypt.

Following in Isaiah's footsteps Jeremiah ascribed this continuing evil to grave inadequacies within the Yahwist cult. Even Yahweh himself, he provocatively declared, saw his own Temple as nothing better than a robbers' den.[27] The reforms of Josiah (Ch.12,ii) seemed to the prophet just an empty, theatrical book-religion. The covenant of Moses had been broken to pieces, and an entirely new version was needed.[28] It must be based on mutual, loving devotion, a covenant of a new and intense spirituality, no longer merely corporate, but personal and intimate, and written in people's hearts.

True, the corporate concept, so dear to Hebrew thinking, was not, could not be, just thrown aside by Jeremiah. But he was preaching his new covenant just after the kingdom and Temple of Judah had been wiped off the face of the earth. So nowadays every man and woman was thrown back on his and her own resources, and the new community had to be based upon their individual decisions. As the Deuteronomist had already stressed, each and every person was directly responsible for his own behaviour (Ch.13,i). Children do not have their teeth set on edge because their fathers have eaten sour grapes, whatever the traditional wisdom might say to the contrary. No, 'the man who eats sour grapes shall have *his own* teeth set on edge'.[29]

Yet the epoch that lay ahead would be an age not only of punishment but of forgiveness. Isaiah had said the same (Ch.13,ii) – and he had also, like others, indicated the need for repentance. To Jeremiah, this concept was central. Forgiveness did not, it is true, have to be *preceded* by repentance, as John the Baptist and the Gospels subsequently declared: for the Jews saw the divine forgiveness as a free, unilateral gift. Nevertheless, a link between forgiveness and repentance did exist – it was explained later that Yahweh overlooks the sins of men in order to bring them to repentance. And repentance, Jeremiah declared, must include a fervent and contrite desire for restoration, a complete, unequivocal, voluntary return to Yahweh's embrace.

Owing to the large amount of tortured gloom in this prophet's outlook, the term 'jeremiad' has come to be a synonym for unrelieved pessimism, but forgiveness, repentance, meant that all would still come well. Just as the message of hope in the *Book of Isaiah* is not entirely a later addition, so, too, Jeremiah's 'Little Book of Hope' is apparently authentic. Admittedly, he told the exiles to settle down quietly in Babylonia – and if they had taken that too literally, there would never have been a later return to their own country. Yet Jeremiah was also sure that, in the end, a Remnant (he uses the word more than any other prophet) would find its way back home: 'I am patient with you,' declared Yahweh. 'Your sons shall go back to your land.'[30] People were seeking anxiously for a theology to comfort them after the disastrous departure into exile, and here it was. Much later, these blended messages of covenant, rejection and future promise were to cause some early Christians to define Jesus himself as Jeremiah born again (Appendix 9).

iv. The Psalms

The hundred and fifty Psalms, the contents of the Psalter, are of incalculable importance to our knowledge of the people of Yahweh, but their composers and editors and revisers cover a great range of centuries. Some psalms, or parts of them, can be dated to Solomon's epoch, and possibly to David's (Ch.7,ii). At the other end of the time-scale, many passages belong to periods after the exile had ended. But the principal creative age of the psalms was the age of the divided monarchy, when their composition proceeded in Judah with unexampled vigour.

Yet the extraordinary diversity of these songs almost defies any attempt to order them into categories. A number of original collections have been detected and distinguished among them, from internal evidence: Psalms 'of David', of David's musician Asaph, of Heman and Ethan the Ezrahites (descendants of Asaph's ancestor Zerah the Levite), of the Sons of Korah, of Yahweh-King, of Degrees or Songs of Ascent (pilgrim songs for festivals) – a category which partly overlaps the 'Hallelujah Psalms', ending with the ritual command 'Praise the Lord.' Attempts have also been made to classify the psalms according to subject and purpose: praises of Yahweh, professions of faith (thanksgiving, communion), national or personal lamentations, supplications in time of crisis, curses upon enemies, prophetic oracles, royal psalms.

This last group expresses the theology of the Davidic monarchy of Judah, and seeks to enhance and renew its effectiveness and potency. The royal psalms, like a number of others, are framed in the first person. This 'I' often purports to be the king himself, speaking for the group and the nation in the collective Hebrew spirit. The king swears to root out evil from private and public life, stressing that dissidents will be severely dealt with, and so will the country's enemies, as many a call for retribution reminds us. The rulers and their peoples feel themselves perilously surrounded by threatening foes, within and without. 'Scatter them, O Yahweh, like thistledown, like chaff before the wind. . . . O Yahweh, break the teeth in their mouths. . . . The righteous man shall rejoice that he has seen vengeance done, and shall wash his feet in the blood of the wicked.'[31]

Love of the Torah, too, remains paramount. And numerous psalms are also close to the moralizing wisdom tradition. Many others display equally strong affinities with the standards of the prophets, interpreting the past or foretelling the future, and sharing the prophetic unwillingness to dwell on sacrificial worship – except sometimes in metaphorical and spiritual terms. There are particularly powerful echoes of Jeremiah's Confessions; and the appeal, 'Save me, O Yahweh, for the waters have risen to my neck, I sink in muddy depths and have no foothold',[32] could be a reference to his imprisonment in a marshy pit.

The scorching, tormenting reality of the sense of sin, and the saving themes of divine forgiveness and repentance, are once again reminiscent of Jeremiah: seven psalms on such topics were later set aside as the Penitential Psalms by the Christian Church. For nothing is stronger in the Psalter than its conviction of the omnipotence of Yahweh.

> If I climb up to heaven, thou art there:
> If I make my bed in Sheol [the underworld], again I find thee:
> If I take my flight to the frontiers of the morning
> Or dwell at the limit of the western sea,
> Even there thy hand will meet me,
> And thy right hand will hold me fast.[33]

The ways in which the psalms celebrate Yahweh are lavishly and eloquently varied. He is the Lord of Jerusalem – Zion. He is also the Lord of nature, in direct succession to the nature worship of the Canaanites, which is never far from the thoughts of the psalmists.[34] He is the divinity who gives the flocks their young, the god of rain upon early crops and of thunder, the killer of the evil monster Rahab, the lord of the sun and moon.

But if these are clear echoes of Canaanite religion, they are also deliberate attempts to supersede and alter it. For the Yahweh of the psalms is above else the God of Israelite history, who has saved his people in the miraculous Exodus, and can be appealed to in however desperate a situation to save them again. He is 'my rock where I find safety, my shield, my mountain refuge, my strong tower':[35] 'he hears me when I call'.

These are not theological treatises or sermons but poems: written in wonderful, flexible, lyrical verse, embodying the concrete images and alluring rhythmical parallelisms that formed the essence of Hebrew poetry (Ch.5,i). And these psalms cover every facet of heartfelt emotion, from the deepest gloom to the most jubilant rejoicing. They played an important part in ritual and liturgy, and were sung to the accompaniment of spectacular dancing and resplendent music – once again inheritances from ancient Canaan. As the great ceremonial procession brings thousands of citizens and pilgrims up the slopes to Yahweh's hilltop of Zion, 'there are shouts of joy and the blast of trumpets ... the singers are in front, the musicians are behind, in between the girls beating the tambourines'.[36]

Parts of the psalms were sung by the entire concourse, parts by a choir or by soloists; a single voice might lead, and the congregation join in the responses, chanting the second of the recurring parallel phrases. Many people wrote and rewrote the psalms at many different epochs, but despite the labels that attempt to identify their authors we do not know who they were. Yet it is they, perhaps, even more than any other Hebrew writers, who most frankly and wholeheartedly present the passions and needs and visions of their people. Their faith in Yahweh, often tested in the gravest distress, is seen in all its sheer, dogged, timeless perseverance. But tranquil piety is not what one finds in these sonorous poems. With an agony and exuberance befitting the turbulent national sagas that lay behind them, they express a religion whose explosive, romantic fierceness knows nothing of and cares nothing for the Hellenic Mean, the gospel of classical moderation.

Part Five

BABYLONIAN AND PERSIAN RULE

CHAPTER 14

PROPHECY AND HISTORY
IN THE DISPERSION

i. Exile: Ezekiel

The Assyrians had deported many people from Israel towards the end of the eighth century; they and their descendants became the Lost Ten Tribes. But it was the men and women of Judah sent away to Babylonia in *c.* 598 and 587 who became the central, nuclear, active element in the *galut* or *golah*, the Dispersion or Diaspora or Exile.

They were settled in various Babylonian regions and especially in a group of towns and villages along the Chebar river-canal which passed through the large commercial city of Nippur, a little to the south-east of the capital Babylon. Although these settlers did not represent a large proportion of the pre-war inhabitants of Judah, they had been shrewdly selected by the Babylonians to include most of the political, social, economic, religious and cultural leaders of the country. So they felt conscious of their responsibility as inheritors and guardians; and it was in Babylonia that Hebrew life had its centre of activity during the decades that lay immediately ahead. Jeremiah, as we saw, recommended them to settle down and make the best of things: 'Build houses and live in them; plant gardens and eat their produce.'[1] And by far the greater proportion of the deportees and their descendants evidently did just that.

Moreover, the banishment was not, it seems, accompanied by persecution. Indeed, after a time the Babylonians took a step designed to encourage the survivors. They realized that the downfall of the royal House of David had inflicted a peculiarly traumatic wound upon the Hebrew exiles. So they endeavoured to rectify this. In *c.* 598 Nebuchadrezzar II had captured the penultimate king of Judah, Jehoiachin (predecessor of his executed uncle Zedekiah), and taken him to Babylonia. But then, more than three decades later, when he was fifty-three years old, Nebuchadrezzar's son Amel-marduk (Evil-merodach) brought him out of prison, gave him a highly privileged seat at the royal table, and endowed him with a pension for life. The Bible tells us the story, and Babylonian records confirm that food rations from the palace storehouse were allocated to Jehoiachin and his five sons – and that he was described as 'the King of Judah'.[2]

Thus established as leader of the Dispersion, he presided over a committee of elders which conducted the exiles' affairs. However, in the absence of an independent political centre, the family and clan again became the central features of the banished community, as in the Israel of the distant past. Genealogical records were preserved. The ownership of property and slaves was permitted. Some of the men became mercenary soldiers and officers in the Babylonian service, others held royal administrative posts; many became agricultural tenants of the king. It was found possible to send costly presents to Jerusalem. And a number of these people played a profitable part in the financial life of Babylonia itself. More than a hundred Hebrew names can be seen in a collection of 730 fifth-century documents found at Nippur. Written in the north-eastern Semitic language of the Babylonians, derived from Akkadian, they constitute the business records of the Murashu family, the city's leading house of private bankers and merchants.[3]

These people of the Dispersion were allowed to live according to their own customs, and maintain the rituals of their faith. In Judah, before 587, rites without the Temple would have seemed utterly impossible; but despite its traumatic destruction the cult of the Babylonian exiles vigorously survived. When portions of the Ten Tribes had been deported to Assyria, they got 'Lost': in other words, they gradually abandoned their Yahwist faith and adopted local beliefs instead. Yet in Babylonia, although once again there were foreign cults all around, no such process of assimilation occurred, at least not on any substantial scale. In contrast to their ancestors in the homeland, who had shown such strong leanings towards the Canaanite religion, these people showed little inclination to absorb the foreign faiths of their new neighbours. Strangely enough, that is to say, Yahweh's power to command submission became most apparent after his people had been defeated. For it was he who was now their only *real* king. In exile, then, these men and women began to see themselves in a new light, and in terms of an even more distinctive and permanent identity, than ever before.

However, by no means everybody was able to settle down in the relative contentment that Jeremiah had advocated. On the contrary, a whole series of psalms, dating from these years, gave eloquent expression to the immeasurable grief of exile.

> By the rivers of Babylon we sat down and wept
>   when we remembered Zion.
> There on the willow-trees

> We hung up our harps....
> If I forget you, O Jerusalem,
> Let my right hand wither away.[4]

And another psalmist urges Yahweh to take vengeance upon the destroyers of the Temple.[5]

The prophet Ezekiel belonged to the same period. Despite reservations because of its weirdness, the book named after him ranked as one of the three major prophetic works of the Bible – along with Isaiah and Jeremiah. That was because of its length. But it could also have been the result of the uncanny potency of its contents.

The book opens with a vision of blinding light and rushing water which accompanied the prophet's call from Yahweh, and for seven days afterwards left him wholly stunned. The next twenty chapters, amid further fantastic images, recount the annihilation, not only, in traditional fashion, of many foreign peoples, but of Judah and Jerusalem as well – ostensibly as a prophecy, but probably after the event (though uncertainties of dating make such speculations hazardous). The Temple is defiled by idolatry: at its gateway sit people wailing for the dying Babylonian god Tammuz (the Sumerian Dumuzi). False prophets and prophetesses abound. Yahweh has forsaken the city, and Ezekiel is ordered to tell the people his words: 'I will set fire to you, and the fire will consume all the wood, green and dry alike.... Cry man, and howl!'[6]

However, like other prophets before him, Ezekiel also added a note of hope, to bring comfort to his shattered compatriots. For when Yahweh, in time to come, would decide to show his judgement and glory to the world, then his people, we are assured, would recognize him as their Lord and reflect his holiness in their own lives, and so they would be able to return to their own country. And the book ends with an elaborate description of the Jerusalem of that happy future age, together with a detailed account of the perfect worship that would be offered in its restored Temple.

The prophet was one of the men of Judah deported to Babylonia in 597. There (apart from a possible return to Jerusalem at the beginning of its final siege) he continued to live, at Tel-abib near the Chebar canal. Five years later, he began to prophesy, and continued, at intervals, until about 570.

The book named after him is an extraordinary mixture of detailed, expert ritualistic discussion and lofty prophetic eloquence, of severe austerity and human compassion, of prosaic prose and elevated poetry, of reasoned argument and bizarre vision. This phenomenal versatility has been regarded as proof of multiple authorship. Yet the constant recurrence of certain phrases and terms, combined with a remarkably orderly chronological sequence, provides strong evidence to the contrary. We see before us a single man, who was at one and the same time prophet, priest, visionary, moralist, legalist, composer of proverbs and gifted literary artist.

The visual imagery of Ezekiel is extremely startling; and he acts out his messages in symbolical mime. For the *oth* (sign) is not only an announcement and a symbol but actually helps to bring about what it symbolizes, and directs the course of the future. Elisha and Isaiah and Jeremiah had likewise performed demonstrations of this kind, accompanying them by the appropriate interpretative commentaries. But Ezekiel adopts this practice in unrestrained fashion, so that whole sections of the book record one peculiar *oth* after another, imposed by Yahweh's instructions. 'Man, take a tile and set it before you ... draw a city on it, the city of Jerusalem ... take a sharp sword, take it like a barber's razor and run it over your chin ... take an iron baking-plate ... you are to eat your bread baked like barley cakes, using human dung as fuel.' And on another occasion Yahweh ordered the prophet to eat a roll of manuscript. He was aware that these curious and cryptic utterances evoked criticism. 'Everyone is complaining', he reported to Yahweh, 'that I always speak in riddles.'[7]

The book is also loaded with a plethora of multi-hued, flame-filled visionary scenes. Trance-like ecstasy was a prophetic tradition, but never before had it been described with such extravagant vividness. The futuristic spectacle which inaugurated Ezekiel's career, subsequently engrossing the enthralled attention of apocalyptics and mystics throughout the centuries, flashed with radiant fire and lightning and fiery bronze and burning coals and sparkling topaz.[8]

Here is the Hebrew taste for colourful description gone wild. Such displays look very like the hallucinatory experiences known to psychologists as photistic, in which voices are combined with brilliant light: the violent sensations that converted St Paul to the faith of Jesus, upon the road to Damascus, and changed the life of Constantine the Great. Ezekiel was also overwhelmed by other shattering sensations: the ghostly fright of the Valley of the Bones (associated by Christians with the resurrection), ferocious rushing noises, phantasmal torrents of hail and urine and blood, inability to move the limbs or utter a sound.[9]

The prophet was convinced that every one of these convulsive disturbances arose from his uniquely special relationship with Yahweh. No less than seventy-eight times does the *Book of Ezekiel* declare 'They (*or* you) shall know that I am the Lord.' But this is not the Yahweh towards whom prophets demanded an intimate love; Ezekiel sees him as completely remote and mysterious. Nevertheless, that does not mean, he insists, that human beings are cast aside and obliterated by divine power. On the contrary, he is at one with Jeremiah in declaring that the fall of Judah has made men and women stand on their own more than ever before, bearing the fullest responsibility for their actions and answering penitently for whatever sins and religious perversities they themselves have committed.

And against these crimes, which had brought the people to their present plight, Ezekiel, as their God-appointed watchman, inveighs with uniquely vivid force. He is not yet confident that the abandonment of Canaanite practices, achieved by the Dispersion, has really and truly come about: or at any rate he blames them for Judah's catastrophe. It is the old story: loathsome idols, 'high places', tree shrines, human sacrifices. And not unlike Hosea (Ch.11,ii), he abusively and obscenely personifies revered Jerusalem as an abominable bastard Canaanite whore. 'You committed fornication with your gross neighbours, the Egyptians ... you committed fornication with the Assyrians and count-less acts of fornication in Chaldaea, the land of commerce ... You are the very opposite of other prostitutes: no one runs after you, you do not receive a fee, you give it.' Ezekiel's contribution to the age-old problem of what Yahweh's people should feel about aliens and their religions is simple and extreme: he regards it as the uttermost heresy to want to be like other peoples – in any way whatever.

When Yahweh said, 'I will give you a new heart and put a new spirit into you', that separateness was what he desired.[10] For once, we have a writer who does not look too far back in the past, and is not even very interested in the Exodus. We must look instead to the days to come, when, amid supernatural manifestations foreshadowing the apocalyptic writings of the future (Ch.18,i), Judah and Israel will be restored and reunified. And over this united realm, the House of David will rule once again; or is this last passage an editorial insertion? For what really interests Ezekiel himself is not so much a possible resurgence of the monarchy, as the creation, in these new stateless days, of a spiritual religious community centred round a Temple rising from the ashes under the name of 'Yahweh-shammah' ('the Lord is there'). And he or his editor presents, with obsessive meticulousness, abundant, legalistic details of the new Temple and cult he has in mind.

For he sees these rituals as highly relevant to his deep concern with atonement, 'at-oneness', a necessary reopening of the channel between human beings and the deity from whom they are estranged. Certainly, like Jeremiah, Ezekiel urges repentance, to be shown by concrete improvement of behaviour, but he has little faith that this self-reform will come about without the ancient, disciplined cult of sacrificial sin-offer-ings and ceremonial expiations. Only through the rigorous performance of such rites will it be possible to decide who is truly a member of Yah-weh's people.[11] This was a formalistic view, appropriate to a writer who probably belonged to the line of priests descended from Zadok. But it braced the demoralized people of the Dispersion to carry on. And it earned Ezekiel the title of Father of Judaism: a new founder of the faith that can soon be described as Jewish (Ch.16,i).

ii. The Deuteronomic History

During the same period of exile, historians of different kinds, once again, looked back upon the former evolution of Israel, reconsidering it in the light of current circumstances. One such enterprise, employing the finest language of the Hebrew Golden Age, proceeded to recast the story of the long period extending from the entry into the Promised Land down to the deportation of the people of Judah. The work, like other basic histories, does not survive as an independent document, but it probably concluded with the release of the ex-king Jehoiachin by the Babylonians in *c.* 561 (Ch.14,i) – a hopeful happening that can even have inspired the composition of the work.

It may have been written by more than one historian, belonging to the same or related schools, but it is even more likely that it is the creation of a single writer. As usual we do not know who he was, but we call him the Deuteronomic historian, because, while adapting, expanding and abbreviating written and oral material from a variety of sources, he is closest in tone and viewpoint to the author of *Deuteronomy*, who had written about the immediately preceding period, comprising the lifetime of Moses (Ch.13,i). However, the historian also adds many comments and interpretations of his own. Their traces seem to be particularly apparent in the *Books of Judges*, and *1 and 2 Kings*. Sometimes he offers revisions, elsewhere he inserts whole explanatory sections and chapters. Moreover, the entire structural schematic unity of this huge segment of the Bible, including its present division into books, is decisively in his debt, or even, to a substantial extent, his own work.

Assuming that we already know the mere historical facts from other sources (including the lost Book of the Acts of Solomon and Annals of Israel and Judah), the Deuteronomic historian pursues the undeviating aim of inculcating religious lessons. From start to end, his only yardstick is obedience to the orders of Yahweh, the supreme power directing the course of all history. It is failure to maintain this required obedience – not just bad luck – that finally led to all the disasters that had overtaken his people, and brought all the high hopes of the settlement and of David's kingdom to nothing. Backsliding to the religion of the Canaanites is again seen as one of the principal forms of this disobedience – as a punishment for which, the Canaanite enemy had been allowed to survive.[12]

It is to the Deuteronomic historian that we owe the exaggerated presentation of Joshua's conquest as a single, comprehensive, nation-wide event, because this was one of Yahweh's greatest salvation-bringing acts. It is he, too, who magnifies the judges, neatly arrayed in chronological sequence, into heroes on a national scale. It seems to be he, once again, who stresses the leading role of Samuel as a predecessor of the kings – perhaps more accurately; but he develops this theme because Samuel was a man of God. And it is he who introduces, or emphasizes, the tradition critical of the monarchy – which had already come to an end, in disastrous circumstances, at the time when he wrote. This last approach results in a particularly hostile assessment of the monarchy's founder Saul. The treatment of Saul's successor David, however, is more complicated. Inheriting and shaping a contradictory collection of favourable and adverse material, the historian seems to be in two minds. He remains conscious that Yahweh does not let bad actions pass unpunished, but he also knows that Yahweh loves David, and he believes strongly in the eternal election of the House David founded, and of Jerusalem, Yahweh's 'chosen city'. And his assessment of Solomon is as complex, and based on as complex an array of sources, as his picture of David.

After the much deplored Disruption, he takes a very jaundiced view of the kingdom in the north. One after another of its kings is condemned as having done evil in the sight of the Lord, entirely regardless of the considerable secular achievements, for example, of Omri, Ahab or Jeroboam II. Although ethical motives are claimed for this censure, what the rulers had really done wrong in the eyes of the writer was, firstly, to aim at Yahwist and Canaanite partnership, and secondly, to refuse to regard Davidic Jerusalem (which was not under their control) as the legitimate centre of Hebrew religion – so that even the fanatical Yahwist Jehu cannot manage to earn wholehearted praise.

The monarchs of the southern kingdom of Judah, with its capital at Jerusalem, might have expected to fare better at the historian's hands, especially as they continued to be members of David's House. Yet with the exception of wholehearted religious reformers such as Hezekiah and Josiah (and even he is not presented as perfect) they receive almost the same severe treatment as the northerners. That is, because they, too, followed the detested policy of Yahwist-Canaanite bipartisanship. Manasseh supplies an object lesson in such apostasy, and there is particularly vivid retributive drama in the horrible fate of Zedekiah, the last of the kings, whose children were slaughtered before his eyes – and then his eyes were put out.

The prophets, on the other hand, receive favourable and deferential attention. It is true that, with the single exception of Isaiah,[13] the Deuteronomic historian does not specifically mention any of them by name, but that was only because he assumed their preachings were known from separate, available works. And their forerunners Elijah and Elisha, who had propounded so many dire warnings, are described and mythologized at reverential length. For he saw them as standing for the prophetic movement as a whole, the communicators of the word of Yahweh, 'who spoke through his servants the prophets'.[14] And the historian is extremely eager to point out that the divine oracles and promises uttered by such 'true' prophets get fulfilled.

Indeed, the books extending from *Joshua* to *2 Kings* are even known as 'Former Prophets'; for, as the Deuteronomic historian has ensured, a prophetic strain runs through this entire portion of the Bible. He sees the divine rebukes administered by the prophets as correct diagnoses of all the subsequent political disasters, when first Israel and then Judah had succumbed to their enemies.

There is no evidence that the Deuteronomic historian belonged to any prophetic group himself. Yet his reassemblage of the past, in accordance with their views, emerges as one of the most tangible results the prophets ever achieved. It was also he who fixed the popular notion of the prophet as a man who not only interpreted Yahweh's will but provided a picture of what it was inevitably going to bring about in time to come.

And here his commitment to the Davidic monarchy was all-important. It had received a terrible blow, fully deserved in this historian's opinion, so that he contrives to explain the catastrophe of the Dispersion in theological terms. Yet he assures us that just as the House of David had been favoured by Yahweh in the past, so also, once more, he would favour it in the future. His drowning people would not die; the descendants of the exiles would return to Jerusalem. Like others, the historian showed astonishing faith in declining to believe that all was lost.

iii. The Priestly History

A second history compiled at about the same time, again only surviving through the insertions of passages in various books of the Bible, is known to us as P, the Priestly Source. It does not deal with the later period covered by the Deuteronomic historian, but reverts to the most ancient epochs handled by those southern and northern forerunners known as J and E (Chs.9,i;11,iii). These collections of material had by now been fused into a single account, which P proceeds to re-edit on lines of his own, providing a framework, and inserting substantial additions, often drawn from very ancient written and oral sources, notably some that had a connexion with the sanctuary of Hebron.

Like J and E, P cannot be identified with any specific 'document'. But the original existence of such a document is not improbable, since the passages attributable to P[15] display an easily recognizable style – clear-cut, formal and precise: dignified, grandiose and often repetitious. A fondness for numerical reckonings, lists, measurements and genealogies is apparent. The historian's vocabulary, too, contains distinctive elements, including legal phrases. He is known as the priestly writer because of a predominant interest in ritual and cult, displaying affinities with Ezekiel (Ch.14,i). The whole purpose of his 'historical' sketch is to serve as a framework for the priestly collection of laws, which, to this author, represents the principal significance of the Torah. His work, which includes ten chapters of *Leviticus* known as the Holiness Code, could have been called 'The Origins of the Religious Institutions of Israel' – institutions which it seeks to represent as eternally valid models not only for the past but for all time to come. P equates salvation history with priestly and cultic legislation. Attempts are made to justify the vested interests of the priests (or a certain group of them), the descendants of David's priest of the Temple, Zadok. Another concern is to reconcile the old tensions between conservative priests and more radical prophets.

As this survey proceeds on its way, emphasis is placed on the ancient, legal sanctity of Yahweh's covenant with Noah, to which the setting up of political authority in the world is traced back. It is presented as the beginning of the age of covenants whereby Yahweh has continually bound Israel to himself. The priestly writer lays down the basic ethical principles that Noah was ordered to uphold: the seven 'Noachide' laws (which medieval rabbis expected even Gentiles to obey). And, in return, Noah and his descendants are promised not only the regular processes of nature that are the basis of farming life, but also control over every other living thing on earth. For Noah's offspring were destined to form the entire human race of the future, as a genealogical Table of the Nations goes on to tell.[16]

And it is in the light of this destiny that Yahweh, according to this writer, proclaimed to Abraham: 'All nations on earth shall pray to be blessed as your descendants are blessed, and this because you have obeyed me.' But he also says: 'Your descendants shall possess the cities of their enemies.'[17] For although salvation was *for* the whole world, it would come, we are assured, through the Israelite progeny of Abraham: a paradoxically courageous assertion, now that its survivors lay in powerless exile. And so the writer goes on to offer a full account of Yahweh's covenant with Abraham, emphasizing the institution of circumcision as its sign.

But the climax of history is the handing down of the Law to Moses on Sinai, which established the unique position of Yahweh's people: whatever the future course of events, asserts the priestly writer, Israel must not deviate in the slightest degree from this prescribed Law, of which he saw Moses' brother Aaron (prematurely described as the first high priest) as the guardian. Dietary prescriptions (*kosher, kashrut*) are prominent (according to these laws, which are of unknown and disputed origin and motivation, only a small proportion of living creatures can be eaten, and the consumption of blood or partaking of meat with milk products is forbidden). The priestly writer concentrates strongly on rules and observances. For example, the sacrificial regulations for atonement have now been turned into a whole day (Yom Kippur).[18]

Nevertheless, he is not so totally devoted to ritual that he forgets about morality. For the whole purpose of Yom Kippur is a cleansing from sin – which is taken more seriously than ever. And sin is enlarged, as so often in Hebrew thought, to include a wide range of social offences. For although, the priestly writer notes, the interests of justice require that you should not lean over too heavily in order to favour the poor, Yahweh condemns every form of oppression. 'An eye for an eye and a tooth for a tooth', deriving from ancient Mesopotamian and Canaanite ideas, is not so much grimly vengeful (as has often been suggested), as constructive and progressive, permitting wronged persons to retaliate in self-defence: though Pharisees and their followers later watered the command down into terms of monetary compensation and restitution.[19]

And one other ethical pronouncement has had a particularly famous history: 'You shall love your neighbour as [a man like] yourself!'[20] *Re'ah*, 'neighbour', means in the Bible the companion to whom one stands in an immediate and reciprocal relationship. This injunction aroused a good deal of debate – following up a continuous theme in Hebrew thought and controversial argument – about whether people should also be expected to love foreigners. Certainly, Jews were unlikely to accept Jesus' instruction that we should love our enemies, because that seemed unrealistic and impossible, and the impossible ought not to be an ideal. Yet the priestly writer, in *Leviticus*, does add quite clearly – like one strand, but not the other, in *Deuteronomy* – that foreigners who were *not* enemies, the non-Jewish, Canaanite and other dwellers in the same land, should be loved just as you ought to love your neighbour, as a man like yourself, 'because you were aliens in Egypt'.[21]

This author's conviction of a universal God partly succeeds in freeing him (like other contemporary writers) from the idea that this belief in God has to be expressed in terms of Israel alone. Certainly, his deity is Yahweh, the Israelite god, yet it is the priestly writer to whom we owe the noble account of this one, single God's creation of the entire world, with which the *Book of Genesis* begins. The process, we are told in formal, incantatory language, was extended over the course of six days. Each successive act of creation is introduced by the words 'And God said ...'.

Day (1) Light and darkness, day and night. (2) Earth's atmosphere, the firmament. (3) Dry land and seas separated, plants and trees. (4) Sun, moon and stars, seasons, days, years. (5) Creatures and birds. (6) Land animals, man and woman. By the seventh day the creation has been completed, and Yahweh can rest.

Here is no longer the man-like divinity who walked in the garden with Adam (Ch.9,i). Now, instead, we see a God who is not only almighty but spiritual and transcendent, the God who on the first day separated light from darkness upon an earth that was 'without form and void, with darkness over the face of the abyss and a mighty wind that swept over the waters'.[22]

The tale that follows has affinities with Mesopotamian creation epics, especially the *Enuma Elish* chanted by priests in the Babylonian spring (New Year) festival.[23] And there are echoes of other, older, and even more popular texts as well. It seems that priests from Judah had come to know these cosmological texts after arriving in the place of their exile. The *Enuma Elish* had told of six days of divine creative acts, and so does *Genesis*, because this conveniently explained and rationalized the Sabbath. And from the same Mesopotamian sources, in particular, comes the account of the second of these days: 'God said, let there be a vault between the waters, to separate water from water.'[24] This picture assumes a sea of water above the earth, and a freshwater sea below its surface: just as the Canaanite god El, 'the Creator of Created Things', had his being 'at the confluence of the two streams', where the upper and lower waters meet (Ch.2,ii).

Yet there are also fundamental differences between the two sets of stories. The essence of the eastern myths was a struggle in which the gods personify different aspects of nature, and Marduk crushes the powers of chaos led by Tiamat. This desire to interpret the creation as a victory over malignant forces reappears in many a psalm, and is seen in other parts of the Bible as well, but here in *Genesis* the entire theme of a conflict has vanished. The God of the priestly writer is not one of the plural, competing forces of nature, nor is he nature itself. He stands apart from the natural world as its omnipotent source and originator. And he makes an absolute *start* – in contrast to the view that 'nothing comes of nothing' (God created the universe, but who created him?), and to the Buddhist doctrine that the earth always was and always will be. This belief that God created the world from the very beginning was not officially defined as a church dogma until AD 1215. The astronomers are still disputing the matter. However, the priestly writer's story is not a philosophical or scientific treatise. It is an unforgettable endeavour to explain the profoundest and most enduring problems by poetical imagination and imagery.

This author also has much to say about the peculiar and exceptional nature of humankind. On the sixth day 'God created man in his own image (*tselem*): in the image of God he created him: male and female he created them'[25] (not, as in the southern history [J], first male and then female). This has been described as the 'Magna Carta of Humanity', but the gift with which man is endowed, through being modelled upon God, has been very variously interpreted. Immortality? The gift of self-conscious reason? Upright bodily form? Probably the key lies in what the priestly writer says in the immediately preceding and following passages, in which he declares (and the theme reappears in the story of Noah's ark) that human beings will be granted power over all animals and birds and fish upon the earth. Nature, that is to say, will no longer be at the beck and call of the Babylonian or Canaanite deities who had stood for its cyclical processes, for it is now under the control of the wholly other, transcendent Yahweh, and he, out of his great bounty, has handed over all its living creatures to the human race. In Greece, too, a century later, Sophocles, was to hymn the vast power of human beings. Greeks did not ignore the power of the gods, but in Jewish thinking there is even greater stress on the belief that everything in the whole of existence – every glorious height to which human beings can rise – is owed entirely to Yahweh. '*You* made him master over all your creatures,' declares a psalmist, 'you made him inferior only to yourself.'[26]

And the priestly writer declares that God saw that the work he did was good: *tob*, a purposeful word. Another author's account of Adam and Eve, to which this tale of the creation is prefaced in the Bible, had ended not in goodness but in total disaster (Ch.9,i). Yet the deviser of the creation story desires to avoid any suggestion that there might be powers of good and evil warring in the world. He wants to show that there is no shadow of Manichean duality in the divine governance of earth (Ch.18,ii): that the world and its contents cannot in any sense be inimical to God, but must be good because the good God has made them. 'Thou hast made all by thy wisdom,' declared a psalm: 'may Yahweh rejoice in his works!'[27]

CHAPTER 15

THE CLIMAX OF HEBREW THOUGHT

i. Job

The condition of Palestine after the successive downfalls of its two kingdoms – Israel to the Assyrians, and Judah to the Babylonians – showed a sad material decline.

The territory of the former northern state, Israel, had provided a new home for settlers brought in by the Assyrians from other parts of their empire, to mingle with the people who had stayed behind. A priest was sent to instruct the new colonists in the worship of Yahweh, which they adopted alongside their own foreign cults, sending pilgrims to Jerusalem from Samaria, Shiloh and Shechem. But we know little about what happened in the country, because the exiled Hebrew writers of these years completely ignored and rejected these developments, and later, when the Samaritans became a separate sect, viewed them with the greatest hostility (Appendix 6).

In conquered Judah, which lost between a fifth and a quarter of its inhabitants in the Babylonian deportations, the first governor appointed by the conquerors, a local Yahwist named Gedaliah, succumbed to murderers (Ch.15,iii; an event still mourned by the Jews as completing their national elimination), and was replaced by a series of successors, some of their own faith and others of different religions and origins. We learn from the five despairing poems of *Lamentations*, written by one of the men left behind amid the ruins of Jerusalem, that the city was virtually uninhabitable for a time, lacking water and food and reverting to cannibalism. And excavations have revealed that many other towns and villages of Judah, too, were utterly destitute, and at the mercy of raiders. Yet life did not cease altogether. The farmers and herdsmen who had remained in the land managed to maintain a certain continuity, and were allowed by their overlords to effect a gradual, partial recovery, distributing among themselves, in the process, the ownerless estates of those who had been deported to Babylonia. However, like their compatriots in Israel, they had to share these lands with a host of immigrants who flocked in to fill the vacuum; some had come from Philistia and others from troubled countries on the eastern fringes, Ammon, Moab and Edom.

Clearly religious syncretism, the coexistence of Yahwism and alien cults which had so often been a feature of the national history, was now positively invited by the circumstances of the epoch. True, worship continued on the site of the ruined, desolate Temple, but the old Canaanite rituals, never defunct, had a good chance to flourish again. Second Isaiah (Ch.15,ii) did not miss the opportunity to revile those who indulged in these detested practices, 'children of sin that you are, spawn of a lie, burning with lust under the terebinths, under every spreading tree, and sacrificing children in the gorges, under the rocky clefts'. But the same prophet also foresaw Yahweh ruthlessly punishing the immigrants who stimulated these outrages: 'I trampled them in my fury, and their life-blood spurted over my garments and stained all my clothing.'[1]

Nevertheless, after all the catastrophes, it was hard not to ask the question: Why do good people suffer, and the wicked prosper? It is a question which monotheistic belief – belief that God not only created the entire universe, but is responsible for everything that happens – inevitably raises, and it presented Yahwists with their most intractable problem; Jeremiah had found it particularly perplexing (Ch.13,iii).

For centuries the answer had been the same: Yahweh will save the virtuous in the end, and will punish their enemies. But now such an answer was harder than ever to accept, and it seems to have been at about this time that someone in the devastated homeland made the most thoroughgoing and penetrating of all attempts to answer this fundamental question. The outcome of his thinking was the unique *Book of Job*.

It consists of a long series of poems, set between a prologue and epilogue written in prose. Job is said to have come from the land of Uz; he is a man of great wealth and great piety. In the prologue Satan, a member of the divine council, alleges that this piety is rooted in self-interest, so Yahweh allows him to act as *agent provocateur*, by depriving Job of all his worldly possessions and all his children, and inflicting upon him a loathsome disease. The time will have to come, says Satan, when the victim of such appalling misfortunes will turn on Yahweh and curse him. But Job still utterly refuses to do this: though, in the heart-rending soliloquy with which the main poetical section begins, he does curse the day he was born.

Three older friends who have come to offer comfort, Eliphaz, Bildad and Zophar, try to convince him that his sufferings have to be accepted: because of Yahweh's irresistible power and unfathomable ways, and because of the sins which Job must surely have committed – since Yahweh always ensures that it shall be the unrighteous who suffer punishment. But Job completely rejects this traditional line of thought. Instead, using the language of the law courts, he demands justice from Yahweh, calling upon some impartial third party or intermediary, a vindicator, to intervene and protect him.

After he has asserted his innocence once again, a young man named Elihu delivers a series of speeches in which he tries to improve on the arguments of Job's other three friends. And then Yahweh himself addresses Job in person. He takes pains to point out the overwhelming divine might displayed in the wonder and variety of creation, which no finite human mind can begin to grasp. Job, in his answer, still does not admit guilt, but he utters words of reverent acquiescence and submission. And then finally, in the prose epilogue, Yahweh rebukes the men who have criticized him, and more than restores his former fortunes. He receives double his original possessions, and lives to a ripe old age.

Job is grouped together with *Proverbs* as one of the 'Poetical Books'. For it contains the largest body of verse composition in the Bible. These poetical sections, formally constructed and making rich use of metaphor and simile, are combined together in the unifying shape of a drama. But that is only one of many ways in which the *Book of Job* can be described, for it is not only drama but folk-tale or fable, prophetic oracle, hymn and epic, lamentation and didactic treatise. In fact, the book partakes of almost every literary *genre* to be found in the entire Hebrew Bible. It is very long indeed – almost a whole literature in itself.

It has been compared to a huge cathedral – built up throughout successive generations and centuries. Owing to textual obscurities and timeless themes, it is impossible to give a date to the work's final completion, but its basic structure may have been established soon after the destruction of Judah, and the main body of its contents composed not too long after that event, say in 580–540. For Job can echo the 'Confessions of Jeremiah', who lived on into the early sixth century, and resembled the same prophet in his refusal to accept that the righteous would be rewarded. The place where the *Book of Job* was written can once again not be determined with certainty, but its desolate atmosphere does not suggest the Dispersion so much as the shattered land of Judah.

Now that they had no kingdoms of their own, the Hebrews saw their problems in an ever more individualistic light, and devoted increasing attention to the power of human evil, and the question why it seems to predominate in Yahweh's creation. The *Book of Job*, confronting this problem with unprecedented sophistication, seems aeons away from earlier pious credulities – though the stricken man's friends still repeat them. We have not moved outside the monotheistic framework, but it is strained almost to cracking-point.

The prose prologue (*Chs. 1–2*)* and epilogue (*Ch. 42, 7–17*) are

---

* As elsewhere, chapter references *in italics* refer to the book of the Bible that is under discussion.

detachable and distinct from the great poetic creation in between. They tell of a traditional Job who, in the face of intolerable hardship, remains the archetype of devout, resigned patience, and is eventually rewarded. These preliminary and concluding sections seem ancient, dating back, perhaps, to the eighth century. The name of Job had already appeared in second-millennium texts. He was one of the proverbially just men of the past, described as the greatest personage in all the east. And it is relevant to the Hebrews' continual preoccupation with the status of foreigners that this paragon of wisdom was believed to have been a foreigner himself. For his home is said to be the land of Uz, which seems to be somewhere in the region either of Edom or of Aram (Damascus); his friends, too, appear to come from Edom. Wisdom literature, of which the *Book of Job* provides the climactic example – personifying the concept of wisdom – had always been associated with foreigners or part-foreigners, among whom Edomites were prominent (Ch.8,ii). Job is a non-Israelite sage, then, like Balaam, the prophet in Moabite employment, and Jethro, the father-in-law of Moses.

So this prologue and epilogue preserved and perpetuated a non-Israelite folk-legend about a wise man of ancient heroic times, who experienced disasters. A Mesopotamian poem of the second millennium had told how illness and suffering befell a righteous man; a 'Poem of the Righteous Sufferer', originating among the Babylonians in the fifteenth century, shows remarkable similarities to the *Book of Job*, and so does a 'Babylonian Theodicy' (*c.* 1000) or 'Dialogue about Human Misery'. Nor would readers of *Job* have failed to know that the Canaanite god Baal, too, had suffered, but finally experienced resurrection (Ch.2,ii).

The prologue serves its purpose by presenting Job's calamities as a test of disinterested faith and loyalty to Yahweh. It seems shocking that Yahweh allows Satan to carry out such a cold-bloodedly cruel test and experiment. Satan, although his name means 'enemy' or 'adversary', is not yet the Devil or chief of devils or the arch-opponent of Yahweh, but a member of the heavenly court. As in other parts of the Bible – which so often sees humankind to be under judicial trial – he appears in the shape of an accuser or prosecuting attorney in search of culprits, ranging over the earth from end to end, and licensed by Yahweh to spy on offenders and hound them down. So Job, a foreigner, is on enemy territory, exposed to arbitrary hostile action, and suffers every misfortune by which a man could possibly be afflicted. Yet, as he sits broken among the ashes of his house and scratches his disgusting sores with the fragment of a pot, he still refuses to revile Yahweh, rebuking his wife with the words: 'If we accept good from God, shall we not accept evil?'

However, the poetic body of the work that now follows displays a considerable contrast: for this phenomenal patience is no more to be seen.

Job's three friends, Eliphaz, Bildad and Zophar, come to visit him. For a week they sit without speaking. And then they offer consolation, of a sort. It is at this stage that Job breaks silence and curses the day when he was born. Then follow the three cycles of speeches from his friends (described with some irony; for one thing, none of them are very good listeners). Job finds their views completely unsatisfactory, and, in a series of incomparable poetic declamations, refuses to admit that he has done anything to warrant the fate that has befallen him. 'Till death, I will not abandon my claim to innocence,' he declares: 'I will never give up.'[2] True, Yahweh has won his cruel wager with Satan, because Job does not curse him. All the same, he subjects his maker to an astonishing series of vitriolic indictments. Yahweh, he declares, although omnipotent and omniscient, shows no interest in individual human beings, who are 'born into trouble, as surely as sparks fly upwards. I tell you, Yahweh has put me in the wrong: he has drawn the net around me', and Job pronounces him unjust and hostile, hedging men in on every side, and himself in particular.[3]

But if Yahweh is relentlessly watching Job, Job for his part declares himself unable to achieve the slightest contact with Yahweh, by which he might induce him to right these terrible wrongs. His greatest problem, indeed, is not the agony of his sufferings but the sense of *estrangement* from Yahweh which they have brought. He wants the plain event of God's visible appearance, so that he may directly challenge his cruelty – and begin to understand even a small part of his plan. 'If only I knew how to find him, how to *enter his lawcourt*, I would state my case before him and set out my arguments in full: then I should learn what answer he would give.' Let him write out his indictment. When he does – even granting that he is judge and witness and executioner all at one and the same time – 'as soon as I have stated my case I know that I shall be acquitted'.[4]

Or at least, if direct confrontation is not possible, their differences could be settled by an arbitrator or redeemer (*goel*), who would bridge the gulf created by God's transcendence and bear witness on Job's behalf and vindicate him, mediating between man and God, just as mediators decide between a man and his neighbour (Ch.13,ii). 'I know that my Redeemer liveth' was later seen as a prediction of Jesus, but Job's vindicator and arbitrator was to be *personal*, not collective or messianic – and posthumous intervention did not interest him: he wanted it, in the Hebrew fashion, during his own lifetime, and in our own world.

After Job's three older friends had finished their speeches and failed to impress him, the young Elihu, who next came on the scene, displayed considerable indignation and anger: because Job, 'with his endless ranting against Yahweh had made himself more righteous than Yahweh himself' (*or* 'was justifying himself and blaming Yahweh'), yet had nevertheless seemed to get the better of the arguments marshalled against him, causing the other men to look like fools. Elihu's torrential orations (not always accepted as an original part of the book) are often not much more than a reworking of the three earlier visitors' arguments. Like them, though with even greater force, he stresses the wondrous works of the sovereign creator, whose rulership on high sets him far above all human weakness and limited, distorted human vision: 'He is so great that we cannot know him'; and Job is an ignorant, senseless, sinful rebel.[5] 'Although you say that you cannot see him [or that he does not see you],' Elihu tells Job, 'the case is before him: so wait for him humbly' – and you will receive your own just deserts in due time. Like Job, he speaks of a mediator, yet *this* mediator will only help by admitting the sufferer's guilt, but pleading that he has paid for it. For Elihu, like the Second Isaiah, believes strongly in the disciplinary value of suffering: 'Man learns his lesson on a bed of pain.'[6]

In the text as we have it, Job does not trouble to comment on the young Elihu's eloquent but cocksure arguments. He has heard most of them before, and is waiting for something else altogether. And now it comes. For Yahweh, who had seemed to be so very far away and inaccessible, suddenly makes himself apparent and speaks to Job in person, 'out of the tempest', like the storm-god of Canaan, vouchsafing one of those shattering direct visions of his majesty that are so rare in the Bible. The discourses that Yahweh now proceeds to utter are accepted, for the most part, as forming an authentic part of the book, but they prove unexpected and disconcerting; and at first sight their relevance seems disappointingly questionable. Yahweh does not by any means heed Job's plea to come into court and vindicate him. Indeed, he does not offer him the slightest comfort of any kind. Instead, he offers a terrifying display of sovereign irrationality. His huge, magnificent rhapsody of hectoring, bullying, sneering rhetorical questions includes a lengthy series of quick-fire riddles about the multifarious creation of the world that had been his work. *You* could not have done any of this, could you? Have *you* an arm like God's arm? Can *you* thunder with a voice like his? Could you, or any other man, have subjugated the land-monster Behemoth ('the Beast') and sea-monster Leviathan? – the ancient Canaanite symbols of primordial chaos and rivalry with heaven.[7]

Yahweh remains incomprehensible. Yet Job has at least been privileged to receive the confrontation he longed for. And it has shown him how the entire human dilemma must be enlarged and expanded into an immeasurably wider context and perspective in which man is not the measure of all things. Such a message brings no immediate help to the wretched miseries that have encompassed him. The problem of good and evil is too grave, and Yahweh is too transcendent, for instant help to be of any relevance whatsoever. But Job has been brought face to face with Yahweh, and has been shown a corner of his momentous mysteries.

And so in some way or other, however dimly, he can see a sort of path ahead. For now his tone becomes strangely altered. In a final poem, he admits that he has been talking about things he did not, could not understand, but now he has seen the omnipotent Yahweh with his own eyes – which has made him ashamed and repentant. Above all, in the face of the overwhelming odds, forced to probe humbly to a new level of meaning, he has been made devastatingly aware that Yahweh's way is not man's, and that he himself is not of the smallest significance. 'What reply can I give you, I who carry no weight? ... I know you can do all things and that no purpose is beyond you.'[8]

Yet these last words of Job's offer formidable food for thought. After all his struggles, he has accepted the power of Yahweh responsibly, neither proud nor abased. But his capitulation is due entirely to inferior strength. He feels shame because he stood out so long against it; but he does not experience any guilt or remorse. He is still a virtuous man who has suffered, apparently through no fault of his own: the whole Deuteronomic system of rewards for the good and punishments for the bad, already questioned by Jeremiah, lies in ruins. We are given no glib or easy answer, in fact no answer at all, to the aching problem of how an all-powerful and all-knowing perfectly virtuous God can possibly have created and permitted all the evil, all the undeserved misery, that we see around us.

And then the short prose epilogue reverts to the simple, calm, archaic atmosphere of the prologue. Job's total restoration is intended for those who like a happy ending. It is described with tongue in cheek, as a sop for the unintellectual who did not want to be shocked by strange doctrines. One of the new daughters, with whom Job is now blessed, bears the name of Keren-Happuch, 'box of eye-shadow'. What a hint that the epilogue is not to be taken too seriously, in contrast to the ineffable profundities of the poetry that has gone before!

ii. Second Isaiah

Some three or four decades after the destruction of the state of Judah, its Babylonian conquerors were overthrown by Cyrus II the Great, king of the Persians (559–530), a people who did not belong to the Semitic cultural zone but spoke an Indo-European language. In a series of lightning campaigns Cyrus conquered his own former overlords and kinsmen the Medes (550), overwhelmed the kingdom of Croesus the Lydian who controlled Asia Minor (546), and irrupted into Mesopotamia, where Babylon succumbed to him (539). Together with the rest of the Babylonian empire, the lands that had formerly constituted the kingdoms of Israel and Judah fell into his hands, and were incorporated into a Persian province called Abarnahara (Beyond the River, i.e. the Euphrates).

Bent on encouraging the local religions of his imperial territories, Cyrus issued an edict authorizing the repair and reconstruction of the dilapidated, partly derelict Jerusalem Temple.[9] The document has been preserved by the Bible, in retouched form. Sheshbazzar, a man from Judah, made plans to undertake this work at the royal expense, perhaps with the rank of local governor. Then a considerable number of exiles returned to Palestine under Zerubbabel. He and Sheshbazzar (if indeed they were not the same person, as has sometimes been supposed) both have Babylonian names, yet both appear to have belonged to the House of David. The Bible gives Zerubbabel most of the credit. Associated with him was Jeshua, grandson of the last priest of the Temple before it had been destroyed. He came to be known as high priest, although the title was not officially employed until later.

Although many Jews still stayed behind in Babylonia, a considerable number were repatriated by Cyrus, on various different occasions – though the reported figure of fifty thousand, including six or seven thousand slaves, seems to represent an exaggeration. Settled in Jerusalem and a small surrounding area, they did not live nearly as well as they had fared in Babylonia, but they came because they felt the people must have at least a minimal territory of their own, to avoid eventual extinction: and Palestine, as all their writers and prophets had reminded them, was the land Yahweh meant them to possess.

The Jerusalem that rose again from the ashes was at first very small, and the reconstruction of the Temple proved disappointingly slow. But immediately after the death of Cyrus (520), the work started again – with the help of the people who had remained in the country all along – and the Second Temple was completed in c. 516. Although the poverty of its materials fell far short of the Solomonian model, and the new building only existed at all because of Persian patronage, it was nevertheless an achievement of which later Jews never ceased to be proud. Many of the psalms record this pride: the Psalter has been described as the 'Hymn-Book of the Second Temple'.

Two prophets, Haggai and Zechariah (Appendix 3), impatient of delay, had urged on the work of reconstruction, but another and much more remarkable prophet arose at the same time in the Babylonian Dispersion. We do not know his name, but call him Deutero-Isaiah or the Second Isaiah.

Like many others throughout the near east, he was deeply impressed by the almost legendary career and personality of Cyrus, who had taken such decisive actions to restore the fortunes of the Jewish people. It is most unusual for any Hebrew writer to speak of a foreigner in the terms Second Isaiah attributes to Yahweh:

I say to Cyrus, 'You shall be my shepherd
  To carry out all my purpose,
So that Jerusalem may be rebuilt
  And the foundations of the Temple may be laid.'[10]

The writer does not formally rank as a 'major' or even a 'minor' prophet, because by the time the Bible was put together his name and identity had already been lost from sight. His oracles appear in the *Book of Isaiah*, of which they comprise most of a very extensive section, from *Chapter 40* to *Chapter 66*.

These passages begin with forecasts of Yahweh's imminent, joyful delivery of his people from Babylonian exile through the agency of Cyrus, in fulfilment of his eternal purpose and covenant, in order to demonstrate to the world that he alone is God and that idolatry is futile. At the same time, the downfall of the Babylonian gods is 'foretold', perhaps retrospectively. Incorporated in this material are four separate 'Servant Songs' describing the mission, troubles and sorrows, justification and triumph of Yahweh's chosen servant. The persecution of this suffering servant is for the sins of others – but the help of Yahweh is near, and Yahweh will enable his servant to bring salvation to the world. About this mysterious figure, more will be said later.

Second Isaiah sometimes echoes the language of Isaiah himself, and may have been written by a later member of his school: which is, perhaps, why the two collections were joined together. But the topical allusions to Cyrus indicate a date subsequent to Isaiah; and in any case the two authors display marked stylistic differences, including (as computer analysis confirms) a strongly divergent vocabulary. The concise, clear-cut speech of Isaiah is replaced, in the second work, by a smooth and ample and self-conscious eloquence, expressing itself by cumulative rhetorical antitheses and repetitions. This is all very deliberately done, because *Second Isaiah* is the best organized and most meticulously polished of all the prophetic writings.

Its composer confers this stamp of unity on a huge range of diverse, traditional material, collected together from various sources, but supplemented by highly original contributions of his own, for he is one of the Bible's outstanding thinkers and artists. His work contains a greater quantity of sustained lyrical poetry than any other prophetic book; its lavish, complex images are exploited to say one thing while recalling or echoing another. The anonymous author refers to oral, 'singing', composition particularly often, but he must be speaking in figurative terms, since some of the oracles recounted here are so long and elaborately structured that, even if they were sung or read out aloud, they must have been written down before this was done.

Indeed, unlike earlier prophets, Second Isaiah may have written them down himself.

He was a great inheritor of the traditions of prophets and of the 'Wise', but presents both these legacies with discriminating adjustments. For Yahweh declares, we are told, that while he 'makes his own servants' prophecies come true',

> I frustrate false prophets and their signs
> And make fools of diviners;
> I reverse what wise men say
> And make nonsense of their wisdom.[11]

Second Isaiah launches a new theological and spiritual epoch. The biblical writings had often before begun to advance ahead of the idea of one-religion-for-one-country towards absolute, unlimited monotheism, but they had, on the whole, tended to remain at the half-way point of saying that our God is stronger than yours. Certainly, earlier prophets had voiced universal monotheistic doctrine in one form or other, but such assertions, when they are again found in *Second Isaiah*, have now become wholly unequivocal. 'I am the Lord, there is no other ... There is no god but me; there is no god other than I, victorious and able to save. ... Who has gauged the waters in the palm of his hand, or with its span set limits to the heavens? ... Who is like me? Let him stand up, let him declare himself and show me his evidence. ... Is there any god beside me?'[12] And Yahweh answers his own question. There are *no other gods* at all, anywhere in the universe. Gazing at the Babylonian pantheon all around him, Second Isaiah makes this his principal theme, enunciating an uncompromising belief in one single God to which Jews and Christians and Moslems have adhered ever since. And the prophet goes on to argue clearly that Yahweh's universal sovereignty requires universal faith. The intimate, tender loyalty towards him which every man and woman in the world must maintain has to be founded upon absolute surrender to his will.

Despite doubts and disputable delimitations of their beginnings and ends, the four 'Songs of Yahweh's Servant', or 'Servant's Songs', can be regarded as integral portions of the work of Second Isaiah. 'Here is my Servant, whom I uphold ... he will plant justice on earth, while coasts and islands wait for his teaching.' In the second of the songs, the servant himself speaks to the peoples of all these territories. 'I will make you a light to the nations, to be my salvation to [*or* that my salvation may reach] earth's farthest bounds.' The third piece is autobiographical. 'Yahweh has given me the tongue of a teacher and skill to console the weary with a word in the morning: he sharpened my hearing that I might listen like one who is taught.' In the fourth poem, Yahweh declares, 'Behold, my

Servant shall prosper, He shall be lifted up, exalted to the heights.'[13] And the servant is also mentioned in other passages of Second Isaiah's work, outside the four songs.

In certain passages he is identified with the patriarch Israel (Jacob), 'whom I have fetched from the ends of the earth'. And elsewhere Yahweh speaks of 'my servants', in the plural, apparently equating them with the whole Jewish people: while in the second song he explicitly identifies the servant, in the singular, with 'Israel, through whom I shall win glory.'[14] In one sense, therefore, he stands for the whole of the community, or at any rate for its faithful, surviving Remnant. And yet, in the fourth song the servant is instead presented not as a collective, corporate personification of Israel but as one single individual who has a message to bring to Israel and the world. But there is no point in trying to identify that individual as a historical personage. The prophet is no longer thinking of Cyrus at this point. Nor, as has sometimes been suggested, is he thinking of his own self. The individual he has in mind will arise and exist in the future, transcending any particular temporal setting.

This duality of Second Isaiah's thought, veering between a corporate and an individual interpretation, seems perplexing to ourselves. But the Hebrew imagination, accustomed to the former range of thinking, found it easy to veer between the two: for example, the *Book of Joshua* has the story of a man named Achan, whose purely personal sin brought disaster upon the whole community. The servant may also be compared to a kingly personage, belonging to a world of royal metaphor in which society and the individual interpenetrate and merge. And his salvation-bringing role echoes the next-of-kin solidarity of clan and family life, in which a man might be an arbitrator or redeemer (*goel*, Ch.13,ii;15,i) in a special sense, when he brings salvation to a relative by claiming him or her as his own (cf. Appendix 4, Ruth).

The servant is a sufferer: although innocent, he is horribly persecuted, all in obedience to Yahweh's will. It is for the sins of others that he suffers. The third poem tells the story, and particularly the fourth. Although 'he had done no violence, neither was any deceit in his mouth',

> He is despised and rejected of men;
> A man of sorrows, and acquainted with grief . . . .
> He was wounded for our transgressions,
>   He was bruised for our iniquities . . . .
>   With his stripes we are healed . . . .
> The Lord hath laid on him the iniquity of us all . . . .
> He is brought as a lamb to the slaughter,
> And as a sheep before her shearers is dumb,
> So he openeth not his mouth.[15]

The *Book of Jeremiah* had stressed that prophet's personal distresses and innocent sufferings. But here the descriptions, although unrelated to any nameable individual, are much more emphatic and detailed and vivid. And, besides, there is this concept of *vicarious* suffering, the ancient oriental conviction that the sufferings of the just are an atonement for the wicked. Once again, there may have been traces of such an idea in *Jeremiah*, but it is *Second Isaiah* who fully and explicitly works the theme out.

It is not suggested that one person can absolve another of his sins. Nevertheless, we are assured that the man who has fully surrendered to the will of Yahweh knows, and is satisfied to know, that his own suffering can be of incalculable value to others. This difficult conception of Yahweh's high purpose was far removed from the *Book of Job*'s intellectual attempt to discuss evil and suffering. And it is to be doubted whether many of Second Isaiah's contemporaries found the concept of redemptive suffering a consolation for their troubles. But St Paul and the Christian evangelists saw these passages as direct forecasts of the crucifixion of Jesus.

For Yahweh also promises, according to *Second Isaiah*, that this suffering will win his vicariously tormented servant eventual vindication and triumph. 'Therefore I will allot him a portion with the great, and he shall share his spoil with the mighty ... After all his pains he shall be bathed in light.'[16] For a start, the new Golden Age was destined to witness (had already begun to witness) a restoration of the faithful Jewish Remnant to their ancestral homelands, where the covenant with the House of David would be revived. And that, above all, is *Second Isaiah*'s most immediate message of comfort, and the reason why he celebrates Cyrus who, foreigner though he is, has made this restoration a practical possibility.

Yet, in addition to this special attention to Yahweh's own people, the servant songs also greatly reinforce *Second Isaiah*'s characteristic monotheism embracing the whole world. For Yahweh will make his servant 'a light to the nations, to be my salvation to earth's farthest bounds'. That is to say, although the Jews were his only believers, he would be worshipped in every other country as well – foreigners would be accepted in his cult. God's universal triumph involved the *submission* of all other states. Their kings and princes 'shall bow to the earth before you and lick the dust from your feet: and you shall know that I am the Lord'.[17] It was a startlingly optimistic forecast to hear from a displaced emigrant belonging to a totally defeated small nation. Henceforward the religion of Yahweh assumed, in the minds of some of its principal thinkers, a missionary character. But the advisability of such enterprises was also questioned, and the Jewish community remained an unresolved synthesis between universal and national characteristics, displaying continual tension between a warm desire to convert the Gentiles (*goyim*) and an equally heartfelt wish to have no dealings with them whatsoever.

CHAPTER 16

THE NEW JUDAISM

i. Nehemiah and Ezra: The Chronicler

The completion of the Temple in *c.* 516 was followed by a period of over seventy years about which we have little information. However, a few contemporary prophets, the anonymous 'Third Isaiah' and Obadiah and Malachi (Appendix 3), put forward complaints about the civil and religious leaders appointed to the restored community by the Persian imperial power. It appears that scepticism and slackness in cult performance abounded, and that men were divorcing their Yahwist wives in order to embark on more lucrative marriages with foreigners.

Such women were available owing to the extensive immigrations that had taken place. Particularly numerous were refugees from Edom. Regarded as unwelcome half-foreigners they had fled from a new power that had overrun their homeland. This was the kingdom of Dedan (Kebar) in northern Arabia, which expanded into Sinai and the Nile valley, seemingly with Persian connivance. Although, in earlier times, Israel may have established commercial relations with the kingdom of Saba (Sheba) in the south of Arabia (the Yemen, Ch.8,i), this was the first time that the impact of the northern Arabians was felt: speakers of a south-western Semitic tongue (related to Sabaean) which eventually developed into the classical Arabic that is still used today for almost all written purposes. Both geographically and ethnically speaking, they were closer than the Yemenites to the Hebrews, with whom they now entered into the contacts, mainly unfriendly, which persisted in the Greek and Roman epochs (Ch.19,i) and have been revived, so formidably and irremediably, in modern times.

During the reign of the Persian King Artaxerxes 1 (464–425), the Jews summed up enough resources and energy to begin reconstructing the walls of Jerusalem, but the king, suspicious of this activity, ordered the suspension of the work. It was this that stirred Nehemiah into action, and inaugurated a new epoch in the history of his country. Although a Yahwist, he occupied an influential post at the Persian court at Susa, apparently as royal cupbearer, and when he requested the king's permission to proceed in person to Jerusalem, he gained his wish, securing appointment as governor or commissioner *(tirshatha)* of the surrounding area.

The accounts of what followed, provided by the *Books of Nehemiah and Ezra*, are well written but of questionable reliability. In particular, despite what we are told to the contrary, Nehemiah evidently arrived in Jerusalem long before Ezra. He seems to have held his appointment for about twelve years *(c.* 445–433/2), but his initial stay had been brief, lasting only about fifty-two days. In this time he erected a new wall for Jerusalem – on the crest of the ridge, since the district on the outside slopes lay in irreparable ruins. The building operation was divided into forty-two sectors, each entrusted to a different set of professional and local groups of his compatriots. The poorer inhabitants, oppressed by their wealthier neighbours and crushed by severe taxes, proved less than cooperative, and Nehemiah's attempt to repopulate the city was coldly received by the surrounding farmers and peasants, who felt reluctant to abandon their ancestral plots of land and go to live among the debris of Jerusalem.

Furthermore, Nehemiah encountered more positive opposition, led by highly influential personages. Chief among them was Sanballat of Bethhoron, whom the Persians had made governor of Samaria. Sanballat, although his name is Assyrian, was a Yahwist (as his son's nomenclature shows); but all the same he proved implacably unsympathetic to the rehabilitation of the ancient capital. And this obstructive policy received strong support from elsewhere. Ashdod, the strongest Philistine city-state at this time, enthusiastically endorsed his attitude, and so did a number of potentates who, like himself, were Persian office holders or clients. One of them was Tobiah of Ammon across the Jordan, leader of a strong Yahwist clan related to priestly and secular families in Jerusalem. And another man who felt like Sanballat was Geshem (Gashmu), monarch of the formidable new kingdom of Dedan (Kebar) in the north of Arabia, which had caused so many Edomites to flee into Judah. These opponents of Nehemiah's activity, surrounding him in a hostile circle, hinted to the Persian court that he was instigating certain rebellious prophets to proclaim that Judah now had an independent king of its own once again.

Nehemiah went back to Persia, but resumed his labours at Jerusalem later on. This time he evidently felt strong enough to take forceful action. Tobiah was thrown out of his room in the Temple precinct, possessions and all. And Sanballat's son-in-law Manasseh (?), though grandson of the Temple priest Eliashib, was expelled from the city.

For if the Samaritans, who were under Sanballat's rule, objected to

Nehemiah, his dislike for them was just as great or greater. When, therefore, they offered their assistance in his attempt to reconstruct Jerusalem,
they earned a snub, and their aid was resoundingly rejected – a decision
(foreshadowed by Zerubbabel and Jeshua according to the biblical
writer) which played a leading part in their secession into a separate
Yahwist sect, of which Sanballat was held to have been the founder
(Appendix 6). Nehemiah loathed the Samaritans because the extensive
racial mixtures they had undergone, since the fall of the northern
kingdom, seemed to him to have totally contaminated the purity of their
Yahwist credentials. By the same token, all other foreigners too were
detestable, and he begged people not to marry any of their women: 'I
argued with these prospective bridegrooms and reviled them, I beat them
and tore out their hair.'[1] The everlasting controversy about such inter-
marriages had reached a decisive, extremist stage.

Another distinguished visitor from Babylonia was Ezra. He was a
scribe 'learned in the law of the God of Heaven'[2] – possibly meaning, in
this context, that he held an official post in the Persian capital, looking
after the interests of his compatriots at court. He was also a priest, reputedly of the line of Aaron. Impressed by this priestly character and
pedigree, the Bible assigns him chronological priority over Nehemiah,
but this is evidently erroneous, for the Artaxerxes 'in whose seventh year'
Ezra came to Jerusalem[3] does not seem to have been the first Persian king
of that name (464–425) but the second, Artaxerxes Memnon (404–358).

According to an alleged letter from the monarch, quoted in the biblical
account, he and his advisers commissioned Ezra 'to find out how things
stand in Judah and Jerusalem with regard to the law of your God with
which you are entrusted'.[4] His commission only related to religious
affairs, but, within this sphere, he was granted extensive powers of
compulsion, not only in Judah, but in other parts of Palestine as well. He
was accompanied on his return from exile by an entourage of priests and
Levites and laymen possibly numbering as many as five thousand; they
brought with them a supply of vessels for the Temple liturgy.

On his arrival, Ezra gathered the people together and read aloud to
them a work described as 'the book of the law of Moses, which Yahweh
had enjoined upon Israel'.[5] This work has been variously identified as
Deuteronomy or its nucleus, or, alternatively, as the whole five books of the
Torah (though not necessarily in their final form). More probably, it was
the priestly code (Ch.14,iii) – which Artaxerxes' government may have
ordained, at this stage, to become the provincial law of Judah. But whatever it was, its recital, so vividly recalling past national glories, was said
to have moved every listener to tears.

Ezra now felt encouraged to press on with an austerer version of
Nehemiah's reforms and purges. Among the exiles in Babylonia a strict

Yahwism had by now become the norm. But this was not by any means the case in Jerusalem, to which members of other races had been flocking ever since the end of the monarchy, so that the stricter Yahwists were counterbalanced, or even outnumbered, by people of mixed religion or the outright adherents of Canaanite and other foreign rituals. Ezra struck out at these practices with uncompromising vigour. In particular, he was determined to reinforce Nehemiah's prohibition of mixed marriages with all possible severity, since such unions had made the land 'unclean from end to end'; the foreign women and their offspring, he declared, should be expelled from the community.[6]

To what extent this determined attempt to create a pure 'holy race' achieved practical results is uncertain. Inevitably, there were abundant protests (Ch.16,ii). It could be argued that the Yahwist religion and community were compelled to adopt such measures out of self-protection. Yet they undermined the prophetic conception that the cult of Yahweh ought to become universal.

But Ezra also had quite another matter in mind at the same time. For he was determined to shift and transfer his compatriots' national aspirations away from political freedom to religious independence instead. So he renewed and reconstituted the priesthood of the Temple, which was henceforward to be shared between the 'sons of Aaron', those who claimed descent from David's joint priests Zadok and Abiathar (the Zadokites, of whom Ezra was one, subsequently prevailed). Gradually these functionaries came to assume the title of 'high priest', which had already, perhaps, entered into unofficial use (Ch.15,ii).

In future, then, instead of the kings, whose day was done, the head of the community would be an anointed high priest, invested with royal insignia and trappings. Supported by a hierarchy of priests and Levites and heads of families, and presiding over a Council of Elders (of disputed composition and character), it was he who would direct the nation under the suzerainty of the imperial power – which gladly encouraged this arrangement in order to scotch political unrest. That the general move towards extreme Jewish purity should bring into being a theocratic Temple State was somewhat ironical, seeing that this was a perfectly familiar and acceptable idea to Persians, Syrians, peoples of Asia Minor, and Greeks, but lacked all Hebrew precedent, except in cloudy theory.

The cult that these high priests fostered was solemnly ceremonial, centring round sacrificial rites. Many psalms of the period utter a warning against the excessive formalism that this situation might cause. However, Ezra, despite his priestly preoccupations, was concerned that no such fault should develop. For the new religious state was to be based, after all, not on the cult but the Torah: to the study of which he personally had devoted himself.[7]

In the hands, then, of men who followed the guidance of Ezra, the Torah became the main pillar and support of the reconstituted community, and was well on the way to its ultimate 'canonical' shape as the normative rule of the Jewish faith (though this was not finally achieved until *c.* AD 90). It is from this time, perhaps, that the Jewish faith, based on these scriptures, can be legitimately called Judaism: and those who professed it, the people of Yahweh or Israelites or Hebrews, can receive the name of Jews (Appendix 11). It was a paradox that Ezra, so confirmed a racialist in matters of marriage, was the man who ensured more than anyone else that the mark of a Jew should not be race, but observance of the Torah.

And the scholar scribes who had to regulate this observance, in accordance with their interpretations of the text, came to be as important as any priest (Ch.18,ii). They were regarded as the spiritual heirs of Ezra, who had accompanied his public reading from the Torah by an *explanation.* Readings from the Law, of course, were nothing new, but this is the first time we hear of the explanatory comments which would later play such a major part in scribal activities, harnessing Judaism to the changing world of each successive generation.

Moreover, Ezra intended to appeal not to an élite but to a much wider public. For both his reading of the text he had produced, and his interpretation which accompanied the reading, were probably followed by translations into Aramaic. This north-west Semitic tongue, related to Hebrew, had earlier been characteristic of the Aramaean states of northern Syria, but subsequently spread elsewhere very widely indeed. In Palestine, in particular, although Hebrew continued to be understood and employed in literary and legal and liturgical circles, from this time onwards Aramaic was displacing it as the common tongue (while the letters of the alphabet gradually acquired the square shape, partly based on the Aramaic script, which they retain today). It was also the cosmopolitan medium employed for Persian official documents, of which examples in that language, very possibly authentic, are preserved in the *Book of Ezra.* Aramaic is still spoken in villages near Damascus.

The *Books of Nehemiah and Ezra*, which claim to describe these events, may perhaps be the work of a single man, writing a short time after the end of Ezra's career. As far as we know, the two books were not separated until the third century AD.

The first seven chapters (and certain other sections) of *Nehemiah*, describing his heroic building of the Jerusalem wall, are known as his Memoir. Clearly and forcefully phrased, this is Jewish history at its most vivid. The account is professedly an autobiographical piece written by Nehemiah himself. Some have suspected that it is not quite that, but a collection of material cleverly put together by a subsequent author or editor. Certainly such a man, as so often, took a hand in preparing the final product, but the original nucleus of the memoir may be taken at its face-value and regarded as an autobiographical work by Nehemiah. By a curious coincidence, the literary genre of autobiography was being developed by Greeks (notably Ion of Chios) at about the same time.

Addressed, it would seem, to Yahweh himself, Nehemiah's memoir may have been lodged in the Temple, so as to secure him a name in the future, a thing he probably could not achieve through direct posterity since his position as royal cupbearer suggests that he was a eunuch.[8] The memoir shows how he had found himself obstructed and attacked by every kind of ridicule, misrepresentation, fifth column and menace, culminating in attempted assassination. However, he sounds like a reformer of single-minded and vigorous perseverance and action. Sometimes he was blunt and deficient in tact; and his temper seems to have been violent. Yet he proved capable of getting on with people as well, and his ruthless attitude to foreign wives was counterbalanced by a keen sympathy with the Jewish poor. He felt completely convinced that he was doing Yahweh's will, and he provided the stable political base which made Ezra's subsequent reorganization possible.

The *Book of Ezra* once again contains his alleged memoir,[9] but like other features of the work, it resembles a literary composition, closely related to *Chronicles*, rather than authentic autobiography. Nevertheless, some picture of Ezra's complicated personality emerges. He was a man who felt ashamed to ask for a military escort, in case this should seem to suggest lack of faith in Yahweh's protection. We can see him fasting and praying and preaching, in the grip of powerful emotion – the man hailed as the Second Moses, the refounder of his people's religion.

The two *Books of Chronicles*, or at least their principal components, may well be by the same man who compiled the *Books of Nehemiah* and *Ezra* from the former's memoir and other materials. *Chronicles* comprises a fresh attempt to write a history of the Jewish people, starting from Adam (although the periods up to the accession of David are only represented by genealogies and lists) and continuing down to the events immediately preceding the reconstruction of the Temple.

At first *Chronicles*, *Nehemiah* and *Ezra* formed portions of one single work; *Chronicles* became detached to constitute a separate book in about 400 BC. It was known to the Septuagint (Greek Bible) as *Paralipomena*, 'Omissions', probably because it contains material omitted from the *Books of Kings* that had dealt with the same period. The Chronicler had access to the Deuteronomic historian, who had contributed so much to *Kings*, and he knew the priestly writer too (Ch.14,ii,iii), though he did not always agree with either of them. Other sources, annals of kings and prophets, are mentioned as well.[10]

The leading theme of *Chronicles* is a straightforward and simple morality, centring entirely upon Yahweh. Thus, since David is 'good', the supreme agent of Yahweh's purpose for his people, any material offering any contrary indication just has to be left out; and David has to be credited with the planning of the Temple. But Solomon, it could not be denied, was its founder, so nothing is said about Solomon's foreign wives or religious compromises, and his embarrassing cession of territory to Tyre, to pay his debts, becomes a free gift.[11] The grandeur of both these monarchs is estimated too highly.

The work also insists throughout, to the point of absurdity, upon the principle questioned in *Job*: that virtue is rewarded by Yahweh, and bad behaviour earns punishment. Thus the illnesses of Asa, Jehoram and Uzziah, kings of Judah, become acts of divine retribution. The uncomfortable fact that Manasseh, although a vigorous supporter of Canaanite religion, enjoyed a very long reign, is explained away by bestowing upon him a fictitious repentance.[12] The no less embarrassing defeat and death of the pious Josiah is accounted for by suggesting that, despite his devotion, he had failed to obey some command he had received from Yahweh.

Yet the state of Judah is still seen as the only legitimate kingdom, and Jerusalem and the Temple stand at the centre of the narrative. It is only when contacts with Judah make some reference inevitable that the northern kingdom of Israel is mentioned at all. And then it is told firmly that it should have mended its ways, reversed the disastrous Disruption for which its first monarch, Jeroboam I, was responsible, and reunited itself with Jerusalem, 'entering Yahweh's sanctuary which he has sanctified for ever'.[13]

Fortunately for later historians, quite a lot of valuable secular information, which had not appeared in the two *Books of Kings*, manages to find its way into *Chronicles*. However, such insertions were entirely subsidiary to the author's main purpose,. which was to display, by edifying, didactic selection, how Ezra's model theocracy had been able to come into existence through Yahweh's direction. With even more single-minded concentration than earlier historians, the Chronicler rates 'what happened' as less important than 'what this happening meant for the people of Yahweh', and, despite all catastrophes, he wants to show that continuity prevails, and that the divine promises are kept.

He is strongly biased against all the people who had avoided deportation, staying behind in the homeland. It is only the exiles who concern him: they are the 'Remnant' that matters, and their future prospects seem to him promising. He entertains a positive hope about their earthly redemption, and the last words in his book reproduce Cyrus' decree inviting them to return to Jerusalem and rebuild the Temple.[14]

ii. Jonah

The short *Book of Jonah* seems to have been written in about the same period; it must have been designed as a protest against the narrow racial policies of Nehemiah and Ezra. We are told how, in ancient times, Yahweh had commanded the prophet Jonah to go to Nineveh, the capital of Assyria, and prophesy catastrophe for its people because of their evil behaviour. Unwilling to obey this divine call, Jonah hastened in the opposite direction instead, proceeding to Joppa (Jaffa) where he caught a ship which set out across the Mediterranean Sea. A great storm, however, arose, and the vessel looked like breaking up and sinking. Lots were cast to discover which of the persons on board should be held responsible for the disaster, and Jonah seemed to be indicated. He was thrown into the sea, and Yahweh arranged that a great fish (mistranslated as a whale) should swallow him up. But after three days and three nights, the fish disgorged him onto dry land.

Once more Yahweh ordered him to prophesy at Nineveh, and this time he obeyed. The Assyrians duly repented of their ways. Jonah, however, felt frustrated because the dire predictions of disaster he addressed to them had not been fulfilled; so he sat outside the walls and prayed that the city might perish, and he himself with it. A castor-oil plant which had quickly grown up and provided him with shelter was attacked by a worm and quickly withered and died; and Jonah too, belaboured by a scorching wind, felt faint, and repeated his prayer for death. He admitted to Yahweh that the destruction of the plant had mortally angered him. But Yahweh replied: 'You are sorry for the plant, though you did not have the trouble of growing it, a plant which came up in a night and withered in a night. And should I not be sorry for the great city of Nineveh, with its hundred and twenty thousand who cannot tell their right hand from their left, and cattle without number'?[15]

The story, a blend of parable and novel, is told in lively language, concealing considerable sophistication under a naïve veneer. Although in the form of a narrative, the book ranks among the 'Minor Prophets' (Appendix 3), because its hero is identified as a prophet, namely Jonah, the son of Amittai, from Gath-hepher in Galilee, who had forecast the expansion of the northern kingdom of Israel under Jeroboam II (c. 787–747). But the theme and language, and various other pieces of internal evidence, indicate that the story was written several centuries later; many scholars would agree with a date between 400 and 350. As usual, we do not know the author's name.

At that date, the ascendancy of Assyria was long since past, and the subsequent imperial career of the Babylonians had come to an end as well. Yet the Jews of the Dispersion were still in Babylonia, and it is banishment in that country that the swallowing up of Jonah by the great fish seems to symbolize, for Jeremiah, too, had used a similar metaphor for the same exile.[16]

The intended moral is made clear by Yahweh's final rhetorical question to Jonah. Like the equally fictional *Book of Ruth* (Appendix 4), and in accordance with the views of the cosmopolitan wisdom tradition, the work constitutes an appeal against narrowness, an appeal not to discriminate against foreigners, a remonstration against the racialism of Nehemiah and Ezra. Their policy excluded from the community every man who could not prove his pure Jewish blood, that is to say, almost all the descendants of those who had stayed on in Palestine instead of going into exile, but the *Book of Jonah* objects to this narrowness. The mercy and compassion which Yahweh feels for human beings in their need, the writer insists, whoever they may be, is powerful enough to override such calculated principles, for Yahweh is not just the God of the few; and we are entering an era when missionary conversions were being seriously considered (Ch.15,ii). The deliberate choice of the hated Nineveh as the setting gives the message sharper emphasis still.

But there was good reason why Yahweh should end the book with a question mark, for its author did not know how the community would respond to such a controversial plea. It is at least evident, however, that Nehemiah and Ezra did not have matters all their own way, and in spite of the deadly seriousness of his theme, the author of *Jonah* contrives, in an oblique fashion, to poke ironical fun at their unrelenting puritanism. His book secured an honoured place in the synagogue liturgy, and is read during the afternoon service on Yom Kippur, the Day of Atonement. Christians saw the swallowing up of Jonah for three days and three nights as the foreshadowing of Jesus' death and resurrection.[17]

Part Six

GREEK RULE AND LIBERATION

CHAPTER 17

LIFE AND THOUGHT
UNDER THE GREEKS

i. The Ptolemies

The last years of Persian rule in the fourth century witnessed a deterioration in the stability of the regions round Jerusalem and Samaria. For when the city-states of Phoenicia revolted against their Persian overlords, unrest probably spread to the Jews as well. This may have been why Artaxerxes III Ochus (359–338) deported a substantial number of them to Hyrcania, beside the Caspian Sea. But then Darius III Codomannus (336–330) was overwhelmed by Alexander III the Great of Macedonia, and Israel and Judah, henceforward to be known jointly as Judaea, were among the countries which passed into his hands (332).

They had possessed contacts with the Greeks for centuries. Latterly, the Persians had provided the region with a silver coinage inscribed with its name (*Yehud*) in Hebrew script but displaying the picture of an owl, imitated from famous silver pieces minted at Athens.[1] But it was not until the conquests of Alexander that the Jews forcibly felt the impact of the European continent, which would henceforward dominate their destinies. As Alexander passed through their land on his way to overwhelm Egypt, there were stories that he treated the Jewish communities kindly, but he showed hostility to the recalcitrant Samaritans who, after their rebuff by Ezra, were forming themselves into a distinct sect (Appendix 6). The Macedonians ejected many of them from Samaria – where Greek colonists took their place – and settled them at Shechem instead.

When Alexander died in 323, his huge empire split up into a number of separate Hellenistic kingdoms ruled by his Macedonian followers and possessing Greek institutions. Three principal dynasties eventually emerged: the Antigonids in Macedonia, the Seleucids in Syria and Mesopotamia and lands farther east, and the Ptolemies in Egypt and certain eastern Mediterranean coastlands and hinterlands. These Ptolemaic possessions included 'Judaea.'

The Ptolemies kept no provincial governor in this dependency, but instead permitted the Jewish Council of Elders, which had apparently existed since the time of Ezra, to continue to administer the country, under the chairmanship of the high priest, who thus became a sort of petty client monarch.

There were occasional signs, however, among its cultural leaders, of an approach far more sceptical than the enthusiastic efforts of Nehemiah and Ezra, and less progressive than the appeal of their opponent who wrote the *Book of Jonah*. This scepticism is very apparent in the assemblage of highly personal reflections and maxims which goes by the name of *Ecclesiastes*. In the Hebrew Bible its author calls himself Koheleth, 'the Preacher'. We do not know what his real name was, but when he claims to be 'the son of King David, king in Jerusalem'[2] – that is to say, Solomon – he is following the recognized practice of pseudonymity, intended to enhance the authority of a book. For in fact, although familiar with ancient Egyptian and Meso-potamian material that goes back far before Solomon's time, he was writing when that monarch had been dead for six hundred years: that is to say, he himself belonged to the third century.

The Preacher correctly requests that Yahweh should be feared and obeyed. Yet the injunction does not ring as convincingly as usual, and he curiously avoids any specific allusion to the divine name, preferring, instead, an almost impersonal method of address. Moreover, like the writer of the *Book of Job* (Ch. 15,i) he stresses the incomprehensibility of the divine ways. Human beings, it is suggested, have been given some sense of the mystery of past and future time, but they have not been granted the capacity to understand Yahweh's work from beginning to end.[3] This conclusion induces a uniquely melancholic, tragic spirit of pessimism. The phrase 'Vanity of vanities, all is vanity' (*or* 'emptiness', *hebel* – origin-ally hot air or smoke) need not, as is sometimes done, be dismissed as a later editorial addition, for it represents the Preacher's viewpoint with perfect exactness.

'It is a sorry business', he remarks, 'that Yahweh has given men to busy themselves with. I have seen all the deeds that are done here under the sun'. His book falls within the familiar category of wisdom literature (Ch.8,ii) – although the Preacher has reservations about the utility of these or any other written works: 'Of making [*or* the use of] many books there is no end, and much study is a weariness of the flesh.' The pursuit of wisdom, like the search for pleasure, or the construction of fine buildings, or the amassing of a great fortune – everything is just 'chasing the wind, of no profit under the sun'.[4]

This Preacher is an educated Jew of the upper class, writing, apparently, in Palestine but detached from his nation's aspirations and struggles. Nor have attempts to detect resemblances to contemporary Greek philosophy proved successful, except in so far as this was everywhere a questioning, disillusioned age. He is pessimistic because, once again like the author of *Job*, he sees only too clearly that good people do not get any rewards, and bad people are not punished, but the Preacher's analysis is much the colder and more deliberate of the two. According to him, in the last resort, time and chance are all that govern human events. The world is an endless recurrence of cycles ending nowhere at all, and death intervenes in a totally senseless fashion, making a human being no better than 'a fish caught in a net, a bird taken in a snare'. So that, although the dead have ceased to exist, they are still better off than the living. And more fortunate still are those who have not yet been born.[5] For this is a world in which *nothing is really worth while*. It is strange to find such an unprecedented questioning of human progress given room in the biblical canon (Ch.16,i). Indeed, the book only secured this anomalous admission because the Preacher had identified himself with Solomon (and perhaps because he had enjoined reverence to Yahweh, even if in somewhat perfunctory terms).

However, the Preacher's final conclusion is not quite so entirely desperate as might be expected. You must carry on, he resignedly suggests. Get on with it, whatever you are doing. True, it would be less trouble never to have been born, but meanwhile, perhaps, a live dog is better than a dead lion after all, so try to have the good time that your labours have earned you, for soon your failing powers will mean that you cannot, even if you want to.

It is undesirable to give oneself a hangover, but subject to that, go ahead, eat your food and be happy, drink your wine and enjoy yourself. It all comes from Yahweh. Women, admittedly, are disillusioning; and yet 'if two lie side by side, they keep each other warm'. Invest your money sensibly, abroad for preference, and not all in one place, since anything may go wrong.[6] And there is a lot more common sense of the same kind, not particularly elevated or inspiring, but redolent of a certain hard-boiled honesty.

In fact, Palestine, under the rule of the Ptolemies, was not an entirely bad place to live in, especially if you were a member of the upper class to which the Preacher belonged.

The leaders of that class were the House of the Tobiads, descended from Tobiah the Ammonite who had made trouble for Nehemiah (Ch.16,i). And now in the reign of Ptolemy III Euergetes (246–221) these Tobiads took advantage of a new opportunity. For when the high priest Onias (Honi) II, of the line of Zadok, chose to withhold taxes from that monarch – probably under the influence of Egypt's Seleucid enemies – the Egyptian government punitively transferred the lay branches of the high-priestly authority to another Tobias (Tobiah), the head of the family at that time, and gave him additional powers as well. Subsequently, Tobias' son Joseph became extremely well-known as a tax collector, businessman and financier on an international scale, regularly to be seen at the Ptolemies' court.

The Tobiads showed a receptive interest in the Greek way of life; and indeed this type of existence was now accessible to many Palestinian Jews. Following the initiative of Alexander himself (who had established a Greek colony at Gaza as well as Samaria), successive Ptolemies created a ring of non-Jewish, Graeco-Macedonian settlements around the edges of Palestine's central plateau, on both sides of the Jordan. The establishment of this screen of fortified Greek-style communities was intended to keep the recalcitrant Jews in order – a function which the colonists were only too glad to perform. At the same time they deliberately challenged the supremacy of the Yahwist faith. In earlier centuries it had always had to battle against rival, hostile Semitic religions – and that situation had not changed, since these remained very active in Phoenicia and elsewhere – but now, in the new settlements, there was Greek paganism to contend with as well.

The Ptolemaic capital was at Alexandria in Egypt, founded by Alexander the Great. There had already been Jews in Egypt for a long time past; and now Alexandria quickly became the largest centre of the entire Dispersion. Some Jews were sent there from Palestine – for example as prisoners of war – and others joined them of their own free will, for the Ptolemies gave these migrants and their descendants many privileges. For example, they were permitted an autonomous urban organization, under their own Council of Elders, alongside the Greek civic community and ranking above the native Egyptian inhabitants. They lived in many parts of Alexandria, but above all congregated in a special ghetto area – by their own choice – and they were free to practise their own worship: the earliest synagogue (Ch.17,ii) known to us anywhere in the world happens to be at Schedia, fourteen miles from the capital city.

Inter-racial tensions, however, became unprecedentedly grave, and although anti-Semitism was by no means new in Egypt, this was the period of the first anti-Jewish literature, which had such an influential and fateful subsequent history. A Greek adviser of Ptolemy I named Hecataeus of Abdera (or a pseudonymous author claiming his name) had written about the Jews with some measure of objectivity, but Manetho, the Egyptian high priest at Heliopolis (On) – or, once again, a Greek using his name – dedicated to King Ptolemy II Philadelphus (283–246) a history of Egypt in which he sharply contradicted the Hebrew account of the Exodus, deeming it offensive to Egyptian national pride. For Manetho, if it was he, asserted the view that the Israelites, far from leaving the country triumphantly under divine protection, had merely been deported by the Egyptian authorities so that they should not spread the infectious diseases, including leprosy, which they had contracted. And at the same time he censured the Hebrews for cruelty, hatred of other people's customs, and deliberate segregation. And a host of similar writers followed his example. Nowhere else in the world, as far as we know, were there such virulent manifestations of racial prejudice at this period.

Shortly afterwards, the Jews of Alexandria embarked on a massive counterblast to this type of disastrous publicity. It comprised, in the first place, a great Greek translation of the Bible. This language was now replacing Aramaic as the *lingua franca* throughout most of the near east, so that in Egypt, as elsewhere, it had become the Jewish community's ordinary medium of speech. The new Greek Bible came to be known as the Septuagint (from Latin *septuaginta*, seventy) because it was supposedly the work of seventy (or seventy-two) translators, working under divine inspiration. They drew on a Hebrew text – which later disappeared – and employed some Aramaic versions as well. The Septuagint also included fifteen books, excluded from the Hebrew canon, which Protestants later described as the Apocrypha (Appendix 7). Legend suggested that the whole of the Septuagint was created at one and the same date, under Ptolemy II. But in fact the translations took shape at various times, a few in slightly earlier periods (Appendix 8, s.v. Aristobulus), but mostly during Ptolemy II's reign or shortly afterwards. The work became immensely influential, because it decisively established the modes of diction and the concepts needed to render Jewish thought into the more cosmopolitan medium of the Greek tongue.

The Septuagint had the obvious effect of bringing Jewish and pagan thought much closer together, but this proved a curiously one-way traffic. The translation was supposedly devised to persuade the Greeks of the correctness of Judaism, but its influence in this direction was negligible or non-existent – even in Alexandria itself, where so many of the two peoples lived together. Indeed, Greek readers would only have found the biblical narratives and prophesies, even after translation, a puzzling and incomprehensible affair. So the version is scarcely referred to by classical authors. But for the Alexandrian Jews it fulfilled an enormous role. It became, in fact, their Bible, in place of the Hebrew Bible which most of them could not understand. And it remained a lasting inspiration. With its aid, these Jews of Alexandria became the only people in the Hellenistic and Roman empires who produced a Greek literature rivalling the contemporary output of the Greeks themselves in size and range. Indeed, in some ways they even outdid the Greeks, since one of these Jewish writers, in the first century AD, was Philo, whose attempt to bridge the gulf between Jewish and Greek thinking remained wholly unequalled. His

efforts, however, proved ultimately unsuccessful, because all such assimi-
lating tendencies were eclipsed and defeated by the entirely different,
more orthodox trends of Judaism that produced the Mishnah and
Talmud (Appendices 8, 10).

ii. Abomination of Desolation

As the third century proceeded on its course, Judaea continued to be a
bone of contention between the Ptolemies and their Seleucid neighbours
and rivals in Syria. In these struggles, the Ptolemies recruited mercenary
troops from the Idumaeans, descendants of the Edomites who had moved
up into the southern reaches of Judah. Finally, however, in 200, the
Seleucid monarch Antiochus III the Great decisively defeated the
Egyptian forces at Panion (Banyas) beside the headwaters of the Jordan,
and the country passed into Seleucid hands.

This transfer was welcome to many of its Jewish inhabitants, because
of their links with their co-religionists in Babylonia, which likewise
formed part of the Seleucid empire. And Antiochus III, on taking Judaea
over, upheld its national customs and autonomous status by a royal edict
(which is generally accepted as authentic).[7] Internal administration was
vested, as before, in the hands of the high priest and Council of Elders,
and at first the new suzerains permitted a considerable measure of autonomy. As in temple states in other Hellenistic kingdoms, the shrine at
Jerusalem was exempted from taxation, and the Zadokite high priest
Simon I the Just (son of Onias II), who had helped to bring about the
Seleucid take-over, was able to earn praise from his Jewish compatriots,
although he maintained a wealthy Greek way of living.[8]

It was at about this time, and no doubt with Simon's active encouragement, that the synagogue began to become a really important force in
Palestinian life. It was a combined 'house of gathering' (Bet ha-Keneset:
the parliament of modern Israel is known as the Knesset) and 'house of
prayer' (Bet Tefillah) and 'house of exegesis' (Bet ha-Midrash). Within
its walls the Torah – kept in an Ark or shrine at the east wall – was read
and taught and interpreted and studied; and fervent prayers were offered
for the revival of the nation, to the accompaniment of the singing of the
psalms, which now assumed their final form. Nor were material
amenities, such as guest accommodation, forgotten.

Although the origin of the synagogues is shrouded in uncertainty, it
should probably be ascribed, not to the time of Ezra, as has sometimes
been suggested, but to the ensuing Hellenistic age, when an example of
such a building is first identified at Schedia near Alexandria (Ch.17,i).
But although synagogues probably originated in the Dispersion, by the
early second century they had appeared in Judaea as well, as Ecclesiasticus

makes clear.[9] And now they multiplied rapidly, and became the focal points of Jewish spiritual and national life. They were vigorous and supple institutions, created by a remarkably literate people in response to their need for collective, congregational activities – the popular religious universities of the age.

However, life in Judaea under the Seleucids soon took a turn for the worse. Taxation increased sharply, until the land-tax amounted to as much as one-third of every crop. Moreover, under Seleucus IV (187–175), the Temple was plundered by one of his representatives (or, perhaps, its plunder was narrowly averted).

This is the juncture at which the shadow of the Romans first falls upon the scene. After their conquest of Italy, they had decisively defeated the Carthaginians of north Africa (240, 202) descended from Phoenician colonists. Next, as the second century began, they were involved in hostilities against the Hellenistic monarchies. In the course of these wars, they won a series of decisive victories against Antiochus III the Great, which deprived him of his position as a dominant eastern Mediterranean power (191–190). The tribute which the Seleucids, as a result of these disasters, were forced to pay Rome meant that the exactions that they themselves imposed upon their own subjects, including the Jews, inevitably became more stringent.

During these years two sharply differing attitudes towards Hellenism became ever more apparent among the Jews of the homeland. Their wealthy aristocracy, with its strong international connexions, led a school of thought convinced that a certain infusion of Greek ways had proved unavoidable, and indeed desirable, if their people was not to fall behind the modern, cosmopolitan world: 'Let us make a covenant with the Gentiles about us, for since we have been different from them, we have found many evils.'[10] Others, however, maintained with the utmost determination that all Greek influence ought to be rejected root and branch.

That was probably the attitude of Ben Sira (Sirach in Greek), the author of *Ecclesiasticus*. On internal evidence, its initial composition took place in about 190–180 BC. The original version, which was in classical Hebrew (though he himself probably spoke the more recent, Mishnaic form of the language, Appendix 10), only exists in substantial fragments, which were found in 1896. The book did not appear in the canonical Hebrew Bible, which was averse to including books attributed to named writers (other than ancient prophets), but a complete Greek version appears in the Apocrypha (Appendix 7), translated, we are told, by Ben Sira's grandson Joshua (Jeshua, Yeshua, transliterated as Jesus), who came to live in Egypt.[11] In consequence, the treatise became known as *The Wisdom of Jesus* – until its popularity in early Christian circles earned it the name of *Ecclesiasticus*, meaning 'the book of the Church'.

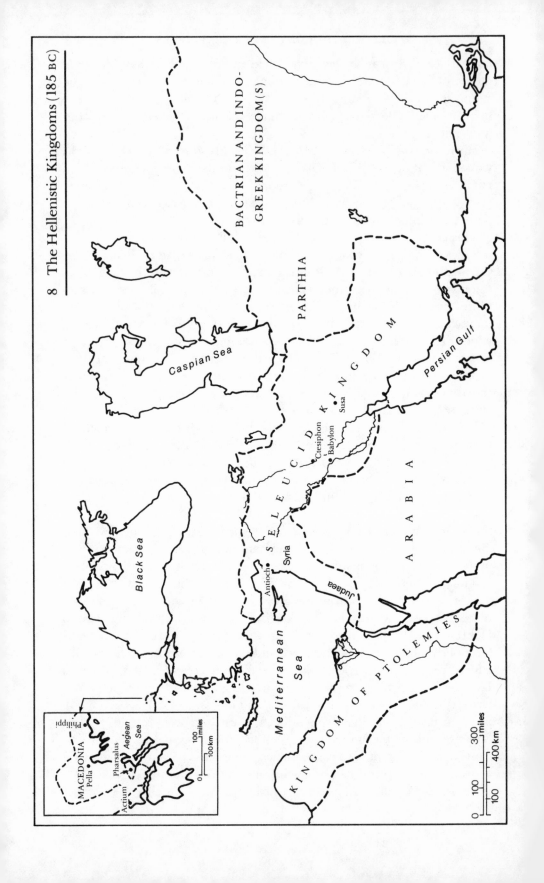

8 The Hellenistic Kingdoms (185 BC)

BACTRIAN AND INDO-GREEK KINGDOM(S)

PARTHIA

Caspian Sea

SELEUCID KINGDOM

Ctesiphon
Babylon
Susa

Persian Gulf

ARABIA

Black Sea

Antioch
Syria

Judaea

Mediterranean Sea

KINGDOM OF PTOLEMIES

MACEDONIA
Pella
Philippi
Pharsalus
Aegean Sea
Actium

0   100   miles
0   100km

0   100   300   miles
0   100   400   km

The former of these titles recalls that the work belongs to the wisdom tradition, which its author eloquently praises, treating wisdom itself as a personification, like the writer of *Job*. Ben Sira provides proverbial utterances and longer reflections upholding the moral aspects of the Torah and the moral accountability of Yahweh's people, and stressing the divine retribution that is visited on the wicked, a doctrine called into question not only by *Job* but by *Ecclesiastes* (Ch.15,i;17,i) – which this work may have been deliberately intended to refute. Unlike other wisdom writers, Ben Sira admires the spiritual values of the Temple and its priesthood. But he also very clearly wants to emphasize that the Torah is the channel by which the divine wisdom comes to Israel – he is the first writer who formally identifies the two.

A scribe and instructor of scribes, well-to-do, it would appear, but not wealthy, Ben Sira points out that a scholar needs ample leisure: 'If a man is to be wise, he must be relieved of other tasks.'[12] He offers a lot of detailed ethical and practical advice, highly conservative, and not unmixed with expediency and self-interest. He is sorry the poor are so poor, but there is nothing to be done about it, because the rulers have to side with the rich. Business is bound to make a man corrupt. Women should be kept in their place. Beating is a good thing, especially for daughters and servants. And, above all, the Jews must follow their own ancestral traditions: 'Let us now sing the praises of famous men, the heroes of our nation's history, through whom the Lord established his renown.'[13] More than once Ben Sira reasserts Jewish values against all others, against, that is to say, the views of the Greeks. 'For every nation Yahweh appointed a ruler, but chose Israel to be his own possession.'[14] The Mishnah would later put it more explicitly, and declare: 'Cursed be the man who would teach Greek wisdom to his son.'[15]

Already that was the very definite view of a puritanical, xenophobe, Yahwist group known as the Hasidim (meaning 'godly' or perhaps 'gracious'). They were first heard of in the early 160s (especially among the poor and in the villages), although they may already have existed at an earlier date. A movement of such a kind, taking up the inheritance of the Rechabites (Ch.10,ii), inevitably stimulated the growing tension between Judaism and Hellenism.

However, it was an issue on which the members of the dominant Tobiad family appeared to be split. They were also divided in their attitude to the unending friction between the Seleucids, now the rulers of Judaea, and the Ptolemies who had controlled the country before. Thus in *c.* 180 the high priest Onias III was suspected of preparing to use the Temple gold for pro-Ptolemaic subversion. But his brother Jason (Joshua, Jesus) remained loyal to the Seleucids, and paid Antiochus IV Epiphanes (175–163) an increased tribute in return for his own appointment to the high-priesthood in the place of Onias, who was assassinated not long afterwards. Backed by the Hellenizing party, Jason also purchased another and even more startling privilege from the king. This consisted of nothing less than the transformation of Jerusalem into a city with Greek institutions – or, possibly, a Greek communal organization (*politeuma*) was established alongside, and in addition to, the Temple-controlled Jewish community.[16]

The new entity, renamed Antiochia in Judaea, included such wholly un-Jewish features as a gymnasium, complete with a corps of young men (ephebes) who were uncircumcised and performed athletics in the nude. This caused enormous shock among orthodox Jews, besides widening still further the already yawning gulf between the rich and the poor, who had no part in the new Antiochia. Jason was overthrown and fled into exile (172), unseated by the even more pro-Greek Menelaus, apparently a member of a second-grade priestly house, so that the high-priesthood passed out of the Zadokite line.

Menelaus secured Seleucid backing for this irregular appointment by promising Antiochus IV even richer gifts than those which his predecessor had provided, including Temple plate; and he even went so far as to admit a Seleucid (Syrian) garrison into the newly built palace citadel in the lower city, the Akra. Not long afterwards, however, Jason came back and regained his former position, consigning Menelaus to prison. Jason also decided that his novel Greek institution of Antiochia had been a mistake – pressing things too far – and so he put an end to its existence, and, for good measure, expelled the foreign troops from the Akra fortress.

Antiochus IV, who was involved in hostilities with Egypt as well as with Parthian secessionists in Iran, suspected him of plotting a pro-Ptolemaic coup (in collusion with Alexandrian Jews), and saw these suspicions confirmed beyond a doubt when grave disturbances began to occur in Judaea, egged on, it appeared, by the new Hasidic movement. So he marched into the city of Jerusalem, pulled down its walls, looted its Temple treasure, and brought back Menelaus and the Syrian garrison, fortifying the citadel for their defence, and for the protection of their Hellenizing supporters, who flocked there for safety (169 or 168).

Antiochus then proceeded to cause this group still greater satisfaction when he forbade the Jews, in all parts of the country, to practise circumcision or celebrate the Sabbath, ordering them instead to offer sacrifices to the pagan gods. Next he took a step which seemed to the horrified Jewish community the ultimate 'abomination of desolation', the abominable thing that causes desolation, or appals,[17] for in 167 he formally rededicated the Jerusalem Temple as a shrine of the supreme Greek deity, Olympian Zeus.

This was part of a general policy of Hellenizing local communities, all over his empire, so that their divergent cultures might be unified, and resistance to the central authority consequently diminished. At a time when the merging (syncretism) of religions was such a fashionable idea throughout the Hellenistic world, it seemed to him and the men around him that the local Jewish god could easily be assimilated to Zeus; after all, under his eastern name of Zeus Sabazios, some Jews already identified him with Yahweh under the latter's name of 'Sabaoth' (which may mean Lord of the Armies). Moreover, the Samaritans (or at least the Greek colonists in Samaria) had actually requested that their shrine should be Hellenized in the same manner (Appendix 6)!

But Olympian Zeus was equated, in local terms, with the Syrian and Phoenician (Canaanite) Baal Shamin, already worshipped by the Syrian troops in Jerusalem. Throughout the entire history of Israel there had existed a connexion and conflict between Yahwist belief and the nature worship of the Canaanites, Phoenicians and Aramaeans. Now, however, this age-old interaction had entered upon a new phase, in which the Hellenistic suzerains were actually identifying Yahweh with Baal.

This was, to say the least, undiplomatic, but so was Antiochus' whole course of action. Elsewhere in his dominions he had never gone so far as to attempt the total obliteration of a foreign temple cult – which was what he proposed now, for Judaism became virtually prohibited. In attempting this, he was badly advised, for if he and his counsellors thought that these aims could be painlessly achieved, they were seriously mistaken. Instead, an irreparable breach occurred, and its outcome was the forcible termination of Seleucid and foreign rule throughout the country.

CHAPTER 18

INDEPENDENCE REGAINED

i. The Maccabean Revolt

The attempt by Antiochus IV to suppress Judaism provoked a popular rebellion. It is known as the Maccabean Revolt because it was led by a family of that name; the word may mean 'hammerers'. They were also called Hasmonaeans, perhaps after an ancestor Hasmon. They belonged to the priestly clan of Joarib – though not to the House of Zadok, descended from Aaron, which until recently had monopolized the high-priesthood.

The outbreak began when an aged member of the Hasmonaean family, Mattathias, refused to offer the first pagan sacrifice at his birthplace Modein (not far from Lydda now Lod), and then struck down a Jew who had shown willingness to comply. Thereupon Mattathias, to escape official retaliation, took to the Gophna hills, up the Beth-horon pass, together with his five never-to-be-forgotten sons, and an increasing number of Jews rallied to his side. The pious Hasidim were among them (Ch.17,ii). Many of those attracted to the cause came from the poorer elements of society, so that the rebellion assumed the aspect of class warfare.

After his death in 166, Mattathias was succeeded by his son Judas (Yehudah) Maccabaeus, a guerrilla genius upon whom subsequent resistance leaders have looked back admiringly as a model. His Hasidic followers, throughout the towns and villages, inspired an exalted enthusiasm for the idea of religious martyrdom, which was to play a prominent part in Jewish and Christian thinking for many centuries to come. In defence of the Law, Judas exterminated people of Hellenizing tendencies, but he also subjected the Seleucid army of occupation to violent attacks, which were crowned by the recapture of Jerusalem. In 164, the Temple was reconsecrated. The event (dramatized by a miraculous supply of oil) has been commemorated ever since by the Festival of the Dedication or of Lights (Hanukkah) – a new sort of feast, because all such occasions hitherto had been based on the Torah. The lights were kindled in a

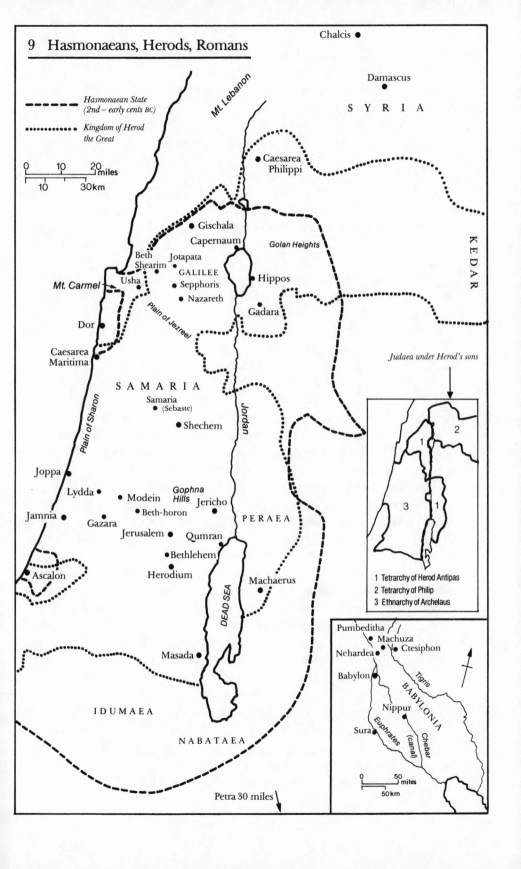

9 Hasmonaeans, Herods, Romans

Hasmonaean State
(2nd – early cents BC)

Kingdom of Herod
the Great

0   10   20 miles
10   30km

Chalcis

Damascus

SYRIA

Caesarea
Philippi

KEDAR

Mt. Lebanon

Gischala

Capernaum

Golan Heights

Beth
Shearim   Jotapata

Usha   GALILEE

Hippos

Mt. Carmel

Sepphoris

Nazareth

Gadara

Dor

Plain of Jezreel

Caesarea
Maritima

Judaea under Herod's sons

2

SAMARIA

1

3

Samaria
(Sebaste)

1

Shechem

Jordan

Plain of Sharon

Joppa

Lydda

*Gophna
Hills*

Jericho

PERAEA

1 Tetrarchy of Herod Antipas
2 Tetrarchy of Philip
3 Ethnarchy of Archelaus

Modein

Beth-horon

Jamnia

Gazara

Jerusalem

Qumran

Pumbeditha

Machuza

Bethlehem

Nehardea

Ctesiphon

Ascalon

Herodium

Machaerus

Babylon

BABYLONIA

DEAD SEA

Nippur

Tigris

(canal)

Chebar

Masada

Sura

Euphrates

IDUMAEA

0   50 miles

50km

NABATAEA

Petra 30 miles

seven-branched candelabrum known as the Menorah, which became the national emblem of the modern Jewish state.

Judas Maccabaeus then proceeded to make a treaty with the Roman Republic, which was only too glad to undermine Seleucid power in any way it could (162–160). This association, renewed nearly twenty years later, came to seem embarrassing and distasteful to later Jewish writers, but it was because the Romans, in the last resort, had stood behind Judas that he was able to survive. Since his origins disqualified him from the high-priesthood, a certain Alcimus (Eliakim), claiming descent from Aaron (though not through the Zadokite branch), took over the office (162). An unsuccessful contender for the post, Onias IV, fled to Egypt where he founded a schismatic copy of the Temple at Leontopolis (Appendix 6). Meanwhile, in Judaea, Alcimus – who despite his priestly background was a moderate Hellenizer – turned against the Hasidim, who had become vociferously disillusioned with the worldliness of the new regime, and had sixty of them executed.

In 160 Judas fell in battle, and was succeeded by his brother Jonathan (Yehonatan). At about the same time the high priest Alcimus died, and after a seven-year interregnum Jonathan, ignoring his family disqualification, allowed a national gathering to appoint him to that office in addition to his secular rulership, thus stirring up trouble for the future. Jonathan also gained access to the Mediterranean by depriving the Seleucids of the port of Joppa. However, he then considered it prudent to provide them with military aid. This enabled him to secure their recognition as 'governor of Judaea', which amounted to virtual sovereignty, though this was still not formally granted. Like Judas, he died fighting.

Their last surviving brother Simon, however, succeeded in asserting formal independence from the Seleucids, expelling their garrison from the Jerusalem citadel (142–141), capturing the fortress of Gazara (Gezer), and compelling the Seleucid monarch, whose kingdom was racked by internal struggles, to acquiesce. Thus the Maccabean Rebellion had finally triumphed – the only successful revolt, in defence of religion, that the history of the ancient world can provide. Henceforward, for eighty years to come (with only a brief intermission), there was to be a free Jewish state once again, the first for four and a half centuries. Simon launched this new order by assuming the hereditary title not only of high priest but of 'ethnarch', a designation which fell short of kingship but signified the ruler of an *ethnos* (nation).

Jewish feelings during the period of the Maccabean liberation are illustrated by the *Book of Daniel*, but it ostensibly deals with events belonging to the reign of Jehoiakim of Judah (608–598). Daniel was a legendary personage of that name, bearing an old Canaanite name.

The book begins by describing how he was deported from Judah to

Babylon and brought up at the court of King Nebuchadrezzar II, together with his three companions Shadrach, Meshach and Abednego. Daniel interpreted to Nebuchadrezzar a dream which had baffled the wise men of Babylon, and received a rich reward. His three companions, however, who refused to worship a golden idol, were cast into a fiery furnace. But Yahweh intervened to rescue them; and Daniel himself, thrown into a den of lions, received similar divine protection.

After another dream, Nebuchadrezzar went mad for seven years, until Daniel restored his sanity, whereupon the king proclaimed the praises of Yahweh. But then came the sacrilegious feast of the crown prince Belshazzar. On this occasion, all who were present offered worship to their gods of gold and silver, bronze and iron, or wood and stone. Suddenly, however, a miraculous writing was seen on the wall,[1] Belshazzar became limp in every limb, and his knees knocked together; Daniel correctly interpreted the portent as forecasting the collapse of Babylonia before the armies of the Medes and Persians (Ch.15,ii).

The second half of the work describes four visions, in which Daniel symbolically reveals the course of history from the sixth to the second centuries, spanning the fall, not only of the Babylonian empire, but of its Median, Persian and Hellenistic successors as well.

The book is a collection of popular fables of various epochs, brought together by an unknown author or compiler, writing in Aramaic in c. 160 (the version that has survived is also partly in Hebrew). Certain other stories about Daniel did not find their way into the scriptural canon (Appendix 4), but respect for his antique figure secured the admission of this principal book bearing his name, which thus became one of the latest writings to qualify as canonical.

Yet although the stories are attributed to the remote past, Daniel's salvation from the lion's den, and the deliverance of his three companions from the fiery furnace, are intended to allude to the persecutions inflicted by the contemporary Seleucid monarch Antiochus IV Epiphanes (Ch.17,ii). Throughout centuries to come, these encouraging and inspiring tales, and Daniel's visions, stirred the emotions of oppressed Jews and Christians.

And so did his theology: for the book strongly revives the old prophetic, utopian assurance that Israel's tribulation shall end when Yahweh's kingdom comes into its own on the Last Day, and the enemies of his people shall be consigned to anguish and affliction. This is the theme, foreshadowed by earlier authors such as Ezekiel (Ch.14,i), which was destined to dominate that abundant mass of 'apocalyptic' Jewish writings (from the Greek verb *apocalyptein*, to reveal or uncover). In telling of the future, if distant, downfall of mighty, hostile monarchs and empires, the apocalyptic authors offer vivid, weird, mysterious, symbolic revelations concerning the Last Day or Days, and the marvels and upheavals that will be a feature of this shattering, glorious time.

Orthodox opinion pronounced that the age of the prophets was suspended (though it would one day revive).[2] But the apocalyptists, their imagination kindled by the crisis under Antiochus IV, were convinced that they themselves stood right at the centre of the ancient prophetic tradition. And indeed their vivid contrasts between the dark, hard, present age and the resplendent epoch that lay ahead seemed to the new generation to express its plight and prospects better than all the promises of the ancient prophets – which had scarcely been fulfilled. In this time of acute convulsion and hardship (as in later disturbed periods of world history as well) their sensational forecasts provided spiritual comfort and psychological escape. And in this task of encouragement the *Book of Daniel* took the lead. Although officially and ostensibly resuscitating the prophetic tradition – and strongly dependent on the wisdom tradition as well – it is essentially apocalyptic in character. Such works are staged in ancient settings because they claim to reveal divine secrets conveyed to famous figures of the past, and written down on secret scrolls.[3]

The apocalyptic portions of *Daniel* are full of anti-Gentile feeling, possibly under the influence of the militant Hasidic movement (Ch.17,ii), and the narrative passages offer a heartfelt invitation to heroic martyrdom, which at the time was beginning to arouse such enthusiasm, whipped up, no doubt, by works such as this. Nevertheless, the Maccabee leaders are not seen as perfect; they still need to be 'tested, refined and made shining white'. And, in any case, Yahweh will intervene at the right moment (not necessarily soon) without the need for any independent action by ordinary men and women. The author of the *Book of Daniel* is following up the belief of Ezekiel that the future Golden Age will assume a supernatural character (Ch.14,i). He also agrees that a liberator or liberators will arrive. Some had said that Elijah would return. The present writer identifies the saviour, at one point, with the archangel Michael: for Persian ideas of angelic intermediaries, already present in earlier parts of the Bible (Chs.9,i;11,i), were becoming increasingly current.

Daniel also declared that the Last Day would be heralded by 'the appearance of one anointed (*mashiah*), a prince'.[4] *Mashiah*, anointed, means no more than a sacred person or legitimate ruler, and the Hebrew Bible never identifies him with an expected superhuman Messiah. Moreover, 'at the critical time . . . he shall be removed with no one to take his part'. The ultimate saviour, therefore, will not be he, but another. For it was revealed to Daniel, in a further vision, that a Son of Man, or One Like a Man (Aramaic *bar nash[a]*), will come with the clouds of heaven, and be invested by Yahweh with everlasting sovereignty and glory, and universal kingly power.[5]

We appear to be back among the ancient concepts of Canaanite religion, in which one god (Baal) was enthroned by another (El). Yet, in keeping with the Hebrew propensity for collective personification (seen in *Second Isaiah* and elsewhere), the *Book of Daniel* appears to endow the phrase 'Son of Man' with a corporate significance – in the immediate context, as a designation embracing all the martyrs persecuted by Antiochus IV, and in a longer view as a symbol for the elect, saved Remnant of the Jewish community as a whole. In the course of the next century, however, as the idea of an eventual cosmic, celestial messianic deliverer (and no longer merely an earthly Davidic leader) rapidly grew, the Son of Man was being spoken and written about as a single saviour, a chosen heavenly personage.[6] The Son of Man with whom the Christian gospels identify Jesus is the direct heir to this way of thinking (Appendix 9).

Another of the *Book of Daniel*'s themes, which influenced Christianity with equally compelling force, was his insistence on the survival of the individual dead. This provides a sharp contrast with the usual Jewish view of an entirely shadowy existence (in Sheol) after death: the Torah is *Torah hayim*, of the living. And the author of *Daniel* did not see this survival as just a recurrence of the heavenly ascensions of particularly venerated figures such as Enoch, Moses and Elijah. For he believed instead that it would apply to the entire Jewish Remnant which would be saved on the Last Day (and to their enemies who would be punished at the same time). He did not envisage immortality of the soul, which was a Greek and not a Hebrew conception. What he had in mind was actual *bodily* resurrection – involving a return upon this earth – to which he offers the only unmistakable, undisputed reference in the entire canonical Hebrew Bible, though the Christians stressed the concept later on.

> At that moment your people will be delivered [*or* will escape],
>   Every one that is written in the book:
> Many of those who sleep in the dust of the earth will wake,
>   Some to everlasting life
> And some to the reproach of eternal abhorrence.[7]

We are back with the old question that had caused *Job* and others such great anxiety: why do the good fail to prosper, and the unrighteous flourish? But now the answer is a new one. Reward and retribution *will* duly and deservedly come – not in our own present life, however, but posthumously, at the end of the world. This was an attempt to harmonize the divine justice with the brutal facts of human existence, an encouragement to defy the oppressions of earthly masters and overlords. It became a cardinal belief of the most influential group of Jews of the ensuing period, whose views will now be discussed.

ii. Jewish Groups and the Monarchy

Although all Jews professed complete devotion to the Torah, this was a time when open divergences of opinion within their ranks were more numerous, mere far-reaching and more productive of lively intellectual exploration than ever before. Among the many religious movements of the time, the Jewish historian Josephus (Ch.20,ii) singled out three. This oversimplified a complex, fragmented picture. Yet the groups or sects he described were of pre-eminent significance.

One of them consisted of the Sadducees, a name which may have been derived from King David's priest Zadok. They were a fairly small group of rich and influential men, landowners for the most part, but also including the hereditary priests in control of the Temple. Its rituals appeared to them more important than attempts to interpret the Torah, which they accepted in its written form just as it was, without seeing any need for additional commentaries. Speculations about the end of the world they dismissed as modern, unauthoritative, and potentially subversive, for allusions to apocalyptic liberators savoured of possible disloyalty to the Hasmonaean regime, which they increasingly supported. But a balanced view of the Sadducees is hard to achieve, because our sources of information all treat them with hostility. For Christian writers detested them, and many Jews, too, misrepresented their attitudes, declaring them, for example, extreme Hellenists, which they were not. If their comparatively passive ways of thinking had prevailed, the future life of the Jews would have been much more static and much less spiritual; but they would probably never have revolted against the Romans (Ch.20,ii).

The second, major group, consisting of the Pharisees, are equally hard to assess fairly, because they too incurred the enmity of the Gospels. Like the Sadducees, they were laymen, but mainly of middle-class origin. Their name seems to have come from a word meaning 'separators' or 'separated', indicating their intention to withdraw from everything that is sinful or unclean. They themselves, however, preferred to be called Haberim, meaning equals or associates or fellow members. Their rise dates from the years when the Hasidim, to whom they owed considerable debts, broke with the Hasmonaean regime because of its secular character. What the Pharisees particularly objected to was Jonathan's assumption of the high-priesthood, for which his family origins technically made him ineligible. However, they were not, at least at this early stage, political activists or agitators. On the contrary, they advocated submissive acceptance of the will of Yahweh, even if that meant endurance of worldly injustice and persecution.

Like the author of the *Book of Daniel*, they believed that individuals would eventually return to the earth, resurrected in bodily form

216

(Ch.18,i). However, in contrast to *Daniel* and other apocalyptic writings, they discounted the expectation of a violent, universal upheaval on the Last Day, for this idea had been foreign to the Torah, and could not therefore, in their view, be right. Some of the Pharisees came to be criticized by their enemies as unduly formalistic and complacent. The charge of 'hypocrisy' was also directed against them by apocalyptically-minded Jews (and then taken up by the Christians), because of their scepticism about the Last Day. But such accusations did scant justice to the Pharisees' progressive qualities. Religion, they felt, should be a source not of gloom but of satisfaction and happiness. Moreover, they were eager to make the Bible applicable to modern needs by offering oral expositions of the text, declaring that this procedure, already adopted by Ezra (Ch.16,i), had been commended to Moses by Yahweh at the same time as the Torah, of which it formed an integral component. For example, in opposition to the Sadducees' inflexible literalism, they interpreted 'an eye for an eye' in terms of monetary compensation. In contrast, once again, to the Sadducees' exclusive emphasis on the Temple, the Pharisees centred their activities on the synagogues (Ch.17,ii), which now existed in every Jewish town. They also took a keen interest in the burning social problems of the day. For Judaea was an impoverished country, and the Pharisaic leaders showed concern for its ordinary people, the poor and oppressed.

In addition, they were active throughout the Dispersion, where their willingness to accept the existing political authorities made it easy for them to flourish, and their missionary success – though the desirability of such enterprises had long been a controversial matter among Jewish thinkers – was recognized even by their enemies.[8] It also exercised an effect on their own methods of biblical interpretation, in Judaea itself as well as other countries. For although they were anxious to avoid pollution by Greek culture, their attitudes could not fail to be influenced, at least indirectly, by contemporary techniques of Hellenistic scholarship, seeping through, in particular, from Graeco-Jewish Alexandria.

The Pharisees' agents and assistants were scribes (*sopherim*) or professional lawyers. There had been scribes, of some kind or other, for many centuries – perhaps going right back to the age of Solomon, when the wisdom tradition appears to have taken shape – and then again in the times of Jeremiah and Ezekiel, and particularly under the guidance of Ezra. The scribes had fluctuated in importance, but now, with men of the calibre of Ben Sira (*Ecclesiasticus*, Ch.17,ii) conducting schools to train their aspirants, they had increasingly come to form a recognizable class, an intellectual élite. In cooperation with the Pharisees, it was they who decided what conduct was required, in all practical details, in order to put the prescriptions of the Law into everyday effect.

Like their Pharisaic allies, these scribes played a leading part in a religious and legislative body known as the *beth din* (court) or Great Sanhedrin (from the Greek *synedrion*, assembly) which became prominent at this time (alongside the political and judicial Council of Elders, presided over by the kings, confusingly sometimes known by the same name). The Great Sanhedrin possessed seventy or seventy-one members, under the joint chairmanship of successive pairs of scholars (*zugoth*) – a president (*nasi*, 'prince') and vice-president (*ab beth din*, 'father of the court') – chosen to represent majority and minority points of view respectively. This committee was much concerned with biblical commentary, but it also passed measures concerning universal education, the rights of women, and proper procedures in courts of law.

By such means the scribes and their associates exerted a large influence on public opinion. The ideal scribe earns superlative praise from Ben Sira,[9] and outside Judaea, too, wherever there was a Jewish community, the same pattern repeated itself: scribes as well as Pharisees became eminent as expounders and interpreters and missionaries throughout the Dispersion.

The third of the principal groups singled out by Josephus consisted of the Essenes.[10] In some respects, they resembled the Pharisees, for they, too, may have been an offshoot of the Hasidim; their name is probably derived from the Aramaic *hasa*, 'pious'. And they too, although both Hellenizers and worldly Sadducees inspired them with equal disgust, tried to make it their practice never to clash with the political power – even maintaining that no ruler rules except by Yahweh's will. And yet, once again like the Pharisees, they felt obliged to show opposition to the leadership of Jonathan, whose appointment to the high-priesthood they deplored and rejected. Moreover, the Essenes went further still, maintaining that the only true representatives of the high-priestly tradition were now themselves. Thus their forecasts of the end of the world seemed to be endowed with peculiar authenticity. But their prophecies differed from those of the Pharisees – unless Josephus is misleadingly equating them with Greek ascetic communities – because they were said to disbelieve in bodily resurrection, adhering instead to the Hellenic doctrine of the immortality of the soul.

However, what particularly differentiated them from Pharisees and Sadducees alike was the way in which they lived. Said to number about four thousand, they (or many of them) withdrew into semi-monastic communities, devoting all their time to observing the Torah in every meticulous detail. The sect which produced the Dead Sea scrolls seems to have been Essene, or related to the Essenes. This was a group, founded in 140–130, whose numerous documents, in the form of leather scrolls, have been discovered near their retreat at Khirbet Qumran, not far from the

Dead Sea. This literature is the work of a devoted, fanatical community. Detesting the Hasmonaean priestly kingship, and claiming a mysterious Teacher of Righteousness as their own leader instead, the Qumran community believed that they alone were members of the new covenant prophesied by Jeremiah, and the faithful Remnant of their time; indeed the final future Remnant at the end of the whole of time.[11]

An apocalyptic, messianic doctrine of the end of the world, accompanied by bodily resurrection, appears in a highly developed form among these austere perfectionists. Their *Community Rule* (*Manual of Discipline*) and *War Rule* saw this cataclysm as preceded by a tremendous struggle between the powers of good and evil.[12] The hosts of evil are led by Satan, no longer a member of Yahweh's court, as in the prologue of *Job*, but now manifestly the Prince of Darkness himself. For the Qumran community had gone very far indeed towards abandoning the traditional biblical concept of the good God's sole control over the world he has created. Instead, they cherished dualistic beliefs in warring forces of light and darkness – beliefs ultimately of Persian origin, but filtered through the general, international, apocalyptic ideas of the Hellenistic age.

And so the Qumran recluses envisaged a primeval, continuing struggle between these two opposing, contrasted forces. A forty-year war between Israel and the nations would follow, but then Israel, spurred on by Yahweh, would win, and judge the world. This polarity between the good and evil forces earned the grave disapproval of more orthodox, monotheistic opinion, and never joined the mainstream of Jewish thought. Strong traces of such views, however, could be detected in Christian writings,[13] and a dualistic faith later formed the basis of a great, international Manichaean religion, founded by Mani in Persia during the third century AD.

When the last of the Maccabee brothers, Simon, had been assassinated by his son-in-law (135), the Seleucid monarch Antiochus VII Sidetes succeeded in reconquering the Jewish state. After his death in 129, however, Simon's son John (Yehohanan) Hyrcanus I (134–104) – who derived this name from a Jewish settlement in Hyrcania on the Caspian – reasserted the national independence. This he did by renewing the Hasmonaeans' treaty with Rome, so that neither the Seleucids nor the Ptolemies dared encroach upon his frontiers. Thus secured, John Hyrcanus extended his possessions very substantially indeed, with the backing of a useful army of mercenaries. The territories of Samaria, Galilee and Idumaea were all annexed. John Hyrcanus particularly disliked the Samaritans, because they belonged to an independent sect (Appendix 6), and had opposed the Maccabee rebellion. So he now proceeded to raze their shrine on Mount Gerizim to the ground, as well as destroying the Hellenized town of Samaria.

In Idumaea, the southern borderland to which the Edomites had fled from the Arabs four centuries earlier (Ch.16,i), the population found itself compelled to adopt the Jewish religion and accept forcible circumcision. Fertile Galilee had already become partially Judaized in earlier times, but John Hyrcanus I, overrunning the territory, vigorously completed the process; so that the country in which Jesus was to preach had not been Jewish for longer than a century and a half. The Pharisees refused to regard these compulsory conversions as valid (thus bringing the king even closer to the rival Sadducee movement). Nevertheless, he recruited many useful soldiers from these newly conquered lands; and he had made his country an important military power.

His influence also extended widely into the large areas of the Dispersion under Roman rule. Thus a decree of the Greek city of Laodicea on the Lycus in Phrygia, which formed part of Rome's new province of Asia, confirms its acceptance of a Roman request, prompted by John Hyrcanus, that the local Jewish community should be allowed freedom of worship; and another city, Tralles in Lydia, was compelled to withdraw its objection to a similar measure.[14] Simultaneously, however, in all parts of the near east anti-Semitic writings were now becoming increasingly abundant, although Jewish authors in Alexandria and elsewhere were busy composing Greek books and pamphlets intended to refute the sometimes wild and ludicrous accusations which these pamphlets put forward (Appendix 8).

At home in Judaea, on the other hand, the *First Book of Maccabees* remains convinced that Hellenism is the root of all evils. The Hebrew original of the work is lost, and its Greek version, which is what we possess, may have been designed for the Jews of Alexandria. The unknown writer, perhaps of Sadducee allegiance, offers a semi-official review of the achievements of the Hasmonaean House, from the time of Antiochus IV's persecutions down to *c.* 125. A second edition was completed after the death of John Hyrcanus I, whose exploits, the editor notes, were also recorded 'in the annals of his high-priesthood.'[15]

Unlike the pietistic compiler of *2 Maccabees* (translator of a work on the period 176–161 by Jason of Cyrene,[16] written for the Jews of Alexandria), the author of the *First Book* possesses many of the qualities of a serious factual historian – although the documents he quotes do not always look authentic. He is a very strong nationalist, utterly dedicated to the leaders of the dynasty: 'Let the high praises of God be on their lips,' in the words of a psalmist, 'and a two-edged sword in their hand.'[17] This ardent attachment denied his book a place in the biblical canon (though like *2 Maccabees* it appears in the Apocrypha, Appendix 7), since the devout guardians of this process objected so greatly to the merger of the monarchy with the high-priesthood. Nor, probably, did they like the writer's failure to make any direct reference to Yahweh – or his eulogy of the Hasmonaeans' allies, the Romans.

Devout Jews also deplored the rapidly increasing Hellenization of the professedly Yahwist court, which, despite these paeans to its militant piety, was gradually assuming the Greek appearance of any small Hellenistic princedom of the time: indeed, Aristobulus (Yehudah) I (104–103), the son of John Hyrcanus I, even adopted the title 'Greek-lover' (Philhellen) as his preferred self-description.[18]

His brother and successor Alexander Jannaeus (Yehonatan, 103–76), who maintained a particularly luxurious, secular way of life, seems to have been the earliest member of his house to assume the title of king,[19] and he may also have been the first to issue a national coinage (though some authorities place this a little earlier). It bears Greek as well as Jewish inscriptions, and displays the un-Jewish maritime symbol of an anchor.[20] This design, imitated from Seleucid issues, proudly recalled that Alexander Jannaeus was able to establish his power over virtually the entire Judaean coast, all the way from Egypt to Mount Carmel. Externally Hellenized though he was, the Greek cities suffered greatly from his brutality, which put an end to any possibility of inter-racial collaboration; alone among them, Ascalon (Ashkelon) in Philistia escaped his clutches.

He also successfully confronted the Nabataeans of northern Arabia. These were Arabs, employing Aramaic as their written language and writing in an Aramaic script (the Arabic alphabet was not created for another millennium), who had become the successors of the kingdom of Dedan (Kebar) in the fourth century, establishing their capital at Petra (the former Edomite capital Sela, in what is now the state of Jordan). As time went on, the Nabataeans extended their influence over the spice route as far as the Mediterranean. Alexander Jannaeus' victories over their army gained him Gaza, and twelve cities across the Jordan as well. Never since the time of Solomon had a Jewish ruler controlled so much territory.

These advances brought him into touch with the Parthians, speakers of an Iranian language who had broken away from the Seleucids and asserted their independence, subsequently expanding from their Persian homeland into Babylonia. Alexander Jannaeus was interested to receive a visit from their envoys, since Babylonia was still densely populated with Jews, descendants of the sixth-century Dispersion. Their communities contributed generously towards the tax payable to the Temple, which was brought annually by great convoys of armed pilgrims.

But the Parthian delegates found a good deal of discontent at Jerusalem. Many of its religious leaders disapproved of the Hellenization of the Hasmonaean court, and they also claimed that the new title of king reduced the authority of the Council of Elders – besides continuing to repeat that the monarch had no right to be the high priest as well.[21] At one stage, numerous Pharisees abandoned their rule of keeping the peace, and broke into active revolt against Alexander. In the course of a savage civil war they even, it now appears, seized Jerusalem and the royal mint, and issued coins of their own in the name of the Council, employing an archaic Hebrew script (c. 88).[22] But the failure of their rebellion cost them hundreds of lives.

Alexander's widow and successor Salome Alexandra (Shelomziyyon, 76–67), totally reversed his religious policy, treating such Pharisees as survived with marked favour. They and their allies the scribes dominated her Council and the Great Sanhedrin – over which her eminent brother Simeon ben Shetah presided – and employed their position to harry the Sadducees. The Jews had not been ruled by a woman since the time of the ill-fated Athaliah (Ch.12,ii). Obviously, a person of her sex could not hold the high-priesthood, which went instead to her eldest son John (Yehohanan) Hyrcanus II. He was not, however, a strong personality, and, when he became king after her death, deferred to the guidance of Antipater, a powerful hereditary chieftain from recently converted Idumaea. The Hasmonaean kingdom now went rapidly into decline. John Hyrcanus II, egged on by Antipater, came into conflict with his brother Aristobulus II; and Antipater invited the Nabataean Arabs to march on Jerusalem and assist his cause. They were doing so with some success when important and ominous news arrived: the Romans had appeared in Syria (63).

During the second and early first centuries, the Roman Republic had been gradually extending control over the entire Mediterranean area; and what had happened now was that its leading personage, Gnaeus Pompeius (Pompey the Great), abolished the shrunken Seleucid monarchy altogether, converting its remnant into the Roman province of Syria. The new province would be welcome to Rome for its riches, but was also intended as a bastion against the hostile Parthian rulers of Iran and Mesopotamia. A new epoch for the entire near east had begun.

Part Seven

ROMAN DEPENDENCY

CHAPTER 19

HEROD THE GREAT

i. The Roman Background

Now that Pompey the Great, on behalf of the Roman Republic, had put an end to the Seleucid kingdom and annexed Syria, it was inevitable that Judaea, too, must fall within the Roman orbit. So its quarrelling Hasmonaean rulers, John Hyrcanus II and his brother Aristobulus II, lost no time in appealing to Pompey. Aristobulus first received his guarded backing, but then proved recalcitrant. So Pompey seized Jerusalem, slaughtered many of its inhabitants, and stepped inside the Temple's Holy of Holies, thus committing an act regarded by the Jews as outrageous and blasphemous.

Judaea became a client-state of Rome, not regaining its full independence until AD 1948. Under Roman suzerainty, John Hyrcanus II – still guided by his Idumaean adviser Antipater – was retained as high priest and titular head of a small and divided territory, including inland Judaea and Galilee, but not their bridge territory of Samaria. Hyrcanus was demoted from the status of king, receiving in exchange the inferior princely designation of ethnarch (the title of Simon Maccabaeus a century earlier). In compensation, however, the Romans confirmed his hereditary right to intervene in matters relating to the Jewish Dispersion,[1] which was increasing in numbers and importance since the disturbances in Judaea had greatly swollen emigration. Five years later, however, after further troubles in the country, the Romans deprived him of his position as ethnarch. He was permitted to retain the high-priesthood, combined with a general supervision of Jerusalem, but the country was carved up into five diminutive units, each under a council of leading local figures, mostly from the ranks of the Sadducee nobility. Antipater, however, who pursued a policy of active collaboration with the Romans, retained a prominent position. He was put in charge of his native Idumaea, and received special powers in Jerusalem itself, including tax-collecting rights.

Meanwhile Rome had come under the virtually dictatorial rule of the first Triumvirate, Pompey, Julius Caesar and Crassus. Crassus plundered the treasure of the Jerusalem Temple, and suppressed a revolt in Galilee; but then he met his death at the hands of the Parthians, at Carrhae (Haran) in 53. Four years later, Pompey and Caesar drifted into civil war. Despite the recollection of Pompey's entry into the Holy of Holies, John Hyrcanus II and Antipater chose to take his side, or were forced to, but after Pompey's defeat at Pharsalus and subsequent death in Egypt (48) (still, precariously, an independent Ptolemaic state), they were able to give Caesar valuable assistance. For, while mediating, ostensibly, between two youthful Egyptian monarchs, Ptolemy XII and Cleopatra VII, but in fact supporting Cleopatra who had become his mistress, Caesar found himself hemmed in by hostile Egyptian forces at Alexandria, and a relief army sent to assist him was held up on the southern borders of Judaea. At this point, however, Antipater, accompanied by John Hyrcanus II and a military force, proceeded to Ascalon and helped the relieving Roman army on its way.

When, therefore, Caesar subsequently defeated his enemies in Egypt and reinstated Cleopatra as his client, he gave the Jews their reward. John Hyrcanus' former state was restored to him, and enlarged to include Joppa and the plain of Jezreel. He himself resumed his title of ethnarch, and his coins describe him as President of the Council of Elders[2]. Antipater was recognized as chief minister, and his fiscal privileges extended to include the collection of the Roman land-tax throughout the country.

Following the precedents of Hellenistic and Roman predecessors, Caesar introduced a series of measures safeguarding the status of Jewish communities in the countries of the Dispersion. Greek cities were ordered to allow them liberty of worship and observance, freedom to dispatch gifts to the Jerusalem Temple, the right to employ their own jurisdiction, and exemption from military service. Pagan cults, after all, tolerated one another's existence; and the Roman administration usually took the view that, provided disturbances of the peace did not occur, communities of all races and faiths should be authorized to maintain their own religious and cultural customs. Despite, however, the frequent reiteration of Caesar's pro-Jewish measures by subsequent Roman rulers, the Greek cities, in which anti-Semitic feelings were strong, proved reluctant to comply.

Nevertheless, the comparatively favourable attitude of the imperial power, and their own determined capacity for hard work, meant that the numbers of Jews throughout the Dispersion continued to rise. At a guess – more we cannot achieve – there may have been eight million people professing the Jewish religion in the world (as against fourteen million today). Something like a million apparently lived in Babylonia, at this time a country under Parthian dominions. Of the remainder, about half dwelt within the Roman empire, and the other half in client states that depended on it, perhaps constituting something over six per cent of the total number of inhabitants of these territories. The provinces of the Roman empire that contained the most Jews were Syria and Asia (western Asia Minor).

In Syria, they apparently numbered more than three quarters of a million, the descendants of people who had been migrating from Judaea and Babylonia ever since the beginnings of the Hellenistic age.[3] A substantial number of settlers had also made their way to Asia Minor, initially under Antiochus III. It is from this region that all the known Roman edicts ordering the maintenance of their privileges happen to come. But that, it would seem, is a historical accident, since there must have been similar decrees applying to other Dispersion lands as well.

The state of Judaea that was now an indirect Roman dependency seems to have possessed a population of about two and a half million. A further million Jews probably resided in Egypt, expanded from the groups who had arrived there under the first Ptolemies (and before). Their autonomous communities were to be found all over the country. At Alexandria in particular, where they came to occupy a separate quarter of their own (Ch.17,i), they comprised almost one third of the city's total inhabitants. No less than thirteen Alexandrian synagogues, of various periods, are known; they came under the control of a self-governing Jewish Council. At Rome on the other hand, where there were between twenty and forty thousand Jews at this time, the synagogues seem to have operated independently of one another, each controlling its own communal property, together with the right to levy contributions and fines. Both at Alexandria and at Rome the Jews engaged in a wide variety of professions; concentration upon money-lending and finance was a later development. A few became rich, but most were poor.

The figures that have just been suggested included a considerable number of proselytes of mixed and varied origins, converted by the missionary activity for which the Pharisees were so well known (Ch.18,ii). People hankered after supernatural backing against the troubles of this world, and were receptive to the simple moral rules, strictly regulated way of life, and strong social consciousness which Judaism offered. Nevertheless, for people living in a foreign country and accepting many of its Hellenizing ways, it was hard to adhere to all the prescriptions of the Law – circumcision for instance (which the Greeks and Romans found disfiguring), or women's ritual baths. In consequence, there arose a large intermediate category of 'Judaizers' or 'sympathizers', who felt favourably inclined to the religion and followed some but not all of the rules of the Torah, and such people, despite objections from the strongly orthodox, enjoyed a recognized status on the fringes of Jewish society.

When Caesar revived and upgraded the régime of John Hyrcanus II and Antipater, the latter's young sons Phasael and Herod were made governors of Jerusalem and Galilee respectively. Herod proceeded to crush a Galilean revolt, amid considerable bloodshed. This earned him such vigorous censure from the Great Sanhedrin (Ch.18,ii) that he had to leave Judaea altogether; but the Roman governor of Syria entrusted him with an important military command, and after Caesar's assassination (44), his murderer Cassius did the same.

When Cassius and Brutus succumbed to the dead man's avengers Marcus Antonius (Antony) and Octavian at Philippi in Macedonia (42), the victorious leaders confirmed the appointments both of Phasael and of Herod, despite Jewish opposition. Soon afterwards, however, the Parthians launched a formidable invasion of Roman Asia Minor, Syria and Judaea (40). John Hyrcanus II was dethroned in favour of his nephew Antigonus, Phasael lost his life, and Herod was forced to flee.

ii. The Kingship of Herod

Herod made his way to Rome, where he met Antony, who had divided up the empire with Octavian, securing the eastern provinces as his share. Antony prompted the Roman government to make a treaty with Herod, and sent him back to Judaea not as prince but as king. This meant that the Hasmonaean dynasty, descendants of the liberators of the country, had been brought to an end, in favour of an Idumaean house of unwelcome race, and recent conversion. The Romans gave Herod this job so that he should help to depose Antigonus, the nominee of their enemies the Parthians. And this he and a Roman fellow-general Gaius Sosius succeeded in achieving after a savagely victorious siege of Jerusalem (37).

Herod earned his reward, and was allowed to unify his kingdom, by the incorporation of Samaria. But various lands on the periphery of Judaea were withheld from him, because Cleopatra VII of Egypt, now Antony's mistress, insisted on annexing them; and a historic Jewish–Egyptian meeting between the two rulers, prompted by Antony in 34, only made their relations worse.

Herod replaced the Council of Elders by an advisory body drawn from among his personal friends, like the privy councils of other Hellenistic monarchs. Moreover, remembering that the Great Sanhedrin had censured him for brutality – and they had also backed the cause of Antigonus against his own – Herod executed forty-five of its seventy-one members. These casualties included many Sadducees who supported the former royal house of the Hasmonaeans. However, the Great Sanhedrin's joint chairmen (Ch.18,ii), the Pharisees Hillel and Shammai, were spared. Ranking among the most venerated Jewish religious leaders of all time, and known as the Elders (Ha-Zaken), these two scholars exercised a strong influence on Jewish law and custom. They were the founders, or directors, of two academies for the exposition of the Torah, which were named after them. According to the Mishnah and Talmud (Appendix 10), the schools professed divergent views in a wide variety of fields, involving no less than three hundred and fifty different controversies, and tradition traces back a few of these disagreements to Hillel and Shammai. Hillel, author of the Golden Rule, 'Do not do unto others that which you would not have them do to yourself' (paralleled in the *Book of Tobit*, Appendix 4, and cast into positive form by the Christians), generally offered milder opinions than Shammai. For example, he opposed him by consenting to the admission of proselytes, even when the conditions they laid down were unreasonable.

But where he and Shammai agreed, it would seem, was in favouring non-resistance to Herod. We learn that a certain 'Shemaiah' – who is probably identifiable with Shammai – directed the Jews 'to love work and shun authority and have nothing to do with the ruling class',[4] and Hillel counselled similar passivity. This attitude enabled their successors in the academy directorships to flourish and get on with their work under Herod and subsequent rulers. It was this series of scholars, known as the Tannaim (Teachers), who modelled the basic forms of scriptural commentary into classical shape, and provided Judaism with the principal content of its oral law up to the time of the destruction of the Second Temple in AD 70.

Since Herod came of a family and a people that could not aspire to the high-priesthood, that office was detached from the kingship and bestowed upon a Babylonian Jew named Hananel. He claimed descent from the Zadokite House with which the post had traditionally been associated, so that Herod was able to point out that Hananel's claims were better than those which any Hasmonaean had ever been able to put forward on his own behalf. However, Herod had married a Hasmonaean princess, Mariamme – in order to raise his political and social status – and her mother Alexandra (the daughter of John Hyrcanus II) angrily complained to Cleopatra VII about this high-priestly nomination, so that the king was forced to appoint Alexandra's young son Aristobulus instead. But Aristobulus conveniently, and suspiciously, died of drowning at a Jericho bathing-party, and Hananel was reinstated. After him came a series of further royal nominees to the high-priesthood, taken from a few Sadducee families which provided Herod with supporters in place of those he had executed.

The defeat of Antony and Cleopatra by Octavian's admiral Marcus Agrippa at the battle of Actium (31), and their subsequent deaths, made it necessary for Herod to protest loyalty to the victorious leader (soon to be known as Augustus) instead. His declaration was accepted and he received back most of the fringe territories that Pompey had removed from Judaea in 63, including the coastal strip. He was also given two Greek cities across the Jordan, Hippos (Susita) and Gadara. Alexandra and Mariamme were put to death, and Costobarus, the governor of Idumaea, alleged to have been their fellow plotter against Herod, underwent the same fate.

Herod remained Augustus' client for twenty-seven years to come. It was incumbent upon him to walk a tightrope, and look like a good pro-Roman and a good Jew at one and the same time. In pursuit of the former image, he must seem an enlightened pro-westerner, able to play his part in the modern world of the Augustan Golden Age – that is to say, in the Hellenized eastern Mediterranean world by which his kingdom was surrounded. So he instituted games in honour of Actium, and constructed a Greek theatre and amphitheatre at Jerusalem. He also transformed Samaria into a fine new Graeco-Samaritan city, which he named Sebaste (after Sebastos, the Greek for Augustus), and equipped with a temple in honour of Rome and the emperor, such as existed elsewhere in the Graeco-Roman world. Herod also built citadels and palaces at other strategic points as well, including Jericho, Herodium south of Jerusalem, Machaerus across the Dead Sea (a former fortress of Alexander Jannaeus), and the formidable rock of Masada on the western bank of the sea, where his residence included a synagogue and ritual bath. In addition, he constructed a splendid Mediterranean port to which he gave the name of Caesarea (Maritima), by far the finest harbour his country had ever possessed.

Herod must also show himself a good enough Jew to retain sympathy at home – and offset the handicap of his Idumaean origin. The climax of his achievements in this direction was his rebuilding of the Jerusalem Temple on an unprecedentedly magnificent scale (22–18), setting it in a huge surrounding courtyard upon a built-up platform (the Haram al-Sharif), where excavations have recently been under way. The Herodian Temple, flanking a new royal fortress palace, the Antonia (which replaced the old Hasmonaean Akra), turned Jerusalem into a much expanded pilgrim city, a major tourist attraction for Jews of the Dispersion, thronged by religious devotees of every kind. Apart from some superb walls, little is left of Herod's enormous constructional activities throughout his kingdom. Yet, although hostile Jewish tradition sought to conceal the fact, his claim to emulate Solomon's works was more than justified, for he was by far the greatest builder his country had ever known.

Augustus now presented him with two large regions of southern Syria, east of the Golan heights and stretching almost up to Damascus, through a region which was vital for the Babylonian pilgrim traffic to the Temple. The transfer took place in two phases, first in 23 and then a year or two later, when Herod himself went to see the emperor, who was visiting Antioch, capital of the Roman province of Syria. On the same occasion he secured the appointment of his brother, Pheroras, as governor of Peraea across the Jordan. However, the Greek city of Gadara, which had been ceded to Herod earlier, seized the opportunity to complain to Augustus about the king's ruthless taxation. As for his Jewish subjects, their feelings about his government were no doubt mixed. They, too, had to contribute very high taxes, in order to pay for all the building activity, but in times of famine Herod acted generously and quickly. Moreover, he was a high-class financier, banker and speculator, and some of his profits percolated downwards to his people.

When Marcus Agrippa was in the east in 15, he came to Jerusalem and visited the Temple, where, in accordance with the Jewish regulations for Gentiles' sacrifices, he offered up a hundred oxen.[5] Shortly afterwards, Herod joined him in a military expedition to the Black Sea; and on the return journey he intervened effectively with the Romans to stop Greek cities from withholding the privileges to which the Jewish communities of the Dispersion were entitled. However, Herod also felt it desirable to make sure that neither these interventions, nor the protests of disaffected cities such as Gadara, should lessen his popularity in eastern Mediterranean lands as a whole, where he was eager to cut an international figure. So he showered presents upon the Greek world, and in 12 secured appointment as President of the Olympic Games, to which his monetary and organizational assistance gave a new lease of life.[6]

This happy picture, however, was darkened at home by the king's pathological suspicion of his sons and other members of his family, resulting in a series of savage executions which left Augustus shocked. The emperor was also deeply displeased when Herod attacked the Nabataean Arabs, his neighbours to the east and south (Ch.18,ii). By this time, their state had become a Roman client, like Judaea itself. Yet the relations between the two kingdoms remained tense, and Herod launched an attempt to solve this Arab problem by force. But the enterprise, which was not brought to a conclusion, subjected his relations with his overlord to a very grave strain, and it was with difficulty that his chief minister Nicolaus of Damascus, a talented Greek diplomat and historian, succeeded – to some extent – in persuading Augustus that the incident had been exaggerated.

Herod then tried to complete his restoration to favour by ordering his people to swear a joint oath of loyalty to the Roman ruler and himself (7 or 6). This practice was customary in Rome's other client monarchies, but orthodox Jews feared that it might involve worship of the emperor's statues, which would be an act of blasphemous idolatry. Ten years earlier, when a loyalty oath to Herod had been introduced, the Pharisees and Essenes (Ch. 18,ii) were specifically exempted. But now that the required oath was extended to Augustus himself, further exemption would have seemed discourteous, if not seditious. When, however, the time came for the Pharisees to associate themselves with the new demand, six of them refused to swear. They got off lightly with a series of fines; Herod cannot have been pleased when his brother Pheroras, who presumably sympathized with their predicament, paid them out of his own pocket.

And the objectors were now talking in exalted messianic language. Hitherto this had not been favoured in Pharisaic circles, and Hillel the Elder himself was on record as sharing this dislike.[7] Yet the recalcitrant Pharisees continued to indulge in high-flown talk of such a kind, and succeeded in persuading Bagoas, a high royal official, that he himself was destined to become the father of the coming messianic king. True, he was a eunuch; but a miracle, they pointed out, might intervene, since *Second Isaiah* had pronounced that a eunuch 'must not say "I am nothing but a barren tree"'.[8]

Talk about messianic kings, unless centred upon his own person, seemed to Herod the most perilous high treason; and Bagoas and others of questionable loyalty, including the wife of Pheroras, were executed (5). Nevertheless, in the following year a group of senior Pharisee scholars instigated serious student demonstrations. Herod had already placed an eagle on his coins;[9] but what he did now was to erect a sculptural representation of a similar bird over the main gate of the Temple. This was promptly denounced as a forbidden 'image'[10] – and (what was probably regarded as worse) one with provocatively Roman associations; and the rioters pulled the ornament down. Herod, in failing physical and probably mental health, departed for Jericho, and once there, condemned the offenders to death. Next he commanded the capital penalty for his own eldest son Antipater, earlier imprisoned for alleged subversion.[11] And then he himself died.

The bloodthirsty upheavals of Herod's last years must be set against the thirty years of flourishing peace that he had earlier provided – an atmosphere in which Jewish scholarship could flourish.

His career sets interesting problems. In spite of spectacular achievements such as the rebuilding of the Temple, he did not give the impression of being a very devout Jew. He belonged, rather, to the tradition of David, Solomon, Omri and Ahab, who had sought to combine Yahwism with the differing religious interests of their other subjects and neighbours. They, however, had remained politically independent, something Herod, in the face of the overwhelmingly numerous Roman legions, could never have achieved. So he collaborated with the imperial power instead.

His penalty, therefore, has been the censure of Jewish posterity, supplemented by gruesome Christian legends telling of his slaughter of the Innocents (from which the infant Jesus was said to have been removed into safety).

Nevertheless, granted that this second-best policy was all he could aim at, he carried it out, for most of the time, with remarkable skill. When he was known, later, as 'the Great', this only meant 'the elder', to distinguish him from later Herods. Yet, if his domestic catastrophes are left to one side, he attained almost as much greatness as was possible for any man of his epoch who was not a Roman.

CHAPTER 20

THE ROAD TO REBELLION

i. Roman Province

After the death of Herod the Great, Augustus divided his state between three of his surviving sons. One of them, Archelaus, was to rule the central region of Judaea itself, including Samaria (from which his mother originated) but without the Greek cities on the country's fringe, which were allocated to the Roman province of Syria. His brother Herod Antipas was given the two separate territories of Galilee and Peraea, and their half-brother Philip was put in charge of the newly acquired lands up in the southern part of Syria. None of these princes was to hold the rank of king; Archelaus became ethnarch (the designation Pompey had allowed to John Hyrcanus II), and Antipas and Philip were given the less distinguished but still princely title of tetrarch (literally, ruler of a fourth part).

Antipas and Philip reigned successfully and for a long time, until 39 and 34 respectively;* the former established his capital at the new city of Tiberias in Galilee (called after Augustus' successor Tiberius), and the latter at Panion or Panias (renamed Caesarea Philippi). But Archelaus only lasted for ten years. By that time, his high-handed behaviour had provoked Jews and Samaritans alike to complain to Augustus, who deposed him and sent him into exile. Judaea ceased to be a state, and instead became a small-scale Roman province, with its capital at Caesarea Maritima. It was to be administered by second-grade governors, with the title of prefect, and later of procurator. These officials belonged to the order of Roman *equites* or knights, below the senators to whom nearly all the important provinces were entrusted – notably Syria, upon whose governors, in times of crisis, they were instructed to lean. And most of them were men of second-grade ability as well. The many success stories of Roman imperial rule did not include the administration of Judaea, bedevilled as it was by irreparable misunderstandings and provocations on both sides alike.

* From now onwards dates are AD unless otherwise stated.

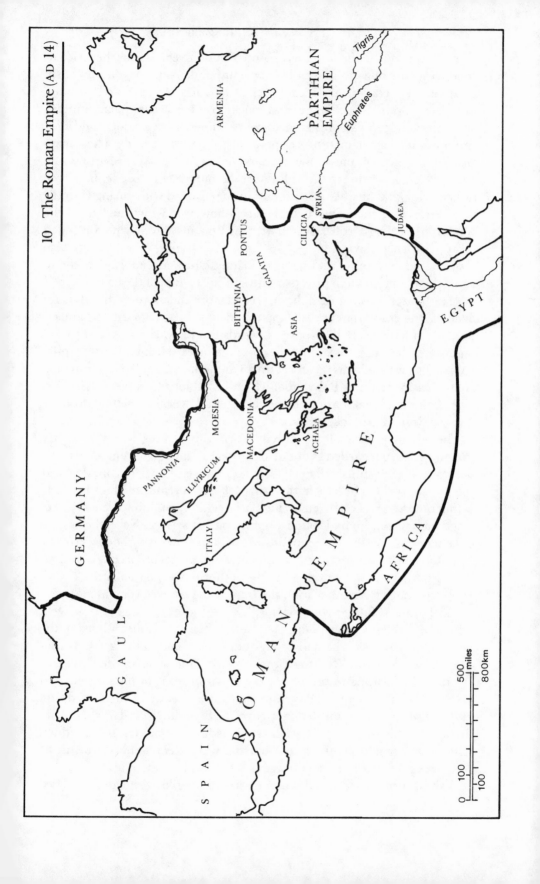

10 The Roman Empire (AD 14)

At the very outset the Romans ran into trouble over a census they tried to conduct in the new province. This was unpopular, because it obviously meant higher taxation, and, besides, criticisms of censuses could be quoted from the Torah. An underground guerrilla force became active under Judas the Galilean,[1] and resistance groups known as the Zealots and *Sicarii* (professional dagger-men) were operating from now onwards. There were also a number of messianic leaders or aspirants, regarded by the authorities as seditious; and the Pharisaic movement, too, retained the radical wing that had become a factor to be reckoned with during Herod's last years. The great Sadducee Houses, however, which had been the supporters of Herod, collaborated with the Romans as well, who continued to appoint successive high priests from their ranks. The prefects also resuscitated the Sanhedrin (in place of Herod's personal advisory body) to assist them and the high priests in the administration of the country.

After his accession in 14, Tiberius relied more and more on the advice of Sejanus, the praetorian prefect (commander of his bodyguard). Sejanus is thought to have been ill-disposed towards the Jews. His suspicions were intensified because two of their co-religionists, Hasinai and Hanilai (Asinaeus and Anilaeus), had set up an autonomous state of their own at Nehardea in Parthian Babylonia, which lasted for fifteen years. Sejanus was afraid that similar ambitions might spread over the Parthian frontier into the Roman province of Judaea.

The fourth prefect of the province, Pontius Pilatus (c. 25–36), has sometimes been regarded as one of his protégés – though he remained at his post long after Sejanus' fall (31), for Pilate enjoyed sufficient confidence at the Roman court to be kept in this office for eleven years: and for the whole of that time he never changed his high priest either, retaining the services of Caiaphas, whom he had found in office on his arrival. Nevertheless, he experienced grave difficulties in dealing with the Jewish offshoot sect of the Christians, whose leader Jesus he executed – in some sort of collaboration, it was said, with the Jewish priestly authorities – just as Antipas had executed Jesus' forerunner John the Baptist in Galilee (Appendix 9).

Furthermore, Pilate attracted the ill-will of more orthodox Jews as well. For they took exception to military standards bearing medallions of the imperial features that he had brought to Jerusalem, on the grounds that they were idolatrous (or too pro-Roman). Following excited demonstrations in Jerusalem, protesters lay down in front of his residence at Caesarea Maritima for five days and nights, and then again in the stadium, and refused to move until Pilate gave in. Soon afterwards he ran into further trouble by using a Jewish religious fund to pay for an aqueduct. This time, when he visited Jerusalem and was beset by angry crowds, he ordered soldiers disguised as Jewish civilians to beat them up.

A third incident occurred when Pilate set up gilded shields, inscribed with the emperor's name and his own, in the former palace of Herod at Jerusalem. Once again vigorous objections were raised – perhaps because the shields bore inscriptions referring to Tiberius' divine paternity (as adoptive son of the deified Augustus), thus offending against monotheistic principles. And finally, after an inflammatory agitator at Samaria had urged a crowd to climb up Mount Gerizim and find Moses' sacred vessels, Pilate's troops intercepted them and caused numerous casualties, followed by arrests and executions.

Under Tiberius' nephew and successor Gaius (Caligula) (37–41), it was the many Jews of Alexandria who took the perilous centre of the stage.

The Greek majority of the population had come to regard them with greater hostility than ever, nursing an explosive blend of ethnic, religious, economic and social grievances. Nevertheless, the Jews had put forward a claim to full citizenship of Alexandria, in contrast to the privileges of an autonomous community which they had hitherto enjoyed. This sparked off a violent retaliatory outburst among the Greeks, producing the first serious pogrom of all time. Pagan gangs forced their way into the synagogues, and set up statues of the emperor within their doors. And then Aulus Avillius Flaccus, the Roman governor of Egypt, who happened, unlike many of his predecessors, to be a strong partisan of the Greek point of view, ordered thirty-eight members of the Jewish Council to be flogged in the theatre, while their womenfolk were forcibly fed with pork, in full view of the public.

Meanwhile, however, a Jewish prince had exerted his calming influence. This was Agrippa I, grandson of Herod the Great and Caligula's personal friend. On the death of Philip and disgrace of Herod Antipas, he had inherited both their princedoms; and he was allowed the rank of king.[2] Now Agrippa made an approach to the emperor, and succeeded in securing the recall of Avillius Flaccus. But the situation at Alexandria remained dangerously tense.

In 40, the Greek and the Jewish communities each sent delegations to Rome to plead their cases. The leader of the Jewish group was the eminent philosopher Philo (Appendix 8), who has left us a vivid account of their perilous mission. Caligula's eccentric, irritable temperament needed very careful handling. He accorded the envoys a brief preliminary hearing. Later they saw him again, and tried to make it clear that, although their religious principles made it impossible for them to sacrifice *to* him, they were always very glad to sacrifice *for* him, which indeed they regularly did. The ruler was unimpressed, remarking that failure to recognize his divinity seemed not so much criminal as lunatic.[3]

While the deputation was conducting these delicate talks, news was brought to them of ominous events taking place in Judaea. At Jamnia

(Yavneh) on the coast, a town of mixed population, the Greeks – who controlled the local administration – erected an altar in honour of the emperor. This was in accordance with the policy of Caligula, who, like his predecessors, but with less regard for tact, encouraged the worship of his imperial self, as a bond of unification between Rome and the numerous subject peoples of the provinces. The Jewish inhabitants of Jamnia, however, refused to regard the altar as a purely Greek affair, but saw it instead as a deliberate provocation to themselves, and shattered it to pieces. The emperor and his advisers took this badly, and it was decided to revive the policy of Antiochus IV Epiphanes (Ch.17,ii): all Jewish places of worship throughout the country, Temple and synagogues alike, were to be transformed into shrines of the imperial cult. So orders were given to Publius Petronius, the governor of Syria (for this seemed an important enough matter to require his personal intervention), to commission a colossal gilt-bronze statue of Caligula, in the guise of Jupiter or Zeus, and, when it had been made, to set it up in Jerusalem. Petronius, recognizing that this could mean rebellion and mass-martyrdom, decided he would need two whole legions to enforce the command, and prepared to lead them south. But Agrippa I finally succeeded in inducing the autocrat to cancel his order – on the condition that the Jews stopped trying to prevent Gentiles from celebrating the imperial cult. Shortly afterwards, Caligula was murdered, and the Jews kept the day on which this news became known as a joyful feast.

His uncle Claudius, who succeeded him (41–54), at once had to face a fresh outburst of rioting and fighting between the Greeks and Jews at Alexandria. The letter he addressed to both groups, in the hope of cooling the situation down, has survived. Urging each side to behave with tolerance and restraint, he added a message to Jewish communities all over the empire, assuring them of his sympathy but urging them not to 'behave with contempt towards the gods of other peoples'.[4]

In Judaea itself, Claudius inaugurated a remarkable interlude in which direct Roman rule was temporarily abolished, and the country recovered the status of a self-governing client kingdom. For the dynamic, restless Agrippa I was allowed to add the Roman province of Judaea to the territories he had obtained in the previous reign, so that his kingdom was now as extensive as that of his grandfather Herod the Great. Unlike Herod, however, he received an excellent reception among the Jews. The Greeks, however, did not like him so much, and his proposal to hold a conference of fellow client monarchs from neighbouring lands was snubbed by the Roman governor of Syria. Nevertheless, Agrippa might have created a measure of interracial harmony, if he had lived – and nobody else stood any chance of doing so at all – but his sudden death in 44, after a reign of only three years, meant that Judaea reverted, fatally, to the status of a Roman province once again.

Under the series of governors who followed, the situation sharply deteriorated. The unstable economic basis of the province created incurable tensions between rich and poor. Ferocious armed adventurers and self-styled prophets and holy men roamed round the land more or less unchecked, and insurrections with a religious or political colouring, or both, broke out in many regions. The procurator Tiberius Julius Alexander (46–48), a renegade Jew, had to deal with a major famine, which was relieved by the rulers of Adiabene (Assyria), recent converts to Judaism. The tenure of Ventidius Cumanus (48–52) witnessed riots, a massacre in the Temple, and clashes between Samaritans and Galileans. The next governor, Antonius Felix (52–60), enjoyed lofty connexions both at the court of the emperor Nero (54–68) and among the Jews themselves. Nevertheless, his vigorous efforts to restore order only produced a higher level of violence, and Judaea was once again filled with armed bands of freedom-fighters and miracle-workers, proclaiming a heady mixture of nationalistic and revolutionary and messianic slogans. In particular, a group of urban terrorists became an increasingly dangerous menace in Jerusalem itself.

Felix also had the difficult task of dealing with the eloquent Christian leader St Paul (Appendix 9), imprisoned by the Romans at Caesarea Maritima after he had clashed with Jewish crowds. On this problem his successor Porcius Festus (60–62) sought the advice of Agrippa II (the son of Agrippa I), whom the Romans had appointed king of the Hellenized city-state of Chalcis beneath Lebanon (Mejdel Anjar), with rights of supervision over the Jerusalem Temple. But Paul, having appealed to Nero himself, was put on a ship for Italy. In Judaea, however, after Porcius Festus had died, the high priest Ananus (Hanan) II, taking charge during an interregnum between governors, executed James the Just, called the brother of Jesus. The next procurator, Lucceius Albinus (62–64), arrived at a particularly critical time, because his emperor had just examined the Jews' demand that, like the Greeks, they should be full citizens of Caesarea Maritima – and the decision had gone against them. Albinus was also beset by violent disputes relating to the high-priesthood. In the course of these struggles, the son and assistants of the high priest of the time, a certain Ananias (Hananiah), were kidnapped by guerrillas, who only released them in exchange for their comrades' liberation from prison.

ii. The First Roman War

Under the procurator Gessius Florus (64–66), a Greek from Asia Minor, everything speedily got even worse. When fighting broke out between

Greeks and Jews in Caesarea Maritima, he detained a Jewish deputation that had come to see him, and placed its members under arrest. Next, because tax payments had fallen into arrears, he seized a large sum from the Temple treasury. Rioting followed, and a house-to-house search which resulted in fights and crucifixions. Troops from Caesarea, called in to control the situation, got involved in an unfortunate scuffle with a Jewish committee of welcome. At this stage an officer was sent by Cestius Gallus, governor of Syria, to try and soothe popular feeling; Agrippa II, too, urged the advantages of collaborating with the Romans, and the priest Joseph ben Hanina said the same, declaring that 'if it were not for the fear of the government, men would swallow one another up alive'.[5]

But such advice received no attention. The First Jewish Revolt, or, as the Jews call it, the First Roman War, could no longer be averted. The struggle was gallant but hopeless. The Romans were firmly in control of the entire Mediterranean region. The Jews, themselves divided, would get no assistance from Parthia, which had just made its peace with Rome; and indeed, even if their co-religionists in the Parthian empire did their best to help, it could amount, in terms of military support, to very little.

The decisive move was made by Eleazar, son of the former high priest Ananias. In August 66 Eleazar, who was captain of the Temple – that is to say, second in its hierarchy after the high priest himself – proclaimed that henceforward no sacrifices would be accepted from any foreigner. This meant that the twice-daily offerings for Rome and the emperor – paid for by the latter – would have to be discontinued. So Eleazar's announcement was an act of rebellion.

He occupied the city, and his political opponent the high priest Mattathias fled to Herod's palace, where a garrison of Roman and Jewish troops protected his life; while his supporters took refuge in underground corridors and sewers. Eleazar then launched an attack on the palace, but his assault was interrupted by the spectacular arrival of Menahem (son of the guerrilla chieftain Judas the Galilean, Ch.20,i), who had made a name for himself by storming the Roman fortress at Masada on the Dead Sea. Menahem accepted the surrender of the Jewish soldiers in the palace, while the Roman troops retreated into its three strong towers. Menahem then proceeded to murder Eleazar's father, Ananias; but before long he, in his turn, was kidnapped by Eleazar, and tortured to death. Thereupon Eleazar allowed the Romans to move out of the towers, telling them they were free to withdraw, but he broke his promise and slaughtered them all, except their commander, who agreed to undergo circumcision.

Excited by these events, Greeks fought Jews at Alexandria, and massacred them at Caesarea Maritima and other cities, while Jews massacred Greeks in Samaria, Galilee and Transjordan. The governor of

Syria now felt obliged to bring an army into Judaea, but it was routed at Beth-horon, north-west of Jerusalem, with the loss of six thousand men. The rebels, their morale enormously raised, seized control of large portions of the country and formed an independent secessionist government, striking large silver shekels inscribed 'Jerusalem is Holy', 'The Freedom of Zion', 'The Redemption of Zion'.[6] An ex-high-priest Ananus II, the *de facto* leader of this new administration, still hoped that the Romans could somehow be induced to offer terms, but such a hope was unrealistic. Nero recalled both Cestius Gallus and Gessius Florus, and upgraded the governorship of Judaea by appointing a senator and ex-consul, Vespasian (Titus Flavius Vespasianus), to the post.

In the summer of 67 the Romans succeeded in recapturing Galilee. But one of the leaders of the territory, John of Gischala (the last Galilean citadel to fall) escaped to Jerusalem with a gang of his men. There, although originally a moderate of the well-to-do urban class, he secretly supported an extreme anti-Roman, anti-priestly group which preserved or revived the designation of Zealots (Ch.20,i), led by a second Eleazar (son of Simon), one of the victors of Beth-horon. As this Zealot gang clashed with the supporters of Ananus II, it was joined by a horde of fanatics arriving from Idumaea, who killed Ananus and many other members of the upper and middle classes. The Romans, however, did not take much advantage of this disturbance. Instead, they continued to mop up outlying centres (including Qumran [Ch.18.ii] whose history thus came to an end). More decisive operations were postponed, because of changes of emperor at Rome, where successive *coups* replaced Nero by Galba (68–69), Otho (69) and Vitellius (69), making it advisable for the new governor Vespasian to remain inactive and watch which way Roman political developments would turn next. But this fortunate delay was not exploited by the rebels of Jerusalem, who were now hopelessly torn between three mutually hostile factions, led by John of Gischala, Eleazar the son of Simon, and another guerrilla leader named Simon the son of Gioras, summoned from Masada by the high priest Mattathias.

In summer 69 Vespasian was recognized as emperor throughout the eastern provinces, and his generals marched on Italy to assert his claim. He left the reconquest of Judaea to his popular son Titus, who collected an army of 65,000 men at Caesarea Maritima. Faced with an imminent siege of Jerusalem, the rebel leadership at long last achieved a certain measure of harmony, after John of Gischala had forced Eleazar and his Zealots into the city's underground labyrinth, and had patched up a sort of agreement with Simon the son of Gioras. Buoyed up by current apocalyptic prophecies,[7] John and Simon faced the imminent showdown with determination.

After urging surrender in vain, Titus pressed on with the siege. In spite of fanatical resistance, he succeeded in capturing the Temple, which was totally consumed by flames. After an existence of six hundred years, the Second Temple had ceased to exist; and it has never been rebuilt. Elsewhere in Jerusalem, however, the Jewish resistance groups, although weakened by famine, continued to hold out, while Titus' soldiers were permitted to plunder, massacre and burn. Finally, after a defence that had lasted for four and a half months, every part of the city had fallen. As in other parts of Judaea, huge numbers of prisoners were taken, destined for execution or starvation or slaughter in gladiatorial shows. John of Gischala and Simon the son of Gioras emerged from their subterranean hiding-places, and gave themselves up. Both were kept alive for the Triumph which Vespasian and Titus celebrated at Rome, their victorious procession depicted on reliefs still to be seen on the Arch of Titus – which display, among the plunder, the seven-branched candlestick or Menorah (later lost from sight altogether). Then John was imprisoned for life, and executioners put an end to Simon. Anyone able to claim a connexion with the House of David was also hunted down and eliminated.

Yet the revolt was not quite over. Masada, Herod's fortress beside the Dead Sea, had been seized from the Romans when the insurrection began. And now, even after the fall of Jerusalem, a determined group continued to hold out there for three more years. They were led by Eleazar the son of Jair, who was apparently a grandson of the freedom fighter Judas the Galilean, and nephew of the murdered resistance leader Menahem.[8] But Roman armies under Flavius Silva surrounded the precipitous hill. Their camp has been uncovered by archaeologists, who have also brought to light many pathetic personal possessions of the defenders and their families in the long siege that followed: fragments of fabrics, leather sandals, skeletons, skulls and plaits of hair. When the Romans finally broke through, nine hundred and sixty members of the garrison, following and going beyond the ancient tradition of martyrdom, committed mass suicide. Only two women and five children were left alive.

The rising had now been stamped out. Damage to the land had reached ruinous proportions, partly because of the scorched earth policy of the rebels themselves. The Jewish population had suffered appalling casualties, and pagan immigrants were allowed to settle in their place. Jerusalem itself was disastrously shattered, and resumption of worship in its gutted Temple forbidden. Furthermore, the Romans now proceeded to abolish the high-priesthood, and the Council of Elders as well. The 'First Commonwealth' had ended when Judah and its Temple fell in 587 BC. Now, in equally catastrophic circumstances, the 'Second Commonwealth', too, was at an end. Both occasions together are mourned by Jews on the 9th day of Ab (July–August) every year.

Our information about the war comes almost entirely from Flavius Josephus (37/38–after 95), one of the greatest Jewish historians of all time – and by far the greatest whom we know by name.

He was strongly against the rebellion, but reluctantly accepted a command from the initial moderate leadership, and proceeded to Jotapata in Galilee. There the soldiers of his garrison, when defeat became imminent, made a suicide pact, and died together. But Josephus, unwilling to lose his life, got away and went over to Vespasian, whose son Titus he subsequently served as an interpreter during the siege of Jerusalem, vainly appealing to the inhabitants to capitulate (and declaring afterwards that Titus had never wanted to burn the Temple down). After the war, he was granted Roman citizenship, and received a house and pension at Rome.

There his first literary work was the History of the Jewish War, intended to explain its character and significance to the Jews of the eastern Dispersion. The Aramaic original is lost, but a Greek translation or adaptation (made by himself and a number of helpers) has survived. About his own questionable role in the rebellion, he writes with a curious blend of fulsome conceit and damaging admissions; but where his own personal affairs are not involved, he is a reliable, first-class narrator. Later he returned to the revolt in his Life, claiming that one part of the rising against the Romans, undertaken at Tiberias in Galilee, had not been fomented by himself, as certain people had charged, but by someone else altogether. He also composed a skilful pamphlet Against Apion, refuting four centuries of anti-Semitic propaganda; and his massive Jewish Antiquities surveyed the entire history of the people in twenty books.

Despite his collaboration with his nation's oppressors and enemies, Josephus remained a passionately devoted Jew. But his attitude to the history of his religion was backward-looking and selective, ignoring the principal opposed currents, apocalyptic and rabbinical, which dominated its present and future development.

EPILOGUE

In Judaea a remnant of the Jews outlived the destruction of the Temple and high-priesthood, and the liquidation of the autonomous government for which they had stood. The leaders who brought their people through the disaster were the Pharisees, the only significant Jewish force to emerge from the calamity. One of their number, an elderly merchant and judge named Yohanan ben Zakkai, obtained permission from Vespasian to proceed to Jamnia (Yavneh) beside the coast, where he established a refugee settlement which became an eminent Jewish centre and academy. Its instructors inreasingly became known by the title of rabbi (lord, master, my superior). It was they who, as searchers, preservers, expounders and interpreters of the Torah, made it possible for Judaism, though the Temple had vanished, to continue its millennial task of self-perpetuation.

Among these Pharisees, the Greek writings of Alexandrian Judaism (Appendix 8) were ignored, and had no future. Yohanan was equally opposed to apocalyptic, messianic speculations (the theme of much contemporary Jewish literature), first, because he knew that the Romans saw them as politically subversive, and secondly, because they aroused such a keen interest among the Christians (Appendix 9). His successor Gamaliel II became so eminent that the title of *nasi* (prince) was revived to describe his directorship of the Jamnia school. Although his own way of life was Hellenistic, he insisted on strict discipline among the Jews. Five hundred of their boys studied the Torah under his auspices; but another five hundred were allowed to study Greek.

The council of the Jamnia academy was gradually recognized by the Romans as exercising control over the religious affairs of Judaea. Yet the revolt had inevitably caused them to adopt a sharper attitude to members of the religion in general. Vespasian levied taxation on all of them, in whatever countries they resided, in order to supersede their own Temple tax, which was abolished. Domitian (81–96) tightened the procedures against evaders of this tax in the city of Rome, and charged converts to

Judaism (who reportedly included members of his own family) with 'atheistic practices', which meant refusal to sacrifice to his own imperial divinity. In Judaea, too, he planned repressive actions, but they came to nothing because he was murdered. The next emperor, Nerva (96–98), must have prided himself on adopting a more lenient policy, since he issued coins commemorating his 'elimination of wrongful accusations (*or* perversions of justice)' concerning the Jewish tax (FISCI IVDAICI CALVMNIA SUBLATA).

Nevertheless, the attempts of his successor Trajan (98–117) to extend the Roman empire to the Persian Gulf were gravely hampered by a chain of violent, unprecedented Jewish uprisings in many parts of the Dispersion. These outbreaks were caused by a fervent mixture of religious hostility, messianic yearning, bitterness about Titus' destruction of the Temple, and resentment because Trajan's conquests would alter the commercial routes to the disadvantage of the Jews who helped to operate this trade. The risings, for all their ferocity, stood no chance of military success. Nor did the Second Judaean Revolt or Second Roman War (132–5), which broke out because the emperor Hadrian had decreed the refoundation of Jerusalem as a Roman colony, under the name of Aelia Capitolina (the emperor belonged to the Aelian family). The talented, vigorous leader of the rebellion, Simeon bar Kosiba (son of Kosiba, or from a village Chezib or Chozeba) was proclaimed as Bar Kochba (Son of a Star), and among those who hailed him (according to a tradition which might not be accurate) was the greatest rabbi of the day, the aged Akiba ben Joseph. Yet Simeon was finally defeated, to the accompaniment of the same appalling loss of life and property that had followed the insurrection of 66–73.

Doubling the local garrison, Hadrian abolished the name of Judaea, with its potentially subversive overtones, and called the province Syria Palaestina instead (for the name, see Appendix 11). He also went ahead with the creation of Aelia Capitolina, and forbade Jews to set foot in the place, and perhaps in the surrounding district as well.

The principal centre of Jewish habitation in the country was henceforward Galilee, to which the Jamnia academy moved, settling first of all at Usha (north-east of Carmel). There, at a time when Christians throughout the empire were beginning to outnumber and out-challenge its Jewish inhabitants, a brilliant new generation of rabbinical teachers emerged; and the Romans, turning once again to the moderate Pharisaic class, authorized a reconstituted Jewish Council, of which the chairmen were permitted to call themselves Patriarchs. The most famous of these leaders, Judah I ha-Nasi (135–219), residing first at Beth Shearim and then at Sepphoris (Diocaesarea), was traditionally regarded as the principal editor of the Mishnah (Appendix 10). Under his grandson Judah II

Nessiah (*c.* 230–86), who transferred his residence to Tiberias, the Jews suffered greatly during the convulsions that were now racking the Roman empire, for which they seemed to be convenient scapegoats. Yet new synagogues abounded, and the rabbis, known at this time as Amoraim (speakers, interpreters), became increasingly influential.

Meanwhile, in Babylonia – which passed during the third century from the Parthians to their conquerors, the Sassanian Persians – the Jewish communities enjoyed a notable efflorescence. Their principal centres were Nehardea (founded in *c.* 212), Sura (214), Pumbeditha and Machuza, whose directors (*geonim*) presided over the creation of the Babylonian Talmud which exceeded its Palestinian counterpart in importance. These communities continued to survive, with mixed fortunes, after the conversion to Christianity of Constantine the Great (306–37) had inaugurated a period of grave difficulties for their co-religionists in the Roman and then the Byzantine empires. Together with the independent sect of the Samaritans (Appendix 6), which was also hard hit, the Jews rallied to the Persian cause against the Byzantine emperor Heraclius I (610–41). But then the Persian empire, and Byzantine Palestine too, were conquered by the second Arab Caliph Omar, whose teacher Mohammed had at first (before his views underwent a reversal) been profoundly influenced by Judaism. The Jews rallied to Omar, and many of them prospered under Arab rule. It was in this epoch that the Masoretes (keepers of the text tradition, *masorah*), applied the finishing touches to the text that is found in all printed editions of the Hebrew Bible. It was not until 942 and 1040 respectively that the academies of Sura and Pumbeditha were closed down.

But the main future destiny of the Jews lay in the centres of the European Dispersion, where they endured harrowing persecution in medieval times. On the other hand the important Khazar kingdom of south Russia adopted the Jewish religion shortly before 800, and retained the same faith throughout the three centuries of its subsequent existence.

Palestine, following the termination of short-lived crusading Latin kingdoms (1100–87, 1229–91), returned to Islamic control, and passed four centuries under Ottoman Turkish rule (1516–1918), followed by three decades of British mandate. Then, after the immeasurable horrors of the holocaust, the country became independent again, in 1948, for the first time for two thousand years.

Amid the unparalleled, awe-inspiring phenomenon of this survival and revival, one of the principal problems of the modern Republic is still that of the ancient state and community: how to reconcile the uniqueness and separatism of Israel with the need to adjust to the external world. And its great achievement will be to win through to this reconciliation more effectively than its ancient forerunners, for all their magnificent creativeness, ever succeeded in doing for very long.

APPENDICES

APPENDIX 1

DATES OF THE KINGS

All dates of the united and divided kingdoms are approximate[1]

(1) THE UNITED KINGDOM

Saul	1020–1000 BC
David	1000–965
Solomon	965–927

(2) THE DIVIDED KINGDOMS

(a) *Israel*		(b) *Judah*	
Jeroboam I	927–907	Rehoboam	926–910
Nadab	907–906	Abijah (Abijam)	910–908
Baasha	906–883	Asa	908–868
Elah	883–882	Jehoshaphat	868–847
Zimri	882	Jehoram	847–845
Omri	882–871	Ahaziah	845
Ahab	871–852	Athaliah (queen)	845–840
Ahaziah	852–851	Jehoash	840–801
Joram	851–845	Amaziah	801–(773)
Jehu	845–818	Uzziah (Azariah)	787–736
Jehoahaz	818–802	Jotham	756–741
Joash	802–787	Ahaz (Jehoahaz I)	741–725
Jeroboam II	787–747	Hezekiah	725–697
Zechariah	747	Manasseh	696–642
Shallum	747	Amon	641–640
Menahem	747–738	Josiah	639–609
Pekahiah	737–736	Jehoahaz II	609
Pekah	735–732	Jehoiakim (Eliakim)	608–598
Hoshea	731–723	Jehoiachin	598
		Zedekiah	597–587

251

(3) THE HASMONAEAN (MACCABEAN) DYNASTY

Judas Maccabaeus	166–160
Jonathan	160–142
Simon	142–134
John Hyrcanus I	134–104
Aristobulus I	104–103
Alexander Jannaeus	103–76
Alexandra Salome (queen)	76–67
Aristobulus II	67–63
John Hyrcanus II	63–40
Antigonus	40–37

(4) THE HERODIAN (IDUMAEAN) DYNASTY

Herod the Great	37–4 BC
Archelaus (ethnarch of Judaea)	4 BC–AD 6
Herod Antipas (tetrarch of Galilee and Peraea)	4 BC–AD 39
Philip (tetrarch in the north)	4 BC–AD 34
Agrippa I	AD 41–44
Agrippa II (various northern territories)	49/50–before 93/94

THE BOOKS OF
THE OLD TESTAMENT
(THE HEBREW BIBLE)

Genesis (Bereshith), Exodus (Shemoth), Leviticus (Wayikra), Numbers (Bemidbar), Deuteronomy (Devarim [Debarim]), Joshua (Yehoshua), Judges (Shofetim), Ruth, 1 and 2 Samuel (Shemuel), 1 and 2 Kings (Melakhim), 1 and 2 Chronicles (Dibre Hayomim), Ezra and Nehemiah (Ezra-Nehemyah), Esther (Ester), Job (Iyob), Psalms (Tehillim), Proverbs (Mishle Shelomoh), Ecclesiastes (Koheleth), Song of Solomon or Song of Songs (Shir Hashirim), Isaiah (Yeshaya), Jeremiah (Yirmeya), Lamentations (Ekha), Ezekiel (Yehezkel), Daniel, Hosea, Joel, Amos, Obadiah, Jonah, Micah, Nahum, Habakkuk, Zephaniah, Haggai, Zechariah, Malachi (from Hosea to Malachi: Tere Asar).

This Hebrew Bible (Tanakh) is subdivided into the Torah (the Pentateuch: Genesis–Deuteronomy), the Prophets (comprising the historical books or 'former prophets' [Joshua–2 Kings], the 'latter prophets', classified according to length as 'major' [Isaiah, Jeremiah, Ezekiel] and 'minor' or 'the twelve' [Hosea to Malachi, Appendix 3]), and the Sacred Writings (Ketubim, Hagiographa: comprising [1] Psalms, Proverbs, Job; [2] the Megilloth or Scrolls [Song of Solomon, Ruth, Lamentations, Ecclesiastes, Esther]; and [3] Daniel, Ezra and Nehemiah, 1 and 2 Chronicles).

Roman Catholics (traditionally employing the Vulgate, the standard version or *editio vulgata* mainly attributable to St Jerome) and Eastern Orthodox name certain books differently; i.e., 1 and 2 Samuel become 1 and 2 Kings, 1 and 2 Kings become 3 and 4 Kings, 1 and 2 Chronicles become 1 and 2 Paralipomenon, Ezra and Nehemiah become 1 and 2 Esdras, and the Song of Solomon becomes the Canticle of Canticles. The same Churches also include in the Bible the 'deuterocanonical' books of Tobit (Tobias), Judith, Wisdom (of Solomon), Baruch, and 1 and 2 Maccabees, all of which are placed by Protestants in the Apocrypha (Appendix 7). However, modern Roman Catholic vernacular translations follow the other (Protestant) versions.

APPENDIX 3

THE BOOKS OF THE
MINOR PROPHETS[2]

AMOS See Ch.11,ii.

DANIEL See Ch.18,i: in the English Bible he is a major prophet.

HABAKKUK End of seventh century BC. The book opens with a lament about the ruthless power and conduct of the wicked, against whom Yahweh does nothing. He replies, however, that he is raising up the 'Chaldaeans' to punish these enemies. Habakkuk, still in some doubt, prepares himself for his prophetic task, and is ordered to write down the divine message, since 'at the destined hour it will come true in breathless haste', and the unrighteous will meet their doom. 'Their leaders are torn from them by the whirlwind, as they open their jaws to devour their wretched victims in secret',[3] but Yahweh will save his anointed.

The 'evil enemy' indicated by Habakkuk has been variously and dubiously identified (at Qumran, centuries later, it was interpreted as the power of Rome). The 'Chaldaeans', on the other hand, are evidently the Babylonians, whose conquest of Judah (Ch.12,ii) the prophet foretells, seeing them as agents of Yahweh's will.

The book is logically and symmetrically constructed, and seems (with the exception of one verse passage) to be the work of a single author. Internal evidence suggests that he was a professional prophet employed by the Jerusalem Temple. He also figures in the story of Bel and the Dragon (Appendix 4).

HAGGAI Dated to the second year of the reign of the Persian King Darius I (522–486). The two chapters of the Book of Haggai contain oracles delivered in Jerusalem, at about the same time as those of Zechariah (q.v.). Haggai rebukes the people for neglecting the reconstruction of the Temple in order to build their own houses, and encourages Zerubbabel and the priest Jeshua (Joshua) to get the work started (Ch.16,i). Seven weeks later, the prophet reassures those who deplored the Temple's inferiority to its pre-exilic counterpart by foretelling that in a new world order, brought about by political convulsions, all nations would bring their tribute to this shrine. A time of prosperity is promised, in which the thrones of enemy nations would be overturned, and on that day Yahweh would exalt his servant Zerubbabel, who was of David's line and is identified as the promised Davidic king.

In sharp contrast to the spirituality of Second Isaiah (Ch.15,ii), Haggai believes that to get worship right is the first priority; the whole duty of the Jews is to shake off their torpor and rebuild the Temple. His prophecies are a primary historic source, reflecting the depressing economic conditions of those who had returned from the exile. Like most post-exilic prophets he writes in a clumsy, heavy style. His teaching that universal convulsions would precede the Day of the Lord was later quoted in the New Testament.[4]

HOSEA See Ch.11,ii.

THIRD ISAIAH is the name sometimes given to the author or authors of the last eleven chapters (56–66) of the *Book of Isaiah*. (For Isaiah and Second Isaiah see Chs.13,ii and 15,ii, respectively.) Written in Palestine in about 500 BC, these prophecies comprise admonitions and reassurances to the Jewish people who are restored from exile and have returned to Jerusalem. It is made known to them that Yahweh will keep his word, and that the faithful can look forward to a new and more glorious future, comprising divine judgement and a new creation. Meanwhile they are adjured to live in righteousness and justice and repentance, and to obey the Sabbath, and to offer sacrifices and prayer. Third Isaiah maintains the Isaianic universalist note by insisting that all Gentiles (notably the Edomites) shall bow down to Yahweh. 'The Grapes of Wrath' (or 'Battle Hymn of the Republic') is one of Third Isaiah's songs. 'I have trampled the nations like grapes ... in my anger, and their blood has stained all my clothing ... I poured out their life-blood on the ground.' But meanwhile it is a time of grim hardship for the Jews; and rebuilding the Temple will not help.[5]

JOEL's prophecies have been attributed to a wide range of dates. Perhaps he lived in about 600, but his oracles were not written down, at least in their final form, for another two or three centuries.

The book begins with a call for a day of prayer to ward off a devastating plague of locusts, accompanied by a severe drought. The locust swarm, with its irresistible onward march 'like flames of fire burning up the stubble', is a sign and warning of Yahweh's invading army on the Day of Judgement. Yet Yahweh is still prepared to accept repentance, and Joel demands that the whole nation should appeal for his mercy, for he will then restore all that has been lost, pouring out his spirit not only on priests and prophets but on ordinary people, regardless of sex, age and class. All evil shall be abolished on that momentous day. 'The mountains shall run with fresh wine and the hills flow with milk', and Yahweh shall make his home in a city and among a people that has at last been made holy. For to Joel, Yahweh is exclusively the God of Israel, 'burning with zeal for his land, and moved with compassion for his people'. It is only in Jerusalem that a Remnant will be saved. Foreign nations, on the other hand, will receive nothing but ferocious punishment; for all they have done is to 'barter a boy for a whore, and sell a girl for wine and drink it down'.[6]

The prophet employs a good deal of familiar liturgical and prophetic terminology, but his dramatic descriptions and powerful antitheses and sharp poetic rhythms stand out as his own original contribution.

JONAH See Ch.16,ii.

MALACHI means 'my messenger', and the prophet to whom this designation is given cannot be identified. The book seems to have been written in Palestine in *c.* 450, shortly before the arrival of Nehemiah (Ch.16,i), though perhaps, in the first instance, its contents were attached to the oracles of Zechariah (q.v.) as an anonymous appendage.

It opens with a demonstration of Yahweh's love for his people, based on the contrasted experiences of Israel and Edom. Worshippers incur rebukes for offering sacrifice with blemished animals. People's sufferings, such as epidemics and plagues of locusts, are a punishment for inadequate tithes and offerings. Those who complain that Yahweh is indifferent to injustice will receive their answer on the Judgement Day, amid a glowing furnace in which all the arrogant and the evil-doers shall be chaff, and that day when it comes shall set them ablaze'. But first Yahweh will send back the prophet Elijah (Ch.11,i), who 'will reconcile fathers to sons and sons to fathers'.

Meanwhile, strict observance of the Law of Moses is required. To combat the low morale and despondent cynicism which are getting in the way of this aim, the prophet adopts a rhetorical pattern of questions and answers anticipatory of the Talmud. He blends strict priestly ritualism with strong expressions of opinion. For example: not only should a man be faithful to his wife, but it is cruel of him to divorce her. Marriage to foreign women is condemned. Yet – paradoxically it might seem – Yahweh's fatherhood means that men must live together like brothers. And the cults of the Gentiles, Malachi adds, may give Yahweh greater satisfaction than his own people's careless, incorrect worship.[7]

MICAH The book bearing his name reflects the historical background of the Assyrian invasions in the last decades of the eighth century (Ch.10,iii). The first part of the work portrays the destruction of Samaria in 722, and the devastation of Judah as well. The oppression of the poor by the rich is denounced, and attacks are launched against unprincipled national rulers, mercenary prophets, and all who oppose the true prophetic cause.

The second part of the book, on the other hand – still against a confused background of troubles – contains prophecies of hope and restoration. An ideal Jerusalem is proclaimed as the focus of human religion and world peace, to which the peoples will stream to learn Yahweh's Law, as he triumphs in the person of a 'governor for Israel', coming from Bethlehem. In a third section, the prophet reminds his people of past favours, and continues: 'Yahweh has told you what is good: and what is it that the Lord asks of you? Only to act justly, to love loyally, to walk wisely before your God.' A series of oracles censure the ingratitude of Israel and Judah alike, the persistence of social injustice and fraud, the abandonment of human loyalties, and the collapse of all reverent and decent behaviour. A day of reckoning is bound to come. Nevertheless, *Micah* ends with a prayer for Yahweh's merciful fulfilment of his promise to Abraham and the other fathers of Israel, accompanied by a renewed expression of hope for the ultimate salvation of its people.

Some of the references to the destruction of Judah look as if they might have been inserted by a later editor, after the collapse of that state in 587; but not necessarily, since the country had already been threatened in the later eighth century, by the Assyrian monarch Sennacherib (Ch.12,ii). Nor does the contrast between earlier gloom and later hope require the supposition of dual authorship.

True, later editors have, as usual, been at work. But it is possible, nevertheless, to identify the haunting, trenchant blend of oracle, lament and dialogue that is characteristic of Micah. He gives classic expression to the need for an individual, ethical, practical response to Yahweh's demands, and he is, above all, following in the steps of Amos, the prophet of social protest on behalf of the oppressed peasantry, from which Micah, too, apparently came.

Succinctly summarizing the prophetic faith, he echoed Isaiah (with whose tradition, or school, he may have been connected) and was quoted by Jeremiah. The gentlest of all the prophets, Micah stressed the forgiveness of sins in verses that are recited in the ceremony of Tashlik, on New Year's Day, beside a stream or river or upon the shore of the sea. His promise of a ruler from Bethlehem (probably not a gloss) embodied a hope that a man of Judah would deliver the country from the Assyrians, but Christians interpreted the words as a forecast of Jesus.[8]

NAHUM was a prophet from Elkosh, an unidentifiable place in the kingdom of Judah. The book named after him was written (except for a few additions) shortly after the fall of the Assyrian capital Nineveh to the Babylonians and Medes in 612. It begins with an incomplete poem (an acrostic, in which the initial letters of consecutive lines spell out a word or phrase), forecasting the coming of Yahweh, 'a jealous God, a God of vengeance',[9] to overthrow his enemies and bring comfort to Judah. Then follows a series of pictures of Nineveh's downfall, together with curses directed against the destroyed city, compared to a prostitute who has enticed the nations into submission and will now receive a prostitute's punishment.

Disregarding the Babylonian menace that now lay ahead, Nahum employs metaphors, hymns, triumphal chants, oracles, satirical comments, and a final dirge to gloat (in contrast to *Jonah*, Ch.16,ii) over the annihilation of Assyrian Nineveh, which he attributes, in graphic, magnificent language, to the saving intervention of Yahweh.

OBADIAH, the shortest book in the Hebrew Bible – only one chapter long – probably dates, in its present form, to the mid-fifth century BC. Its writer launches a concentrated attack on the hated Edomites, who despite their fortresses and their boasted wisdom had been forced to emigrate from their homeland (to Idumaea, on the southern borders of Judah, Ch.16,i). Every man of them, the prophet declares, will be cut down and wiped out, and this vengeance, he feels, will be well deserved, because when the Babylonians conquered Jerusalem, the Edomites had sympathized with them and stood aloof. But soon the Day of Judgement will come upon Edom, and overwhelm all other nations as well. The land of the people of Yahweh, on the other hand, will be fully restored, expanding to north, south, east and west: 'Exiles of Israel shall possess Canaan as far as Zarephath [Sarepta, in Phoenicia, the modern Sarafand], and exiles of Jerusalem in Sepharad [probably Sardis in Asia Minor, a centre of the Dispersion] shall póssess the cities of the Negeb.'[10]

In some cases Obadiah uses similar phraseology to Jeremiah's, and it appears that both prophets are employing some earlier oracle against Edom, which had described its people as haunting 'the crannies among the rocks', probably referring to their capital Sela, which later became Petra, the principal city of the Nabataean Arabs (Ch.19,ii).

ZECHARIAH prophesied in 520–518 and was associated with the plea of Haggai (q.v.) that Zerubbabel and the priest Jeshua should rebuild the Temple (Ch.15,ii). After a call to repentance, the first eight chapters of the book present eight visionary dreams. In the first, four heavenly horsemen bring news that, although the world of the great powers is at present uneventful, Yahweh nevertheless promises that he will intervene on behalf of his people. Four iron horns, representing oppressive foreign rulers at the four points of the compass, are cut off by four smiths. A man with a measuring line signifies the enormous increase of population expected in the new Jerusalem. The high priest Jeshua is accused before a heavenly tribunal by 'the Satan' but acquitted. A lampstand with its seven lamps (the eyes of Yahweh) represents the divine vigilance, and two olive trees stand for Jeshua and Zerubbabel. A flying scroll inscribed with divine curses symbolizes the purging of evil-doers. A woman called Wickedness who is shut up inside a barrel and carried off to Babylon is another symbol of Israel's purification. Four chariots are sent out to different parts of the earth to suppress Israel's enemies and punish 'the land of the north' (Babylonia, the seat of the Persian administration).

By divine command, the priest Jeshua is to be the ruler of the Jews ('with a priest at his right side' – so 'Jeshua' may be an error for 'Zerubbabel', with Jeshua at his side). But just dealing is declared superior to priestly ritual and fasting; and provided that this moral injunction is heeded, Yahweh proclaims a glorious future for his people and for Jerusalem, where he will return to make his home. Righteousness, peace and plenty will prevail in the city, as men and women of every nation flock to it in order to find him; they will pluck the robe of a Jew and say, 'We will go with you because we have heard that God is with you.'[11]

For Zechariah, the absence of international troubles – a disappointment after Darius I's accession (522) had been beset by encouraging disturbances – is only a prelude to Yahweh's imminent, violent restoration of Israel. Satan has the role of an accuser, as in *Job*, and does not yet play his future part of Yahweh's adversary. Although Zechariah, like Haggai, is dedicated to the restoration of the Temple, his interests are much larger. His symbolic imagery is almost as fantastic as Ezekiel's, and this and a bizarre profusion of angels mark him out as one of the forerunners of apocalyptic writing.

Chs.9–11 of the book, regarded as the work of a Second Zechariah (though the hand of more than one contributor is detectable), describe the destruction of the cities of Phoenicia and Philistia (probably by Alexander the Great, 336–323), the hopes of an imminent messianic kingdom, and the coming revival of Jewish military power (to drive out the Ptolemies). The prophet sees himself as the shepherd of Yahweh's flock, but they have strayed and broken the covenant – for example, when they destroyed the unity of Judah and Israel long ago.

Then follows a pair of apocalyptic oracles (*Chs.12–14*), sometimes described collectively as Third Zechariah, but the two pieces are, in fact, the work of two different authors. The first depicts the supernatural deliverance of Jerusalem from a united assault by all the peoples: 'Like a brazier in woodland, like a torch blazing among sheaves of corn, the clans of Judah shall devour all the nations around them, right to left', but, at the same time, there shall be mourning for a martyr, 'who has been pierced' – seen by Christians as a prophecy of the crucifixion.

The other oracle attributed to Third Zechariah once again vividly forecasts the Day of Judgement, when false and lecherous prophets shall be eliminated, and the flesh and eyes and tongues of the Jews' enemies shall rot. If, however, any of these foes do somehow manage to survive, they must go to Jerusalem and worship Yahweh, or no rain will fall upon them and they will die of thirst.[12]

These curious mixtures of obscure historical and apocalyptic allusions, labelled as the work of the Second and Third Zechariah, were destined to receive keen attention from the New Testament.

ZEPHANIAH declares (or is made by his editor to declare) that he received his divine commission during the reign of King Josiah of Judah (c. 639–609). If so, the abuses which he sees around him suggest that the book preceded Josiah's religious reforms, which were intended to put a stop to such evils. But it is possible, instead, that the work was composed under Jehoiakim (c. 608–598) – because he undid the reforms. (The 'forecast' of the downfall of Judah in 587 BC, and of the Dispersion that followed, seems to have been added by an editor after the event.)

Among those who will suffer punishment on the forthcoming Day of Yahweh the writer specifies the following: idolators who worship the sun, moon and stars, and Baal, and the Ammonite God Milcom; apostates from Yahwism; imitators of foreign customs and ways; men of business; and those who remain just indifferent, 'sitting in stupor over the dregs of their wine'. An exhortation that 'all who live humbly by God's laws' should never abandon this pursuit of righteousness – for 'it may be that you will find shelter in the day of the Lord's anger' – is followed, in the third and final chapter, by a prediction of catastrophe for Philistia, Moab, Ammon and Assyria. The final passages of the book do not spare Jerusalem and its leaders from this general indictment, and yet, all the same, the prophet foretells the survival of a Jewish Remnant on the Day of the Lord. The work is by no means original, containing, for example many echoes of *Isaiah*. Its presentation of the Last Day may have influenced the writer's younger contemporary Jeremiah. And indirectly, the same passage, by providing selections employed in the Office of the Dead, inspired the medieval hymn *Dies Irae* (Day of Wrath), incorporated in the Requiem Mass.[13]

APPENDIX 4

SHORT STORIES AND ROMANCES*

BEL AND THE DRAGON is a fictitious account of two happenings in the reign of King Cyrus II the Great of Persia (559–530 BC, Ch.15,i).

(1) This story tells how Daniel (Ch.18,i), the king's most honoured friend, refused to worship the Babylonian god Bel (Marduk) and, in answer to Cyrus' protests, maintained that the abundant food and drink which the priests set before the god every day were not consumed by that deity, who 'is only clay inside and bronze outside, and has never eaten anything at all'. Cyrus bade the priests prove their case against Daniel, on pain of death for whichever side failed. They laid out the provisions in the shrine and sealed the doors – and since they had a secret entrance under the table, everything was gone by the morning. But Daniel had secretly scattered ashes on the floor of the shrine, so that the footprints of the priests gave them away. In consequence, they were put to death.

(2) The Babylonians also worshipped a huge snake or dragon. But Daniel, once again, rejected the king's belief that this was a living god, and obtained permission to be allowed to try to kill it – on the condition that he did not use either a sword or a stick. So Daniel took pitch, fat and hair, boiled them together, and made them into cakes which he fed to the snake. It ate them – and burst into fragments. This infuriated the people of Babylon, who made the king hand him over to them for punishment, and threw him into a den of lions. 'Every day, two men and two sheep had been fed to the lions. But now they were given nothing, to make sure they would eat Daniel.'[14]

Meanwhile, however, the prophet Habakkuk (Appendix 3) was preparing a stew to take to the reapers in the field. As he crumbled bread into the bowl, the angel of Yahweh appeared and ordered him to take the food to Daniel in the lions' den. Habakkuk showed reluctance: whereupon the angel grasped his hair, and swept him through the sky to the city of Babylon, by the blast of his breath. Daniel ate the stew, and the lions did not touch him. Seven days later the Babylonian monarch, coming to mourn his lost friend, was amazed to find him still alive, and cried out in praise of his rescuer Yahweh. Daniel was hauled out of the pit, and the men who had tried to put an end to him were thrown in instead. The lions immediately tore them to pieces and devoured them, before the king's eyes.

* In the Old Testament, the Apocrypha and other Jewish sources.

These two narratives, celebrating Daniel's legendary prowess as an attacker of pagan idols, can be dated to the second or first century BC. They do not find a place in the Hebrew Bible but are appended to the Book of Daniel (Ch.18,i) in the Greek Septuagint and St Jerome's Latin Bible (the Vulgate), and form part of the Protestant Apocrypha (Appendix 7). See also below, s.v. Susanna and the Elders.

THE BOOK OF ESTHER tells how a Persian monarch (Xerxes I, 486–465; or Artaxerxes II [Ahasuerus], 404–359, according to the Septuagint), deposed his queen Vashti and married a beautiful Jewish girl Esther in her place. With Esther's assistance, her cousin and foster-father Mordecai was able to warn Ahasuerus (through Esther) of a plot against his life. But the hostile grand vizier Haman induced the king to decree that not only Mordecai himself but also all the others Jews as well, who lived anywhere in the Persian empire, should be massacred, upon a day fixed by lot. However, by Esther's skilful intervention, and the king's recognition that such an act would be a poor reward for Mordecai's service, the tables were turned and Haman was hanged on the gallows that had been designed for Mordecai, who was now appointed grand vizier in Haman's place. On the day appointed for the extermination of the Jews, they were permitted to defend themselves forcibly against their foes, of whom they slew more than seventy-five thousand.

Henceforward, because Haman had fixed the date of the proposed massacre of the Jews by lot (*pur*),[15] the two days of this slaughter of their enemies, in February or March, were celebrated by the Feast of Lots (Purim), the most joyful carnival in the Jewish calendar, primarily a holiday for children. The *Book of Esther* is read at two services on the Feast's successive days. Although the work makes no mention of Yahweh (a deficiency rectified by references to Esther's and Mordecai's piety in the Septuagint), it was included in the Hebrew Bible to provide sanction to this festival, which was not of Mosaic origin (though it had existed at an early date, under some different name). *Esther* is one of the five festal Megilloth (scrolls) (the others being the Song of Solomon [Song of Songs], Ruth, Lamentations and Ecclesiastes).

The story may date, in its present form, from the second century BC. It is not based on historical fact. There was never, as far as we know, a Persian queen called Esther, or a minister Haman, or a Jewish counsellor called Mordecai. Despite the tale's fervently nationalistic tone (deplored as murderous by Martin Luther) it had probably originated (as a piece of 'wisdom') among Persians and Babylonians rather than Jews: Esther is the Aramaic name of the Babylonian goddess Ishtar, and Mordecai – whose legend may at one time have been separate – means 'worshipper of Marduk', the Babylonian god. This is a story for the Dispersion, assuming close contact with the Gentile world.

JONAH See Ch.16,ii.

JOSEPH The Biblical story of Joseph, the son of Jacob (Ch.9,i), with its brilliant construction and vivid content, could be described as a short novel.

JOSEPH AND ASENATH is the story of the Egyptian girl Asenath (Aseneth), daughter of Potiphar (Potiphera), priest of On (Heliopolis). The pharaoh gave her in marriage to Joseph, to whom she bore two sons, Manasseh and Ephraim.[16]

Asenath, a great beauty, became a convert to Judaism, and was initiated into the faith by eating from a miraculous honeycomb. The son of the pharaoh, with the connivance of her brothers-in-law Dan and Gad, tried to rape her, but the plot was discovered in time. The monarch's son was killed, and Joseph became his heir.

This work was written in Greek during the second or first century BC (and then translated into many other languages). It may be the oldest Greek novel in existence. Its author, however, was a Jew, though he presents Judaism as a mystery religion on a par with the many other Hellenistic faiths of that kind, involving elaborate initiations, which pervaded the Hellenistic world. *Joseph and Asenath* is not in the Hebrew or Christian Bible, but there were Christian versions of the work, in which the heroine appeared as the daughter of Shechem and Dinah (see below, s.v. Ruth), only adopted by Potiphar as his foster-child.

JUDITH This book tells how Nebuchadrezzar (Nebuchadnezzar), described as king of Assyria, dispatched his general Holofernes on an expedition to Syria and Phoenicia. At the siege of the Israelite city of Bethulia (perhaps Bethel), an Ammonite general named Achior warned Holofernes of the danger of attempting to storm its walls. But a beautiful and devout widow named Judith came out of the city, making out that she was a refugee, and foretold to Holofernes that he would be victorious. Invited to visit him, she dressed in her most elegant clothes, put on elaborate jewellery, and entered his tent. But there, as he lay in a drunken stupor, she cut off his head – and brought it back to her people in a bag. The Assyrian army was defeated, and during the rest of Judith's lifetime (she lived to the age of a hundred and five), her country remained at peace, and free from invasion.

The *Book of Judith* does not form part of the Hebrew Bible, and its Hebrew original is lost. It survives in a Greek translation or adaptation in the Septuagint, in a Latin version made by St Jerome from a shorter Aramaic text, and in the Apocrypha. Judith means 'woman of Judah' or 'of the Jewish faith'; while preparing to entice the foreigner, she only eats *kosher* food.[17] The account is not historical; Nebuchadrezzar was king not of Assyria but of Babylonia, and there are many other inconsistencies.

The narrator, who seems to have been writing in the second century BC, was probably attempting to encourage his co-religionists to display heroism in the Maccabean revolt against the Seleucids. Various *midrashim* (Appendix 9) link the tale with the Feast of the Hanukkah (Dedication, Lights), instituted when the Seleucid domination came to an end. And indeed, the entire *Book of Judith* itself is framed in the form of a *midrash*. Its blend of piety and eroticism, resembling the atmosphere of Greek novels, has attracted the attention of numerous European painters.

RUTH In the days of the judges (Ch.5,i), famine compelled Elimelech of Bethlehem, accompanied by his wife Naomi (Neomi) and their two sons, to move eastwards across the Dead Sea to Moab. There he died, and his sons died as well, leaving behind them Moabite widows, Orpah and Ruth. Naomi decided to return to Bethlehem, but urged her daughters-in-law to stay behind in Moab. Orpah reluctantly complied, and returned to her family, but Ruth insisted on leaving with Naomi, declaring that she would stay with her and embrace the Yahwist faith.

When they reached Bethlehem, Ruth tried to make them a living by gleaning in the fields; and the owner of the land, a relative of Elimelech named Boaz (Booz), treated her kindly. At Naomi's suggestion, Ruth paid an alluring visit to Boaz on his threshing-floor at night, and appealed to him to fulfil the role of next-of-kin by buying Elimelech's estate and making her his wife. After inducing another kinsman to forgo his prior claim, Boaz accepted both responsibilities. The son whom Ruth subsequently bore him, through the guidance of Yahweh, was Obed, the grandfather of King David.

This popular legend makes a lively short story, reminiscent of a romantic, miniature novel or novella. Internal evidence indicates that the book was not completed until the Exile was over. However, many elements seem to date back to pre-exilic times: for example, the same theme of a widow's trick to win her legal rights had appeared in the much earlier account of Tamar, who deceived Judah into sleeping with her by disguising herself as a prostitute.[18] The story ends with a genealogy of David, going back to Ruth, and this link may well have had some basis of historical fact, since a Moabite ancestress of David would not have been something to invent.

'Why', Ruth asks Boaz, 'are you so kind as to take notice of me when I am only a foreigner?' The tales of Ruth and Tamar, like those of Rahab (another harlot-saint, who supposedly betrayed Jericho to Joshua) and David's wife Bathsheba, all echo the Jews' constant oscillation between the rejection and acceptance of aliens: can a mixed marriage produce legitimate children? The tale of Dinah (in *Genesis*) whose Canaanite lover Shechem was slaughtered for seducing her and seeking to make her his wife, indicated that people (e.g. Nehemiah and Ezra, Ch.16,i) were right to refuse to allow any Jewish man or woman to marry a foreigner at all. But the *Book of Ruth*, on the other hand, as well as inculcating honourable kindness towards converts to Judaism, is a direct protest against such vetos on foreign marriages.

Loyalty is also strongly praised. The custom of the levirate (from levir, brother-in-law: strictly, a man's obligation to marry the wife of his dead brother; though Boaz was not in the literal sense the brother-in-law of Ruth) is admiringly combined with stress on the responsibilities that fell on an arbitrator or redeemer (*goel*, Ch.13,ii,15,i,ii) in the special sense of a kinsman whose duty it is to redeem or protect his near relations.

The book is one of the Megilloth (see above, s.v. Esther). Its imagery is closely linked to the harvest; and it is read as part of the Liturgy of the Feast of Weeks (Pentecost). In the Septuagint and Christian Bibles it is placed immediately after *Judges*. The utterance of Boaz, 'The Lord be with you',[19] is repeated three (or sometimes four) times in the Latin Mass.

SUSANNA AND THE ELDERS (Daniel and Susanna, The Book of Susanna). Susanna is described as the wife of a Babylonian Jew named Joakim in the sixth century BC. Two of his friends, who were elders and judges, became infatuated with her beauty, and in the hope of getting a glimpse of her hid together in her garden – where they encountered each other face to face. Admitting what they were after, they fixed a time to make another visit to the garden, on this occasion together, so as to catch her alone. They duly made their appearance, and came up to her while she was bathing. 'If you will not do what we want,' they declared, 'we shall give evidence in a court of law that there was a young man with you, and that this was why you sent your maids away.'[20] She still rejected their overtures, and was hauled into court for adultery. Despite all her pleas of innocence, the elders' account was believed, and the judges condemned her to death. But Yahweh inspired the young Daniel to take up her cause and protest, and he demanded and obtained a fresh trial. Interrogating her two accusers separately, he caught them out as liars; and it was they, instead of Susanna, who suffered the death penalty.

This moralizing theme of *Susanna and the Elders* is typical of the Jewish literature of the second and first centuries BC; and a special emphasis is placed on the right of an accused person to be given a proper trial, because the Pharisees attached particular importance to this. But above all the story is a literary masterpiece: an early, small-scale example of detective fiction, sketching its succession of sparkling incidents in a series of deft and rapid strokes.

Illustrating the wisdom of Daniel (like *Bel and the Dragon*, described above), this little work was made into the thirteenth chapter of the book bearing his name in St Jerome's Vulgate. An earlier Christian scholar, Origen, had believed that the tale had originally been an authentic part of *Daniel*, its Hebrew original having suffered suppression, according to his view, because of the poor light in which it displayed the Jewish elders.

TOBIT tells how the man of that name, a Jewish exile deported to Nineveh by Shalmaneser V (*c.* 727–722), does much to help his co-religionists – for example by burying the bodies of those who have been executed by Sennacherib – but becomes blind, and despairingly prays to Yahweh to end his life. At the same moment in Ecbatana (Hamadan in Iran), his relative Sarah offers a similar prayer, because the demon Asmodeus has killed her seven successive husbands, on each occasion during the course of their wedding night. Yahweh hears both of these prayers, and decides to send the angel Raphael to bring help to Tobit and Sarah in their distress. So Raphael (disguised under the name of Azarias) joins Tobit's son Tobias, whom his father has dispatched to recover ten talents of silver he has left with a certain Gabael at Rages (Rhagae in Media), and they start on their journey, with Tobias's dog. When they reach Ecbatana, Tobias marries Sarah and overcomes the demon by pursuing instructions conveyed to him by the angel. They all return to Nineveh, where Raphael cures Tobit's blindness. Many years later Tobit, at the point of death, warns his son to move away from Nineveh, which is doomed, and he leaves again for Ecbatana. On his arrival there he learns of Nineveh's destruction (a song of thanksgiving and an epilogue are later additions).

This story, adroitly blending narrative, piety, romance and family sentiment, was first composed in the imperial (official) form of Aramaic, but translated before long into Hebrew and then into Greek. Its author has assimilated a variety of ancient folklore and fairy-tale themes, sometimes imperfectly. For the most part, he transforms the nomenclature of the legendary characters into Hebrew, but he retains the Babylonian name of Ahikar for a nephew of Tobit's,[21] thus acknowledging the influence of the Babylonian Wisdom of Ahikar, a collection of proverbs and stories about Sennacherib (a copy was found at Elephantine, Appendix 6). The appearance of Asmodeus (the Persian *aeshma daeva*) reflects the dualistic idea that demons, in conflict with angels, are responsible for moral and physical evil (Ch.18,ii).

Whether the writer lived in Palestine or the Dispersion is uncertain. His chronological position, too, is disputed. Proposed dates have ranged widely between the fifth century BC and second century AD; the reign of the Seleucid Antiochus IV Epiphanes (175–163 BC, Ch.17,ii) is perhaps as probable an epoch as any, since his sanctions against the Jews included a refusal to allow them to bury their own dead,[22] a prominent theme in the book. Its writer also wants to encourage honour to parents, and levirate marriage (see above, s.v. Ruth). He (or an editor) urges generosity in almsgiving, and offers a classic formulation of the Golden Rule emphasized by Hillel the Elder (Ch.19,ii): 'Do not do to anyone what you yourself would hate.' Tobit and his dog became a favourite motif of medieval Christian art, and the work became part of the Protestant Apocrypha.

APPENDIX 5

HEBREW LOVE POETRY

Love poetry is represented in the Bible by the *Song of Songs* or *of Solomon* (Shir Hashirim, called the *Canticle of Canticles* in St Jerome's Latin Vulgate). This is a collection of poems – originally, it would seem, quite separate one from another – in which, for the most part, a man and woman speak in alternation. They express passionate love in fervent lyrical language, spiced with sensuous, elaborate imagery.

The girl's appeal, in the opening words of the book, sets the tone: 'O that you would kiss me with the kisses of your mouth! For your love is better than wine.' The young women who are her companions reply to her, and she tells them that, like Ruth (Appendix 4), she comes from a strange land:

> I am dark but lovely, daughters of Jerusalem,
>> Like the tents of Kedar
>> Or the tent-curtains of Shalmah.
>> Do not look down on me; a little dark I may be
>> Because I am scorched by the sun....
> Tell me, my true love,
>> Where you mind your flocks....

'I am an asphodel in Sharon,' she declares, 'a lily growing in the valley.' 'No,' her lover answers: 'my dearest girl is a lily among thorns.'

She sees him coming towards her.

> There he stands outside our wall,
> Looking in through the window, glancing through the lattice.
> My beloved answered, he said to me:
>> Rise up, my darling!
>> My fairest, come away!
>
> For now the winter is past,
>> the rain is over and gone.
> The flowers appear on the earth,
>> the time for singing has come,
> And the voice of the turtledove
>> Is heard in our land.

> The fig-tree puts forth its figs,
>> And the vines are in blossom;
>> They give forth fragrance.
> Arise, my love, my fair one,
>> And come away.

In a dream, the girl experiences the desolate feelings of separation, and the joy of reunion. Her friends tell her of the splendid procession which had celebrated the wedding of King Solomon. Then she glories in the beauty of the man she loves:

> My beloved is fair and ruddy,
> A paragon among ten thousand.
> His head is gold, finest gold:
> His locks are like palm-fronds, black as the raven.
> His eyes are like doves beside brooks of water,
>> Splashed by the milky water
>> As they sit where it is drawn....
> His legs are pillars of marble in sockets of finest gold;
> His aspect is like Lebanon, noble as the cedars.
> His whispers are sweetness itself, wholly desirable.
> Such is my beloved, such is my darling,
>> Daughters of Jerusalem.

And he, too, finds rapturous images to describe his beloved:

> The curves of your thighs are like jewels,
>> The work of a skilled craftsman.
>> Your navel is a rounded goblet
>> That never shall want for spiced wine.
>> Your belly is a heap of wheat
>> Fenced in by lilies.
> Your two breasts are like two fawns,
>> Twin fawns of a gazelle....
>> My loved one, daughter of delights!
> You are stately as a palm-tree,
>> And your breasts are the clusters of dates.
> I said: 'I will climb up into the palm
>> To grasp its fronds.'
> May I find your breasts like clusters of grapes on the vine,
>> The scent of your breath like apricots,
> And your whispers like spiced wine
> Flowing smoothly to welcome my caresses,
> Gliding down through lips and teeth.

The girl answers:

> I am my beloved's, his longing is all for me.
> Come, my beloved, let us go out into the fields

> To lie among the henna-bushes;
> Let us go early to the vineyards
> And see if the vine has budded or its blossom opened,
> If the pomegranates are in flower.
> There will I give you my love.

And he pays tribute to the power and violence of love:

> Love is strong as death,
> Passion cruel as the grave;
> It blazes up like blazing foe,
> Fiercer than any flame.
> Many waters cannot quench love,
> No flood can sweep it away:
> If a man were to offer for love
> The whole wealth of his house,
> It would be utterly scorned.[24]

It is because the Hebrew title mentions King Solomon as its author that the book's alternative title is 'the Song of Solomon', but his name only appears in the third person,[25] and stylistic and thematic features (including evident echoes of the Hellenistic pastoral of Theocritus) ascribe the work to a far later epoch than Solomon's, namely the third or second century BC.

It was no doubt the ascription to Solomon, founder of the Temple (as well as versatile lover), which secured the admission of this unexpected material to the Hebrew Bible (it is the first of the festal Megilloth or scrolls, Appendix 4, s.v. Esther), and the process was rationalized by theories detecting an allegory of the relationship between Yahweh (bridegroom) and Israel (bride). This comparison was already familiar from the prophets,[26] who had themselves been prompted by near-eastern precedents, drawn, for instance, from the love lyrics of Egypt (including pieces believed to relate to the cult of the goddess Hathor), and from texts reflecting Sumerian rites of sacred marriage (in which the king played the part of the fertility god Tammuz). Canaanite documents from Ugarit reflect similar rituals and poems, notably in relation to the marriage of Yerah the moon-god and his consort Nikkal, and recount the legend of the monarch Krt, the son of El, in which the beauty of his bride Hry receives celebration.[27]

Whatever the traditional background of the *Song of Songs* might be, its poet or poets had probably more or less forgotten its existence, since the work that emerged, in its existing form, has become virtually an anthology of secular poems of courting and mating. They were no doubt sung at wedding festivities, like psalms written for royal marriages.[28] Later on, rabbis did not approve of people singing these pieces as secular compositions. Yet the great Akiba ben Joseph, in the second century AD, pronounces the *Song of Songs* 'the Holy of Holies',[29] that is to say the most sacred of the group of biblical books known as the Sacred Writings (Appendix 2), and certainly the poems harmonized with the scriptural teaching 'Be fruitful and multiply',[30] honouring the belief that the *shekinah*, the divine presence and immanence, floats between bridegroom and bride. For a Jew who does not try to procreate a family was considered by the Talmud as if he had shed blood and diminished the image of Yahweh, causing his presence to depart from Israel.[31]

APPENDIX 6

TEMPLES OUTSIDE JERUSALEM

ARAD in the eastern Negeb, 20 miles north-east of Beersheba and 15 miles west of the Dead Sea, dates back to the fourth millennium BC. Excavations have revealed a place of worship, measuring 65 by 49 feet, belonging to the fortified city built by Solomon. Some archaeologists have identified this as a temple of Yahweh, with the implication that Solomon's temple-building was not limited to Jerusalem. But although certain resemblances to Solomon's Jerusalem Temple, as described by the Bible, can be detected, there are also divergences which leave it uncertain whether the Arad sanctuary was, in fact, dedicated to Yahweh, rather than to one of the many foreign cults which Solomon sanctioned as well.

ELEPHANTINE is an island on the River Nile at the point where the Aswan Dam has now been built. During the Persian occupation of the country (from 525 BC), it harboured a Jewish military colony, but there had also been Jews at Elephantine before 525. Its first Jewish colony may go back to the later eighth century, or at least to the seventh or early sixth, under the XXVIth Dynasty pharaohs Psamtik (Psammetichus) I or Ahmose (Amasis) II.

Some of the settlement's fifth century archives have been discovered, in the form of papyri in imperial Aramaic, close to the language of Nehemiah and Ezra.[32] From these documents it appears that the colonists possessed a temple where they worshipped Yahu (a form of the name Yahweh); evidently they paid no heed to *Deuteronomy*'s demand for cult-centralization at Jerusalem. Nor were they any more attentive to orthodox insistence on monotheistic Yahwism, since among other objects of their worship were Herem-Bethel, Asham (Eshem)-Bethel, and Anat-Bethel, who seem to have been distinct Canaanite or Aramaean deities rather than manifestations of Yahweh. These appellations indicate that some of the Jewish inhabitants of Elephantine came from Bethel, though a substantial contingent also seems to have arrived from Judah, after its fall to the Babylonians.

The religious autonomy of these settlers was encouraged by the Persians, whose King Darius II wrote to Arsham, his satrap in Egypt, ordering that the Feast of Unleavened Bread should be meticulously observed (419). However, at a time when Arsham was out of the country, the priests of the Egyptian god Khnum, probably hostile not only to these religious practices but also to the

Persian occupying power, attacked the temple at Elephantine and razed it to the ground. The Jews, over a period of years, sent petitions to various personages requesting permission to rebuild the shrine; and worship was in due course resumed. But when the Egyptian XXVIIIth dynasty eliminated Persian control (c. 405–401), the colony seems, before long, to have disappeared.

GERIZIM, Mount (the Samaritans). There had long been tension between Jerusalem and Samaria, founded by Omri and Ahab to become the capital of the northern kingdom of Israel. But the seeds of a decisive breakaway were sown by the attitude of Nehemiah and Ezra (Ch.16,i), when they returned to Jerusalem from Babylonia. For they took the view that the Samaritans, polluted by an influx of immigrants after the Assyrian deportations (Ch.10,iii), provided a classic example of the tricky, undesirable category of bastard semi-foreigners, practising impure religion. In consequence, when the Samaritans offered assistance in the reconstruction of the city, their offer was turned down (the Bible suggests that there may have been an earlier rejection by Zerubbabel and Jeshua). As a result, they have continued to execrate the memory of Ezra ('the accursed'). The Jews, in reply, maintained that the hostile governor of Samaria Sanballat, who did everything possible to obstruct Nehemiah and Ezra, became the founder of the Samaritan sect that now began to emerge. The development of the schism, however, was a gradual affair, culminating when the Samaritans erected a rival temple (of which the remains have been found) on Mount Gerizim (2,860 feet high in the Ephraim hills), with the declaration that this, and not Jerusalem, was Yahweh's chosen place. It is not known if the building was put up before, during, or after the time of Alexander the Great. While he was alive, however, the people of the region rebelled against his governor, with the result that Samaria was transformed into a Greek military colony, and much of its population moved to Shechem, which became the future dwelling place of most of the Samaritan sectaries.

Samaritans as well as Jews were settled in Egypt under the Ptolemies, and their synagogues were to be found in many other countries of the Dispersion as well. Men like Ben Sira, the author of *Ecclesiasticus*, particularly hated them, regarding their cult as a deplorable heresy. Another very hostile witness, the historian Josephus, declares that it was at the wish of their own local authorities (notably the Greek colonists?) that the Seleucid king Antiochus IV Epiphanes Hellenized their temple on Mount Gerizim, dedicating it to Zeus Xenios, 'protector of strangers' (or possibly to Zeus Hellenios, 'of the Greeks').[33] However, the Hasmonaean monarch John Hyrcanus I demolished the shrine altogether (129).

Subsequently the territory of the Samaritans was incorporated in the Roman province of Judaea. But they were frequently restive, and Pontius Pilate (AD 26–36) put down a religious demonstration on Mount Gerizim by force, suspecting subversive messianic intentions (Ch.20,i). The Samaritans stood aside from the First Revolt (AD 66–70), though the Romans, once again, had to crush incipient messianic disturbances. At the time of the Second Revolt (132–5), their writings were burnt by Hadrian.

After a brief renaissance in the fourth century AD, they chose to abandon the

Byzantine cause in the seventh, in favour of the Persians, who were superseded shortly afterwards, however, by the Arabs. Thereafter the Samaritan sect continued to survive, though usually as an oppressed minority. It is still represented in 1983 by a population of five hundred at Nablus (Shechem) and the new town of Holon (a suburb of Tel Aviv), under the high priest Pinhas ben Mazliach. He and his followers still celebrate the Passover on Mount Gerizim with abundant animal sacrifice every year.

The Samaritans claim to go back to the time of the judges and to trace their descent from the Ten Tribes, denying the biblical report that the latter were deported *en masse* by the Assyrians. In fundamentalist fashion, they accept only the five books of the Torah as sacred scripture, and call themselves *Shamerim* (observant) rather than *Shomeronim* (Samaritans) on the grounds that they alone preserve Moses' authentic teaching. The text of their Torah, which employs an archaic alphabet resembling Phoenician characters and deriving from the Early Hebrew script (the only descendant of that script still in use today), dates in its present guise from the late second or early first century BC. It differs slightly from the orthodox Jewish version. In particular, additional references to Mount Gerizim have been introduced[34]; and a number of regulations are differently interpreted.

The Samaritans divide their history into a period of Divine Pleasure (*rahuta*), when their temple still existed, and Divine Displeasure (*fanuta*) ever since it has been destroyed. But they also believe in a future Day of Retribution and Reward when a Restorer (*taheb*) will appear to revive their fortunes, and the dead will rise again to enter paradise or roast in hell-fire for all eternity.

LEONTOPOLIS During the persecution of the Jews by the Seleucid monarch Antiochus IV Epiphanes in 167–164 BC, and the subsequent Maccabean Revolt, many refugees fled to Egypt, led by Onias (Honi) IV (son of the murdered Onias III), who had been dispossessed of his high-priesthood at Jerusalem by the Hellenizing party, in favour of Alcimus (Eliakim). Onias IV and his following were settled by King Ptolemy VI Philometor at Leontopolis, not the provincial capital of that name but an otherwise unknown place near the southern tip of the Nile delta, where they formed a military colony. Onias IV founded a schismatic temple, forming a branch of a movement (another was at Qumran) rejecting the Temple and priests of Jerusalem.[35] Its Palestinian origin limited its attraction for Egyptian Jews. Nevertheless the shrine survived until the Romans closed it down in AD 73.

SAMARITANS, see GERIZIM, Mount.

APPENDIX 7

THE APOCRYPHA

The name comes from *Apocryphon* (hidden away), referring to writings that were either concealed in a literal sense (though it is not known that this happened) or seemed too profound or too unorthodox for general circulation (cf. legend in 2 Esdras).[36]

Saint Cyril of Alexandria and Saint Jerome used the term for books they found in the Septuagint but not in the Hebrew Bible. When Jerome, therefore, called these writings *apocrypha*, he meant 'uncanonical' ('deuterocanonical' became the preferred Catholic term). Martin Luther sought to establish the Apocrypha – enlarged by the inclusion of a few works outside the Septuagint – as a separate section of Scripture between the two Testaments, and was followed in the Authorized or King James (Church of England) Version of the Bible, which includes the following works under this heading: (⊕ indicates original composition in Greek, ‡ in Hebrew, * in Aramaic): (1 Esdras ‡ * and 2 Esdras * [3 and 4 Esdras in Jerome's Vulgate]: an adaptation of the Book of Ezra, with passages from 2 Chronicles and Nehemiah not in the Septuagint), Tobit * (Appendix 4), Judith ‡ (ibid.), The Rest of Esther * ⊕ (a supplement to Esther, ibid.), Wisdom 'of Solomon' ‡ or ⊕ (Appendix 8), Ecclesiasticus‡ (Ch.17,ii), Baruch ‡ (alleged writings by the secretary of Jeremiah, Ch.13,iii), Epistle of Jeremy (Jeremiah) * (formerly attached to Baruch), Song of the Three Holy Children ‡ (Shadrach, Meshach and Abednego, Ch.18,i), Susanna and the Elders * (Appendix 4), Daniel, Bel and the Dragon * (ibid.), The Prayer of Manasseh or Manasses (not in the Septuagint)‡, 1 Maccabees ‡ and 2 Maccabees ⊕ * (Ch.18,i).

Various other extra-canonical works as well, including many no longer in existence, can be loosely described as 'apocryphal', notably the *pseudepigrapha* (including apocalyptic writings, e.g. the Books of Enoch – 1 Ethiopic, originally in Aramaic; 2 Slavonic, or The Book of the Secrets of Enoch; 3 Hebrew – and legendary lives of the prophets; cf. also Joseph and Asenath, Appendix 4), and the abundant literature of the Qumran sect (Ch.18,ii).

APPENDIX 8

JEWISH WRITINGS OF
ALEXANDRIA

i. Alexandrian writings other than Philo

ARISTEAS, LETTER OF A Jewish author (*c.* 100 BC, or possibly a little earlier) professed to be a pagan official Aristeas writing to his brother Philocrates in order to give a (legendary) account of the compilation of the Septuagint – which stimulated all this Graeco-Jewish writing (Ch.17,i). His purpose was to tell the Jews that they can share Greek ways without compromising the essentials of their religion. He identifies Yahweh with Zeus.

ARISTOBULUS, a philosopher (*c.* 100 BC), wanted to prove in his allegorical Exegesis of the Law of Moses that Jewish wisdom was much older than Greek philosophy – and had provided its source and model. Fragments of his work survive; one passage records that a Greek translation of some sections of the Torah existed before the Septuagint.

ARTAPANUS, at a similar date and with the same aim, made Jacob and his sons the builders of pagan temples, and attributed the foundation of the Egyptian cult of sacred animals to Moses, about whom many legends of Hellenistic type are added. Fragments survive.

DEMETRIUS, towards the end of the third century BC, was the author of a work On the Kings in Judaea, the first Jewish history in Greek. Now lost, it was apparently composed in a simple style, and did not Hellenize the great figures of Jewish history or claim superiority over paganism.

EUPOLEMUS, who was Judas Maccabaeus' envoy to Rome in 161, wrote On the Kings of the Jews, a popular history which was framed in a rhetorical style and took great liberties with the biblical tradition. Eupolemus declared that Moses introduced writing to the Jews, and that they transmitted it to the Phoenicians, who in turn passed their knowledge on to the Greeks. Fragments survive.

EZECHIELOS, second century BC, wrote tragedies on Jewish subjects. 269 lines of his Exagoge (Exodus) still exist, bringing together various chronologically separate episodes (early examples of biblical exegesis and paraphrase) in Hellenistic style, with echoes of Euripides. These passages are the only extant Jewish dramatic verses in Greek, and the longest surviving specimens of Graeco-Jewish poetry.

JOSEPH AND ASENATH See Appendix 4.

MACCABEES, SECOND BOOK OF See Ch.18,i and Appendix 8.

MACCABEES, THIRD BOOK OF Written after the Maccabean period (but before AD 70), the work gives a fictitious, miraculous account of a persecution of the Jews by King Ptolemy IV Philopator of Egypt (221–204 BC). The idea that Jews can accommodate themselves to Greek ways is refuted. (4 Maccabees, a philosophical discourse, was probably written at Antioch in Syria in the first century BC.)

PHILO THE ELDER, c. 200 BC, wrote the first Graeco-Jewish epic poem, On the Kings of the Jews, adhering closely to the biblical tradition. The 24 surviving verses display a style that is obscure to the point of being almost unintelligible. (Philo of Byblus, who wrote on Phoenician antiquities, is a different man: and so is the famous Philo – see below).

THEODOTUS, second century BC, wrote an epic poem about Jewish history, employing a clear and simple manner.

WISDOM (WISDOM OF SOLOMON in Greek manuscripts). It is uncertain whether the original was in Hebrew or Greek. The work did not find its way into the Hebrew Bible, but is in the Septuagint and forms part of the Apocrypha (Appendix 7). It was composed in the first century BC by a Jew who probably lived at Alexandria; he was a man of high intellectual calibre, who wrote with passion and fire. Condemning idolaters at length, the writer harmonizes Jewish religion and Greek philosophy with great boldness, declaring the body to be evil, and accepting the Platonic doctrine of the pre-existent immortality of the soul. He adopts the Stoic doctrine of the universal immanence of wisdom (*hokmah*), personified as in *Job* and *Ecclesiasticus*, and regarded as a sort of attribute of the divinity. She is shown as the defender of the righteous and the judge of God's enemies: and above all she is identified as the all-pervading Word (*logos*, based on the Hebrew *dabar*), in the sense of everything that gave order and shape to the universe and human affairs: a doctrine designed to bridge the gulf between Jewish and Hellenic ideas.

ii. Philo

PHILO (Philo Judaeus), c. 30 BC–early 40s AD, provided an even more comprehensive endeavour to conclude the long history of tensions between Judaism and Hellenism by blending them together and making them one.

His numerous theological-philosophical writings (some of them, originally, composed as sections of larger compositions) include On Providence, On the Indestructibility of the Universe (of which his authorship is not certain but probable), On the Contemplative Life (ditto; expressing admiration of the Essenes [Ch.18,iii] and Therapeutae, Jewish ascetics in Egypt), three major commentaries on the Pentateuch (Torah), and the voluminous Allegorical Expositions of the Holy Laws, explaining the whole of Jewish history by the method of allegory (according to which the contents symbolize an inner, spiritual meaning), which had already been applied to Homer and other Greek poets by the Alexandrians. He also wrote a series of works setting out the Jewish religion for pagans, including an essay On the Decalogue (Ten Commandments) and Biographies of the Wise (Abraham and Joseph are preserved: there is also a Life of Moses, written in the Greek manner but repeating the assumption that Greek philosophers were indebted to him for their views).

Although Philo wholeheartedly admitted Gentile proselytes who 'saw God', considering them to be as unquestionably Jewish as the physical descendants of Abraham, he nevertheless insisted (against certain of his more permissive Alexandrian co-religionists) upon obedience to the Jewish Law, and denounced polytheistic practices. Yet the Bible he used (and treated as oracular) was the Greek version, the Septuagint, and his continuous endeavours to show the resemblances between Greek and Jewish observances draw freely upon the Greek philosophers and display a greater closeness to Greek than to Jewish culture. Finding it difficult, like the author of *Job* and dualists at Qumran and elsewhere (Ch.18,ii), to bridge the gulf between an omnipotent, good God and the imperfect or evil world of matter, Philo accepted the existence of intermediary beings representing the different aspects of God's existence and thought, notably the Logos (see above, *Wisdom of Solomon*).

He also laid great stress on the transcendence and ineffable incomprehensibility of God. Nevertheless, he maintained, human beings are able, by God's grace, to be united within a direct, mystical communion, an experience which he described as 'ecstasy' – a divine frenzy like that of the prophets, but joyful and serene. But this ecstasy is only a stage towards the soul's entire liberation from the body and re-ascension to God. Like Plato, he saw the body as a prison, coffin or grave for the soul, which constantly seeks to rise again to the heights from which it has fallen. These beliefs, blending borrowed elements in so highly original a fashion that they almost amounted to an entire new philosophy, were little studied or cared for by later Jews, but greatly affected the thought of the Christian apologists who were trying to make their religion comprehensible to pagans, and influenced St Augustine's distinction between the two cities in the City of God.

Philo described contemporary events, and recorded the important part he played in them, in his writings Against Flaccus (the governor of Egypt) and On the Embassy to Gaius, accounts of the oppression of the Alexandrian Jews under the emperor Caligula (Ch.20,i). These works reflect the idea that persecutions of this kind inevitably evoke divine punishment.

APPENDIX 9

JEWS AND CHRISTIANS

JOHN THE BAPTIST After Judaea became a Roman province in AD 6 (Ch.20,i), Galilee and Peraea (across the Jordan) continued to constitute the princedom of Herod Antipas (4 BC–AD 39), who like his father Herod the Great ruled as a client of Rome. On the desert fringes of this dominion, in *c*. 28–29, John the Baptist, hailed as the successor of Elijah and Elisha, proclaimed to his fellow Jews the imminence of the Kingdom (Kingship) of Yahweh, following the apocalyptic tradition of the Day of the Lord (Ch.18,i). He also insisted on repentance, a complete change of heart, *after* which, he stressed (differing here from certain of the prophets), all Jews would be forgiven their sins. And he converted the familiar ceremony of periodical ritual ablutions into solemn and significant baptisms.

But Herod Antipas saw John's emphasis on dawning heavenly rule as a potentially subversive belittlement of earthly kingdoms, and had him executed at Machaerus, a fortress built by his father on the border of Peraea.

JESUS, according to the Gospels (from which, although they date from thirty-seven years and more after his death, the principal features of his career can be partially reconstructed), was one of those whom John baptized. He probably came not from Bethlehem (inserted to fulfil a prophecy by Micah,[37] Appendix 3) but from Nazareth or some other place in Galilee, a territory only converted in fairly recent times to Judaism (Ch.18,ii), and looked down upon by Jerusalem as bucolic and productive of theological errors; many of the itinerant, charismatic preachers of the epoch were Galileans.

Jesus added an amendment to John's preaching: the Kingdom of God was not just imminent, because *it had already begun to arrive*, by his own agency, under God's direction. This placed everything in a new light. Like John, he insisted on repentance, and he claimed that his mission empowered him to forgive sins. To his fellow Jews, who regarded the forgiveness of sins as a free gift belonging to Yahweh alone, this claim seemed a usurpation of the divine authority and an infringement upon monotheism.

All Jesus' thoughts and social and ethical teachings (closely adapted from Judaism), as well as his healings and other actions (often hailed as miraculous), were dominated by this single idea, to which social and ethical precepts, however

277

strikingly formulated, remained secondary. His belief that all Jews, without exception, were embraced by the dawning Kingship prompted him to devote particular consideration to the Jewish poor, because they were 'poor in spirit', depending so much on God's help. Repentant sinners, too, lacking the complacency of the consciously virtuous, would easily qualify for admission. And, by the same token, the simple, unspoilt directness of children must make them readily receptive to Jesus' message. He also welcomed women around him, since obviously the Kingdom could not be limited to only one sex.

But Pharisees and scribes (Ch. 18,ii) were not accustomed to being surrounded by women in such a way. Moreover, his injunction to love your enemy as yourself – because petty worldly enmities paled to nothing in face of the unique opportunity – seemed to them impracticable, and therefore mistaken (although *Proverbs* had said one should give one's hungry enemy food to eat).[38] Nor did other Jewish teachers consort, like him, with the Samaritans (Appendix 6), or go outside the synagogues, as he did, in order to attract a much wider Jewish public (including scarcely any Gentiles, it would seem, though he no doubt proposed to reach out to them at a later stage, in pursuance of the universalistic proclamations of the prophets).

Jesus' adherents and listeners saw him in various lights. They declared him to be a member of the House of David. They hailed him as the heir to the prophetic succession, believing, for example, that he was Elijah or Jeremiah reborn. The story of the Transfiguration told how Moses and Elijah appeared beside him. He was also envisaged as the messiah or anointed one (*Christos*), whose coming was said to have been forecast by *Second Isaiah* (Ch. 15,ii), or was seen as the Son of Man foretold in the *Book of Daniel* (Ch. 18,i). His disciples also declared him to be the Son of God – in a new, literal, special sense of one born of a virgin (translating the 'young woman' of Isaiah's prophecy[39] in this sense). Jewish thinkers were familiar with miraculous elements in the births of Samson, Isaac, Jacob and Samuel. But they felt that the Christians' assertion that Jesus had no earthly father at all endowed him with a divinity that blasphemed against Yahweh's uniqueness.

For these reasons his mission to the Galilean Jews encountered extensive opposition. In consequence, Jesus abandoned the region and proceeded gradually towards Jerusalem (*c.* AD 30 or 33). But he must have foreseen the rejection and death that awaited him there, recalling the stories of heroic past martyrdoms and *Second Isaiah*'s poems describing a suffering servant (Ch. 15,iii), and a host of other prophecies that seemed to prefigure his career. For, like other Jews before him, he wholeheartedly accepted the concept of 'typology': that is to say he believed that his experiences fulfilled, in precise detail, the predictions supposedly offered by the Torah and prophets and psalms.

And Jesus purposefully ensured that fulfilment by directing all his actions accordingly. Thus the manner of his coming to Jerusalem was adjusted to fulfil a text of *Second Zechariah* (Appendix 3), and, after his arrival in the city, he was said to have quoted passages from *Jeremiah* and *Second Isaiah* to forecast and justify his ejection of traders from the Temple precinct by force.[40] This action helped to cause his arrest by the Temple's powerful controllers the Sadducees, with the connivance of one of his own twelve apostles Judas Iscariot, disappointed, like others, by his rejection of an earthly leadership role.

Jesus appears to have been accused of threatening to destroy the Temple, and claiming to be the messiah and Son of God and king of the Jews, charges to which, believing in the wholly unique, and therefore not so easily definable, character of his mission, he gave no clear answer. Tiberius' provincial governor Pontius Pilate took the case over, and convicted him of sedition on the last-named charge. It is not impossible (with due respect for vigorous arguments to the contrary) that the high priest Caiaphas and the Sanhedrin acquiesced. But by a total *non sequitur*, many Christians held the entire Jewish race to blame for his death for all time to come, under the curse of Cain (it was absolved of deicide by the Second Vatican Council, 1962–5). Three days after Jesus' death on the cross, his followers declared that they witnessed his bodily resurrection (a concept going back to *Daniel*, Ch.18,i) and subsequent ascent to heaven, as Enoch, Moses and Elijah were believed to have ascended in ancient times.

PAUL The conversion of this tragic story into a posthumous triumph was the work of Saul – a Greek-speaking Jew of the Dispersion, belonging to a Pharisee family of Tarsus in Cilicia (S.E. Asia Minor) which obtained Roman citizenship, whereupon his name was changed to Paul.

Following the crucifixion, local Jewish councils took vigorous action against the supporters of Jesus, and Paul travelled round to reinforce this repressive aim. While on his way to Damascus, however, where many Jews resided, he was overcome by a visionary experience consisting of a voice and a light (the phenomenon of photism, described by Ezekiel, Ch.14,i), and converted to an unshakeable belief in Jesus' divinity. Paul's subsequent activities are known to us not only from the later *Acts of the Apostles*, but also from his own vigorous, excitable, yet powerfully intellectual letters, of which the earliest date from the 50s, scarcely twenty years after Jesus' death.

At first the centre of the minute following of Jesus was Jerusalem, under his principal disciple Simon Peter and then James the Just known as Jesus' brother, who with Paul's participation organized missions to the Jewish Dispersion. But then in *c*. 45–47 began Paul's own major journeys to numerous countries, wonders of perseverance and endurance which brought him into violent conflict not only with the Jews but also with Jewish Christians, who deplored his permissive attitude to unqualified Gentile converts. As a result of these frictions, he increasingly addressed and converted audiences of Gentiles in place of the Jews whom he had first sought to approach. On returning to Jerusalem in *c*. 58, he was accused of blasphemy by the Jewish authorities, and detained in order to save his life – by the Romans. Shortly afterwards they moved him to Caesarea Maritima, where judicial hearings were held, and then, in response to his appeal (as a Roman citizen) transferred him to Rome, where Nero was emperor. There, following trials which may have been instigated not by Jews but by Jewish Christians, he was executed, perhaps in 64 when the Christian community at Rome suffered persecution as scapegoats for the city's great fire.[41]

Paul had become converted because he could no longer accept the Torah as a guide to life, declaring that its unrealistically perfectionist legalism had failed, throughout the ages, to rescue the Jewish people from its miseries. He felt that the whole of the world's history had been set on an entirely new course by Jesus, the second Adam who, reversing the original sin of the first, brings all men to life. Paul seems to have been uninterested in any and every occurrence in Jesus' career before the Last Supper. Yet he maintained a total conviction that the tales of the crucifixion and resurrection and ascension possessed the unique saving power to obliterate men's sins and thus set the overwhelming revolution into effect. It was these events, maintained Paul, which by God's grace (beside which human initiatives amounted to nothing) had given everyone an opportunity for the redemption which had figured so largely in Jewish ideas. All other traditional 'wisdom', he declared, was negligible and useless. The Jews, on the other hand, felt that this assertion that sins were cancelled by Jesus' death invalidated God's free forgiveness of the penitent; and that the total humbling of the heart to receive God's grace, upon which Paul insisted, struck at morality by paralysing the human will.

AFTER PAUL After Paul had vanished from the scene, his churches for Gentile converts did not seem to have come to very much, and such Christian communities as survived were more often to be found among the Jews, who still cherished Jesus' memory. But the First Jewish Revolt (AD 66–73) totally reversed this situation, since the Jewish Christians became discredited among the Romans along with the Jews (from whom the Roman authorities imperfectly distinguished them), and gradually dwindled into a number of minor, eccentric sects, which did not outlast the ancient world. The Gentile Christians, on the other hand, seeing the destruction of Jerusalem as a fulfilment of biblical prophecies (and adding interpolations to Josephus [Ch.20,ii] so as to make the point clearer), escaped this stigma and persisted and multiplied.

Within a very short period after the revolt, it was they who began to produce the four Gospels – preaching a sharp dissociation from the Jews, and displaying the Jewish Christians also (exemplified by Jesus' apostles) in a by no means favourable light. In the second century AD, when belief in Jesus Christ and the practice of Judaism had been found to be incompatible, feelings moved still further in Paul's favour. It is true that an attempt by Marcion of Sinope in Pontus (N. Asia Minor) to raise him to a startling eminence – by a total rejection of the entire Old Testament, which seemed to him bloody and licentious – proved abortive, and the dominant tendency instead was to damp down the more awkward, radical aspects of Paul's thinking. But it was he who had adapted the Jewish religion of Jesus to the Gentile world with which the future of Christianity remained.

MIDRASH, MISHNAH
AND TALMUD

MIDRASH (from Hebrew *darash*, to search or investigate). A term applied to certain methods of biblical exposition and to a class of Jewish writings employing these methods. The Midrashim are divisible into (1) Halakha (Tannaitic, 'of the academies'), comprising the deduction of the oral from the written Law, (2) Haggada, intended for the purpose of edification rather than legislation – lore rather than law. Midrash proper originated during the last centuries BC, the great period of the scribes (Ch.18,ii), though the earliest extant collections, notably the Mekilta on *Exodus*, only date from the second century AD. The Talmud describes Midrash as a hammer that wakes to shining light the sparks that slumber in the rock.[42]

MISHNAH A collection of precepts which set out to teach the oral Law without binding it directly to the text of Scripture. This method (from *shano*, repeat, i.e. study) went back at least to the first century BC, and by the second century AD was gaining preference over the Midrash. It was at this period that the material comprising the Mishnah was systematized into its present form, reputedly by the Patriarch Judah I ha-Nasi (*c.* 135–219). Gaining immediate recognition, this massive repository of diversified traditions became the most conspicuous landmark in Jewish literature since the Torah and the prophets, and, next to them, exerted the greatest influence on the language. It is written in Mishnaic Hebrew, a development (through 'rabbinical' Hebrew) of the classical, biblical language. The Mishnah contains little about ethics, except in a single treatise, the *Aboth* (a guide to private conscience, not necessarily containing only late material, as is sometimes supposed). And Messianism and the coming Kingdom of God receive very little attention indeed.

The Mishnah forms one of the two main parts of the Talmud.

TALMUD (Hebrew 'learning'). Strictly speaking the Talmud, long revered by the Jews as a sacred book, comprises two main sections, the Mishnah (see above) and the Gemara ('completion'). The designation of 'Talmud' is generally applied to the latter, which provides an interpretative commentary on the Mishnah. There are two Gemaras: the Palestinian or Jerusalem Talmud written in the western dialect of the Aramaic language, and completed in the fourth century AD; and the Babylonian Talmud in eastern Aramaic, dating from the following century.

The Talmud is an almost inexhaustible mine of information about Jewish and near-eastern and middle-eastern theology, law, history, ethics, legend and folklore. Its deliberate retention of contrasted and rejected viewpoints is particularly valuable.

THE NAMES OF THE COUNTRY
AND THE PEOPLE

To name correctly, in any specific period, the land and people described in these pages is often not very easy.

I have spoken of 'Israel' in the title of the book, though the term has to be employed with care. The problem is not so much that it had originally designated only the central tribal uplands, because that definition was soon extended. More productive of confusion is the fact that from the death of Solomon onwards, for some centuries, Israel was only one of the two kingdoms into which the territory was divided, the other being Judah. As for Canaan – another term often used by the biblical writers to describe the land they took over from the Canaanites – the designation had appeared in Akkadian (north-eastern Semitic) texts of fifteenth-century date, and thereafter recurred with fluctuating meanings (the Amarna tablets use it to signify a province – western Palestine and Phoenicia – whose people called themselves Canaanites, and part of Syria, itself a country of variously estimated dimensions[43]).

Often Palestine, known as Syria Palaestina to the Greek historian Herodotus,[44] is as convenient a designation as any. Originally signifying Philistia (land of the Philistines), the term was extended inland so as to comprise the whole country. Its employment, therefore, in connexion with the ancient world need not be thought to imply support or rejection of any specific modern political thesis.

For the Greek and Hasmonaean periods the term Judaea is available – including (usually) the regions now defined as Judaea and Samaria, but in other respects subject to geographical fluctuation. The Roman province, too, continued to be known as Judaea, until Hadrian abolished the name in favour of Syria Palaestina.

Equally serious difficulties arise when we try to decide what to call the men and women who lived in the country. 'The people of Yahweh' is often a convenient term. 'Jew', 'Hebrew', 'Israelite' are sometimes regarded as interchangeable, but that is not always strictly the case. The word 'Jew' (originally defining the descendants of Jacob's son Judah) carries a wide range of implications – religious, cultural, ethnic, biological[45] – which mean that the term can hardly be employed without misleading effect before the fall of the kingdoms of

Israel and Judah, or even, some would say, before the return of the exiles, when Judaism came to possess many of the characteristics that it subsequently retained.

The designations 'Israelites' or 'people of Israel' are available for the earlier periods, though not, perhaps, for the very earliest: since some believe that they can only be accurately used *after* the Exodus and subsequent settlement, though it is convenient to accept, for practical purposes, their biblical extension backwards to cover the period of the patriarchs. But once we have reached the epoch when the country has become divided between the kingdoms of Israel and Judah, 'Israelites' and 'people of Israel' will evidently have to be abandoned as a generic term. And so at that period 'Hebrews' may be used instead – until the time comes when 'Jews' seems a sufficiently descriptive appellation. (Some like to speak of the people of the much earlier times of the patriarchs and judges as Hebrews, too, especially as all the biblical uses of the word, except one, relate to the period before 1000 BC. And yet, for these early epochs, it is perhaps best to avoid the term all the same, because of the controversial obscurity of words that may be etymologically related to it: the cryptic Habiru or Apiru, and Eber the ancestor of Abraham, Ch. 1,ii;3,i.)

TABLE OF DATES

CANAAN, ISRAEL, PALESTINE	MESOPOTAMIA, SYRIA, ARABIA, PERSIA
8300–4000 BC. Neolithic epoch: Jericho	
4500. First pottery	
3150–2200. Early Canaanite (Early Bronze) Age: ending in widespread regression	3500 BC. Oldest inscribed tablet at Kish (Sumerian)
	2600. Supremacy of Ur (24th cent., Great Palace)
	2370. Mesopotamia annexed by Akkadians
	2300. First climax of Ebla (N. Syria)
2200–2000. Semi-nomad invaders (shaft graves): (Middle Canaanite–Middle Bronze Age I or transitional between Early and Middle Canaanite)	
2000–1800. Amorite invasions and immigrations: (Middle Canaanite–Middle Bronze Age IIA)	1800. Script at Byblus
19th–16th cents.(?) The patriarchs Abraham, Isaac, Jacob	18th cent. Golden Age of Mari under Zimri-Lim
1800–1550. Economic and cultural prosperity under Egyptian domination (Middle Canaanite–Middle Bronze Age IIB)	1728–1687. Hammurabi of Babylon
	1365–1250. First Assyrian Empire
14th cent. Labaya the 'Lion Man' at Shechem	14th–13th cent. Tablets at Ugarit (Ras Shamra)
1300. Departure of Joseph for Egypt	
12th cent. Invasions and immigrations of Joshua and others	12th–11th cent. Rise of Aramaeans and Phoenicians
12th–11th cents. The Judges: the First Commonwealth begins	
12th–11th cents. Settlement of Philistines	
1050. Philistines defeat Israelites at Aphek	
after 1050. Samuel	
late 11th cent. Saul: killed by Philistines at Mount Gilboa	
1000–965. David	

EGYPT	GREECE, ROME
2325–2275 BC. Pepi I (VIth Dynasty): fought against sand-dwellers	
1971–1928. Sesostris II (XIIth Dynasty, Middle Kingdom): records of Sinuhe	2000–1400 BC. Height of Minoan civilization in Crete
1925–1875 and 2nd half 19th cent. Execration texts	
1900–1890. Tomb-paintings at Beni-Hasan	
1720–1580/67. Hyksos rule (XVth-XVIIth Dynasties)	
1479. Victory of Thothmes III (XVIIIth Dynasty, New Kingdom) over Canaanite coalition at Kàdesh	
1417–1379. Amenhotep III: Amarna letters	
1379–1362. Amenhotep IV (Akhenaten): Amarna letters: religious reforms	1400–1200. Height of Mycenaean civilization in Greece and Aegean
1304–1290. Seti I (XIXth Dynasty): arrival of Joseph in Egypt (?)	
1287/6. Rameses II fights battle of Kadesh against Hittites	
1225–1187. Wars against Peoples of Sea (Philistines, etc.)	
1213–1203. Merneptah: Exodus of Moses from Egypt (?)	
1185–1152. Rameses III (XXth Dynasty)	
1100–1085. Rameses XI: Mission of Wen Amun	
	11th cent. Dorian immigrations to Greece
	825–800. Euboean settlers at Al-Mina (N. Syria)
	8th cent. Urbanization of Greek city-states

CANAAN, ISRAEL, PALESTINE	MESOPOTAMIA, SYRIA, ARABIA, PERSIA
965–927. Solomon: the First Temple	970–936. Hiram I the Great of Tyre
926–722. The Divided Kingdoms: Israel and Judah	10th cent. 'Queen of Sheba' (Saba, Yemen)
9th cent. Elijah, Elisha	885–870. Ben-hadad I of Damascus
	881–859. Ashur-nasir-pal II of Assyria
	873–842. Ittobaal (Ethbaal) of Tyre
	870–842. Ben-hadad II of Damascus
	854/3. Assyrians fight battle of Karkar against Syro-Israelite coalition
mid-8th cent. Amos, Hosea	733. Damascus destroyed and annexed by Assyrians
742. Isaiah begins to prophesy	
722. Fall of Israel (Northern Kingdom) to the Assyrians: Deportation of the Ten Tribes	722. Conquest of Israel by Shalmaneser V and Sargon II of Assyria
	701. Sennacherib of Assyria invades Judah
600. Jeremiah begins to prophesy	612. Babylonians destroy Nineveh
597, 587. Fall of Judah (Southern Kingdom) to the Babylonians: end of First Commonwealth: Deportation (Dispersion)	597, 587. Conquest of Judah by Nebuchadrezzar II of Babylonia
	539. Conquest of Babylonia by Cyrus II the Great of Persia (Achaemenid Dynasty)
early 6th cent. Ezekiel	
537. Edict of Cyrus II the Great of Persia permitting exiles to return	
later 6th cent. Second Isaiah	525. Conquest of Egypt by Cambyses of Persia
516. Second Temple completed by Sheshbazzar and Zerubbabel	
later 5th cent. Nehemiah	490, 480–79. Wars between Persians (Darius I, Xerxes) and Greeks
early 4th cent. Ezra	464–425. Artaxerxes I of Persia
	5th cent. Geshem of Dedan (Kebar) in N. Arabia
	404–358. Artaxerxes II Memnon of Persia
332. Conquest by Alexander III the Great	4th cent. Nabataean state founded in S. Arabia

EGYPT	GREECE, ROME
945 – 924. Sheshonk (Shishak) I (XXIInd Dynasty)	
	750 – 700. Completion of the Homeric epics (Iliad and Odyssey)
	750 – 550. Colonial expansion
610 – 595. Necho II (XXVIth Dynasty; Saite Kingdom)	7th – 6th cents. Social revolutions
589 – 570. Hophra (Apries)	6th cent. Climax of power of Etruscan city-states
525. Conquest by Persians	509 – 31. Roman Republic
	508. Constitution of Cleisthenes at Athens
	499 – 494. Ionian Revolt against Persians
	490, 480 – 479. Persian Wars
	477. Delian League, followed by Athenian empire
	5th cent. Golden Age of Greek literature: Aeschylus, Sophocles, Euripides; Herodotus, Thucydides
	mid-5th cent. Supremacy of Pericles at Athens
	447 – 438. Construction of Parthenon at Athens
	399. Trial and execution of Socrates
332. Conquest by Alexander III the Great	338. Philip II of Macedonia defeats Greek city-states at Chaeronea
	4th cent. Plato, Isocrates, Demosthenes, Aristotle
	4th cent. Rome's conquest of Italy
	336 – 323. Alexander III the Great of Macedonia

CANAAN, ISRAEL, PALESTINE	MESOPOTAMIA, SYRIA, ARABIA, PERSIA
323 – 200. Ptolemaic rule	334 – 330. Darius III Codomannus of Persia: conquered by Alexander III the Great
	312 – 63. Seleucid empire
200 – 142. Seleucid rule	247. Parthians break away from Seleucid empire
	223 – 187. Antiochus III the Great: annexes Palestine from Ptolemies (200)
167. Measures of Antiochus IV Epiphanes against Jews lead to Maccabean Revolt	175 – 163. Antiochus IV Epiphanes: measures against Jews (167)
166 – 37. Hasmonaean (Maccabean) rule	
164. Temple reconstituted	
mid-2nd cent. Sadducees, Pharisees develop	
140 – 130. Qumran community established	
135 – 104. John I Hyrcanus: Galilee and Idumaea annexed	
103 – 76. Alexander Jannaeus: assumes title of king	
63. Judaea becomes Roman client	63. Pompey annexes remnant of Seleucid empire (province of Syria)
37 – 4 BC. Herod the Great	
AD 6 – 41 and from 44. Judaea a Roman province	
30 or 33. Crucifixion of Jesus	
64. Execution of St Paul	
66 – 73. First Jewish Revolt (First Roman War): ends with fall of Jerusalem (70) and Masada (73)	

EGYPT	GREECE, ROME
323 – 30. Ptolemaic kingdom	323 – 30. The Hellenistic kingdoms (Ptolemaic, Seleucid, Antigonid, and then Indo-Greek)
	264 – 241, 218 – 222. Rome's victories over Carthage in First and Second Punic Wars
	2nd cent. Rome's victories over Hellenistic kingdoms
	58 – 44. Julius Caesar's Gallic Wars and dictatorships
30. Death of Cleopatra VII and Roman annexation	31. Octavian (Augustus) defeats Antony and Cleopatra VII at Actium
	31 BC – AD 68. Julio-Claudian dynasty (Augustus, Tiberius, Gaius [Caligula], Claudius, Nero)
	68 – 69. Year of the Four Emperors
	69 – 79. Vespasian: his son Titus captures Jerusalem (70)

NOTES

(pp. 17–60)

CHAPTER 2
The Canaanites

1 Joshua 11.10.
2 R. de Vaux, *Early History of Israel*, I, pp. 95f., 103f.; W.L.Albright, *Cambridge Ancient History*, 3rd ed., II, 2, pp. 114–16.
3 Ibid., pp. 139f. and pp. 148–60 respectively.
4 Psalms 14.1; 53.1.
5 F.Jacoby, *Fragmente der griechischen Historiker*, III, 802.
6 Genesis 14.19.
7 Jeremiah 44.15–19.
8 J.Finegan, *Light from the Ancient Past*, I, p. 168.

CHAPTER 3
The Patriarchs

1 Genesis 14.13.
2 Genesis 17.5
3 Genesis 49.1–27.
4 Genesis 32.28
5 Sources in R.deVaux, op. cit., pp. 271f., 275–8.
6 Exodus 1.8.
7 J.B.Pritchard, *The Ancient Near East in Pictures Relating to the Old Testament*, 3rd ed., fig. 3.
8 Psalms 78.12, 43.
9 J.B.Pritchard, *Ancient Near Eastern Texts Relating to the Old Testament*, pp. 376–8.

CHAPTER 4
Moses

1 Papyrus Anastasi VI (J.B.Pritchard, *Ancient Near Eastern Texts*, op. cit., p. 259).
2 Exodus 2.10.
3 Exodus 24.12; 31.18.
4 Deuteronomy 34.10–12.
5 Exodus 3.6,15; 4.5.
6 Deuteronomy 32.8
7 Exodus 6.2f. etc. against Genesis 4.1,26 etc.
8 Judges 5.5.
9 Exodus 3.14.
10 Exodus 20.2; Deuteronomy 5.8
11 Exodus 33.20.
12 Deuteronomy 6.4f.
13 Exodus 6.7.
14 I Samuel 2.30.
15 Exodus 20.12–17; Deuteronomy 5.16–21.

CHAPTER 5
Conquest and Settlement

1 Joshua 24.30.
2 Joshua 13.1.
3 Psalms 105.12f.
4 Judges 6.32.
5 Ezekiel 16.3.
6 Judges 5.13, 19, 20f.
7 Judges 9.46.
8 Numbers 23.9; Deuteronomy 26.19.
9 Exodus 20.11.

293

10 Psalms 119.97f.
11 Exodus 29.44.
12 2 Samuel 15.24.
13 Exodus 12.12; 12.13, 23, 27.

CHAPTER 6
The Philistines, Samuel and Saul

1 W.F.Edgerton and J.A.Wilson, *Historical Records of Ramses* III, pp. 30f.; R.D.Barnett, *Cambridge Ancient History*, 3rd ed., II, 2, pp. 371f., 507f.
2 J.B.Pritchard, *Ancient Near Eastern Texts Relating to the Old Testament*, pp. 25–9.
3 1 Samuel 13.19–21.
4 J.A.Thompson, *The Bible and Archaeology*, p. 130; Numbers 22. 4–6.
5 Jeremiah 23.22.
6 1 Samuel 10.5.
7 1 Samuel 15.3.
8 1 Samuel 8.5.
9 1 Samuel 10.11f., 19.24.
10 2 Samuel 1.18.
11 Proverbs 16.18.

CHAPTER 7
David

1 1 Chronicles 14.15.
2 Psalms 89.3, 27; 45.6
3 Psalms 110.4.
4 2 Samuel 21.19; 1 Chronicles 20.5 (son of Jair, slayer of Goliath).
5 2 Samuel 6.16, 20.
6 2 Samuel 7.16.
7 2 Samuel 22.2.
8 2 Samuel 1.26f.
9 N.K.Sandars (ed.), *The Epic of Gilgamesh*, pp. 91ff.
10 Ecclesiasticus 47.8.
11 E.g., Psalms 18; 55; 68; 78.
12 2 Samuel 6.5.

CHAPTER 8
Solomon

1 J.Bright, *History of Israel*, 2nd ed., p. 211, note 74.

2 1 Kings 11.5–7.
3 1 Kings 5.13 (against 9.22).
4 1 Kings 4.21.
5 J.B.Pritchard, *Ancient Near Eastern Texts Relating to the Old Testament*, p. 320.
6 1 Kings 4.31.
7 1 Kings 4.30.
8 R.D.Barnett, *Illustrations of Old Testament History*, pp. 33ff.
9 Proverbs 22.17–24.
10 H.W.F.Saggs, *The Greatness that was Babylon*, pp. 439ff.
11 Proverbs 25.21.
12 Proverbs 6.29–35.
13 Proverbs 8.13.
14 2 Samuel 14.2–20; 20.16–22.
15 Proverbs 25.1–29.27.

CHAPTER 9
The Invention of History

1 G.W.Anderson, *A Critical Introduction to the Old Testament*, p. 31; J.A.Soggin, *Introduction to the Old Testament*, p. 103.
2 Genesis 3.19.
3 Daniel 4.10; cf. Ezekiel 31.9.
4 Numbers 21.8f.; 2 Kings 18.4.
5 Micah 6.7; cf. Exodus 34.19.
6 Genesis 8.21.
7 Genesis 9.25.
8 Genesis 10.21.
9 Genesis 11.9.
10 Genesis 12.2,7.
11 Luke 17.32.
12 Genesis 18.25.
13 Exodus 34.14–26.
14 2 Samuel 18.19–30; 17.17–21.
15 2 Samuel 12.1–4, 9–12.

CHAPTER 10
The Northern Monarchy: Israel

1 1 Kings 12.20.
2 Exodus 32.4–35.
3 Y.Aharoni, *The Land of the Bible*, pp. 202f., 241.
4 J.B.Pritchard, *Ancient Near Eastern Texts*, op. cit., pp. 320f.

5 1 Kings 16.25.

6 R.D.Barnett, *Illustrations of Old Testament History*, pp. 48f.

7 1 Kings 16.31f.

8 1 Kings 18.19; 13.

9 1 Kings 18.21; 20.1–34; 21.26, 16.30.

10 2 Kings 10.31.

11 R.D.Barnett, op. cit., p. 50.

12 J.B.Pritchard, *Ancient Near Eastern Texts*, op. cit., 320f.

13 D.W.Thomas, *Documents from Old Testament Times*, pp. 204–8.

14 Hosea 7.11.

15 R.D.Barnett, op. cit., p. 55.

CHAPTER 11
Northern Prophecy and History

1 1 Kings 18.17; 22.24–6.

2 1 Kings 18.21, 39

3 1 Kings 19.12.

4 2 Kings 1.8.

5 2 Kings 2.23f.

6 2 Kings 9.6.

7 Ecclesiasticus 48.12.

8 2 Kings 6.1.

9 Amos 7.14f.

10 1 Kings 22.23; Isaiah 28.7f.; Micah 3.5; Deuteronomy 18.22.

11 Amos 3.8.

12 Amos 2.7.

13 Amos 8.3; cf. 5.18–20; 6.11.

14 Amos 3.2.

15 Hosea 13.1; 11.1f.; 14.8.

16 Hosea 6.2.

17 Hosea 4.5; 6.9; 9.7.

18 Hosea 14.5, 7.

19 Hosea 2.16f.

20 G.W.Anderson, *A Critical Introduction to the Old Testament*, p. 35; J.A.Soggin, *Introduction to the Old Testament*, p. 107.

21 Genesis 22.13f.

CHAPTER 12
The Southern Monarchy: Judah

1 1 Kings 14.23f.

2 1 Kings 15.11.

3 2 Chronicles 24.7.

4 2 Kings 16.3.

5 R.D.Barnett, *Illustrations of Old Testament History*, p. 60.

6 2 Kings 21.9.

7 J.B.Pritchard, *Ancient Near Eastern Texts*, op. cit., p. 291; 2 Chronicles 33.11–13 (garbled account).

8 2 Kings 22.8; 23.2.

9 Jeremiah 22.15f.

10 R.D.Barnett, op. cit., p. 74.

CHAPTER 13
Southern Legend and Prophecy

1 Deuteronomy 17.18.

2 Deuteronomy 4.44–26.28.

3 Deuteronomy 7.7; 9.5.

4 Deuteronomy 32.6f.

5 Deuteronomy 24.16, against 5.9.

6 Deuteronomy 12.29f.; 19.1.

7 Deuteronomy 10.18f; 15.1, 3; 23.20.

8 Deuteronomy 31.19, cf. 11–13.

9 Isaiah 8.1.

10 Isaiah 6.5.

11 Isaiah 1.16f.

12 Isaiah 30.18.

13 Isaiah 6.9f.

14 Isaiah 28.7 (*Good News Bible*).

15 Isaiah 7.14; 9.6.

16 Isaiah 11.6.

17 Isaiah 11.9.

18 Jeremiah 8.8f.

19 Jeremiah 4.6.

20 Jeremiah 46.17.

21 Jeremiah 11.20–3; cf. 20.10f.

22 Jeremiah 15.18; 20.14.

23 Jeremiah 20.7; 12.1f.

24 Jeremiah 20.12; 4.19.

25 Jeremiah 2.8; 10.5.

26 Jeremiah 7.9; 17.2; 2.20; 2.28; 7.30.

27 Jeremiah 7.11.

28 Jeremiah 31.31–4.

29 Jeremiah 31.29f.

30 Jeremiah 23.5–8; 3.14; 31.17.

31 Psalms 83.13; 58.6; 58.10.

32 Psalms 69.1f.

33 Psalms 139.8f.

34 Psalms 18, 29, 68, 72, 74, 78, 80, 82, 86, 88, 89 etc.

35 Psalms 18.2, 6.
36 Psalms 47.5; 68.25.

CHAPTER 14
Prophecy and History in the Dispersion

1 Jeremiah 29.5.
2 J.B.Pritchard, *Ancient Near Eastern
   Texts*, op. cit., p. 308.
3 M.D.Coogan, *Biblical Archaeologist*,
   XXXVII, 1974, p. 6–12.
4 Psalms 137. 1f., 5.
5 Psalms 74.4–11.
6 Ezekiel 20.47, 21.12.
7 Ezekiel 4.1.; 5.1; 4.3; 4.12–14; 3.1–3;
   20.49.
8 Ezekiel 1.4–28.
9 Ezekiel 37.12f.; 3.13; 13.11; 7.17; 24.6;
   3.15 etc.
10 Ezekiel 16.3, 26, 28f., 34; 20.32; 36.26.
11 Ezekiel 43.18–27; 45.13–46.15.
12 Judges 2. 11–23; cf. 1.27–35.
13 2 Kings 20.1–11.
14 2 Kings 21.10.
15 G.W.Anderson, *A Critical Introduction to
   the Old Testament*, p. 46; J.A.Soggin,
   Introduction to the Old Testament, p. 144.
16 Genesis 10.1–7.
17 Genesis 22.18 and 17.
18 Leviticus 16.29; 23.26 (cf. Babylonian
   Talmud, *Yoma*).
19 Leviticus 19.15; Exodus 21.24.
20 Leviticus 19.18.
21 Leviticus 19.34.
22 Genesis 1.2 (one of three possible
   translations).
23 T.W.F.Saggs, *The Greatness that was
   Babylon*, pp. 409f.
24 Genesis 1.6.
25 Genesis 1.27.
26 Psalms 8.6, 5
27 Psalms 104.24, 31

CHAPTER 15
The Climax of Hebrew Thought

1 Isaiah 57.4f.; 63.3.
2 Job 27.5f.
3 Job 5.7; 19.6; 9.21–3; 3.23.

4 Job 23. 3f.; 13.3; 31.35; 23.7.
5 Job 36.26; 34.35–7.
6 Job 35.14; 33.23; 33.19.
7 Job 38.12f., 40.9, 40.15–41.8.
8 Job 40.4; 42.2.
9 Ezra 1.1–4, 2 Chronicles 36.23.
10 Isaiah 44.28.
11 Isaiah 44.25.
12 Isaiah 45.18; 45.21; 40.12; 44.7–8.
13 Isaiah 42.1; 42.4; 49.6; 50.4; 52.13.
14 Isaiah 41.8f. (cf. 44.1f.), 43.10; 49.3.
15 Isaiah 53.3, 5–7(*Authorized Version*).
16 Isaiah 53.12, 11.
17 Isaiah 49.23.

CHAPTER 16
The New Judaism

1 Nehemiah 13.25.
2 Ezra 7.12.
3 Ezra 7.7.
4 Ezra 7.14.
5 Nehemiah 8.1.
6 Ezra 9.11; 10.3.
7 Ezra 7.10.
8 Cf. (Second) Isaiah 56, 3–5 on the
   memorials of eunuchs.
9 Ezra 7.12–9.15.
10 1 Chronicles 9.1; 2 Chronicles 9.29;
   13.22; 16.11; 24.27.
11 2 Chronicles 8.2.
12 2 Chronicles 33. 12f.
13 2 Chronicles 30.8.
14 2 Chronicles 36.23.
15 Jonah 4.10f.
16 Jeremiah 51.34, 44.
17 Matthew 12.40.

CHAPTER 17
Life and Thought under the Greeks

1 Y.Meshorer, *Jewish Coins of the Second
   Temple Period*, pp. 116f., nos. 1–4.
2 Ecclesiastes 1.1.
3 Ecclesiastes 7.24; 3.11.
4 Ecclesiastes 1.2; (cf. 12.8); 1.13f.;
   11.12; 2.11; cf. 4.8.
5 Ecclesiastes 9.11; 1.9; 3.19; 9.12; 4.3.

6 Ecclesiastes 9.4; 12.1; 10. 17; 2.24 (etc.); 7.26–8; 4.11; 11.2.

7 Josephus, *Jewish Antiquities*, XII, 138–44.

8 Ecclesiasticus 50.1–21. Or was Simon I (4th–3rd cents.) known as 'the Just'?

9 Ecclesiasticus 51.23.

10 1 Maccabees 1.11.

11 Ecclesiasticus, *Preface*.

12 Ecclesiasticus 38.24.

13 Ecclesiasticus 44.1f.

14 Ecclesiasticus 17.17.

15 Mishnah, *Baba Kama*, 82B.

16 2 Maccabees 4,9; Josephus, op. cit., XII, 40.

17 Daniel 9.27; 11.31; cf. 1 Maccabees 1.37–40.

CHAPTER 18
Independence Regained

1 Daniel 5.5.

2 1 Maccabees 14.41.

3 2 Esdras 14.5, 44, 46.

4 Daniel 9.25.

5 Daniel 7.13f.

6 1 Enoch 37–71 (The Similitudes or Parables of Enoch), etc.

7 Daniel 12.1f.; cf. Isaiah 26.19 (later interpolation).

8 Matthew 23.15.

9 Ecclesiasticus 39.1–11.

10 Josephus, *Jewish Antiquities*, XIII, 171, XVIII, 18; *Jewish War*, II, 140, 154–9; Pliny the Elder, *Natural History*, V, 15, 73.

11 *Damascus Rule*, B II.

12 *Community Rule*, IV; *War Rule, passim*.

13 Matthew 12.26–8; 1 John 2.18, etc.

14 Josephus, *Jewish Antiquities*, XIV, 241.

15 1 Maccabees 16.24.

16 2 Maccabees 2.19–21.

17 Psalms 149.6; cf. 83 and 84.

18 Josephus, *Jewish Antiquities*, XIII, 318.

19 Strabo, *Geography*, XVI, 2.40, against Josephus, op. cit., XIII, 301 (Aristobulus I).

20 Y.Meshorer, *Jewish Coins of the Second Temple Period*, pp. 118ff.

21 Babylonian Talmud, *Kiddushin*, 66a (? reign).

22 D.Jesselsohn, *Palestine Exploration Quarterly*, CXII, 1980, pp. 11–17

CHAPTER 19
Herod the Great

1 Josephus, *Jewish Antiquities*, XIV, 196 (attributed to Caesar).

2 Y.Meshorer, op. cit., pp. 121ff.

3 Sources in E.M.Smallwood, *The Jews under Roman Rule*, p. 121.

4 Babylonian Talmud, *Shabbath*, 31a; Mishnah, *Aboth* 1, 10.

5 Josephus, op. cit., XVI, 14.

6 Josephus, op. cit., XVI, 149; *Jewish War* I, 426–7.

7 Mishnah, *Aboth* 2,7.

8 Isaiah 56.3.

9 Y.Meshorer, op. cit., p. 130, no. 54.

10 Josephus, op. cit., XVII, 151.

11 Ibid., XVII, 187.

CHAPTER 20
The Road to Rebellion

1 Josephus, *Jewish Antiquities*, XVIII, 2–5.

2 Josephus, op. cit., XVIII, 237; Y.Meshorer, op. cit., pp. 138ff.

3 Philo, *Embassy to Gaius*, 45.367.

4 F.G.Kenyon and H.I.Bell, *Greek Papyri in the British Museum*, 1912.

5 Simeon ben Yohai, *Sifre* (halakhic midrash) *on Numbers* 42 (ed. Friedmann, fol. 13a).

6 Y.Meshorer, op. cit., pp. 154ff.

7 2 Esdras 13.6ff., etc.

8 Josephus, *Jewish War*, VII, 253.

EPILOGUE

1 *Coins of the Roman Empire in the British Museum*, III, p. 15, no. 88.

APPENDICES

1 Various differing chronological systems are employed (listed by

J.H.Hayes and J.M.Miller, *Israelite and Judaean History*, pp. 680–3). The dating adopted here is that of J.Begrich (1929) as revised by A.Jepsen (1964). According to alternative calculations the dates of e.g. Jeroboam I of Israel would be 932=31–911/10 or 931/30–910/09 or 925/23–905/3 or 922–901.

2 For the classification of prophets see Appendix 2. Daniel is placed with the 'major' prophets in the English Bible.

3 Habakkuk 2.3; 3.14.

4 Haggai 2.6, 21; Hebrews 12.26.

5 Isaiah 66.19f.; 63.3,6; 66.1.

6 Joel 3.18; 2.18,32; 3.3.

7 Malachi 4.1,6; 2.14–16; 1.11–14.

8 Micah 5.2; Matthew 2.5.

9 Nahum 1.2.

10 Obadiah 11–15, 20.

11 Zechariah 6.11,13; 8.23.

12 Zechariah 12.6,10; John 19.37; Zechariah 14.12, 17.

13 Zephaniah 1.12; 2.3; 2.5–15; 3.11–20; 1.14f.

14 Bel and the Dragon 7,32.

15 Esther 3.7.

16 M.Philonenko, *Joseph et Aséneth* (1968); cf. Genesis 41.45; 46.20.

17 Judith 12.2.

18 Genesis 38.13–16.

19 Ruth 2.10 and 4.

20 Susanna and the Elders (Daniel and Susanna) 1.21.

21 Tobit 1.21.

22 2 Maccabees 9.15.

23 Tobit 4.15.

24 Song of Songs 1.1f., 5–7; 2.1f., 9–13; 5.10–12, 15f.; 7.1–3, 6–12; 8.6f. The Translations are from the *New English Bible*, the *Good News Bible*, and the *Authorized (King James) Version*.

25 Ibid. 3.7,11.

26 Jeremiah 2.2; (2) Isaiah 54.4ff.; (3) Isaiah 62.4ff.

27 J.Gray, *The Canaanites*, p. 113, 150.

28 E.g. Psalm 45.

29 Mishnah, *Yadaim*, 3.5.

30 Genesis 1.28; 9.1,7.

31 Babylonian Talmud, *Gittin*, 57a.

32 Sources in J.Bright, *A History of Israel*, p. 377, nn. 4–7.

33 2 Maccabees 6.2.

34 Deuteronomy 27.4; similar injunction inserted after Exodus 20,17 and Deuteronomy 5.21.

35 Josephus, *Jewish War*, I, 31–3 and VII, 423–32, against *Jewish Antiquities*, XII, 387f., and XIII, 62–73.

36 2 Esdras 14.46.

37 Micah 5.2; Matthew 2.6; John 7.42.

38 Proverbs 25.21.

39 Isaiah 7.14; Matthew 1.23.

40 (2) Zechariah 9.9; Matthew 21.2, 4f.; Jeremiah 7.11; (2) Isaiah 56.7.

41 Tacitus, *Annals*, XV, 44.

42 Babylonian Talmud, *Sanhedrin* 34b.

43 Cf. D. Diringer, *The Alphabet*, I (1968), p. 185; G.Adam Smith, *The Historical Geography of the Holy Land*, 25th ed. (1966), p. 27.

44 Herodotus, II, 104; III, 5 and 91; VII, 89.

45 R.Patai, *The Jewish Mind* (1977), pp. 15–24, 543 n. 12; A.Unterman, *The Jews* (1981), pp. 13–18; on why be, or remain, Jewish see D.Marmur, *Beyond Survival* (1983).

BIBLIOGRAPHY

Some General Books

AHARONI, Y., *The Archaeology of the Land of Israel* (London 1982)
   The Land of the Bible: A Historical Geography, rev. ed. (Philadelphia 1979)
ALBRIGHT, W.F., *The Archaeology of Palestine*, 4th ed. (London 1960)
   The Biblical Period from Abraham to Ezra, rev. ed. (New York 1963)
ALT, A., *Essays on Old Testament History and Religion* (London 1966)
ALTER, R., *The Art of Biblical Narrative* (London 1982)
ANATI, E., *Palestine Before the Hebrews* (London 1963)
ANDERSON, G.W., *The History and Religion of Israel* (Oxford 1966)
AVI-YONAH, M. (ed.), *A History of the Holy Land* (London 1969)
BAKER, D.L., *Two Testaments: One Bible* (Leicester 1976)
BALY, D., *The Geography of the Bible* (New York 1957)
BARON, S.W., *Social and Religious History of the Jews*, 17 vols., 2nd ed. (Philadelphia 1957–67)
BARR, J., *Old and New in Interpretation: A Study of the Two Testaments* (London 1982)
BEN-SASSON, H.H. (ed.), *A History of the Jewish People* (London 1976)
BEWER, J.A., *The Literature of the Old Testament*, 3rd ed. (New York 1962)
BLENKINSOPP, J., *Wisdom and Law in the Old Testament* (Oxford 1983)
BRIGHT, J., *The Authority of the Old Testament* (London 1967)
   A History of Israel, 3rd ed. (Philadelphia 1981)
BRUCE, F.F., *Israel and the Nations* (London 1973)
CAPPS, A.C., *The Bible as Literature* (New York 1971)
CORNFELD, G. and FREEDMAN, D.N., *The Archaeology of the Bible: Book by Book* (San Francisco 1982)
DAVIDSON, R. and LEANEY, A.R.C., *The Pelican Guide to Modern Theology*, Vol. 3: *Biblical Criticism* (Harmondsworth 1970)
DAVIES, W.D., *The Territorial Dimension of Judaism* (Berkeley 1983)
DAVIES, W.D. and FINKELSTEIN, L. (eds.), *The Cambridge History of Judaism*, Vol. 1 (Cambridge 1983)
DENTAN, R.C., *The Knowledge of God in Ancient Israel* (New York 1968)
DOTHAN, T., *The Philistines and their Material Culture* (New Haven 1982)
EDWARDS, I.E.S. (etc., eds.), *The Cambridge Ancient History*, 3rd ed., Vols. 1–3 (Part 1), (Cambridge 1970–82)
EHRLICH, B.L., *A Concise History of Israel* (London 1962)
ENGNELL, T., *Critical Essays on the Old Testament* (London 1970)
FILSON, F.V., *Which Books Belong to the Bible?* (Philadelphia 1957)
FINEGAN, J., *Light from the Ancient Past* (Princeton 1969)

FRANK. F.T., *Discovering the Biblical World* (Maplewood 1975)
FRYE, W.N., *The Great Code: Bible and Literature* (London 1982)
de GEUS, C.H.J., *The Tribes of Israel* (Assen-Amsterdam 1976)
GORDON, C.H., *The World of the Old Testament* (London 1960)
GOWAN, D.E., *The Bridge Between the Testaments* (London 1980)
GRANT, M., *The Jews in the Roman World* (London 1973)
GRAY, J., *Archaeology and the Old Testament World* (Edinburgh 1962)
    The Legacy of Canaan, 2nd ed. (London 1964)
GUTHRIE, H.H., *God and History in the Old Testament* (London 1961)
HAHN, H.F., *The Old Testament in Modern Research* (London 1956)
HARKER, R., *Digging up the Bible Lands* (London 1972)
HARRISON, R.K., *A History of Old Testament Times* (Grand Rapids 1957, 1970)
HENGEL, M., *Jews, Greeks and Barbarians* (London 1980)
HENN, T.R., *The Bible as Literature* (Oxford 1970)
HAYES, J.H. and MILLER, J.M. (eds.), *Israelite and Judaean History* (London 1977, 1980)
HEATON, E.W., *The Hebrew Kingdoms* (Oxford 1968)
HERRMANN, S., *A History of Israel in Old Testament Times*, rev. ed. (London 1980)
HESCHEL, A.J., *The Prophets* (Philadelphia 1962)
JACOBSON, D., *The Story of Stories: The Chosen People and its God* (London 1982)
JAGERSMA, H., *A History of Israel in the Old Testament Period* (London 1982)
JOHNSTON, L., *A History of Israel* (London 1964, 1978)
KEDOURIE, E. (ed.), *The Jewish World* (London 1979)
KELLER, W., *The Bible as History*, rev. ed. (London 1963)
    Diaspora (London 1971)
KENYON, K.M., *Archaeology in the Holy Land*, 4th ed. (London 1979)
    The Bible and Recent Archaeology (London 1978)
KITCHEN, K.A., *The Bible in its World* (Leicester 1978)
KOCH, K., *The Growth of the Biblical Tradition* (London 1969)
KUGEL, J.L., *The Idea of Biblical Poetry* (New Haven 1981)
LANCE, H.D., *The Old Testament and the Archaeologist* (London 1983)
LAPP, P.W., *Biblical Archaeology and History* (New York 1969)
LEANEY, A.R.C., *The Jewish and Christian World 200 BC to AD 200* (Cambridge 1983)
MACCOBY, H., *The Sacred Executioner* (London 1982)
MACKENZIE, R.A.F., *Faith and History in the Old Testament* (Minneapolis 1963)
MACKIE, J.L., *The Miracle of Theism* (Oxford 1982)
MAGNUSSON, M., *B.C.: The Archaeology of the Bible Lands* (London 1977)
MARGOLIS, M.L. and MARX, A., *A History of the Jewish People* (New York 1965)
MARTENS, E.A., *Plot and Purpose in the Old Testament* (Leicester 1981)
MAZAR, B., *Canaan and Israel* (in Hebrew) (Jerusalem 1974)
MELLOR, E.B. (ed.), *The Making of the Old Testament* (Cambridge 1972)
MILLER, J.M., *The Old Testament and the Historian* (London 1976)
MOOREY, P.R.S., *Biblical Lands* (London 1975)
    Excavation in Palestine (Guildford 1981)
MOSCATI, S., *L'Enigma dei Fenici* (Milan 1982)
NETANYAHU, B. and MALAMAT, A. (etc., eds.) *The World History of the Jewish People*, Series
    I–IV (Jerusalem and London 1964–79)
NEUSNER, J. (ed.), *Understanding Jewish Theology* (New York 1973)
NOTH, M., *The History of Israel*, 2nd ed. (London 1960)
    The Old Testament World (London 1966)
O'CONNOR, J.M., *The Holy Land: An Archaeological Guide* (Oxford 1980)
ORLINSKY, H.M., *Understanding the Bible through History and Archaeology* (New York 1972)

OSTERLEY, W.O.E. and ROBINSON. T.H., *A History of Israel*, 2 vols. (London 1932)

OTZEN, W., GOTTLIEB, H. and JEPPESEN, K., *Myths in the Old Testament* (London 1980)

OWEN, G.F., *Archaeology and the Bible* (Westwood 1960)

PATAI, R., *The Jewish Mind* (New York 1977)

PAUL, S.M. and DEVER, W. G., *Biblical Archaeology* (Jerusalem 1973)

PEARLMAN, M., *Digging Up the Bible* (London 1980)

PETERS, F.E., *Children of Abraham* (Princeton 1982)

PFEIFFER, C.F., *Ancient Israel* (Grand Rapids 1965)

PFEIFFER, C.F. (ed.), *The Biblical World* (Grand Rapids 1966)

PRITCHARD, J.B. (ed.), *Archaeology and the Old Testament* (Princeton 1958)

RAMSEY, G.W., *The Quest for the Historical Israel* (London 1982)

RAPHAEL, C., *The Springs of Jewish Life* (London 1983)

ROBINSON, H.W., *The History of Israel*, 2nd ed. (London 1964)

ROGERSON, J.W., *Anthropology and the Old Testament* (Oxford 1978)

ROWLAND, C., *The Open Heaven: A Study of the Apocalyptic in Judaism and Early Christianity* (London 1982)

ROWLEY, H.H., *The Growth of the Old Testament* (London 1950)

ROWLEY, H.H. (ed.), *The Old Testament and Modern Study* (Oxford 1951)

SANDMEL, S., *The Hebrew Scriptures* (New York 1978)

SCHECHTER, S., *Studies in Judaism* (New York 1958)

SCHMIDT, W.H., *The Faith of the Old Testament* (Oxford 1983)

SCHOVILLE, K.N., *Biblical Archaeology in Focus* (Grand Rapids 1978)

SCHÜRER, E., *History of the Jewish People in the Age of Jesus*, rev. ed. (G. Vermes etc.), Vols. I–II (London 1973, 1979)

SEVENSTER, J.N., *The Roots of Pagan Anti-Semitism in the Ancient World* (Leiden 1975)

SHAROT, S., *Judaism: A Sociology* (Newton Abbot 1976)

SHULVASS, M.A., *The History of the Jewish People*, Vol. I: *Antiquity* (Chicago 1982)

SILVER, A.H., *Where Judaism Differed* (New York 1956)

SMALLWOOD, E.M., *The Jews under Roman Rule* (Leiden 1976)

SMITH, G. ADAM, *The Historical Geography of the Holy Land*, 25th ed. (London 1931)

SMITH, M., *Palestine Parties and Politics that Shaped the Old Testament* (New York 1971)

STERN, M. (ed.), *Greek and Latin Authors on Jews and Judaism*, Vol. I (Jerusalem 1974)

STOLZ, F., *Interpreting the Old Testament* (London 1975)

STONE, M.E., *Scriptures, Sects and Visions: A Profile of Judaism from Ezra to the Jewish Revolt* (Oxford 1983)

TCHERIKOVER, V., *Hellenistic Civilization and the Jews*, new ed. (Philadelphia 1961, 1975)

THOMAS, D.W. (ed.), *Archaeology and Old Testament Study* (Oxford 1967)

THOMPSON, J.A., *The Bible and Archaeology* (Grand Rapids 1962)

THOMPSON, T.L., *The Historicity of the Patriarchal Narratives* (Berlin and New York 1974)

TRAWICK, B.B., *The Bible as Literature: The Old Testament and the Apocrypha* (New York 1982)

UNGER, M.F., *Archaeology and the Old Testament* (Grand Rapids 1954)

VAN RULER, A.A., *The Christian Church and the Old Testament* (Grand Rapids 1971)

DE VAUX, R., *Ancient Israel* (London 1961)
The Bible and the Ancient Near East (London 1972)
The Early History of Israel (London 1978)

VERMES, G. and NEUSNER, J. (eds.), *Essays in Honour of Yigael Yadin* (*Journal of Jewish Studies*, XXXIII, 1–2) (Oxford 1982)

WELLHAUSEN, J., *Prolegomena to the History of Ancient Israel* (Edinburgh 1885, New York 1957)

WESTERMANN, C., *What Does the Old Testament Say about God?* (London 1979)

WILLIAMS, W.G., *Archaeology in Biblical Research* (Nashville 1965)

WISEMAN, D.J. (ed.), *Peoples of Old Testament Times* (Oxford 1973)
WRIGHT, G.E., *Biblical Archaeology*, rev. ed. (London 1962)
WRIGHT, G.E. (ed.), *The Bible and the Ancient Near East* (New York 1961)
YAMAUCHI, E.M., *The Stones and the Scriptures* (Leicester 1973)
ZEITLIN, S., *The Rise and Fall of the Judaean State* (Philadelphia 1962)
ZIMMERLI, W., *The Old Testament and the World* (London 1976)

Introductions to the Old Testament (Hebrew Bible) are offered by the following:
B.W.Anderson (3rd ed., 1978), G.W.Anderson (rev. ed., 1974), G.E.L.Archer (1964),
H.K.Beebe (1970), A.Bentzen (4th ed., 1958), B.S.Childs (1979), O.Eissfeldt (1965),
G.Fohrer (1968, 1970), R.K.Harrison (1970), H. St.J.Hart (1951), J.H.Hayes (1979,
1982), O.Kaiser (1975), O.J.Lace (1972), J.Lindblom (1973), R.H.Pfeiffer (1957),
S.Sandmel (1963), J.A.Soggin (rev. ed., 1980), R.C.Walton (1970), A.Weiser (1961),
C.Westermann (1969).

General accounts of Jewish theology and religion are provided by: B.S.Childs (1970),
R.E.Clements (1978), W.Eichrodt (1961, 1967), I.Epstein (1945, 1954, 1959),
L.Finkelstein (ed., 1960, 1971), G.Fohrer (1972), E.Jacob (1958), L.Jacobs (1973),
W.C.Kaiser (1978), J.Kalir (1980), Y.Kaufmann (1960–1), J.L.McKenzie (1974),
J.Neusner (ed., 1973), J.B.Payne (1962), G.vonRad (rev. ed., 1975), H. Ringgren
(1966), J.W.Rogerson (1983), L.Roth (1960), H.H.Rowley (1956, 1967),
J.N.Schofield (1969), S.Terrien (1978), A.Unterman (1981), T.C.Vriezen (1967),
G.E.Wright (1969), W.Zimmerli (1978).

INDEX